BEYOND REASONABLE DOUBT

Reasoning Processes in Obsessive-Compulsive
Disorder and Related Disorders

BEYOND REASONABLE DOUBT

Reasoning Processes in Obsessive-Compulsive Disorder and Related Disorders

Kieron O'Connor

Frederick Aardema

and

Marie-Claude Pélissier

Fernand-Seguin Research Center, Louis-H. Lafontaine Hospital, University of Montreal, Canada

John Wiley & Sons, Ltd

Other Wiley Editorial Offices

John Wiley & Sons Inc., 111 River Street, Hoboken, NJ 07030, USA

Jossey-Bass, 989 Market Street, San Francisco, CA 94103-1741, USA

Wiley-VCH Verlag GmbH, Boschstr. 12, D-69469 Weinheim, Germany

John Wiley & Sons Australia Ltd, 33 Park Road, Milton, Queensland 4064, Australia

John Wiley & Sons (Asia) Pte Ltd, 2 Clementi Loop #02-01, Jin Xing Distripark, Singapore 129809

John Wiley & Sons Canada Ltd, 22 Worcester Road, Etobicoke, Ontario, Canada M9W 1L1

Wiley also publishes its books in a variety of electronic formats. Some content that appears in print may
not be available in electronic books.

Library of Congress Cataloging-in-Publication Data

O'Connor, Kieron Philip.
    Beyond reasonable doubt : reasoning processes in obsessive-compulsive
disorder and related disorders / Kieron O'Connor,
Frederick Aardema, and Marie-Claude Pélissier.
      p. cm.
    Includes bibliographical references and index.
    ISBN 0-470-86876-7 (cloth : alk. paper) – ISBN 0-470-86877-5
(pbk. : alk. paper)
    1. Obsessive-compulsive disorder–Treatment.   2. Reasoning
(Psychology) 3. Reasoning.   I. Aardema, Frederick. II.
Pélissier, Marie-Claude.   III. Title.
RC533.O34 2005
616.85'22706–dc22

                                   2004011339

British Library Cataloguing in Publication Data

A catalogue record for this book is available from the British Library

ISBN 0-470-86876-7 (hbk)
ISBN 0-470-86877-5 (pbk)

Typeset in 10/12pt Palatino by Dobbie Typesetting Ltd, Tavistock, Devon
Printed and bound in Great Britain by Antony Rowe Ltd, Chippenham, Wiltshire
This book is printed on acid-free paper responsibly manufactured from sustainable forestry
in which at least two trees are planted for each one used for paper production.

CONTENTS

About the Authors vii

Preface ix

Foreword by Paul M.G. Emmelkamp xiii

Acknowledgments xv

1 Cognitive Approaches to Obsessive-Compulsive Disorder:
   An Overview.   1
   Obsessive-Compulsive Disorder   1
   Cognitive Approaches to OCD   4
   Intrusions and Inferences in OCD. 10
   Phobic and Non-Phobic Models of Development in OCD 12
   Treatment Considerations 13
   Conclusion 16

2 Reasoning in Everyday Life 17
   Formal Logic and Informal Thinking. 17
   Making Sense of the Senses. 32

3 Reasoning and Narrative 53
   Conversation and Conviction 53
   Inference and Imagination. 67
   Conclusion 80

4 Reasoning and Psychopathology 81
   Reasoning in Clinical Populations 81
   Reasoning Therapy 96
   General Conclusion. 110

5 An Inference-Based Approach to Obsessive-Compulsive
   Disorder 113
   Clinical and Phenomenological Investigations
   into Inferential Confusion 113

Critical Concepts in an Inference-Based Model 115
Psychometric Measurement of Inferential Confusion. 121
Experimental Studies of Inferential Confusion 131
Clinical Trials of an Inference-Based Approach to Therapy (IBA) . 140
Conclusion 146

6 Using the IBA Treatment Manual 149
Introduction to Treatment 149
Step-by-Step Program 149
Common Queries from Clients 166
Troubleshooting Guide 170
Case Studies 178

7 Future Directions 199
IBA and Other Cognitive Therapy. 199
Future Development in IBA 211
A Final Comment 213

Appendix 1 Overview of Our Treatment Program for
             Obsessive-Compulsive Disorder 215

Appendix 2 Worksheets, Exercise Sheets and Training Cards 227

Appendix 3 279

Appendix 4 281

References 285

Index 301

ABOUT THE AUTHORS

Kieron O'Connor completed his research and clinical training in psychology at the University of Sussex and the Institute of Psychiatry and Maudsley Hospital London (UK). In 1988 he was awarded the first of a series of fellowships by the Fonds de la Recherche en Santé du Québec, and established a clinical research program at the Fernand-Seguin Research Center, Louis-H. Lafontaine Hospital, University of Montreal. The multidisciplinary research program, which focuses on obsessive-compulsive disorder, Tourette and tic disorder, and delusional disorder, is currently funded by the Canadian Institutes of Health Research. Kieron O'Connor is also Associate Research Professor at the Psychiatry Department of the University of Montreal and is scientific advisor to the Quebec OCD Foundation. He has over 100 scientific publications. Forthcoming publications include *Cognitive Behavioral Treatment of Tic Disorders* (Wiley, in press).

Frederick Aardema studied clinical psychology at the University of Groningen and the University of Amsterdam in the Netherlands under the supervision of Prof. P.M.G. Emmelkamp in affiliation with the Fernand-Seguin Research Center located in Montreal, Canada. He currently resides in Canada and has published in international journals in the field of obsessive-compulsive disorder. In particular, his research interests include psychometric and experimental methods in the measurement of reasoning processes in OCD, as well as the application of inference and narrative based models to obsessions without overt compulsions. He is a licensed psychologist and has a private practice in Montreal, Quebec.

Marie-Claude Pélissier studied psychology at the University of Quebec at Montreal in Canada and did most of her clinical training in London, England. She has been working for almost eight years in clinical research on obsessive-compulsive disorder and other OCD related disorders, which has resulted in publications in two international journals. As a licensed psychologist, she recently started her own private practice. She is also actively involved in local mental health community groups where she teaches and acts as scientific consultant on OCD.

PREFACE

In this book, we bring together three traditionally separate lines of enquiry to try to understand the clinical phenomenon of obsessional compulsive disorder, namely, reasoning research, philosophy of mind and language, and cognitive therapy. Developments in these three areas in the past 50 years seem to have led naturally to a fruitful cross-talk about the way we think. Each area in its way has grown dissatisfied with former constraints on its paradigms and has emerged with new perspectives on thinking, resulting in a potential convergence of approaches to understanding thinking disorders.

Sir Frederick Bartlett in his influential work on thinking, later resumed in his 1958 book, *Thinking*, subtitled *An experimental and social study* highlighted how the complexities of thinking pervade all areas of daily life. Thinking, he proposed, was an autonomous process, best considered a skill, which, like other skills, can be learnt. Importantly, Bartlett also recognized that thinking always has 'direction' and 'agency'. In other words, thinking is, above all, a human skill.

Reasoning research emerged from the philosophy of logic to develop insightful applied experimental paradigms. Most early studies operationalized thinking in terms of deduction to enable study of the processes by which conclusions are confirmed or disconfirmed according to the content of the premise. Such research has revealed that most people do not always think or act logically and that in everyday life they are susceptible to a variety of cognitive illusions. The puzzle is, despite this, how do they manage to function adaptively?

Johnson-Laird has suggested that formal rules of logic are replaced in everyday life by what he termed mental models. People construct their own idiosyncratic multi-modal mental models of possible outcomes and refer to these possibilities, rather than rules, to infer consequences. The models are drawn from experience and both the content of these models themselves and access to these models depend crucially on other psychological factors.

The main tenet of cognitive therapy is of course that thinking critically influences mood and behavior. Since its inception in the 1950s as a result of dissatisfaction with psychoanalytic notions of the unconscious, cognitive therapy has focused on thinking in the here and now and cognitive behavior therapy has developed to be a mainstream treatment of choice for a number of psychiatric disorders. Cognitive therapy unravels thinking errors that lead people to react in maladaptive ways. Often the thinking is conceptualized within the templates of conditional reason, 'If I don't do X, then I must feel Y', 'If X happens, then Y is inevitable'. However, rather than draw on reasoning paradigms and research to underpin the application of reasoning in clinical practice, cognitive therapy, particularly of the Beckian kind, has turned to a more remote cognitive structure of beliefs to explain reasoning. The concern with cognitive structure has also led cognitive therapy to seek an experimental base in the information processing theory branch of cognitive science. Even empirical findings using reasoning paradigms are referred back not to reasoning processes but to problems in biased memory, attention, or information gathering.

Recent developments in the philosophy of mind and language have, however, highlighted the close link between thought and language, and suggested this link precedes any relationship between thinking and other cognitive structures. In order to think, we first need the language to think. The unit of language most closely connected to reasoning is the narrative unit, not the isolated thought or statement. The dynamics of the narrative carries our thinking from point A to B and the conclusions we arrive at are often tempered more by the form of the narrative than any objective facts, statements or thoughts on their own. Indeed, thoughts in this sense cannot be 'biased' as compared against an objective standard because they only ever arise and make sense within a personal narrative, whose context extends horizontally and vertically beyond the inference of the moment, into the person's life story, not outwards to an objective reality.

In such a narrative approach to cognition, we move away from the 'black boxology' and modular thinking of an input–output mediational model, to a mental model where even core beliefs are understood and grounded principally in the observable reasoning narrative around them, rather than connected to remote hypothetical cognitive structures beyond them.

We suggest later in the book that adoption of a narrative constructionist approach facilitates the application of reasoning models to cognitive therapy. After all, it is much more straightforward to modify a manifestly misguided reasoning process than access and correct a hypothetical schema. Furthermore, in this way, cognitive therapy genuinely becomes a 'thinking therapy'. A reasoning approach may also overcome some incoherences in current clinical cognitive theory and help resolve the growing gap between cognitive principles and cognitive practice for clinicians, who seem by default to be increasingly adopting experiential-based therapies to complement formal cognitive thought challenging techniques.

The development of the current inference-based approach to treating obsessive-compulsive disorder (OCD) began effectively from our dissatisfaction with current cognitive explanations. The Beck model has been very successfully applied to treating emotional disorders where a few firmly held beliefs guide the depressive or anxiogenic interpretation of normal sensations and events. The seminal work of Jack Rachman, Paul Salkovskis and other thinkers, inspired by the Beckian approach, applied the model successfully to obsessions. These pioneers offered an exciting and refreshing vision of a disorder, once considered intractable, but now accounted for by cognitive appraisals of otherwise normal intrusions. But do all obsessional types fit this model? Are all obsessional disorders best considered an anxiety disorder or are some subtypes closer to belief disorders such as delusions? In our clinical work in the past 10 years, it became clear in certain types of OCD, particularly where there was a strong personal investment in the obsessions, that the initial intrusion was actually an inference about a state of affairs. In other words, the intrusion was the end point of a reasoning process, not the inadvertent beginning of an appraisal process, which subsequently produced the obsession independent of the intrusion. In this case, the content of the intrusion needed to be addressed in therapy. Even when we looked at other obsessional cases with less conviction, we still found that the initial intrusion frequently took the form of an inference but in these cases more a 'doubting inference' ('maybe...'). Furthermore, some single case studies showed that modifying the content of the intrusions impacted on OCD symptomatology and further appraisals of the obsessions. These doubting inferences did not seem to arrive normally and had pathological characteristics. They also seemed to result from a peculiar style of reasoning, a cognitive illusion, which we identified as 'inverse inference'. In inverse inference, instead of beginning with evidence from the senses and then drawing conclusions, people with OCD draw conclusions despite contradictory evidence of the senses. So, in a sense, they work backwards from what could be to what is, instead of from what is to what could be. Inverse inference is distinct from other reasoning errors such as 'reverse inference' (reversing the usual 'if P, then Q' sequence to assuming a consequence implies a premise P) and 'converse inference' (assuming that because if P, then Q, then conversely not P means not Q).

Although inverse inference always characterizes the resulting OCD reasoning style, other reasoning or narrative devices play a role in producing the cognitive illusion and we designated the end state of all these processes under the term 'inferential confusion'.

The middle chapters of the book chart the empirical validation of the concept of 'inferential confusion', operationalized through experimental reasoning research, psychometric instruments and clinical intervention and resulting in a manualized application of the intervention: inferential-based approach (IBA) therapy. Much research still needs to be done, and the IBA program is still evolving, as the accompanying sections make clear.

Since the program focus is on unravelling the idiosyncratic thinking processes of the client (as one might expect of a 'thinking therapy'), it is from our experience more client-friendly than therapist-friendly. However, we feel confident enough about the program's utility to place it in the public domain. In fact, we encourage qualified professionals who use the manual to return feedback and comments to us.

Kieron O'Connor
Frederick Aardema
Marie-Claude Pélissier
Montreal, March 2004

FOREWORD

I am delighted to write this introduction to *Beyond Reasonable Doubt: Reasoning Processes in Obsessive-Compulsive Disorder and Related Disorders.* Since Freud, who considered in 1926 obsessive-compulsive disorder (OCD) as 'unquestionably the most interesting and repaying subject of analytic research', a number of different theoretical accounts of the etiology of OCD have been proposed. When I started studying the cognitive treatment of OCD in the eighties of the past century, I was rather skeptical about the effectiveness of cognitive therapy in OCD, given the good results which we and other clinical researchers had achieved with behavioral approaches, i.e. exposure and response prevention. The results of studies of my research group, however, proved me wrong. Cognitive therapy proved to be as effective as the gold standard treatment for OCD: exposure *in vivo* and response prevention.

Since these earlier studies into the effectiveness of cognitive therapy in OCD, the field of cognitive approaches to obsessive-compulsive disorder is in a period of considerable activity. The Obsessive Compulsive Cognitions Working Group, an international consortium of clinical researchers, was established in 1996, devoting much time and energy into research into the cognitive underpinnings of OCD with an emphasis on specific beliefs that cause this disorder, but neglecting reasoning processes involved in OCD. The authors of this book identified this deficiency and set out to remedy it. They take the position that a process-oriented approach may be more fruitful than a focus on specific beliefs and appraisals in OCD, and they emphasize the reasoning processes that are associated with the occurrence of obsessions and propose an inferential-based approach to the treatment of OCD.

The reasoning-based cognitive therapy proposed in this volume draws on different theoretical positions, including research into reasoning processes, narrative approaches and cognitive theory and therapy. The generic cognitive model derived from these different theoretical influences has been tailored to the specific characteristics of OCD.

Although reading through these theoretical backgrounds does not make easy reading for most clinicians, it is worthwhile and enhances an understanding of the new inference-based treatment approach of OCD proposed by the authors. This novel inference-based approach considers that the initial intrusion is actually a faulty inference. It is argued that an idiosyncratic reasoning process maintains the initial doubt or inference.

This book is not only a seminal book, it is also a courageous book, in that the authors take stand against the prevailing view among most current OCD researchers that specific beliefs and appraisal processes are central in understanding OCD and against the view that OCD follows a phobic model of development.

The authors have succeeded extremely well in proposing an alternative account of the development of obsessions and in an alternative reasoning-based therapeutic approach to remedy them. These accounts are clearly written and the relevance for the understanding of OCD is clear. However, the implications of this work go beyond OCD. The volume provides potentially useful theoretical and therapeutic approaches to a range of anxiety disorders (e.g. generalized anxiety disorder) and mood disorders (e.g. dysthymia).

Psychological treatment of OCD will be effective if it is theoretically founded and empirically verified. It is hoped that this work will inspire investigators to test the proposed treatment in this book in controlled clinical trials. In short, the book is undoubtedly a most important addition to the literature on OCD.

Paul M.G. Emmelkamp
Professor of Clinical Psychology
University of Amsterdam, The Netherlands

ACKNOWLEDGMENTS

We would like to thank the following people and institutions:

Sophie Robillard for clinical collaboration in development of the IBA program.

Annette Maillet, Vicky Leblanc, Julie Charette and Julie Brochu for material contributions to the preparation of the book.

François Borgeat and Christo Todorov for their psychiatric expertise.

David A. Clark, Paul Emmelkamp, Mark M. Freeston, Richard Hallam, Phil Johnson-Laird, Gail Steketee and Steve Taylor for thoughtful comments on our thinking.

The management and personnel of the Centre de Recherche-Fernand Séguin, Hopital Louis-H. Lafontaine, Department of Psychiatry, University of Montreal for providing infrastructure support and a nurturing environment for our research programs.

The Fonds de la Recherche en Santé du Québec, Canadian Institutes of Health Research (formerly the Medical Research Council) and the Fondation Louis-H. Lafontaine for providing projects funding and research fellowships over the last 10 years.

All the students, professionals, assistants, technicians and volunteers who have worked on our research projects.

Angela Ambroise for her translation skills.

All clients who have participated in our clinical program and projects without whom this book would not be possible.

Finally, we thank Deborah Egleton, Ruth Graham, Lesley Valerio and Vivian Ward of Wiley for ably guiding the text from paper to proofs to print.

CHAPTER 1

COGNITIVE APPROACHES TO OBSESSIVE-COMPULSIVE DISORDER: AN OVERVIEW

OBSESSIVE-COMPULSIVE DISORDER

Obsessive-compulsive disorder (OCD) is a serious mental health problem. It is among the most prevalent of anxiety disorders with estimates of 1.9–2.5% lifetime based on cross-national epidemiological studies involving more than 40,000 people in seven countries (e.g. Weissman *et al.*, 1994). It is characterized by a chronic fluctuating course and can lead to significant handicaps in professional, social and family life among people who would otherwise function quite well (see Rasmussen & Eisen, 1992; Steketee, 1993). OCD may also increase risk for other conditions such as depression and alcoholism or substance abuse (Angst, 1993; Rieman *et al.*, 1992).

The hallmark of OCD is the presence of obsessions and compulsions (DSM-IV; American Psychological Association, 1994). Obsessions are defined as recurrent, persistent ideas, thoughts, images or impulses that intrude into consciousness and are experienced as senseless or repugnant. Compulsions are repetitive, purposeful forms of behavior that are performed because of a compulsive urge to do so. Obsessions may revolve around a wide variety of themes although the most common obsessions reported are related to contamination, making mistakes, aggressive thoughts, need for symmetry or order, somatic thoughts, religious or sexual thoughts and superstition. The most common compulsions are checking and cleaning (Rasmussen & Tsuang, 1986).

In some cases obsessions will not lead to an overt ritual but rather a covert attempt to neutralize the thought by mental effort to control or attenuate the negative impact. Compulsions can be linked functionally with the content of the obsession. So a person washes their hands because they are preoccupied with the thought that they may be dirty. On the other hand the form of the compulsive ritual may only be loosely tied to the content of the obsession. A person might counteract the thought that the day will go badly with a situationally convenient ritual (tapping the coffee mug that happens to be there) rather than a fixed ritual. Apart from rituals a person may use other neutralization techniques or coping strategies to suppress, or avoid the impact of the obsession (Freeston & Ladouceur, 1997).

Subtyping of OCD

Early analysis of OCD symptoms revealed subtype clusters around washing, checking, rumination and precision rituals. Hoarding, impulsion phobia, health obsessions, dysmorphobia and some aspects of eating disorders have since been proposed as additional subtypes of OCD (Clark, 2004).

However, several problems discourage a definitive separation of subtypes on the basis of symptom clusters. Firstly, different studies have revealed different and sometimes conflicting symptom clusters (Calamari *et al.*, 2004). Second, the majority of people with OCD have more than one subtype. Indeed, it is rare to find a person ranking high on only one discrete subscale of the obsessional inventory. In a recent study (Julien *et al.*, 2004), only 52% of a sample of 80 consecutively referred cases of OCD showed a significantly high enough score on one Padua Inventory subscale compared to others to be classified even with a dominant subtype. A third reason for doubting the efficacy of symptom subtyping is the wide individual differences even within major subtypes. Should a woman who washes repeatedly because she is preoccupied that she might be contaminated by a sexual encounter be identified in the same category as a woman who washes because she feels there may still be dirt from her garden on her hands? The old clinician maxim, 'When you've seen one case, you've seen one case', applies with bells on to OCD, and begs the question of whether more qualitative approaches to case formulation may be appropriate.

At any rate, there is currently debate over whether symptoms or other performance or cognitive factors might better serve as denominators (McKay *et al.*, 2004). For example, the belief that a person should at all costs be a good mother and protect her family might lead to both checking and washing rituals. It may be that any topic could develop into an obsession, and that the different symptom clusters simply represent the different ways harm can occur: infection, violence, robbery, accident, illness, disorganization, lack of care, verbal insult, punishment by higher authority, etc.

Natural course of OCD

Onset of OCD can occur at any age from a few months to late life. The peak age of onset is in adolescence to young adulthood (Karno *et al.*, 1988), and onset is usually gradual, often starting in childhood as a concern with routine and order, with tic-like gestures, and developing with more cognitively complexity (Geller *et al.*, 2001). If onset is during maturity, it is frequently triggered by a critical incident, although in all cases seen in our clinic, there is always evidence of pre-morbid subclinical precursors. Although obsessions and compulsions may evolve over time and wax and wane in intensity, there are no reported cases of spontaneous remission.

Diagnostic Boundaries

OCD compulsions can be distinguished from complex tics, habit disorders and stereotypies on the basis of intent and emotion (O'Connor, 2001), while obsessions are distinct from worries, depressive ruminations and normal thoughts regarding the content, frequency, egodystonocity and controllability of thoughts (Clark, 2004).

According to standard diagnostic categories, OCD is classified as an anxiety disorder. But it is an atypical anxiety disorder. OCD populations do not consistently show attentional biases characteristic of anxiety disorders, or even show anxiety as a dominant symptom, and guilt, blame and frustration can also accompany OCD. Anxiety may be secondary to the obsessional belief and some authors have argued that OCD would be better conceptualized as a belief disorder within a continuum between OCD overvalued ideation and delusional disorder (Insel & Akiskal, 1986; O'Connor & Grenier, 2004).

Treatment of OCD

The most successful behavioral therapy to date was developed from a phobic model of OCD development. Vic Meyer (1966), in an original case series, showed that the expectation of increased anxiety was not met when clients were exposed to the feared obsessional stimuli; but only when refraining from performing the compulsive ritual which Meyer realized delayed habituations. He termed the treatment exposure with response prevention (ERP). Subsequently, Eysenck, Rachman and colleagues hypothesized that OCD might follow Mowrer's two-stage theory of fear development and maintenance, whereby an initial conditioned anxiety response is subsequently reinforced by actions that lead to avoidance. The logic behind ERP then is to extinguish the compulsive ritual and avoidance by demonstrating spontaneous decline of anxiety over time during exposure in the absence of the negative reinforcement of the ritual or avoidance. This procedure requires initially tolerating a high level of anxiety.

In a now classic series of experiments, Rachman and colleagues (see Rachman and Hodgson, 1980) established that the prevention of the compulsive behaviour is essential if exposure is to be effective in reducing anxiety. But compulsive rituals and other forms of safety behaviours aimed at 'neutralizing' the obsessional anxiety are often subtle and difficult to detect. Mental neutralizations may impede exposure by defocusing attention of invalidating its effects by counterproductive thought patterns. The early recognition that thinking could actively maintain anxiety has led even strongly behaviourist practitioners to attend to thinking as a preliminary step towards motivating exposure (Foa & Franklin, 2002).

Cognitive behavioral therapy (CBT), based largely on exposure and response prevention, is the treatment of choice for OCD, either alone or, especially in more severe cases, in combination with pharmacological treatment (March et al., 1997). The CBT model predicts that exposure to the anxiety-provoking thought or object without performing compulsive rituals, other neutralizations or avoidance, will reduce the importance accorded to the thought and result in decreased obsessional preoccupation and associated anxiety. Meta-analyses on more than 30 studies with CBT treatments indicate large effect sizes that would generally support the claims of leading researchers that between 75–85% treated in these studies benefit from CBT (Abramowitz, 1996, 1997, 1998; Hiss et al., 1994; Steketee & Shapiro, 1993; van Balkom et al., 1994). However, despite these claims, there are large numbers of patients (estimates may be up to 40%) who either refuse treatment or drop out (Steketee, 1993), and there remain a number of subtypes of OCD who do not benefit substantially from CBT. Recent work has identified cognitive factors that play a role in maintaining obsessional behavior, such as beliefs, and appraisals about initial intrusive thoughts and cognitive challenges now play a significant role in CBT (Salkovskis, 1985, 1999).

COGNITIVE APPROACHES TO OCD

Cognitive models of obsessive-compulsive disorder (OCD) emphasize cognitive distortions and beliefs in the development and maintenance of this disorder. The initial clinical application of cognitive principles in the treatment of OCD was carried out by the pioneering work of Emmelkamp and colleagues (Emmelkamp & Beens, 1991; Emmelkamp et al., 1980; Emmelkamp et al., 1988) who investigated treatment based on changing irrational beliefs (Rational Emotive Therapy; Ellis, 1962). Since then, attention has shifted away from a focus on irrational beliefs in general towards identifying specific dysfunctional beliefs in OCD, based on Beck's (1976) cognitive specificity hypothesis, which holds that different psychological disorders are characterized by different dysfunctional beliefs (see Taylor, 2002a). The theoretical application of cognitive models to OCD, in particular, Beck's model of psychopathology, found its most coherent formulation in the work of Salkovskis (1985, 1989) who argued it is not the unwanted thought or intrusive cognition that leads to distress and compulsive behaviors, but how the person appraises these thoughts in terms of personal responsibility. Similarly, Rachman (1997) has argued that it is not the intrusive cognitions that cause distress and compulsive behaviors, but the consequences of these thoughts in terms of personal significance.

In these appraisal models the occurrence of the obsession came to be sharply delineated from the subsequent appraisal of the obsessional thoughts. The 'normal' nature of obsessions was indeed supported in several studies which found that intrusive cognitions share a similar content with obsessions in approximately 80%–90% of non-OCD populations (Rachman & DeSilva, 1978; Salkovskis & Harrison, 1984). However, it is worth noting that there was not a consensus across these studies defining intrusions, and not all intrusions were included. Also, it has recently been suggested that this argument may have been taken too far in that there are important inference processes, which go beyond content considerations, that may play a role in the production of obsessions before appraisals or beliefs come into play (Clark & O'Connor, in press).

The original work of Rachman (1997) and Salkovskis (1985, 1989) has guided most of the research on OCD, and the main impetus of research since then has been to identify other types of beliefs and appraisals that may play a role in the development of OCD, while pre-existing concepts such as over-estimation of threat (Carr, 1971), intolerance to uncertainty (i.e. 'intolerance to ambiguity', Frenkel-Brunswick, 1949), and perfectionism (Frost et al., 2002) still struggle to find their place in the appraisal model of OCD as specific obsessive-compulsive beliefs, rather than markers for anxiety disorders in general. More recent beliefs that have been proposed to be relevant to OCD are beliefs concerning the necessity to control thoughts (Purdon & Clark, 2002), Thought–Action Fusion (Rachman & Shafran, 1999), and beliefs or appraisals in general concerning the over-importance given to thoughts (Freeston et al., 1996).

The Obsessive Compulsive Cognitions Working Group (OCCWG) has attempted to identify the most important belief domains in order to bring clarity to the multitude of cognitive variables proposed to be relevant to OCD (OCCWG, 1997). This work has ultimately resulted in the Obsessive Beliefs Questionnaire (OBQ), focusing on six belief domains, namely intolerance to uncertainty, importance of controlling one's thoughts, perfectionism, inflated responsibility, over-estimation of threat and over-importance of thoughts (OCCWG, 2001, 2003). Although this measure does not claim to be exhaustive with respect to the measurement of cognitive beliefs that may be relevant to OCD, it has advanced the measurement of cognitive factors involved in OCD, and improved the ability to answer important research questions, which were previously limited by the sheer multitude of cognitive constructs proposed to be relevant to OCD. However, none or only some of the OBQ domains can claim to be specific to OCD (Clark, 2002; Taylor *et al.*, 2002), and the ability of these cognitive variables to explain OCD symptoms has been rather disappointing. Also, problems of overlap among these domains remain, and the question has been raised whether the OBQ measures irrational beliefs in general (Taylor, 2002a) or is better accounted for by negative mood states (Emmelkamp, 2002). It has also been suggested that the cognitions proposed to be relevant in OCD themselves require an explanation (Jakes, 1996; Taylor, 2002a). In fact, these authors argue that if appraisals and beliefs play some role in causing OCD, it is important to identify the causes of these beliefs and appraisals.

There is also the question of potential overlap between OCD-related cognitive measures and personality traits. For example, Aardema (1996) found that scores on measures such as the Irrational Beliefs Inventory (Koopmans *et al.*, 1994) could in large part be explained by personality (54%), in particular neuroticism (45%). In this regard, it is disturbing that the trait-like characteristics or beliefs that have been identified to be relevant to obsessive-compulsive disorder are often reminiscent of the same characteristics that have been identified in obsessive-compulsive personality disorder (OCPD). For example, perfectionism and mental control are characteristic of OCPD in DSM-IV-TR, while the link between inflated responsibility and OCPD is easily made. Even a concept such as intolerance to uncertainty, which appears to originate in the early work of Frenkel-Brunswick (1949), on 'Tolerance to ambiguity', and which was originally primarily associated with rigidity, has indirectly become wound up with OCD through the work of Hamilton (1957) who found obsessive-compulsive patients tended to avoid ambiguity on self-report ratings. Clearly, the advent of the appraisal model has inherited several concepts already in place. Yet, OCPD has not been shown to make a person more vulnerable to develop OCD (see Baer & Jenike, 1998). Thus, the initial enthusiasm of this endeavor to 'explain' OCD in terms of cognition by gathering a sufficient amount of measures of cognitive variables that would accommodate the entire spectrum of obsessive-compulsive symptomatology has lost some of its lustre. Indeed, it is starting to become increasingly clear that OCD is not akin to a personality disorder, which may be partially described, but not explained, in terms of an exhaustive set of beliefs and trait-like variables.

One of the main reasons for the tendency of cognitive models to focus on beliefs or trait-like characteristics in OCD is the assumption that all psychological disorders must be characterized by specific beliefs relevant to this disorder as per the cognitive specificity hypothesis of Beck (1976). The emphasis on beliefs to explain OCD has led to perhaps somewhat contrived and unnecessary attempts to phrase cognitive variables in terms of beliefs, while in fact some of the cognitive domains in the OBQ are more reminiscent of process variables or biases rather than particular beliefs. For example, the OCCWG has defined over-estimation of threat as 'beliefs indicating an exaggerated estimation of the probability or severity of harm', or intolerance to uncertainty as 'beliefs about the necessity for being certain' (see Taylor, 2002b, p.7). The tendency to phrase cognitive distortions or process variables in terms of specific beliefs is rather surprising, since the appraisal model of OCD was derived from Beck's theory of psycho-pathology, which does make an explicit distinction between cognitive beliefs and cognitive distortions or processes (Beck, 1976). However, cognitive accounts of OCD have failed to make such an explicit distinction between process and content characteristics of OCD, or at least, the distinction between content and process has become quite blurred in the past decade. Thus, the cognitive specificity hypothesis may have been applied in a rather selective manner focusing solely on beliefs at the expense of cognitive distortions and processes.

Traditionally, cognitive process variables have been associated with an information-processing paradigm and are often taken to refer to processes such as attention, perception and memory. However, other types of cognitive processes have been identified, which find their origin in clinical observations and reasoning-based paradigms rather than pure information-processing theory. The best-known of these are Beck's cognitive distortions such as over-generalization, all-or-nothing thinking and personalization. These types of cognitive processes have been almost completely ignored in popular cognitive models of OCD, and no attempts have been made to explicitly identify if these types of cognitive distortions operate in OCD.

Characteristically, process variables operate independently from specific mental content, and may apply to a wide variety of mental contents. For example, the cognitive distortion 'over-generalization' is not necessarily concerned with any particular content, but can apply to a variety of types of information. Even so, the delineation between process and content is often not entirely clear. The lack of delineation between process and content is intrinsic to the nature of these concepts. Generally, process variables deal with cognitive features of OCD that are not bound to *specific* thoughts and beliefs, but concern themselves with the *operation* of cognition. However, cognitive processes require content to operate upon, and without content there would be no process. Thus, process variables can differ with respect to their domain width, ranging from formal approaches dealing with information processing in general, and not limited to a specific category of information, through to cognitive processes that pertain to a specific content domain (i.e. over-estimation of threat). An example of an approach focusing purely on the form of obsessions would be Reed's (1985) cognitive structural approach to OCD that identifies a central process characterizing OCD as a tendency to over-classify events and information regardless of the content of the thoughts. In the words of Reed (1985, p. 214): 'if radio reception is distorted, we examine our receiver rather than the newscaster's announcements'.

Thus, despite the inherent symbiosis between process and content, the distinction is important, since it inevitably leads to different cognitive formulations of psychological disorders, research questions and even interpretation of results. For example, in early experimental research on OCD, Milner *et al.* (1971) suggested obsessional patients show a need for certainty to terminate ordinary activities. In a task that required the identification of a particular sound amidst white noise, the obsessional patients asked more often for a repetition of the sound than a control group. However, these results can both be interpreted as a *need* for certainty representing a particular belief or trait-like characteristic of OCD or as a tendency to doubt what was seen or heard correctly as the result of particular process characteristics operating in OCD.

Historically, doubt has always figured as an important characteristic of OCD (Janet, 1903), but is presently only given a marginal role in cognitive accounts of this disorder. However, several authors consider pathological doubt and uncertainty a prominent cognitive characteristic that pervades obsessional thinking (Rasmussen & Eissen, 1992; Reed, 1985; Ribot, 1905). While initially the application of Beck's model to OCD by Salkovskis (1985) almost appeared to equate doubt with intrusive cognitions (see ibid., p. 578, Figure 1), it has almost completely fallen out of favor since then. The neglect of doubt as a pervasive characteristic of OCD in current cognitive accounts is not entirely surprising. The concept of doubt does not lend itself well to appraisal formulations of OCD, since doubt is a mental state, which is more reminiscent of a particular cognitive process operating independently of specific content, rather than a particular belief. Besides the 'normalization' of intrusive cognitions, which inadvertently subsumed doubt under the same category, as mentioned before, the tendency has been to identify specific beliefs relevant to OCD rather than process characteristics or cognitive distortions.

However, there are several reasons to assume that a process-oriented approach to OCD may be a more fruitful line of research than a focus on specific beliefs and appraisals in OCD. Phenomenologically speaking, OCD is not as clearly defined in terms of pervading beliefs and feelings such as in depression where themes such as hopelessness and worthlessness come to the foreground in a relatively uniform way. In fact, the clinical manifestations of OCD are so varied that some authors have doubted whether all these varieties can be subsumed under the label 'obsessive-compulsive disorder' (see Reed, 1985). Obsessions do not exist in a vacuum, and while the senseless and ego-dystonic nature of obsessions is sometimes emphasized as a characteristic of OCD, this disorder tends to find its way towards content domains that in one way or another, and often indirectly, have some sort of personal relevance or importance to the individual involved. Hence obsessions often take a (semi-)idiosyncratic form. The idiosyncratic content of obsessions can be striking, and even though there are clearly subgroups of OCD patients with particular types of obsessions, clinical evidence suggests that the reasoning behind the same type of obsessions shows great variety in terms of cognitive content. Recognition of the idiosyncratic content of cognitive variables in OCD has led some to suggest that more idiosyncratic measures may be needed to assess cognitive characteristics in OCD, since current measures of obsessive beliefs such as the OBQ may reflect mood states rather than deeper cognitive structures (Emmelkamp, 2002). However, the difficulty with identifying specific obsessional beliefs may be intrinsic to the phenomenology of obsessive-compulsive disorder. That is, there may be no schema containing *specific* beliefs that cause this disorder, but rather patterns in reasoning that may revolve around *any* type of mental content or belief.

An inference-based approach (O'Connor & Robillard, 1995, 1999) bypasses the problem of idiosyncratic content in OCD, since instead of identifying specific beliefs or appraisals in OCD it emphasizes the reasoning *process* that is associated with the occurrence of obsessions. As mentioned before, without cognitive content there is no cognitive process, since cognitive processes require mental content to operate upon, but rather than identifying *specific* mental content, an inference-based approach locates specific reasoning processes proposed to be specific to OCD in idiosyncratic narratives that form the justification behind a particular obsessional doubt. Such an approach is entirely cognitive in nature and is loosely affiliated with information processing and neuropsychological paradigms without losing contact with the phenomenology of OCD and clinical applications, but it deviates from other cognitive models of OCD in that it does not locate the origin of obsessions in intrusive cognitions, nor in specific appraisals guided by specific beliefs that make these intrusive thoughts seem beyond control. In fact, it has been argued that appraisals and beliefs follow logically from the primary doubts in OCD, and as such may not represent essential elements in the development of OCD (Aardema & O'Connor, 2003). However, the exact relationship between appraisal and cognition requires empirical identification.

INTRUSIONS AND INFERENCES IN OCD

The quality of 'intrusiveness' in obsessions was first systematically elaborated by Rachman and Hodgson (1980) who noted that the essential characteristics of intrusive thoughts was their unwanted and unwelcome entry into consciousness, and this quality fitted well with clients' phenomenal experience. It is the unwanted nature, rather than the intrusiveness, which causes distress, since pleasurable spontaneous ideas tend to be more happily embraced as our own. Rachman and Hodgson also note that 'intrusive' does not mean entering consciousness from somewhere 'out there', that obsessions are prompted by external and internal prompts, and not 'inserted', but that although this conceptualization may be unsatisfying, it is difficult to discern another function for the content of obsessions other than their intrusiveness. The word 'intrusion' is of course used in other psychiatric domains where the intrusion may correspond better with a sense of thought insertion (Mullins & Spence, 2003), but is it an accurate term for obsessions? Intrusions have been variously defined as spontaneous, aversive or intrusive, although spontaneous thoughts may not count as intrusions if they are not ego-dystonic. Put bluntly, is it not more misleading than informative, if obsessional thoughts do not really intrude, to call them intrusions?

James (1890) noted our thoughts tend to evolve in a stream of consciousness with ideas chaining one onto the other in a continual flow, but the crucial element maintaining a preoccupation with obsessions is the personal significance attached to the 'intrusive' thought. The point of contention is how this personal significance gets attached. Historically, any intrinsic value attached to the content of the thought has been dismissed from the equation. Several studies have indicated that the content of intrusive thoughts is an universal experience shared with approximately 80% of non-OCD populations (Rachman & DeSilva, 1978; Salkovskis & Harrison, 1984). But as these studies noted, the intensity and frequency of the thoughts are greater in OCD populations, so we might surmise that even if the content is normal, the context in which the content appears is not always normal.

In fact, in any case the content of *all* obsessions has not been shown to be normal. In the original study by Rachman and DeSilva (1978), the obsessions associated with overt compulsions were under-represented, in particular more bizarre over-valued ideas, and further, some of the obsessions would now be recognized as mental tics (such as mentally replaying a song or phrase) which have a distinct etiology (O'Connor, 2004). Other items might be now considered more anxious than obsessive thoughts. Subsequently, Purdon and Clark (1993) have shown elegantly that the content of obsessional intrusions is distinct from both anxious and depressive automatic thoughts. Apart from the question of context, there is also the question of the form of the intrusive thoughts which is not well captured in simple statements of the subject matter. As several authors from Janet (1903) onwards have noted, doubt is an important quality of obsessional thoughts, particularly when talking of obsessions associated with overt checking or washing compulsions (example: 'perhaps the oven is left on', 'maybe my hands are dirty'). However, this doubting seems not to take the form of a genuine questioning doubt (example: 'I wonder if it will rain tomorrow', 'maybe this time next year I could be in London'). It rather takes the form of an inference of doubt about an actual state of affairs. Furthermore, the doubt is not posed in a spirit of impartial enquiry (example: 'now did I leave the stove on or did I not? Let's weigh up the probabilities either way and see what evidence best supports the hypotheses').

The appraisal argument would be that it is exactly the consequences which imbue the initial 'intrusion' with personal significance. The automatic negative appraisals become indistinguishably associated with the intrusion so that the intrusive thought evokes the same negative reaction. However, there are a couple of blips in this argument. First, as initially underlined by Jakes (1996), the processes by which intrusions turn into obsessions have never been fully elaborated. Second, appraisals do not relate to the specific content of intrusions, although some appraisals may be more specific to one rather than other subtypes of compulsion, e.g. appraisals of responsibility are hypothesized to be more relevant to checkers (Rachman, 2002), control of thoughts to ruminations (Julien et al., 2004). If intrusions were just haphazard thoughts, then the appraisal model would not need to accommodate the content. But even thinkers within the appraisal model recognize that the content can be thematic (Rachman et al., 1995; Trinder & Salkovskis, 1994). The themes, of course, relate generally to negative events, to harm and danger, yet in clinical practice, the themes of intrusions remain disarmingly personal and idiosyncratic. A person suffering from contamination fears constantly has the same doubt about germs landing on her skin (example: 'maybe airborne microbes have transferred onto my skin'). Similarly, a person with severe health anxiety is constantly seeking reassurance for her doubt 'maybe I have cancer', but not for any other disease. Thoughts of heart disease, diabetes, dementia, all statistically probable, cause no reaction. As pointed out elsewhere (O'Connor, 2002), doubts apparently comparable to the obsessional doubt seem never to occur even under duress. For example, the person with contamination fears about microbes landing on the skin is not afraid to touch plastic bags or shop counters or to breathe in air for fear of microbes. But objectively speaking, these activities could be equally infectious. She has no problems touching food or even real dirt in her apartment. A checker has a constant recurring doubt 'maybe something has fallen from my pockets'. He verifies his wallet has not fallen out of his pocket several times per day. He verifies that nothing has fallen out of his car when he leaves it. But he does not verify his doors or windows when he leaves the house because these stimuli do not activate his theme. Now it seems difficult to accommodate these 'incoherences' purely within an appraisal model. The appraisal model of course explains very well how an increased perception of harm or responsibility would augment the intensity of the compulsive neutralizing. But it seems unable to offer a satisfactory account of why a particular theme of obsession is repeated to the exclusion of others. Why, for example, wouldn't manipulation of increased responsibility in the checker above induce additional doubts related to windows, or in the case of the washer, to airborne microbes as well as augmenting the intensity of existing obsessional themes? Although studies with non-clinical populations have demonstrated a general effect of manipulating responsibility on performance, clinical populations tend to react differently in and out of pertinent OCD domains. The majority of people with OCD tend to suffer from one major subtype (56% of our cases) but even where people show more than one subtype, within each subtype, the obsessional theme still remains constant. For example, a homemaker with obsessions about cleanliness, tidiness and hoarding relates all the obsessions to a common theme about being a good enough mother.

PHOBIC AND NON-PHOBIC MODELS OF DEVELOPMENT IN OCD

A conceptualization of obsessions as inferences was initially inspired by clinical observation of OCD with over-valued ideation (OVI) (O'Connor & Robillard, 1995). Fixed beliefs with a strong personal investment have been observed in a variety of psychiatric complaints, but OVI is generally located on a dimension between obsessions and delusions (Jaspers, 1913; Spitzer *et al.*, 1991). The overlap between OCD and Delusional Disorder has been a matter of debate for some time, and the nature of OVI is an important element in determining whether OCD itself is best characterized as an anxiety disorder or a schizotypal disorder (Enright & Beech, 1990; O'Dwyer & Marks, 2000). It is recognized that similarities between both disorders may only be partial in that delusional disorder has several other dimensions such as systematization of belief, lack of insight about the belief causing distress and the type of emotions typically associated with the belief (O'Connor *et al.*, in press).

As noted, an inference-based approach conceptualizes OCD as a belief disorder rather than locating its causal development in the exaggeration of normal passing thoughts. The imaginary nature of representations has always figured as an important cognitive characteristic of delusional and related disorders where the person's beliefs deviate to a great extent from objective and/or consensus reality, but has not been given wide application in current cognitive models of OCD that emphasize rather the role of exaggerated and catastrophic interpretations. However, if the main obsessional concern revolves around themes only distantly related to objective events and objects as they occur in the here and now, then there may be reason to assume that OCD does not primarily follow a phobic model of development (O'Connor & Robillard, 1995). Instead of conceptualizing OCD solely as the result of appraisal of objective events (or intrusions), OVI highlights the remoteness of obsessional cognitive representation from the objective qualities of the feared object or event. This to the extent that 'the person with OCD does not react to what is there, and not even to the exaggerated of what is there, but to what might possibly be there even though the person's senses say otherwise' (ibid., p. 889). This would locate OCD in the different spectrum of related disorders than those of an appraisal model (see Figure 1.1).

While the concept of inferential confusion was inspired by observation of OCD with OVI, the exact nature of this relationship is still unknown. The concept of OVI itself is ill defined, and Veale (2002), while providing a conceptual analysis of over-valued ideas, argues for a better understanding of over-valued ideas, and that an advancement in assessment is required for this often neglected area of psychopathology, as well as novel treatments that specifically target over-valued ideas. However, it still remains to be seen whether over-valued ideation is a concept that is particularly relevant to a subgroup of OCD patients, or whether it represents a process characteristic operating in OCD in general. For example, inferential confusion (i.e. a tendency to negate and distrust the senses) may operate on a continuum ranging from obsessional doubt to pathological certainty, and represent a separate dimension from the high conviction levels seen in OCD with OVI. Empirical studies of the construct of inferential confusion are discussed in Chapter 5.

TREATMENT CONSIDERATIONS

Despite advances in cognitive-behavioural formulations of OCD, this has not led to improvements in treatment outcome. The early studies of Emmelkamp and collegues did not show any added benefit of including cognitive interventions in the treatment of OCD as compared to exposure *in vivo* (Emmelkamp & Beens, 1991; Emmelkamp *et al.*, 1988). Treatment

Anxiety Disorders

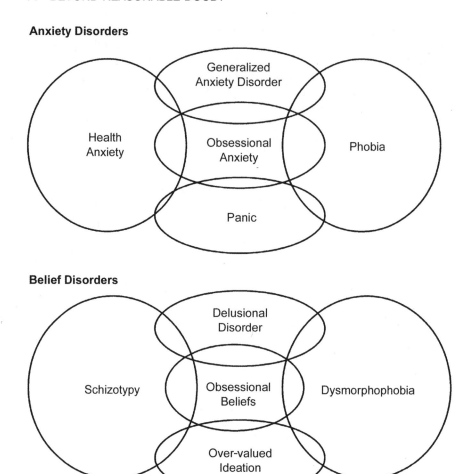

Belief Disorders

Figure 1.1   Diagnostic spectrum of anxiety and belief disorders

studies carried out since then, focusing on changing specific obsessive-compulsive beliefs, have yielded similar results (van Oppen *et al.*, 1995a).

In part, the lack of additional benefit from cognitive interventions in OCD treatment may be due to the self-imposed restriction of appraisal models which address the appraisal of intrusive cognitions, rather than the 'intrusion' or primary inference. However, if the content of the initial intrusion or inference holds an intrinsic meaning reflected in a higher than normal conviction, it will dictate the strength of subsequent reactions.

Hence, where obsessional conviction is high, the intrusion and appraisal are inherently linked and the obsessional sequence begins with the intrusions.

Clinically speaking, an inference-based approach (IBA) would suggest that all intrusions, even non-bizarre ones, are in fact inferences. However, in non-OVI or low obsessional conviction where the content of the initial intrusion is 'normal', the focus of the distress may not be the initial doubt, but the reaction and further consequences, which may be dealt with independently of addressing the doubt. However, even though addressing the initial doubt or primary inference may not be *necessary* to dispel distress, it should be *sufficient* to dispel distress since, in the IBA model, it is ultimately the trigger for the secondary distressing appraisal.

Exposure and response prevention remain the treatment of choice for OCD with, however, a high treatment refusal rate and with variable effects on cognitive and emotional factors. Also implicit in the IBA model is that OCD should be treated as a belief disorder, so in a sense one could view exposure *in vivo* and the appraisal model as dealing with the anxiogenic thought and behavior feeding discomfort *after* the belief formation and the IBA model as dealing with reasoning processes preceding belief formation. All three models are not incompatible, particularly if one considers that in non-OVI OCD, according to IBA, it is not the *content* of the intrusions, but the *context* of its arrival on the scene which is problematic. In other words, even if the content of the intrusion may frequently be normal, the reason for the same doubt arriving in a non-OCD sample may be more realistic and, in an OCD sample, more the product of subjective reasoning.

Although the appraisal and inference model can complement each other in practice (see Clark & O'Connor, in press), there are some points of contention in case formulation, since for the inference approach the obsession begins with the initial doubt. For example, let's consider an obsessional doubt about sexuality. A client is distressed by constant doubting about whether he is homosexual or not. The primary inference is: 'maybe I could be homosexual'. The appraisal approach to this problem would be to normalize the initial intrusion 'maybe I'm homosexual' and encourage the person to tolerate the uncertainty (Gyoerkoe, 2003). The inference approach would be, however, to consider the doubting as an obsessional doubt, not founded in reality, and so explore the narrative producing the doubt (and associated reasoning errors). The person might be basing the doubt of their sexual attraction on a series of category errors ('looking at a man is the same as being attracted to him'; 'in a recent film I saw two men meet at a gym, I work out in a gym, so that could be what I'm doing') rather than any genuine sense-signals of sexual arousal (such as spontaneous erection, arousing fantasies). Of course such clients often pursue a course of confirmatory testing behavior, where they will set up a 'sexual' situation and test their subsequent behavior (such as stand close to a target person while massaging their penis to see if they achieve an erection). The ensuing warmth from rubbing then risks being interpreted as evidence of arousal. The inference treatment approach here would be to return the client to making decisions about sexual orientation based on reality sensing, not on the basis of doubt-inducing narratives, and this approach contrasts with encouraging the client to tolerate the doubt through exposure.

An inference-based approach would share with cognitive behavior therapy the aim of detaching the person from the reality-value and importance of the intrusive thought. However, rather than identifying a thought as just a thought, the inferential confusion model would seek to identify the narrative which convinces the person that a hypothetical possibility is a real (even if small) likelihood or, in the case of 'fusion' obsession, identify the cross-over point when the person enters the imaginary world and the obsessional doubt becomes lived-in, and how subsequent rituals and other neutralizations are a natural consequence of a confusion between an imaginary and a real problem. This confusion of a subjective discourse with reality we term *inferential confusion*.

CONCLUSION

This chapter has situated the reader within current debates and controversies within cognitive theory of OCD. It has hopefully clarified how attention to reasoning and inferences may provide a helpful, and to some extent, novel perspective on OCD. It has also raised queries about the nature of IBA, namely: How does this approach relate to more formal approaches to the experimental study of reasoning? How does reasoning research address belief disorder? What other therapies have addressed reasoning? How does a focus on reasoning impact on other cognitive areas of functioning? Then there are the more direct questions on the validity of the approach. Can inferential confusion be reliably measured? Does it discriminate OCD from other disorders? Does modifying inferences produce change in symptoms? Does it add to other current treatments? How is it best implemented and delivered? The following chapters attempt to address these concerns. We start by examining reasoning in everyday life.

CHAPTER 2

REASONING IN EVERYDAY LIFE

FORMAL LOGIC AND INFORMAL THINKING

Introduction

Advanced forms of thinking such as deduction and induction are often said to differentiate humans from other species. The process of reasoning is specific to human beings and has allowed us to create a world that is so technically advanced, so artfully complex that it is no surprise philosophers, scientists and other observers of the human species have wondered about this ability of abstraction. How is it produced, for what purpose, and do all humans reason in the same manner? Are humans born with logic or do they learn to be logical? Under what circumstances are we logical and non-logical?

Psychological study of reasoning has largely evolved in the past 50 years. But cognitive psychology of thinking really gained prominence after Wason and Johnson-Laird's *Psychology of Reasoning: Structure and Content* was published, in 1972. Essentially, these authors developed a comprehensive theoretical account of reasoning as well as paradigms to describe and test everyday reasoning processes. Johnson-Laird (1983), and Johnson-Laird and Byrne (1991) developed a mental model theory of thinking which viewed these processes outside of formal logical theories of reasoning. We will describe the mental model theory further but, first, we will examine classic types of reasoning that have been studied and reported on in the literature.

Deduction

Traditionally, a difference is made between deductive and inductive reasoning. In deductive reasoning, a conclusion is drawn on the basis of true premises, whose truth value can be assumed. Hence, deduction produces correct conclusions which must be valid given that their premises are valid (Johnson-Laird, 1999). The valid nature of the conclusion is given not by the content of the premises *per se*, but by the structure of the argument (Manktelow, 1999). In its pure form, this would be represented in the following manner:

Major premise:	All A are B
Case:	A
Conclusion:	B

If you add content to such a proposition, you could read the following:

> All cats from this pet shop are Persian breeds.
> This cat was bought from this pet shop.
> This cat is a Persian breed.

In deductive reasoning, all the information required to draw a conclusion is implicitly found in the premises. Other forms of deductive arguments are presented by stating the major premises through a conditional statement, so for example: 'if p, then q'. Four particular cases derived from this conditional statement would produce specific forms of deductive reasoning. The first of these forms is what is also known as a *modus ponens* (MP) as in the following:

If it snows, then it is cloudy.	(If p, then q)
It is snowing.	(p)
It is cloudy.	(q)

It is possible to negate the antecedent (p) and then draw a different conclusion. An example of denying the antecedent (DA) is the following:

If it snows, then it is cloudy.	(If p, then q)
It is *not* snowing.	(not p)
It is *not* cloudy.	(not q)

Another possibility is the affirmation of the consequent (AC) as in the following:

If it snows, then it is cloudy.	(If p, then q)
It is cloudy.	(q)
It is snowing.	(p)

And finally, when the consequent is denied, we call this form a *modus tollens* which states 'if p, then not-q' as shown in the following example:

If it snows, then it is cloudy.	(If p, then q)
It is *not* cloudy.	(not q)
It is *not* snowing.	(not p)

Only two forms of deduction yield valid conclusions and they are the *modus ponens* and *modus tollens*. A valid deductive conclusion is one that is true if the premises are true. So if we assume that it is true that if it snows, then it is cloudy, the *reverse* (if it is cloudy, then it is snowing) is not necessarily true (DA) and neither is the *converse* (if it is not snowing, then it is not cloudy) (AC), so DA and AC do not lead to valid conclusions. In other words, a conditional rule is one of implication where p implies q but the rule is not one of equivalence, that is, p is not equivalent to q. That is precisely why DA and AC are not valid conclusions. For example, weather conditions other than 'snowing' can occur when it is cloudy (rain, thunderstorm, hailstorm, etc.) but snowing implies that it is cloudy, so it MUST be cloudy if it is snowing.

The following are clinical examples of how the different forms can seem valid but are effectively invalid, in a deductive sense.

An example of a *modus ponens* (MP) with a client's thoughts would be the following:

If I am first in everything, then I am perfect.	(If p, then q)
I am first in everything.	(p)
I am perfect.	(q)

The same example when denying the antecedent (DA) would yield the following:

If I am first in everything, then I am perfect.	(If p, then q)
I am not first in everything.	(not p)
I am not perfect.	(not q)

Affirmation of the consequent (AC) as in the following:

If I am first in everything, then I am perfect.	(If p, then q)
I am perfect.	(q)
I am first in everything.	(p)

And finally, the *modus tollens* as shown in the following example:

If I am first in everything, then I am perfect.	(If p, then q)
I am not perfect.	(not q)
I am not first in everything.	(not p)

All four examples are disputable from a clinical point of view simply because the initial premise is disputable (being 'first' in everything does not imply being 'perfect'). But from a logical point of view, both *modus ponens* and *modus tollens* forms are correct, and DA and AC could be debated with the patient because they take an illogical form.

Conditional Reasoning

It was Piaget in the mid-1960s who tried to explain how individuals were able to reason logically. His theory of abstraction suggested that, by adolescence, individuals were able to arrive at formal reasoning processes because such cognitive ability developed by an interaction between maturation and experience. In this view, adequate experience can lead to sophisticated thought processes. These cognitive processes are developed in different stages which are cumulative: sensorimotor, pre-operational, concrete operations and formal operations. However, Manktelow and Over (1990) make several criticisms of Piaget's theory and argue, for example, that ignorance may be at the root of poorer performance rather than lack of maturation and that memory capacities are necessarily better in adults than in children which would explain the differences in these abilities. In any case, mental logic has played a key role in research on the development of cognitive abilities. In fact, one of the first experimental tasks to apply the principles of deductive reasoning to look at thinking abilities was developed by Wason, in 1966. The 'Wason Selection Task' (WST) can claim to be the most investigated experimental procedure in the reasoning literature (Manktelow, 1999). One of the reasons must be that it is quite simple, yet extremely informative about human logical strategies.

The Wason Selection Task

For the readers in reasoning research, the description of this reasoning task will be very familiar but you at least hold the privilege of knowing the answer! For the others, be aware that in the normal population, not more than 10% of people correctly solve this task (Wason & Johnson-Laird, 1972) which means that it is just about normal NOT to be able to solve it! The experiment is the following.

You are presented with four cards set out like this:

The experimenter then presents you with the following conditional rule: '*If there is a vowel on one side, then there is an even number on the other*'. Your task is to point out which card(s) MUST be turned over in order to find out if the conditional rule is true or false.

The reason why this task informs us about deductive reasoning is because you need to use the abstract rule of logic concerning conditional reasoning ('if p, then q') which is to seek evidence that would disconfirm the rule (if p, then not-q) in order to come up with the right answer. Effectively, the logical reasoning here is not only to try to confirm the rule by turning over the 'A', which is what more than two-thirds of people choose (Manktelow & Over, 1990), but also to try to disconfirm the rule by turning over the '7' (the 'not-q' card). The rationale here is that even if the rule is confirmed, this does not tell us with complete certainty if it is true or false. However, turning over the card that is liable to disconfirm the rule yields the complete answer. As aforementioned, fewer than 10% of people try to falsify the rule and this result has been consistently replicated over the last two decades (Evans *et al.*, 1993). Researchers have tried to find ways of making this task easier by finding out the elements that caused difficulties. But Wason (1968) and Johnson-Laird and Wason (1970) proposed that the absence of falsification signified the existence of a *confirmation bias* in human reasoning, that is, the tendency to look for confirming evidence without looking for disconfirmation.

In trying to explain the WST results, Evans (1989) proposed evidence for a *matching bias*, which was explained by the tendency of the participants to check only the cards that had the information named in the rule (so, the vowel and the even number). This matching bias has prompted attention to the 'relevance' and 'context' in which reasoning takes place. To illustrate the idea of relevance, let's try another example with the following conditional statement: 'If you drink milk, then you are a cat'. How would you find out if this rule is true or false? Well, your first thought would NOT be to put a typical cat in a room with a saucer of milk and show me that he does indeed drink milk, because even if he did, we still would not know for sure if the rule is true or false. More likely, you would prove me wrong, maybe by drinking a glass of milk and saying, 'I drink milk and I am not a cat!' which is falsifying evidence that proves that the conditional rule is not true. So the rule is false in that sense, because one false case (you drinking milk and being human) shows it to be.

In the 'milk and cat' example, one could have replied: 'It is common sense that species other than cats drink milk! So the rule is false.' There is no need to look to and use abstract rules of reasoning to solve this particular 'cat and milk' task because knowledge and context can yield the correct answer. This point does illustrate a wider part of a debate that concerns researchers in the reasoning literature, as to how we reason. How do we arrive at conclusions? The debate is still open and some of the main positions will be discussed in the following section.

Arguments on Rationality

The first argument about logical tests of rationality is whether or not people reason with the mechanism inferred by the experimenter. Cohen (1981) sets out the 'normative system problem' by stating that, for example, people may be using a more personal system of probability (based on experience) while the experimenter expects and intends a more modern probabilistic mechanism of reasoning to be used. A second argument against a normative system of reasoning concerns the problem of the cognitive load such abstract tasks can put on a participant. It is thus argued that it is incorrect to qualify someone as being irrational if that person cannot solve a task that is beyond the limits of their human cognitive processing abilities.

The argument over cognitive processing abilities has been considered by Oaksford and Chater (1993) as a problem of 'external validity', where a normative system theory does not transpose well into real-life problems because previous knowledge and beliefs are taken into account in 'real-life reasoning'. Cohen (1981) has also argued that external validity was in danger because laboratory experiments were artificial and not represen-tative of normal thinking and reasoning.

A third argument of 'interpretation' may account for why participants may not be interpreting the reasoning problems in the way intended to be interpreted by the researcher. Henle (1962, cited in Evans & Over, 1996) argued that people's personal representation of the problems would yield conclusions that were logical in respect to that person's specific representation.

Finally, Evans and Over (1996) are concerned with the interpretation of these reasoning research results: they assert that experimental errors should not stand as proof of human irrationality. Their theoretical position is to try to resolve some of the proposed arguments of the normative system, interpretation and external validity. They have proposed a 'two kinds of rationality' solution. Rationality1 describes a personal way of reasoning based on knowledge, experience and beliefs while Rationality2 deals with following principles of logic. It is proposed that people use a combination of these two types of rationality where they will reason within a normative system (Rationality2) only if it supports their personal goal and personal logic, (Rationality1), to achieve these goals. According to Johnson-Laird (1999), this theory accommodates too much, and hence is circular and unverifiable.

Syllogistic Reasoning

We have just seen how conditional reasoning can be examined but we now turn to a more traditional and thoroughly investigated way of under-standing reasoning which dates to Aristotle: the use of syllogisms. The utility of abstract reasoning problems lies in their lack of use of prior knowledge or beliefs in order to achieve a 'pure' reasoning condition. As explained by Evans (1982), tasks in which real-life problems are examined increase the probability that some memory of a similar task instead of reasoning will be used. So the only way to avoid this dilemma is to create problems that do not use any examples referring to similar events (analogies). However, creating such a 'pure' condition is precisely what makes the debate on the external validity argument so important. That is, it becomes questionable to know if pure reasoning forms are really expressing the way we reason in everyday life. So as Manktelow (1999) puts it, there is a trade-off in any reasoning research.

Nevertheless, syllogisms are a restrictive form of reasoning which are typically exposed by stating a major premise and a minor premise in order to draw a conclusion. For example, the following sequence:

Major premise:	All A are B
Minor premise:	All B are C
Conclusion:	All A are C

Concluding on the relation between A and C, which has not been explicitly stated but inferred by the use of the minor premise 'All B are C', is at the root of syllogistic reasoning. A less abstract example of syllogistic reasoning would read as follows:

Major premise:	All athletes are healthy
Minor premise:	All healthy people drink lots of water
Conclusion:	All athletes drink lots of water

Syllogisms can be difficult to solve, as is suggested by certain empiric findings reported by Manktelow (1999) concerning overall adequate performance. So why do people make errors? Since the 1930s, many researchers have tried to understand why. For example, it was proposed that certain pairs of premises could suggest a 'mood' and lead to a 'type' of conclusion. This was called the 'atmosphere theory' (Woodworth & Sells, 1935, cited in Manktelow, 1999) and meant that, for example, a universal conclusion could be drawn from two universal premises or that two affirmative premises would lead to an affirmative conclusion. However, it was argued by Evans *et al.* (1993) that the atmosphere theory only explains the manner in which people *perform* syllogisms and not the reasons *why* participants react this way. Manktelow suggests that the atmosphere theory refers to a mechanism of response and that it can really be considered to be a response bias theory.

Deductive Reasoning

In an annual review article, Johnson-Laird (1999) proposes two ways of understanding deductive reasoning which form the basis of slightly conflicting theories. One is by measuring *deductive competence*, which yields theories of content, that is, *what* the mind is computing. Another is understanding *how* the mind is carrying out these computations, which leads to theories of *deductive performance*.

Deductive competence

We have already talked about Evans and Over's theory of two kinds of rationality which is part of deductive competence theories. Another example of a theory that examines *content* of reasoning is a model by Anderson (1990) where rational analysis is seen as an efficient evolutionary adaptation to the environment. For example, Cosmides (1989, cited in Newstead & Evans, 1995) reports on a way of reasoning that is guided by 'checking for cheaters' which would have evolved from our ancestors. In other words, it would be adaptive for survival to be on the lookout for people who break social contracts, and this would have evolved in consequence to natural selection. But this idea has been refuted on the grounds that experimentally, when the theory fails to be validated, it is then recognized that not all ways of reasoning are guided by adaptation to the environment. Johnson-Laird thus points out the tautological nature of the theory and that it does not yield to any scientific conclusions.

Theories of rationality have also been criticized in a recent review article by Shafir and LeBoeuf (2002). First, some authors criticize the very idea of rationality on the basis of validity and relevance of the findings that show that people make 'errors' and have 'biases'. Shafir and LeBoeuf reviewed studies of logical reasoning which clearly show that these biases are systematic and do not depend on whether or not participants are interested, motivated or even experts about the tasks. This does not mean that humans are illogical *per se* but maybe that the tasks are unrealistic in their demand of logical processing and that participants are reacting in a normative way. Other arguments concern the difference in how the experimenter construes the task vs the construal of the participant's view. In this case, the experimenter would be wrongly coding the participants' response. Another argument is that the participant may be wrongly interpreting the connection between two premises and not necessarily reasoning incorrectly. For example, in deductive tasks requiring probability judgements, the participants may not always be spontaneously thinking in terms of *mathematical* probabilities which is the correct way of resolving probabilistic tasks. Finally, overall format of the tasks may improve or reduce ability of resolution as well as cognitive capacity to compute the information given in a logical problem.

Deductive performance

There are three primary models explaining *how* the mind computes information, and how deduction takes place. One theory states that performance is derived from factual knowledge and that the repetition of an association of inferences transforms itself into a content-specific rule. A second school of thinking asserts that formal rules of inference are based on laws of logic which account for laws of thoughts. Third, a theory of mental models acknowledges that reasoning is based on manipulation of mental models representing situations.

In his review article, Johnson-Laird (1999) points out that a theory based on knowledge does not account for when a person draws conclusions about the unknown, that is, a logical argument that you know nothing about could yield a valid conclusion:

> If it's spwitching, then it's frashing.
> It's spwitching.
> Therefore, it's frashing.

The alternative inference rule-based theory also presents problems because it relies on ancient ideas that the laws of logic are, *ipso facto*, the laws of thinking. However, Johnson-Laird questions the testability of this argument since laws of logic can be tested in so many ways that it is difficult to know which process is really at work.

Finally, the mental model approach is based on semantics because understanding discourse depends on both meaning and knowledge. So a mental model represents a possibility and the structure of the mental models is construed by the form that these possibilities take. The mental model theory is described later in this section.

Inductive Reasoning

In inductive reasoning, a conclusion is drawn on the basis of some evidence. An inductive conclusion increases information but is not necessarily true, since it is drawn from one's own experiences, hypotheses, opinions and knowledge. For example:

> This is a Persian cat.
> This cat belongs to my sister.
> All of my sister's cats are Persian.

The conclusion here is a valid inductive conclusion because it is drawn perhaps on the knowledge that my sister only buys Persian cats. This knowledge mediates the conclusion 'all of my sister's cats are Persian' which increases the information we had (this is a Persian cat and it belongs to my sister') but, at the same time, reduces the possibility of coming to other conclusions, that is, the inductive conclusion here rules out that my sister may have other types of cats. This is precisely what differentiates inductive logic from deductive logic. In other words, conclusions in inductive reasoning add information that is not necessarily in the premises which means that, contrary to deductive reasoning, here, the content of the argument cannot be separated from the form. The meaning of the premises and what they imply are at the heart of induction (Myers *et al.*, 1986). The point is well explained and a comprehensive definition of inductive reasoning is proposed by Johnson-Laird (1993). It states that induction is 'any process of thought yielding a conclusion that increases the semantic information in its initial observations or premises'. Again, what the definition implies is that the content of the proposition has the implication of ruling out certain states of affairs. Manktelow (1999) underlines the distinction between general and specific induction. General inductive reasoning stems from combining several states of affairs to draw a general conclusion (reasoning from the particular to the general). Specific inductive reasoning is going from a particular case to a particular conclusion.

In his theoretical article on induction, Johnson-Laird (1994a) reports on two main lines of ideas about induction which have been of historical importance. The first idea is that induction is looking for the common characteristics of a set of observations. These common elements are necessary but sufficient to classify instances. For example, only ducks quack, so if you quack, you are a duck and if you don't, you are not a duck. The second idea contradicts the 'common elements' theory by proposing a 'prototype' theory which states that understanding stems from having typical images mentally represented and in store in order to classify instances. For example, having an image of a typical duck in mind as an animal that quacks, paddles with its feet in the water and can fly long distances permits the classification of an instance by how representative it is of the prototype.

An important question that has preoccupied researchers is one concerning the 'correctness' of an inference, that is, how is induction justified? For Johnson-Laird (1994a), current research on induction is in a state of uncertainty and 'no adequate theory of the human inductive process exists' (ibid., p.14). He argues that the mechanism of induction is almost inseparable from normal mental activity since it is part of how we make sense of the world and the way we do that is by having models based on the availability of pertinent knowledge (see the 'availability heuristic' in Tversky & Kahneman, 1982) to the state of affairs that we are reasoning about. This leads us most of the time to use inductive reasoning in everyday life, which, as was explained earlier, does not always lead to true conclusions. But it is the form that we use in everyday reasoning because valid deductions are not possible in the absence of all true or necessary information.

Manktelow (1999) also reports on the dilemma that has prevailed for years on how one instance can yield a generalization while at other times, many instances that should lead to a particular inference do not form the basis for generalization. A common clinical example illustrating this would be characterized by a depressed person who on account of one single negative event would conclude that they have had a 'bad day' and on a day of plenty of positive events occurring would fail to report that they have had a 'good day'. Johnson-Laird (1994b) suggests that what makes the strength of an argument depends on the relation between the premises and the conclusion but also on the proportion of possibilities that are compatible with the premises, in which the conclusion is true. Johnson-Laird's theory of mental models will be discussed in the following section.

Mental Models

Inspired by the work of Kenneth Craik (1943; cited in Johnson-Laird, 1994b) on how the mind has created 'small-scale models' of reality, Johnson-Laird (1983) initially developed his theory of Mental Models (MM) to explain verbal comprehension. When people try to make sense of a narrative, it is hypothesized that they create a model in their mind of the situation that is discussed. The model itself can be a visual image or a word but most importantly, its structure corresponds with the way humans consider the structure of the world to be (Johnson-Laird, 1994a).

The theory was revised by Johnson-Laird and Byrne (1991) in order to explain deductive reasoning. The MM theory suggests that there are three levels of thinking that people go through when they are trying to draw conclusions. They first try to understand the premises by using what they know in general and according to their level of language as well. Then, they will construct models about what has been understood from these premises. The models can be images, words or instances of each premise. The next level involves combining the models in order to draw a description of the state of affairs they are trying to compose. This description must yield to a conclusion which includes new information, outside of the given premises. If the person doing the reasoning does not find such a conclusion, he or she will not answer that anything follows from the premises. However, if he or she does find a conclusion, the last stage will have the reasoner searching for alternative models which would be coherent with the premises but where the supposed conclusion would be false. This last level then involves validating that no falsifying model compromises the conclusion, that is, that the conclusion is valid. If alternative models do falsify the conclusion, then it is false and the reasoner must search for a new conclusion which no alternative model can falsify.

The MM theory makes three predictions about reasoning processes. First, the more models which need to be invoked for a given inference, the more difficult the task will be to solve. Johnson-Laird and Byrne (1991) effectively introduced the psychological element of a cost–benefit ratio where one will naturally try to construct as few models as possible in order to avoid cognitive overloading, the capacity of model representation being restricted by working memory constraints. The second prediction of MM theory is that invalid conclusions will be drawn if they are based on a faulty model, that is, a model that is incomplete and overlooks other possible models. This problem can be tested by noting if erroneous conclusions are consistent with erroneous premises. The third prediction is that reasoners will search for alternative models much more when the conclusion is not believable. Hence, knowledge influences the reasoning process. These three predictions have been tested using reasoning paradigms and yielded empirical support (for a full review, see Johnson-Laird & Byrne, 1991).

Biases in Reasoning

The majority of research focusing on reasoning biases stems from experiments in syllogistic and conditional reasoning. In syllogistic problems, participants seem to be influenced by two main and almost standard influences: the logic of the problem and the 'non-logical' issues (Evans & Over, 1996). Logic of the problem refers to performance, hence, the degree to which people possess logical deductive abilities. 'Non-logical' components refer to the extent to which reasoners are influenced by aspects of the task which are not meant to interact with its resolution. For example, the belief bias is the tendency for people to accept invalid arguments because they have believable conclusions, not necessarily correct ones. Evans (1983) suggests that the belief bias may be in place because people don't find logic necessary, which he calls 'misinterpreted necessity'. In other words, for most people, the fact that an argument *may* follow from a premise is good enough to conclude that it is valid, whereas in logic, a conclusion *must* follow from an argument to conclude that it is valid.

Some researchers have tried to reduce the belief bias by adding information in the instructions to help the participants avoid using prior knowledge and understand that a logical valid conclusion *must* follow from the given premises and only IF they do, should they conclude it is valid, regardless of whether the conclusion is plausible. Experiments by Newstead and colleagues (1992; 1994; cited in Evans & Over, 1996) showed that the belief bias could be greatly reduced with the use of these 'augmented instructions' but not completely eliminated.

Another example of a reasoning bias is the confirmation bias that was discussed earlier and illustrated by Wason (1966) in his Selection Task results. People naturally tend to be satisfied with evidence that confirms what they already believe and do not try to disconfirm such a belief. Evans (1989) has underlined that confirmation bias arises not because people don't want to falsify information but rather because there is an inability to do so.

Probabilistic Reasoning

Probabilistic reasoning is concerned with the estimates that people make when they are uncertain about a statement. In everyday life, people make inferences on the basis of *subjective probability*, that is, the subjective amount of confidence they have in a proposition (Manktelow & Over, 1990). People also make decisions based on *subjective utility* which describes the degree to which someone has a use for a possibility. Some of the interesting questions about probability judgement concern finding out how people develop and maintain their degrees of belief as well as the way in which they acquire such an ability. Another area of research examines how experience affects beliefs that have already been formed. As has been shown by the Wason Selection Task experiment, it seems that people are prone to look for confirming evidence so that experience may be 'fitted' into beliefs.

Another very important experiment which empirically validates the idea of confirmation bias was devised by Wason (1960). It is known as the '2-4-6 Problem' and it tests inductive reasoning. Participants are presented with a series of three numbers (typically: 2, 4 and 6) and they are told that they need to discover a rule that the experimenter has in mind, which governs the order of the three numbers. For the participant to find out what the rule is, he or she needs to write down a series of three numbers that would illustrate it. For each set of numbers, the experimenter will indicate whether their guess conforms to the rule but participants are instructed to announce the rule only once they are sure it is the correct one. The participant writes down each of his hypotheses. So, for example:

Instances	(+ or −) (conforms or not)	Hypothesis	
2 4 6	Given.		
32 34 36	(+)	Adding 2 to even numbers.	
7 9 11	(+)	Adding 2 to any numbers.	
22 28 34	(+)	Any increasing even number.	
62 73 81	(+)	Any increasing number.	Correct.

So the rule is 'any increasing number' but the major finding is that participants have a tendency to test only positive instances of the hypothesized rule which shows that falsification is not a primary reasoning strategy used by people in general. In other words, the confirmation bias found from the results of the Wason Selection Task is also apparent in this task.

Reasoning with Heuristics

The work of Tversky and Kahneman in the early 1970s concerns reasoning as a decision-making operation where premises are judged according to a restricted number of heuristics. These heuristics are principles which allow people to avoid calculating probabilities or predicting values. However, these heuristics can lead to systematic errors because the assessment of premises is based on data of limited validity. So, for Tversky and Kahneman (1982), just as people's perceptions can deceive reality, heuristics activate a bias on judgement of probability.

Representativeness heuristic

For example, the representativeness heuristic leads a person to rely on the degree to which A resembles B, or how much A is a representative of B. So, if you are given the following characteristics about a man: 'talkative, sociable, good with numbers and always on the run', how would you try to figure out the probability that this man is an accountant?; a salesman?, a librarian?; a researcher? The representativeness heuristic would lead you to the stereotypical judgement that these characteristics most likely represent a salesman. While this may be true, it is not always the case because base rates (i.e. how many salesmen in proportion to accountants, etc.) are not considered when the representativeness heuristic filters judgement.

Another example of the representativeness heuristic is the misconception of chance or what is called the 'gambler's fallacy'. Chance through this heuristic is perceived to be a self-correcting mechanism where people expect that the appearance of A is 'due' after many Bs have appeared. For example, if you roll two dice and don't get doubles after 10 consecutive draws, the gambler's fallacy would have you believe that rolling a double is 'due' where in actual fact, random chance could dictate that another 10 rolls of the dice will appear before getting a double.

Tversky and Kahneman (reported in Manktelow & Over, 1990) devised a simple problem to illustrate the representativeness heuristic bias which is known as the 'Linda problem'. Essentially, it shows that people commit what is called the conjunction fallacy, that is, concluding falsely that a conjunction is more probable than its own case. The problem is the following:

Linda is 31 years old, single, outspoken, and very bright. She majored in philosophy. As a student, she was deeply concerned with issues of discrimination and social justice, and also participated in anti-nuclear demonstrations. Which is more likely?:

Linda is a bank clerk.
Linda is a bank clerk who is active in the feminist movement.

The correct answer is the first one: Linda is a bank clerk. The reason is there are only a small amount of bank clerks who are feminists so it would be less probable that Linda would be both. But the representativeness heuristic would suggest that Linda's actions and values are representative of being a feminist, hence she is likely to be active in the feminist movement.

Availability heuristic

The availability heuristic explains how people estimate the frequency or probability of the occurrence of an event by bringing to mind the easiest example of a class of event, that is, instances of large classes of events are recalled quicker than infrequent ones. For example, Tversky and Kahneman (1973; cited in Tversky & Kahneman, 1982) presented a list of famous men and women to participants, instructing them to read it once and then judge whether the list contained more men then women. The lists were manipulated where, in some of them, the men were relatively more famous than the women, and vice versa on some of the other lists. Results demonstrated that the lists containing the class (gender) that had the more famous people were judged to include more of that particular gender. The authors conclude that familiarity yields erroneous decisions, according to the availability heuristic. Other biases created by the availability heuristic include bias due to the effectiveness of a search set, that is, the ease with which certain sets of words come to mind will affect a probability estimate; bias of imaginability occurs when one imagines a set of probabilities so vividly that it actually incorrectly qualifies the actual likelihood estimate of the occurrence of such a probability; and bias of illusory correlation (Chapman & Chapman, 1969, cited in Tversky & Kahneman, 1982) describes the tendency to judge the occurrence of two events based on the strength of their association, that is, because of their strong bond, these events will be judged to have occurred together more frequently than they actually have. As will be explained later, this tendency has clinical implications.

Anchoring (or adjustment) heuristic

The anchoring heuristic describes the fallacy of starting with an initial value biased to fit the final answer. In other words, the base rate seems to be suggested either by the formulation of the problem or by the result of a partial computation. An illustration of such a bias was demonstrated by Tversky and Kahneman (1982). Their study involved spinning a wheel in front of participants and asking them to estimate if various quantities, stated in percentages (i.e. 'What is the proportion of African countries participating in the United Nations?'), were higher or lower than the arbitrary spin number. The assessments of participants were significantly derived from the arbitrary starting point which clearly shows that accuracy is influenced by anchoring. Another example concerns decision-making where experts need to estimate a quantity in the form of a probability distribution. Participants have been observed to estimate very narrow confidence intervals, reflecting an over-confidence in their judgement not justified by their knowledge.

Conclusion

This section has outlined the main differences between deductive and inductive reasoning and described the main reasoning paradigms that have been used to test these inference processes. The key finding from this extensive research is that people in the general population have trouble resolving logical tasks. Effectively, they are prone to different reasoning biases which lead them to false conclusions. Moreover, certain forms of deduction are invalid and yet, people do not seem to be able to differentiate between those which are valid (*modus ponens* and *modus tollens*) and those that are not valid (affirming the consequent and negating the antecedent). This has led reasoning researchers to hypothesize about how people reason. Effectively, theories like Johnson-Laird's mental models theory or Tversky and Kahneman's heuristics theory have helped to view reasoning as guided by factors other than formal logic. For example, the mental models theory tells us that people have representations of 'how the world is' and they will draw inferences based on these models. So if the model is incorrect, invalid conclusions may be drawn from it. Tversky and Kahneman (1982) have provided evidence that heuristics seem to guide reasoning so that it is understood that people will look for the easiest way to judge a probability, not necessarily the most valid judgement. Hence, it appears that context is important to inference and the next section will explore this notion in detail.

MAKING SENSE OF THE SENSES

Logic and Experience

As we saw in the previous section, reasoning research is increasingly concerned to extend paradigms to accommodate everyday reasoning. Put another way, apparently rational people seem, in overwhelming number, misled when following the rules of reason under most circumstances. Their reasoning depends more on the evaluation of context and self-interest than formal logic and they are happily susceptible to a range of cognitive illusions arising from apparently invalid inferences. Furthermore, this illogical thinking, if not normative, is clearly normal and adaptive. People *do* reason. They are constantly drawing inferences. They infer meaning, causality, future courses of action. But they do it their way.

So why do people reason illogically? In this section we turn this question around and ask, what are the processes by which people reason in the real world other than by formal rules? Do we need perhaps to abandon the logical template in everyday life and adopt other more psychological models of inference? The previous section has already discussed the antagonism between rule-based and mental model approaches to reasoning, and in particular between deductive and inductive logic. Deductive logic is a closed system where theoretically anybody starting at one place can end up at another without any external input. It would seem tailor-made to arrive at impartial decisions. Yet, for most people, this deductive logic goes awry even in the most contrived deductive situations; even, indeed, when the goal is to perform well in an academic experiment in syllogistic reasoning. People do not follow logic even when logically they should, to the evident frustration of logicians, who have variously suggested training people to think logically (Evans, 1989); or that we humans should abandon all hope of reasoning with our folksy ways and mentalistic psychology, until a more appropriate machine-based technical vocabulary is available to reason for us (Churchland, 1986; Feyerabend, 1963/1970).

An alternative is to seek human logic in human experience itself. Inductive logic is inferring from experience. But here again we seem to have a paradox. Two people cannot share the same experience, so how could they converge on induction? Yet people can arrive at an inductive consensus. Indeed, whole cultures can agree when the induction is about received experiences. Conversely, deductive logic is itself influenced by inductive experience, especially in the formation of initial premises. The initial inference usually has a taken-for-granted truth value but if it is faulty, it can lead to faulty conclusions even where the subsequent deduction is faultlessly logical. In everyday life, reasoning seems a mix of both induction and deduction. One easy route to accommodating the alternation between induction and deduction is to say that the two reasoning modes operate together; that induction supplies the premises and deduction produces the subsequent conclusions. The problem with this argument is that it assumes people can switch from deductive to inductive mode at appropriate stages in reasoning, which does not seem to be the case. In talk aloud experiments, people usually manifest a continuous back and forth between reason and experience (Wason *et al.*, 'Mensa Man', quoted in Manktelow & Over, 1990) and context, emotion and personal investment seem to be the operative factors in conditioning the outcome of reasoning.

In effect, it is clear, as Tversky and Kahneman's (1982) work shows, that people use thinking selectively not in pursuit of objective truths, but in pursuit of the most adaptable outcome, which, of course, is itself a multi-dimensional and moveable goal. Adaptable, that is, not to the situation in general but to their personal situation at the moment. In other words, thinking works by logic only when abstracted from experience. In everyday life the logic is part of experience, not the other way round. In real life, reasoning is 'hot' and we are frequently dealing with surprises, incoherences, paradoxes amidst our reasoning, not the even progression of rule-based logical postulates.

Evans and Over (1996) have proposed a kind of dual process model whereby two discrepant inference processes exist at the same time. One is holistic, affective, association-driven and automatic – Evans and Over (1996) term this Rationality1 – for achieving everyday goals. The other, normative and rule-based Rationality2, requires effort to arrive at normative 'inferences' which can then over-ride the automatic irrational-ities. Although, as Shafir and LeBoeuf (2002) point out, this approach would find a resonance with cognitive theories (e.g. Shiffrin & Schneider, 1977) which distinguish automated and controlled processing or immediate and effortful responses (Zajonc, 1980), it is unclear whether such differences in reasoning (unlike automated and controlled processing) are generated by task demand. It seems more parsimonious to argue that Rationality2 is a special case of Rationality1 and only when reasoning is abstracted from context, or imposed on the context, are normative rules followed in themselves. Indeed, in everyday life, those who attempt to take refuge in cold logical rules would seem to be the inadapted ones. This refuge in rules has a particular relevance for OCD, as discussed later.

In life, reasoning becomes adapted to and by context. *In logic*: Socrates is a bachelor, bachelors are men, so Socrates is a man. *In life*: Jane says she's a bachelor, bachelors are men, yeh, but Jane's definitely a woman. So perhaps Jane means she's a bachelor girl or maybe she's lying, or perhaps she's implying a different sense because she doesn't know the proper use of the term. So let's start again and qualify the premise. Jane is a girl who calls herself a bachelor...A whole context of social, biographical, topical issues arise around even the simplest inference. In fact, going back to Tversky and Kahneman (1982), it is evident that factors such as topicalness, remark-ableness, proximity, or accessibility influence judgement calls simply because they keep reasoning close to home, and constitute the context here and now.

The Effect of Context in Reasoning

One crucial demonstration of the effect of context on reasoning is the 'framing effect', whereby reasoned decisions can be modified as a function of the way a problem is presented. In the framing effect, the same inference problem can lead to completely different conclusions, solely on the basis of the context in which it is presented. We have already discussed this in reference to the Wason Selection Test. A classic example of framing is found in Tversky and Kahneman (1982), where a choice between two different programs for combating a disease was framed in terms of lives saved or lost. Program A will save 200 lives out of 600. Program B has a 1/3 probability of saving 600 lives and a 2/3 probability of saving no one. Put in this way, the majority of participants preferred program A. But, when the choice was reframed in terms of loss – Program A will lead to 400 deaths; Program B has a 1/3 probability of no deaths and a 2/3 probability of 600 deaths – the majority chose program B. The framing effect extends to other problems in deductive reasoning and may be due to relatively unequal subjective values attached respectively to loss and gain, or it may be, as Legrenzi et al. (1993) suggest, due to a focus on restricting thoughts only to what is explicitly presented in mental models.

In another example (Owen White, personal communication), a 'framing effect' influences solutions to the following two logical problems. (1) There are three cards face down, two black and one red, and you must select the red card from the three. After you have indicated your choice, one of the two cards you did not pick is removed at random. You now have the chance to rechoose between the two existing cards. Is there any advantage to changing your choice? (2) There are three accounts, only one of which is truthful. You must choose one account from the three. After you have chosen, one of the two accounts you did not pick is removed at random. You now have the chance to rechoose from between the two remaining accounts. Is there an advantage to now changing your choice?

The answer in both cases is that there is no advantage to changing choice if one of the three cards or accounts is removed. But generally this is more obvious in the second than the first example, because the first seems framed as a probability task, and choosing one out of two gives a higher chance than picking one out of three. In the second example, the reference frame is more substantive than statistical.

Also, despite Pascal's famous phrase about the heart having its own reasons which reason doesn't know, we can also reason emotionally using 'affect heuristics', also known as emotion-based reasoning (Engelhard *et al.*, 2001). One clinically relevant example of affective heuristics is ex-consequentia reasoning (Arntz *et al.*, 1995) where feeling anxious that something is wrong leads to the intellectual conclusion that there is danger. Feelings can also form a key source of reference for deciding on a course of action. People may reason on the basis of their own feelings that an event is important, or infer from feeling that a certain situation or person has certain attributes. Evaluative conditioning has established that preferences based on unconditioned reactions can be generalized to other essentially irrelevant properties (Levey & Martin, 1987). People may also consciously over-ride logic out of feelings (e.g. such as compassion). Often the emotive appeal of a subject may over-ride its rational appreciation. In therapy, clients will often feel compelled to do an action because it just doesn't 'feel' right not to do it. Clinicians in research protocols can have a hard time administering treatments which seem to offer less, because it feels intuitively as though the client would benefit from 'the more the merrier' maxim (regardless of proof to the contrary). For example, there was a celebrated case of a Canadian doctor (see 'l'affaire Poisson', la Presse, December 1st, 1995) taking part in a clinical trial to test the effectiveness of two cancer treatments, who falsified protocols and gave all his clients one treatment because he *felt* ethically unable to refuse them the benefit (despite no evidence that it was superior). In fact, aphorisms can often provide the source and received wisdom for strong emotively appealing premises, until, that is, one finds that the aphorisms themselves need to be contextualized, since in absolute terms they are often self-contradictory (example: 'many hands make light work' vs 'too many cooks spoil the broth').

In everyday life, as we saw with the Jane example above, premises frequently need to be complex, relational, and qualified by experience. As Johnson-Laird (2001) notes, in logic, connectives such as disjunctions and conditionals have idealized meanings as truth functional but natural language is not truth functional and connectives conveying temporal or spatial relations and modulation in general violate logical constraints of reason. One problem is that the premises may be conditioned by distinct sources of experience (reflective, affective, sensory experience) often leading to conflict. Indeed, the formation and automatic acceptance of a conditional conflicting premise can lead further deduction astray.

Exchange (in Montreal)

A. I bet you ten bucks I can prove logically that I'm not here.
B. OK. Because you can't. That's ridiculous.
A. Well, I'm not in Russia, am I?
B. No. Of course not, you're here.

A. If I'm not in Russia, I must be somewhere else.

B. Yes, OK.

A. But if I'm somewhere else, I can't be here.

B. Mmm...I guess.

A. Ten bucks, please.

B. OK... but you're not here so I can't give it to you.

This trivial example is a good illustration of how terms of reference within a reasoning cycle can rely on different sources and contradict themselves. In this case, the conflict is between sensory evidence and semantic points of reference. A less comic example of the same conflict would be:

A1. I'm having a great time here enjoying myself.

A2. But if I'm happy, that means I'm not sad any more.

A3. But if I'm not sad, I'm not being serious.

A4. If I'm not serious, I can't be acting properly.

A5. Now I'm not enjoying myself here any more.

As several authors (ex. Popper & Miller, 1983) have argued, there may be no such phenomenon as inductive logic, there is only deductive logic but there may be inductive psychology and inductive behavior. The fact that induction looks outwards to the world of experience is perhaps best shown by the lack of standardized inductive tests (as compared to tests of deductive logic), and the need for such tests to leave large leeway for connecting with individual experience. One of the most systematized forms of inductive reasoning is Bayesian decision-making which bases estimates of prior personal probabilities on personal utility and continually updates probabilities according to the current states of affairs. Such inductive methods of inference, which incidentally conflict with the more standard scientific procedures of hypothetico-deductive reasoning (O'Connor, 1985, 1990), emphasize how inductive psychology is intimately bound up with evaluating the world. In other words, people use their senses and experiences to arrive at relevant inductive inferences about states of affairs. Inductive logic is then behavioral logic and in the service of psychological laws. Hence, in order to understand inferences, we need to understand the psychology of knowing rather than improve formal logical constraints *on* our knowing. So how do we know the world and make enough sense of our experiences to draw inferences?

Knowledge and Experience

Our experience of the world is always with us, it is the totality of meaning surrounding us at any given time. In contradiction to the Monty Pythonesque query, 'What is the meaning of life?' the reality is we can never escape meaning. The philosopher Edmund Husserl (1973) made the point that experience is what we are always certain of and the more we move away from direct experience, the less certain we are of anything. I know from my experience that I am sitting here in front of a table writing with a window on the communal garden. I'm certain of it. Of course, I may not be certain of a variety of features in the garden or the room, the names of flowers, the type of wood in the table. But that I am experiencing this as a reality is certain. I also know there's a room next door. I'd bet a lot of money that room has a table and a window but I can't be 100% sure of it in the way I am sure of this room. Of course, when it comes to inferring conclusions or future courses of action on the basis of my senses, I can be mistaken and the evidence of my senses certainly does not translate naturally into a guaranteed correct course of action. But I am nonetheless always certain of what appears before me. If I smell donuts, I smell donuts. There may be no donuts. There may even, objectively speaking, be no smell of donuts, it might be cleaning fluid smelling like donuts. But I'm still certain of what I smell. If my experience gives me certainty, it makes sense to call on it in times of uncertainty.

Similarly, the physical dimensions of the world are always around me, and equally part of my experience, and I always am able to place myself in relation to the world and others in time and in place. If I'm disoriented then my lack of such ability only emphasizes its importance in locating me in the world. My experiences are always grounded in a world around me, I am always in the world, and in an active relationship doing this or that or not doing this or that. Indeed, I can't think or do without being in the world whether I like it or not, since such is the human condition. So if I do not exist as a solitary self but as a relating self, then my unit of experience must always take the form of a self–world relation. In other words, I experience by interacting. No interaction, no experiences. So how does this self–world relation define my experience?

One popular account, known as both the realist account and the 'common-sense' philosophy, is that the world precedes me, is independent of me, and constitutes a physical universe which I negotiate, or if not bump into. This negotiation in the process creates my experience of the world and myself, entirely by one major defining hybrid characteristic: physical-out-thereness. Most realist philosophers do not adopt a radical realism which would be akin to living like the character in the Samuel Beckett play *Mime* pushed and pulled willy-nilly by external forces. So most realist models include different degrees of mediational arguments. Physical things are out there. They go on out there independent of me. I, with my senses, notice them, or don't notice them, because my senses are tuned or not tuned to pick up physical characteristics relayed to my brain through ambient light or sound, or by touch. The brain through its mediational (i.e. cognitive) faculties makes sense accordingly. I can, of course, choose what I attend to, I can ignore or disregard, or attend by degrees. I can think about what I notice, categorize it, convert it, react to it, treat it symbolically, but in all cases reality must be represented in my mind in order to go any further. This representation must 'correspond' to a reality out there, and there is a right and a wrong correspondence. If there is an elephant and I see a hat, my representation is inaccurate. It may be 'biased' rather than inaccurate, so that if someone greets me and I view selected features as a menacing threat, I may be said to have a threat bias. Here, I would still see the right thing (a person saying hello) but my bias would be due to interpretation not representation. The term 'bias' has of course crept stealthily into the cognitive vocabulary, but the term is borrowed from electronics, where bias is created in a circuit to direct current flow. Inevitably since the realist model views information processing as an input–output problem, it draws heavily on electronic metaphors and the black box instrumentation of the cognitive brain keeps apace with the advance of technological wizardry, from the resistance-capacitance filter models of the 1950s, transistor theory in the 1960s, cybernetics of the 1970s, information technology of the 1980s, and parallel distributed networks in the 1990s. As an operational heuristic for getting about and living day to day, the realist model is clearly useful. Apart from a few hiccups under ambiguous (illusionary) conditions, the notion of independent physical reality accords an unproblematic and unreflective continuity to everyday life, rather as a geocentric model of the sun orbiting the earth could superficially account for the everyday experience of night and day. But as an account of how we actually know the world, the realist account is deeply flawed.

Whatever its heuristic value in dealing with everyday life, realism accounts very poorly for the way we humans collect information and gather knowledge. In the first place, we never attend to what is merely there, indeed, what is even just there. Second, the physicality of what we notice is not sufficient to explain its impact on our behavior. In fact, third, we must always infer more than what is there. My sense of reality includes the fourth table leg I can't see, the extension of the room out of view, the wider world beyond my building which I cannot see but know is there. This gap-filling is not a cognitive deficit, we simply have no choice, since to see objects in isolation would be dysfunctional. We are always filling in holes in the physical texture of reality, inferring more than we can see. Like St Exupéry in *The Little Prince*, we can see both an elephant and a hat within the same physical shape. Material qualities of objects and events (their facticity) are never sufficient to guarantee their emergence into my view. I can only have partial information about any object I see, the rest of the information being hidden from me, and filled in. In addition, all the objects I see at any one time seem connected as part of the same unified world despite often having distinct material textures.

In fact, to only see just what is there may be deficient. The material for gap-filling reality is constructed from our experience.

Hence, an alternative account of how our knowledge and experience are generated in relation to the world is called the constructionist version. In this version the self–world relation is dynamic and reciprocal, not static and one-way. In the constructionist version we create our reality as a function of the way we interact with the world. This is not a solipsistic account *à la* Bishop Berkeley where the world is simply an extension of my mind. When I leave a room, the furniture is still there, it doesn't dissolve into a mental qualia or flux..., luckily for those in the house-moving business. Although physicalness is there, it is as we have seen, not sufficient to account for what I see, hear and experience and how I do so. Indeed, our surest reference point to knowing is our immediately surrounding experience. It is more likely by appeal to my experience than to physicality that I confirm my reasoning. Compare the two following reasonings:

(1) This apple is green and hard.
     Green and hard apples are juicy.
     Therefore this apple is juicy.
(2) This apple is green and hard.
     Green and hard apples are juicy and *I've eaten such apples before*.
     Therefore I'm sure this apple is juicy.

The gap between object and inference about object is bridged more surely by experience in the second case than by the more abstract deduction in the first case.

We must here make a distinction between constructivism and constructionism. Constructivism accords our cognitive mediational processes more agency in selecting information and tuning responses to a world (Mahoney, 2003), but within a mediational realist approach. The constructionist perspective, however, sees perception as not just active but creative. I do not selectively attend to salient features to gather information but rather whatever I see already has a momentum and a direction, and this momentum brings salient features into view since it defines the relevant sphere of my interaction with the world. My gaze behavior acts not as a series of search and find missions so much as a continually directed flow which leads me neatly on to my next point of reference in time and space. This direction, depending on which constructionist author you are reading, is variously ascribed to telic purpose, goal context, project, intentionality, affordance. We still settle here for the oldest term 'intentionality', to evoke how my thinking is always 'about something in the world'. It is always directed. The important claim of intentionality is that what I experience has already been set up to be experienced before I see it, and that is why I always see what fits with my projects, and my intentions towards the world. In other words, it is not that the world impacts on me and then I determine my reaction. It is rather that my intentions towards the world at that moment pre-determine the set of events likely to impact on me. The world, of course, always has the qualities of physicalness, otherness, unforeseenness, but these qualities adapt to fit my projects at the moment. They adapt due to my intentionality.

It might seem we are being reductionist here and essentially saying the world is determined by my agency and hence by a little homunculus figure who organizes my projects in front of a window of the mind. But the argument is rather that intentionality is the thread running through my self–world relation. Hence, it is not located in me or in the world, but rather forms a necessary part of my interaction with the world. We are condemned to purpose and to activity and so it is by acting that we experience. This act is not 'cognitive', it is experiential. Cognition is part of experience, not all of it. But the whole of my experience *is* organized by my intentionality, so if intentionality is pre-cognitive, intentionality is not reducible to a cognitive intention as in 'I intend to do it'. Hence intentionality is the background to my agency, not the agency itself.

Of course, this view is in contradiction to the cognitive science viewpoint which seeks a command economy explanation of experience, relegated to an increasingly remote higher-order bureaucracy which controls all sense modalities through a descending chain of lesser modules. Generally speaking, current cognitive theory does not like raw experience very much, unless it is scaffolded in terms of cognitive structure (such as schemata). The cognitive approach to dealing with complex experiences is to postulate different modes producing distinct elements of cognition which join together to be activated multimodally at a schema level. The constructionist approach would argue that even apparently stable internal precepts are effectively at the mercy of ongoing experiences. Hence it's not surprising that we can arrive at completely different, even contradictory inferences, depending on our intentions towards the world.

An example of the way themes of knowing transcend cognitive content is that perceived material properties of objects and places can change quite drastically depending on the conditions under which we constitute them. If I am brought into a room on trial, what I notice about the room may be very different compared to what I notice about the same room when I am brought in to receive a prize. I may label the same percepts as 'room', but my experience of the room in each case will be flexible and movable, as a function of my way of knowing the room, rather than of any inherent physical properties of the room. This change in experience is not a question of reattributing different meanings to the same objects, since the experience decides the way reality and non-reality appear tangibly before and around me. This unity and identity of the 'real' (and 'unreal') at any moment are, according to Husserl (1973), fundamentally constituted by thematic consciousness which is neither subject nor object, but is approached via intentionality.

Cognition and Experience

A good example of how this relative relation between cognition and experience affects inference is the phenomenon of bridging (also termed 'given-new contracts', Clark, 1977) where the significance of the same two statements changes depending on how the gap between them is filled. Of course, the power of experience to alter significance depends on the number of choices we have available, should we wish to draw on experience. So experience can lead us up many a pathway. This role of experience in reasoning could also explain the framing effect and how the descriptive context of a task can alter inference. The amazing point about bridging is how we are able, by drawing on experience, to connect the most remote and unlikely statements, and accord such invented relatedness not only a sense but an inevitability.

Take the following pairs of bridging statements:

(1) The girl smiled at me. The train for Baltimore was late.
(2) The girl smiled at me. Nixon said he wasn't a crook.
(3) The girl smiled at me. I decided to go bungee jumping from the Eiffel Tower.
(4) The girl smiled at me. A smile costs nothing.

Some sample bridging connections could be:

(1) The girl smiled at me as I gulped down my coffee because she knew the train for Baltimore was late.
(2) The girl smiled at me in the way I guess people smiled when Nixon said he wasn't a crook.
(3) The girl smiled at me in disbelief when I said I had decided to go bungee jumping off the Eiffel Tower.
(4) The girl smiled at me but then a smile costs nothing.

Interestingly, in bridging, the more distant the link present, the greater role for and facility in appealing to experience for a bridge. The most semantically similar pair (no. 4) is the most difficult to connect informatively, except by a simple conjunction. Notice from the bridging examples how experience not only fills in and connects but constructs a meaningful sub-world. Each of the bridging examples above (except perhaps no. 4) could easily be linked in a continuous fashion to previous experience or lead to a future set of experiences. Each example recounts a distinct life story beyond it.

In order to highlight the role of bridging clinically, let's reverse the bridging procedure and view the following self-statements as potential bridging links:

(1) Whatever the day, I feel rotten because I know good times, good weather, good people are only temporary, and they go away, leaving you sad at the end of the day.
(2) I generally control my mood by activity and exercise and I work out at home even if it's raining, doing aerobics and using a bicycle machine to work up quite a sweat.
(3) It doesn't matter how careful you are, there's always danger and you could feel perfectly safe but you wouldn't be sure even if you took precautions since they don't really help you.

See now how apparently logically incompatible statements make sense when connected by each of the respective bridging experiences.

(1) It was a brilliant sunny day. So I felt miserable.
(2) It's cold and wet, pouring down with buckets of rain. So now I'm too hot.
(3) My door has every security device you can buy. So, of course, I'll be robbed.

In effect, bridging allows us to connect disparate objects or events and create a joined-up reality with a narrative filling. Radical constructionism would accord no permanence whatsoever to reality, which is continuously being created and recreated by our current projects (Gergen, 1994; Parker, 1999). Things always appear to be real, but this illusion of permanence out there is in itself created by my current projects and practices as an attribute of reality. In the same way that if I create a model of a camel I need to put legs and a hump on it to make it credible, so constructed reality needs to have the air of permanence and out-thereness in order to be 'real'. There are many ontological dilemmas associated with the radical constructionist position (see Burkitt, 2003; O'Connor & Hallam, 2000). Basically radical and social constructionists have not quite resolved the problem of whether reality does exist in some form, and often seem to suggest so implicitly while denying it explicitly (Edwards *et al.*, 1995). Some constructionist thinkers admit reality but proclaim its irrelevance to experience, and posit parallel worlds inhabited by real and constructed selves (Harré, 1991). However, luckily such debates don't need to preoccupy us herè since our concern is with 'knowing' and inferring at the epistemological level, not 'being' at the ontological level. In other words, we can simply ask, how accurately does constructionism account for our way of knowing the world?

The answer is very well and more economically than mediational realist accounts, which take loans out on intelligence to support claims about hypothetical mental structures. It does a particularly good job of accounting for the contextual nature of knowing, and the relational coupling between perception and action, knowing and doing which we live every day.

The principal ways this coupling is explained in constructionist thinking is through grounding the unit of experience within a dynamic self–world interaction which always has a direction. Another point about constructionism is that it legitimately appeals to experience through all the constituents of experience, including the body, as points of reference for inference. Contrary to cognitive information processing models, constructionism *de-intellectualizes* experience. We said earlier that induction is in the service of psychology. In a constructionist approach, cognition or understanding is in the service of experience. We make sense of statements through an appeal to all varieties of experience. Such varieties of experience include all senses, the body, feelings and the imagination. For Lakoff (1987), reason is only made possible by the body and meaning is derived not from its correlation with things but from the embodied experience of humans in the world. According to Lakoff (1987), all human thought has as one of its elements 'ecological structure'. Thus, conceptual structure takes its form, in part, from pre-conceptual embodied structure. For Lakoff, the latter has two elements, first, a basic level structure, composed of gestalt perception, body movement and rich mental imagery; second, a kinaesthetic image–schematic structure, which gives rise to an embodied sense of, for example, balance in one's body movements (Burkitt, 2003).

The relation of embodied sense to reason is even clearer in the case of Merleau-Ponty (1962), perhaps the most ecologically minded of the constructionist philosophers (Abrams, 1988), who held that all our awareness presupposes our immersion in a physical world, not in the sense of objective parameters but rather in human terms of proximity, horizon, depth perspective. This conception contrasts with the cognitive point of view which sees an input of information and then an attribution of meaning, and it contrasts with the Gibsonian 'direct realist' approach which explains perception action coupling in terms of affordances picked up directly from the physical environment by the optic array. Gibsonian 'direct realism' rules out our conscious reflection, which makes it difficult to account for creative conceptual or even emotional elements of perception. In contrast, in the phenomenological approach, both Merleau-Ponty (1962) and Heidegger (1962) grounded thought in everyday doings, where people are not objectively positioned or angled in ambient light, but are purposively leaning or being held, or embracing in a humanly positioned way. For Merleau-Ponty, it is the multitude of background speakings, gestures, glances, intersubjective experiences, which make up a sensible world rather than an objectified world. Such humanized 'living invisibility' constitutes the visible world.

Contextual behaviorism has likewise embraced perception and action as a reciprocal, dynamic and personalized unit. O'Connor (1987) drawing on the motor model of mind (Weimer, 1977) suggested behavior should be considered as a response act, its beginning and end determined by a complex personalized goal-oriented definition. Hayes and Hayes (1992) noted that contextual behaviorism leads to a focus on contextual rather than cognitive variables in the first instance as part of the thinking–acting cycle. When an individual establishes a stimulus response relationship, this occurs in a context established by a social–verbal community. Hayes and Hayes identify a context of literal meaning, a context of evaluation, a context of reasoning, and a context of cognitive and emotional control, all of which can vary independently. An act in context is defined by its purpose and can be ecologically long or short, but acts are whole units with all elements working together. The intimate creative connection between perception–action and context inference in mime illusion supports the constructionist account of inference (O'Connor, 1996).

Mime as Context Inference

Essentially, the mime artist, by his/her action, can lead the spectator to infer an imaginary context against which his/her actions make sense. Because this inferring goes beyond observation and assigns a particular action a wider significance. So, mime shares similarities with other inferences based on partial knowledge, such as causal and probabilistic inference. Mime, then, as O'Connor (1996) noted, is perhaps not a visual illusion but rather a cognitive illusion of inference, involving a particular type of context inference.

The 'simulation' heuristic in probability judgement (Kahneman et al., 1982) involves the elaboration of a plausible scenario that leads from realistic initial conditions to a specific end stage and is often used to support the judgement that the likelihood of the end state is high. Similarly, a mime artist who wishes to establish an elephant (or a hat) in the kitchen would begin with the plausible scenario of the kitchen or the elephant and then lead up in credible stages to the initially incredible conclusion. What makes a good scenario in mime? A good scenario is one that bridges the gap between the initial and end state by a series of plausible intermediate events, and this is precisely Kahneman et al.'s (1982) conclusion about good scenarios which lead to implausible probability judgements. But whatever the skill of the actor, mime illusion can only work because the audience has a rich and readily available array of contexts to be inferred about the action.

A mime context can be widened or enriched or updated by more elaborate actions on the part of the mime but the 'illusion' is not built up piecemeal, rather, it arrives intact around the mime gestures. For example, if a mime artist moves a foot up and down miming a pedal-bin, then the audience infers not just a pedal but the whole bin. A mime artist who credibly mimes banging a nail into a wall can credibly release the hammer behind the back without first defining a table behind to put it on, or use a small finger movement to position an imaginary picture without further elaboration of the frame on the wall since these elements are implied as part and parcel of the inferred context. The richness of the imaginary context that can be inferred from even the smallest action, raises the possibility then that actions have a set of latent possible contexts associated with them. The mime audience then may have a personal distribution of plausible latent contexts associated with different gestures, and the exact one is continually sharpened and updated by the mime actions. This notion is concordant with Johnson-Laird's (2001) position that inference depends on possible mental models available.

If so, then experience does not arrive pure from the outside-in, to be later filtered, represented, stored and retrieved as the more mechanistic mediational realist models have proposed. If, instead, experience is constructed contextually and continuously anew with each project, we undertake to be selectively imposed on the 'out-there' and subsequently updated as our projects progress. This being the case, then our mental representations must represent experience to us as the first reference point of inference rather than the world of objects, people and things, and this is exactly in order that we can connect the objects, events, people and things into the continuous film we call everyday life.

Experience and Language

What device or code, then, would at the same time be able to create and represent experience, communicate experience on different levels and update it continually, at the same time as rendering itself accountable and accessible as a reference source? Well, such a code already exists. *Language*. It's what in fact we use daily to represent and convey our experiences. Recently philosophers of mind from cognitive linguistics to discourse analysts have indeed turned to language to understand experience, in particular, intentionality, the determining factor of experience and telic action.

Although in one sense the preoccupation with language as the medium of thinking follows naturally from the constructionist model of knowledge and the focus on experience, the notion departs dramatically from the focus of current cognitive theory, in particular, information processing paradigms which reify cognitive faculties such as attention, memory, schema, etc. unproblematically in the treatment of information.

In a sense, the linguistic constructionist model is saying to the cognitivists, hey, wait a minute, you've jumped to investigating these cognitive faculties as though they exist in the brain but you've missed the obvious point that they are first of all talked about in everyday language before they are investigated. In one sense, terms such as attention and memory are also acceptable ways of talking about and accounting for what we do. They are language devices, communicating an understood meaning rather than just entities. So why not at least start by looking at the language in which we refer to cognitive faculties such as attention and memory to see how they convey a meaning about our mental life that leads us to infer they are mental faculties?

However, if language is our vehicle or medium of experience, if its nuances and turns of phrase in a sense systematize and solidify our grasp of experience, how do we know that experience is not itself created by language? In other words, does language represent the world of experience to us, or does it create itself? Perhaps there is nothing behind language, except language itself. In other words, when we talk of processes such as 'mind', 'inner being', 'self', perhaps these terms are what Wittgenstein (1953) termed 'language games' and do not have any real existence other than as a way of speaking within a culturally accepted narrative. In other words, 'mental states' may simply be words that have meaning in a psychological story. Mental states as things may not need to exist with real referents outside of the text in which they are spoken. In other words, curing 'anxiety', 'obsession', 'panic', etc. may simply be a case of teaching the person to speak a new language, rather than addressing a reified aberrant internal state. As Hacking (1983, p. 136, cited in Tibbetts (1988)) noted:

> It will be protested that reality, or the world, was there before any representation or human language. Of course. But conceptualizing it as reality is secondary. First there is the human thing, the making of representations. Then there is the judging of representations as real or unreal, true or false, faithful or unfaithful. Finally comes the world, not first, but second, third or fourth.

Now, some language philosophers are less radical about this position than others (Bechtel, 1988). Indeed, one group, which are called variously 'functional linguists' or 'intentionalistic psychologists', argue that language does indeed talk about real events and mental states. In this way, language always has effectively the same functional role for everybody in talking about what really exists and allowing us to infer on the basis of language.

It's just that between individuals, there will be a difference in 'denotation' of terms. In other words, I call the piece of furniture I'm sitting on a 'chair', you call it a 'smurf', but when using these terms to discuss the same object to sit on, the terms 'chair' or 'smurf' are interchangeable since effectively they refer to the same real bit of furniture.

Because language represents to us a world of fixed relations, so language itself must have fixed relations for us to make sense of the world. Jerry Fodor (1987) (a former colleague of Chomsky) holds this position. But this does not lead to a perfect world since semantics can create apparent liaisons and confuse us, particularly since, according to Fodor, cognitive language is necessarily modular and restricted in its functions at any one time. This has led some linguistic theorists to think effectively that only a computational theory can be adequate to represent the infinite combination of our complex experiences. Churchland (1986) suggested further that reducing language to numerical combinations might prove to be more biologically coherent. Such a computational approach to language does not account well for its self-reflexive and referential functions. For example, language can have one immediate sense but an ultimate different and distant reference point. So, how can language capture my intentionality? Intentionality in language philosophy is usually defined as a propositional attitude, e.g., I believe that Charles is the Prince of Wales, which linguistically captures the directed 'aboutness' of my thinking experience. But how can this propositional statement be represented in order to capture distinct intentionalities? I can be talking about Prince Charles, the Prince of Wales, or the next King of England, or if I lived adjacent to Buckingham Palace, 'the bloke next door', and be referring to the same person. But in each case the sense is different and not always interchangeable within the same sentence and so each phrase represents a different intentional experience. It is also clear that some states are non-referential. For example, language can refer to things which do not exist, which can lead to an apparently conflictual intentional stance. There may be a conflict between the content and the meaning of a proposition. Intentionality as a reference point for my actions about the world may conflict with intensionality of a unique proposition referring to a current mental state (Emmett, 1989). If acting under intensionality and intentionality, one could be contradictory but coherent. 'I know that the world is round but in my state of mind right now, I believe in a flat world.' Attempts to answer the queries about the quirks of language have led philosophers either: (1) to fragment the function of language and postulate internal languages to decode language, one code for the senses, and another higher order symbolic code for more remote terms of reference; or (2) to simply seek solutions in natural language use itself and tie use in an utilitarian fashion to ongoing behavioral projects.

The functionalist attempts to resolve these problems have involved reducing language to symbolic information systems (Dretske, 1981). Fodor (1987) suggested we need an internal language ('mentalese'), which represents all the eccentricities of our language to us in a computation of rules and representations. Dennett (1978, p. 10), for example, broke away from computational theory to hold that 'propositions are graspable only if the predicators of propositional attitude are well behaved predictors of human behavior' (Bechtel, 1988). In other words, rather than try to reduce language to a set of codes, symbols or essences which can explain its generation, we should classify language as a function of how we behave and what we do with it. In the phenomenological position, intentionality represents an attitude towards the world, a way of doing, rather than a set of propositional statements. In language terms, this leads to what Quine (1969) termed the 'need for meaning holism' rather than functional relations. Language, according to Quine, is a fabric fitting over experience, not a simultaneous translation coding device. This reverses Fodor's claim that in order to make any sense of the world of experience, my language must be conceptually articulate with the counter-claim that in order to be conceptually articulate language must make sense.

Austin's (1956–1957/1970; 1962) conception of the speech act involves not only the content of the speech but the actions of the speaker in performing the speech, including their intention, the locutionary force of the speech act and the effect of its utterance on the speaker. Austin looked to language use itself to uncover subtle distinctions in nuance and meaning. This involves collecting vocabulary and idiom used to tell about a particular domain, such as responsibility, then examining in detail the nuances involved in the use of terms and idioms. For example, there are many different ways to communicate the same intention. Q. 'How long will it take?' A1: 'I'll do it in a jiffy', A2: 'I'll be quick as a flash', A3: 'It'll take me two flicks of a beaver tail'. These answers differ figuratively and semantically, but the same message is understood if I wish to know how long the job will take. But of course the content and context of the message may have different implications for other actions. Each speech act effectively includes the intentions behind the speech.

So one group of language philosophers analyzes speech function in linguistic and syntactical terms in the hope of computationally representing language function. Another group tries to account for the experiential structure of language by requiring a holistic approach to speech as an act not reducible to composite parts. The functionalist studies of the formal relationships of linguistic terms inside language may help us understand how our brain synthesizes experiences. However, the attempts to relate language to a cognitive linguistic code do not explain the creative aspect of language and how we play with it. There is difficulty in explaining the impact of poetry and non-verbal language, particularly when nothing is spoken. The content of language can be very figurative, imaginative, abstract, even non-existent and still be acceptable, particularly when it comes to representing intentional states.

The dilemma is that functional linguistics is striving to tie language to a fixed reference point to explain the fact that language is always referring beyond itself, even sometimes in contradiction to itself. Language cannot, as Quine (1969) noted, be reduced to sensory experience, nor can it exhaustively be represented by computational notation. One answer to the dilemma may be to enlarge the context of words and propositions to encompass more of the experience in which they were uttered. Rather than attempt to atomize language into smaller and smaller units, the unit can be extended horizontally, to locate each phrase within its past and future and vertically to take account of the multi-layered possibilities for the meaning of a linguistic reference. A phrase such as 'Charles was a royal who was not royal' is meaningless nonsense, until we extend its context to the complete news report which preceded the phrase with 'Charles' behavior was not in accordance with royal protocol, so in this instance...'. The multi-layered use of the word royal gives an apparently non-sensical phrase a depth, literally, through its contrast of the different levels of meaning of the term 'royal'.

It seems then that the more powerfully we wish to relate language to reflect the richness of experience, the more we are forced to rely on the vertical context beyond the language term itself. The apparent logical paradoxes of phrases such as 'there is honour amongst thieves' or 'to live outside the law you must be honest' are understood because our knowledge can appeal to separate but vertically parallel terms of reference for the same words. Someone can be honest in one sense but not in another and be outside one law but inside another without contradiction. The importance of context is most evident where we wish to create irony, sarcasm, or sardonic wit and humor. Humor frequently depends on implicit knowledge of the topical sense of a word inferred from a current context of use not even remotely coded in or accessible from the words themselves, as illustrated in this post-Enron joke:

A1. I've just been at my accountant's place.
A2. Which prison was that?

So language conveys experience not just by words but the context of their use, and it is this horizontal and vertical context of use, ultimately reflecting a wider self-world positioning, which creates their particular 'intentionality' or 'aboutness' at any moment.

Conclusion

Earlier in the chapter, we discussed how reasoning is influenced by everyday concerns and projects, and how our inferences change depending on content, context and presentation. So, in order to understand thinking or any other cognitive process, we need to place it in the context of how we experience the world. We have 'intentionality', we are always acting teleologically and our projects define our knowledge and our functioning. When we reason inductively, we must draw from personal experience. The way we present our experience is through language, and hence language use is crucial to guiding and justifying inferences. Staying at a computational linguistic level does not capture the flow of language use, its multi-layered meanings and its role in pointing to what is not said or implied in making sense of the world. Human conversation is always about something and this intentionality of language is best captured in a humanistic personalized way through its context of use. Hence the unit of language we use in reasoning needs to be one that captures intentionality experientially. This unit needs to encompass horizontal and vertical context around isolated thoughts or propositions, and is termed the *narrative unit*.

Language does not just represent the world to us, at the same time it brings it to us, understandable in terms of our own positioning. It connects the world around us and to us, and so it essentially defines our self–world relation. Language does this connecting in the form of a narrative. In fact, when we think, we think along the lines of continuous stories. Perhaps not explicitly but implicitly everything I see, hear and do can be located on a story line. It is clear that the richer the language (such as with the use of metaphors and metonyms), the greater the impact of the story. Oxman *et al.* (1988) showed how the language used to describe altered states of consciousness was closely tied to different categories of experience. The same state which could be classified as schizophrenic or ecstatic was talked about differently by different groups. Clinicians readily recognize the importance of contextualizing client accounts within a wider biographical narrative. The use of narrative in mood induction and in modifying psychological state is already well recognized in the clinical literature, although the role of the narrative is often not explicitly recognized in cognitive therapy. Scripted narratives are a key way to impact on attitude and mood. The work of Hansen (2003) has shown how a 'stream of affect' or a 'stream of anxiety' evolves during the continuous reading of a text to a greater degree than when the reader alternates between separate statements. But considering narrative as a unit of thought and language has not formed part of standard cognitive approaches. In the next chapter, we look in more detail at how the narrative process controls our inferences.

CHAPTER 3

REASONING AND NARRATIVE

CONVERSATION AND CONVICTION

The Structure of Narrative

A narrative is a story with a beginning, a middle and an end. But the internal structure of a narrative is ordered essentially by its human dimension, and narrative takes its form from human experience. Paul Ricoeur (1984) noted that human experience is storied because of the way we need to understand actions organized in time. Time becomes human time to the extent that chronology takes the form of a narrative and portrays a temporal existence. Someone is always telling the narrative, so narratives tell us not only about past actions, but also how the individuals understood those actions. Jerome Bruner (1986) has noted that 'narrative mode', as opposed to the more impersonal 'paradigmatic mode' of relating events, is especially useful for personalizing ambiguous events and when words need to convey more than their literal meaning. Listening to a narrative is itself a process and good stories give birth to many different meanings. There is no one true interpretation of a narrative, and the listener is always an interpretative agent (Riessman, 1993). Narrative language, as Burke (1950) said, does not just tell people how things are but also tries to move things along in a human way. The language of narrative, according to Halliday (1973), has an ideational function which expresses referential meaning and an inter-personal function which expresses social and personal relations through talk and textual function which connects text syntactically. Likewise, McAdams (1997) considers that narratives require settings, characters, initiating events, transforming attempts, consequences, reactions and a denouement in order to be storied. According to Burke's (1945) classical analysis, all language stories paint a complete geographical and historical picture and relate what was done, when, why, where, how and to whom. What is clear is that narratives have both a performative and a textual function, and that they are reflective as well as self-reflective, referential and self-referential. In other words, they talk about the world, the person in the world, and the thoughts of the person about being in the world.

Narrative Approach to Thoughts

We all exist on a narrative flow. We have a past and a present and a future. We know where we come from and where we are going towards. We are always in the middle. Of course, our stories can take different orientations. They can be professional stories, personal ones, interpersonal ones, cultural stories. Our narratives may be multi-layered and cover physical, emotional, intellectual domains. We may abbreviate our experience but we cannot do without our stories. I might ask you how you arrived home today. You might reply 'by bus' or 'by car'. But if these captions were all you could recall of the journey, you would be worried since your journey home related moment by moment would make up a detailed story. Effectively, it is more worrying to lose a connecting story than lose an odd fact here and there.

Clients also talk about their problems as stories. Obviously they have their own life stories, but they also situate their problem in narrative terms and recount the problem as a narrative.

> Example: Q: So give me an example of your worry.

> A: I saw my sister's boyfriend just ignoring us, reading the newspaper and I thought he's in one of his moods again. He's going to be annoyed at her later because of me. I start worrying they were going to argue over me and maybe he'll hit her. I imagined them having a fight. He could really hurt her. Then I start to panic. I phoned my friend to get her opinion. But she only agreed with me which made it worse, so I couldn't relax until I knew she's alright about six hours later.

We could see this as a series of cognitive thoughts or statements chained together. But this idea loses the natural multi-layered nature of the narrative. As we'll see a little later, it is the dynamic nature of the narrative plus other aspects of its narrative quality which give it a persuasive power. Isolating and changing any one term in a chain of discrete thoughts does not necessarily change the narrative and it is doubtful if the diverse nature of the narrative can be replaced with a single cognitive term, by a kind of psychological reduction technique.

For example, consider the distinctiveness of the following two narrative units touching on the same theme of responsibility, taken from Hallam and O'Connor (2002):

(1) You could give me that paper to read and I'll be sure. I'll have no problem. I'll read it now quickly, because it's not mine. But when I'm writing something, doing my CV, it's *me* doing it. *Me*, I'm not capable. I'll spend hours reading it just in case there's something there, and even

then I put it aside and check it again because it's *me*, you see, it's *me* who's doing it all...and that's the difference.

(2) Well, I could be back home, doing the cooking, or something, or listening to the radio, waiting for the kids to come home, and I suddenly think – oh, my God, did I fill that memo out properly – what if I didn't – no one else will check it properly – it's my job to do it – they'll act on it and if it's not right, the person will get the wrong information – and, well, everyone will know it was me.

The cognitive idea of treating thoughts as isolated units encourages us to see thoughts as contextless and absolute rather than seeking their meaning embedded in the narrative. Ironically, in order to clinically explore and confront assumptions about, say, responsibility, it is necessary anyway to go back to the richness of the text, in order to nuance the clinical meaning. However, isolating thoughts from their horizontal and vertical context has another major implication. It tends to let cognitive therapy think in terms of information processing distortion or 'lens correction', while the narrative approach thinks in terms of adaptive experience. In fact, the narrative approach would go so far as to say that the presence of cognitive distortions is solely an artifact of taking thoughts out of their natural narrative context. To illustrate the point, let's look at the following narrative:

I heard a noise outside the door. It turned out the noise was a pile of egg boxes which I had forgotten I had left outside the door, falling over and breaking. Someone had unexpectedly walked into the boxes knocking them all down. So I had wasted a lot of eggs and I blame myself for being careless.

In this narrative there are no obvious distortions. However, let us join two separate ideas from the narrative.

I heard a noise outside the door.
I blamed myself for being careless.

There are a number of Beck-style cognitive distortions here: (a) catastrophic thinking; (b) jumping to conclusions; (c) personalization...to name just a few.

So when we classify discrete thoughts as distortions, in fact it may simply be that the narrative context is missing. A narrative approach seeks the narratives leading up to the discrete thoughts or assumptions in order not only to contextualize and understand what appear to be distorted thoughts, but to link them to an adaptive context.

In order to be persuasive, a narrative must be complex and contain relations, transitions and contingencies. Russell and van den Broek (1992) have noted that the structure of narratives required the key persuasive elements of events, relations, transitions and contingencies, simply in order to make a convincing story. The three main dimensions of narrative structure relevant to clinical practice are: relational structure of the represented events (the structural connectedness), the psychological relations between the events (the representation of subjectivity) and the complexity or style of the narrative linguistics. The main sub-classes of structural connectedness are event categories, i.e. temporal relations, causal relations, co-referential relations, and propositional relations. Representation of subjectivity details the way the account is narrated and the intensity of experience of events, i.e. how events are described in relation to emotional intensity and depth of experience. Linguistic complexity includes the competence of the person, the sub-clause structure, and the number of plots and sub-plots available in the story.

As an example, if I simply state: 'There is a bear in your kitchen', I probably won't appear very convincing. But if I say: 'I heard a growling sound as I walked past your kitchen, and saw wet claw-like footprints leading to the sink', you may begin to be more convinced. If I say: 'I read in the newspaper that a bear had escaped and that he was seen heading this way. It's known by experts that such bears usually head for kitchens since they like to search for food', you may become more and more convinced . . . and so on. Note, in all this change in conviction, no sightings of bears have entered. It's all narrative construction.

According to Russell and van den Broek (1992), a new narrative is most usually persuasive when developed in a zone of proximal development to rival representations, neither exceeding too dramatically nor staying complacently within the exact current narrative structure. In other words, to maximize persuasive power the alternative narrative must be new but comparable in structure to the old.

The main parameter which makes a narrative 'believed in' is termed variously the degree of 'absorption' or 'transportation' attached to the narrative. Its believability (believe it or not) has nothing to do with whether it is 'fact' or a 'fiction'. Facts by themselves can be less convincing than stories with a cultural or emotional resonance, and making a narrative account more factual does not necessarily influence its credibility (De Rivera & Sarbin, 1998). This finding can account for how people can have *believed-in imaginings* (example: alien abductions).

In modifying a narrative, we do not try to change facts, distortions, or misattributions. Rather, an alternative narrative is constructed which complies with the believability parameters (as noted above). This is 'narrative restorying' rather than 'lens correction'. The narrative approach begins with textual narrative and treats this story as the basic account of the problem. It does not attempt to isolate the problem from the narrative. So, for example, take the following text: 'I can't stand this problem. These anxiety attacks, I'm not able to tolerate them. I told my sister. She agreed. She said they are too much. No one should suffer them like I do. So that's it. I've decided I'm not living another year with this problem. I'm not putting up with it. It's got to go.' An initial evaluation might consider that the person has an anxiety problem which in addition they are tolerating badly. But talk of the anxiety is embedded in a narrative whose principal theme is tolerating anxiety problems. A narrative approach would explore the theme as expressed in the person's narrative, not suppose the person was really referring to a state beyond the narrative. In other words, the language use of a referent term pointing outside the narrative does not necessarily establish this reference point as existing independent of the narrative. Modifying the theme of the narrative will necessarily modify the person's experience of the problem as, for example, if the narrative becomes: 'These anxiety attacks are a problem but in the end I go on regardless, I'm able to think and carry out everyday jobs satisfactorily.'

Narrative Positions

Narrative language has dynamism so that a narrative form such as a life story emerges in the process of the telling. It is not a fixed form. As Freeman (1995) notes, the cognitive structure of a story is hence not fixed and may vary depending on the context of the telling and its purpose. Sometimes the focus may be on the present, sometimes on the past. According to Knudsen (1990), a life story is not a story of life but a conscious strategy for self-preservation, a legitimatization of moves and counter-moves and of projections for the future.

The temporal dimension also gives stories a plot-line. Narratives are our life stories and our life-lines. We are 'in' them, indeed, they are our identity, even if the identity shifts with the story. Stories essentially are organized by theme, not syntactic form. Our narrative reflects our intentionality, our way of talking 'about', but in a lived-in fashion. It has various devices to draw us into its living space. If the narrative is our unit, then we need to adopt a holistic approach to understanding its impact and grasp meaning through the form and structure of narrative rather than just its linguistic structure. In discussing narrative techniques, we discover a whole series of devices that help narrative achieve psychological qualities such as transportation, conviction, absorption.

Language has the power to connect the person to their experience and the world at all times and help make inferences about states and events partly by positioning the person in the here and now. So narrative language positions us. At the same time as it opens up a living space, it also traps the person in the space. Language has a number of devices for commandeering, engaging or immersing the person in the narrative here and now in different ways. Language can be commanding, accusing, or flat and factual. Its power lies in its ability to position the person differently with respect to their experience and the world and both literally and experientially put them on the spot. Imagine the following two notices stuck to the same wall. (1) 'The Red Cross is setting up a blood donor clinic at X shopping mall today. Why don't you become a donor today?' (2) 'The army needs YOU now!' Both notices are recruitment drives, both on billboards, which someone can walk by without any further consequences. But the tone of the notices evokes two different emotions and stances and thus elicits distinct types of self-reflection, and reading them is suddenly 'about' distinct experiences.

Narrative, then, can be said to have two distinct threads, elaborating and representing experience and, at the same time, ecologically positioning us in a human way, our personally human way, to our world. In a sense, then, if we see narrative as the vehicle of inference, the paradoxes of illogicality in resolving, say, the Linda problem (see Chapter 2) make existential sense, since the immediacy of the narrative and its referents has primacy and pull. Its strong pull has to be actively resisted and disregarded in order to successfully impose a formal logical template. The way Linda is presented to us in the narrative leads to the inference that she is a feminist bank teller even if this is statistically unlikely.

Unspoken Narrative

Narratives also have a non-linguistic referent which permits non-verbal sequences to establish narrative context. For example, I might have enough experience of meta-language available to make a coherent propositional attitude out of any old gobbledegook. If I enquire: 'How are you today?' and the reply is 'Spliff, spliff, biddledeedo, bondabonk, spludgesplee', then that could lead me to infer well-being. Inferring meaning here depends on prior knowledge, experience of the setting, and an available heuristic. Obviously the fact that I can convey the same meaning non-linguistically or with many different phrases underlines the experiential rather than purely semantic nature of narrative talk.

Language can also make sense by meta-referring to other external referents, often several times removed. This meta-reference enables, as John Shotter (1994) has noted, a rhetorical poetic use of language whereby apparently articulate meanings may be deduced from what is unsaid or said obliquely; paranoid preoccupations frequently center on uncertain or ambiguous signals. Often the less said, the more meaning. Hence the ability of poetry to invoke more keenly experiential states than prose. Take the following:

(a) I picked a flower out of the bunch because it seemed the most prominent one with a good red head and a strong rose smell. The petals were a little bit drooped but still fresh and green. I bought it because I know my girlfriend likes red and she has a pattern like roses on her bedroom wallpaper. It was my Valentine's Day present and I also bought heart-shaped chocolates, well wrapped up in red paper with a heart and a tag on it.

(b) A flower..., a good red head...
a strong rose...
like roses on wallpaper was my valentine...
heart-shaped and well wrapped up...
a heart and a tag.

Which of these two accounts elicits a more touching response, the full text or the poem-like synopsis which uses a sample of the same textual terms? Why, indeed, does this poem make sense at all? We fill up the gaps with our own personal story and experience. This accounts for the generative and creative aspect of stories and how two people can derive opposite experiences from the same story. Note how the poem discards its textual clothes precisely in order to transport us. In its very disjointedness, the poem takes us beyond the senses of the here and now. We make sense of disjointed statements and we 'mind the gap' with reference to experience. In many ways the persuasive aspects of narrative argue against the functional linguistic ideas, which would suggest, for example, that a more involved linguistic mechanism would lead to a richer representation and fuller experience. Whereas, in fact, often in narrative, the less said the better, because then the more personalized the opportunity to thematize, and hence the more chance for absorption. We have seen earlier how experience as a reference point can lead us astray. Use of narrative language devices can also misguide our inferences and convince us.

Narrative Devices

One way that we can be overpowered by narrative language is in our use of metaphor or metonyms, which serve to create illusion. I really feel 'life is a ship and I'm tossed about'. I act 'as if' I'm playing a role in 'life's tragedy'. It should be noted that metaphoric expression is not some meta-reflective high order meta-cognition to be entered in or not. Narrative is real-time thinking. I may have a choice of language but I have no choice but to choose a story, express it in language and live it. But the choice of the language can affect credibility. A story can become accepted literally as the truth, similar to what Whitehead and Russell (1910) termed 'misplaced concreteness'. There is also the opposite device of giving mundane events a symbolic meaning in story lines.

Q. 'Why are you working so hard?' A. 'I'm like Sisyphus bending my back always to the stone.' Here, use of a figurative context could be an acceptable connection between internal and external state. Conversely, 'life's just a bummer' would also be a competing figurative term.

Another narrative device is miscategorization when an event either becomes exaggerated into a more severe category due to its description, or comes to represent a completely separate category by mislabelling. A good example here comes from a recent *Time* magazine article by Chris Taylor (2004) where a religious group argued against same sex marriage by saying: 'The word equality is being misused to rob all the sacred things of their uniqueness. What's next? Legalized heroin? Prostitution? Polygamy? Incest?' Another version is when an inadvertent insult becomes classified as a major harassment. Example: 'Oh, so you're not free to help me on Saturday, so you don't like me then, so I'm nothing to you, I see.'

Such category errors may seem similar to some of Beck's distortions: personalization, overgeneralization, catastrophization. However, in mis-categorization, there is no process of exaggeration; rather, the reasoning problem is the miscategorization itself. If, say, a small skin abrasion is miscategorized as a major accident, naturally the response will be exaggerated. Sometimes there may be an inability to separately categorize objects, an example being if all insects from moths to spiders are considered poisonous and capable of biting. Here, naturally, the person will react to a small ladybird 'as if' poisoned, but this reaction is a consequence of miscategorization and not because of an 'exaggerated sensibility' to insects. There is evidence that people with OCD do tend to oversimplify or broaden concepts (Persons & Foa, 1984).

This may happen because a dominant, one might say imperative, language/discourse is already in place and available, or it may be simply a learned association or confusion of terms. In another narrative device, a conversation goes off on a tangent and connects to another barely associated narrative which is, however, experienced as if the join is seamless. 'I think John broke his leg and that's why he's up at the hospital, you know the same one they shut down last year because of Legionnaires' disease. It was terrible, my mother had to be moved and she'd just been diagnosed with cancer. Oh my, I hope John doesn't have cancer.' There is also a hierarchy of stories and myths with a culturally higher status story preferred to a lower status one. For example, a person helping another across the road may prefer the self-reference to a 'knight in shining armor', rather than a 'busybody trying to take control'. A more insidious device involves overlapping narratives which mix incompatible terms, or where a kind of short-hand is created termed 'conceptual blending', and two terms from different discourses are compacted into one term. For example, blended terms such as the 'noble savage', the 'iron lady', the 'jail bait' integrate separate meanings into a new identity network. As Fauconnier and Turner (2002) note, we are constantly blending different terms, different times, different spaces in the course of our daily narratives. When somebody tells us they used to weigh 100 lbs, we transpose the past image onto the present. When we see a Persian rug in a shop, we transpose it in our mind to a wall in our home. As well as projection, blending allows us to compress and also to clash. Such blending can also be useful. Musical groups are good at stimulating blends and clashes, e.g. 'Cowboy Junkies', 'Barenaked Ladies', 'Jesus and Mary Chain'. As Fauconnier and Turner (ibid., p. 115) note, 'a linguistic system to be useful at all has to have a wide and powerful array of resources for prompting compression and decompression. Identity seems to be primitive but it is instead an achievement of the imagination.' Obviously all these narrative devices can lead to starting off on the wrong premise and so lead convincingly on to a faulty story.

One could even suppose that inference is a by-product of narrative sequence, in the sense that narrative always goes from there to here and we are never talking on the spot, as it were, so we are essentially bound to infer from then to now or from this now to the next. The structure of narrative accommodates well the ever present tension between my experience now and my past and future experiences, in effect the tension between the near and the remote, which effectively requires a coherent linking for me to live. We have noted that one function of narrative is to convince, but what is the nature of a conviction within a narrative constructionist approach? Within a cognitive model, of course, belief is a key organizing cognitive structure. In narrative, a belief then may be seen rather as the meeting point of several narrative streams. Such a notion is not in conflict with earlier ideas of routine thinking as an acquired skill (Bartlett, 1958).

Narrative and Belief

If narratives convince us that they are not just stories, they do also lead to beliefs. So, is a reasoned belief simply the end point of a convincing narrative? In an enduring conviction or belief, has the person basically chosen one narrative and just stuck to it? One clue that this might be the case is that a narrative is always behind a belief. How do we know? Because by definition it is always reasonable to ask how a belief is arrived at, unlike, say, a sensation, which just arrives. But how in that case would we decide on one belief among apparently equivalent competing narratives? A point to note here is that as well as being at the juncture of past and future we are always at the juncture of several competing narratives to do with life, status, job, family, predicament. Obviously therapists of both narrative and cognitive persuasions have noted for some time that constructing alternative accounts of biographies is useful in modifying mood and sometimes appraisals and beliefs. However, beliefs in cognitive theory are generally conceptualized according to a depth metaphor, where core beliefs or assumptions produce more superficial appraisals or interpretations. Working away at lower order appraisals may lead eventually to a modification of schema, but the schema are considered less accessible.

There are many incoherences in this notion of fixed core beliefs, somehow stored in a mode or schema like hard-to-remove residue in a well used saucepan. First, people's beliefs can change quite dramatically over very short periods of time. Indeed, one of the key findings in recent research monitoring delusion beliefs is the fluctuation in intensity and preoccupation of belief over time (O'Connor et al., 2003b; Sharp et al., 1996). Attitude conformity is also clearly contextual and varies with social environment (ex. Asch, 1956). Also, as Sarbin (1996) has pointed out, there is no firm support to the cognitive argument of concept formation and concept attainment as a series of complex steps in developing the ability of conceptualization. Sarbin has, indeed, argued that concept formation is not a series of stages but results from the acceptance of background stories that form the basis for identity making. Our concepts and beliefs follow from our narrative actions. Kelly (1955) has shown that we develop constructs in close relation to elements of our world. That is, our constructs are guides to relating to people and events and both can be meaningfully represented in the same two-dimensional space. In other words, what is in my world and how I organize my world are closely related and I am defined by my interactions with the world. Narrative defines the meaning and the units of my actions: 'going to work', 'doing a good job', 'taking the kids to school'. These descriptive actions are also accounts of who I am and each action can be translated into a coherent self-referent term. An industrious worker does a good job, a responsible father takes his kids to school. Where our narrative–action couplings are repeated and habitual, so our beliefs appear to remain fixed. Over a lifetime, a person is likely to have built up many overlapping layers of narrative–action coupling. All for the most part are mutually supportive. Recounting a story centered on leisure pursuits, work activity, social activity is likely to converge on a strong unifying (if rich and complex) identity which is coherent with past and planned actions. Indeed, one way of building new narratives is through clinical role playing which can persuade a person to change behavior (e.g. to quit smoking) by exacerbating conflict within identity through realization of the incoherence of, say, parenting and smoking as joint activities (O'Connor, 1989).

Indeed, at this point we may ask ourselves what is belief? Sarbin would answer that beliefs result from stories that are told, and a fixed belief persists because the person has not been told another story. There is some evidence for this, in that over-valued ideas, even seemingly bizarre ones, can be modified by reframing information through education (Zucker *et al.*, 2002). The difference between giving information and telling a story is that although information may be credible, it has to fit into a story in order to lead up to belief. What we can say, however, is that every belief in some way positions the person at the center or junction of dominant stories. These stories, as we have noted, have 'intentionality' or 'aboutness' in general since they have content. They are stories but also immediate guides to current goings on and actions. When people note beliefs in a static form, 'I'm an honest person, I'm a conservative', asking what they mean by 'honest', etc., leads to expanding the condensed statement into an action story, and what this belief means in terms of everyday interactions, goals and agency. In fact, all narratives in some way position the person directly or indirectly in relation to the world. In other words, all have self-referent plot lines. When we talk of self-attributes, it is short-hand for a narrative about projects defining who I am. When we ask people to tick off self-defining adjectives on a checklist, they elaborate the adjectives into a series of narratives coherent with the implied actions/attributes. In fact, often when people are ambivalent in their reply to checklists, we help them as clinicians by relating these adjectives coherently to their actions. Incoherent stories of action can lead to self-doubt. But this is exactly how people can come to doubt who they really are, since they constantly need to seek identity with reference to how they will act. But here we're suggesting that strongly held beliefs are *not* any deeper than superficial beliefs, but simply supported by more overlapping narratives and hence are perhaps more habitual and automatic. A firmly held belief then may simply be one that finds itself at the crossroads of several self-referent and self-supporting stories so that the challenge to one story will be countered by a parallel story with a similar plot-line.

Supposing I am confronted with the three following stories concerning a dirty stain on a handkerchief. 'The stain came about accidentally because of a spilt glass of wine', 'The handkerchief has been stained deliberately out of malice', 'The stain is a sign of fate and reveals who you are.' Note I cannot appeal to any certain experience to decide my choice of belief. I can, however, choose with cross-reference to other narratives based on other's experience. For example, I can appeal to the authoritative experience of witnesses. But if I need to choose by myself, how do I decide which narrative to believe? Assuming, of course, I care enough to pursue the matter. The answer seems to depend on where each account leaves me positioned with respect to key self-referent themes. Where does each account leave me positioned not only regarding the stain but within the greater scheme of life? The following narrative leaves little doubt. 'The stain on that handkerchief is a sign of who you are in the universe.

It represents in its natural shape the ups and downs of your life. It resumes your past and prophesies your future. It represents the very essence of your being. Lose it and you lose yourself. Value its significance and you value yourself.'

Placing mundane acts or events symbolically at the center of much larger coordinates of self-reference accords both the events and the person a seductive and persuasive sense of powerful importance, usually unavailable in the real world. Such persuasive techniques are part of a rhetoric and rhetorical devices also reveal the power of language on thinking and inference.

Reason and Rhetoric

Rhetoric is essentially the use of words to form attitudes and induce actions (Burke, 1950). As Maranhão (2002) notes, in the Ancient Greek world, the teaching of rhetoric was not only considered socially appealing but was considered a bastion of emerging democracy positioning itself against the old values of traditional religion and culture. Narrative was placed by the Greeks between epic poetry and dialogical discourse as one of the great modes of persuasion. In particular, rhetoric argued against the rigid morality of the epic poems. Indeed the Sophists, an influential group of peripatetic educators of the fourth–fifth century BC, devoted themselves entirely to teaching and perfecting rhetoric which they considered the highest expression of wisdom. Rhetoric right up until medieval times was a key discipline in universities and was considered an excellent formation for thinking. Rhetoric now tends to have a negative connotation and these days is applied to vacuous self-serving and deceptive political argument. Rhetoric puts language on the stage. The rhetorician has to sense the mood of the audience, and play on opportunities. The rhetorician must initially come with a strong story line and ethos which establishes status. This may be uniform, insignia, authority, identifiable race, class or status. Another important aspect is emotional stimulation in order to engage the person in the rhetorical account. Finally, argument must employ metaphors, stories, myths and images to convey the central idea as important and beyond the person, and in which they can now share if they transcend their own concerns, intelligence and sensory input.

In its skilled form, rhetoric draws on reasoning and narrative devices by its ability to conjure up illusions of thinking to change conviction level. Jerome Frank (1987) wrote a particularly illuminating piece on how psychotherapy may share goals and means with rhetoric. Therapy may be little more than rhetoric, simply a question of convincing someone to think and talk differently about their problem. This view makes sense if we accept the constructionist argument that people's problems are anyway partially about the use of language and are part of a wider discourse. But in other ways therapy is often aimed at undoing or 'deconstructing' the results of rhetoric. This deconstructing may also involve challenging common-sense meanings phenomenologically, as, for example, stripping away assumptions and acquired ideologies. Or in social constructionist terms, over-riding the dominant discourse with a personal voice-over. Or by re-authoring parts of the conversation to see where the language use was inherited from an earlier figure (e.g. a role model, a teacher, an unfinished conversation). A technique common to all narrative therapies involves distancing the person from acquired meanings or imposed narrative meanings in order for them to focus on the literal meaning of the words, thus helping the person to realize that their strong reaction is not to what is there but to an unrelated or blended association of what is there. For example, rhetoric may create a tension by introducing conflicting narratives about a person's identity. Rhetoric then blends distinct and conflictual meanings into a narrative identity. We have already noted the key properties of narrative discourse of connectivity, relatedness and reference to other events 'outside' of itself. The 'tricks' of rhetoric often involve making connections where none previously existed, in order to make someone feel that one experience necessarily refers to another and thus to confuse and blend categories. Alternatively, consequences are drawn, logically, but on the basis of a faulty premise. Finally, people can be led to distrust their own experience in favor of a larger, more dominant discourse. Obviously psychological character-istics such as suggestibility (in hypnotism) may play a role in persuasion, and the setting of the rhetoric must be conducive to a transfer of credibility.

Arguably, the most sinister study in the use of rhetoric was its systematic use by the National Socialist German Workers Party (Nazis) of Germany between 1933 and 1945. What is peculiar about the Nazi use of rhetoric was the recognition by the Nazi leaders, particularly Josef Goebbels, that their persuasive power rested practically exclusively on the mastery of rhetoric. Unlike, say, Stalinism, which made some quasi-appeal to Marxist ideology underpinning its actions, Nazism's sole reference was to rhetoric itself and it made no claim to articulate a scientific ideology (apart from eugenics, but this was more a means than a central platform). On the contrary, there were continual conscious attempts to mystify Nazism religiously with symbols. The spirit of the movement was constantly appealed to in a mystical fashion.

In fact, there was a Reich's propaganda school of rhetoric which issued a house journal (*Unser Wille und Weg; Our Will and Way*) at regular intervals where advice and counsel on Nazi rhetoric were published. Some quotes illustrate the privileged position of 'the rhetorical art' in Nazi Germany. Frauenfeld (1937), a party propagandist, writes that never in the history of

Germany or indeed of whole humanity did the spoken word have such significance. He goes on to note the primacy of personal experience in rhetoric to the detriment of indirect representation. The written word is abstract, impersonal. Also reading is usually done alone, while speaking is communal; many hundreds or thousands sharing in the enthusiasm allow the spoken word to pass from simple understanding to the depths of feelings and drives. He also distinguishes in rhetorical status the lecture, talk and meeting. The highest level is ceremonial gatherings which allows a unified program of music, flags and a speech. The opposite to this form of rhetoric is the talk and the lecture. Whereas the mass meeting transmits experience, the talk directs itself to the mind to teach and educate. Needless to say, Frauenfeld is not in favor of the talk since it goes against the wish for the hearer to be motivated, to be swept along by the movement. The sentiment that successful Nazi rhetoric rests on, transporting the audience away from their own thinking and experience into emotional identification with the speaker's world, is continually repeated in the pages of *Unser Wille und Weg*. Ringler (1937), another propagandist, notes in an article, 'Heart or reason?: what we don't want from our speakers', that the last thing the Party wants is speakers who deliver 'facts' and who carve up their subject with scientific exactitude when they should be preaching a world-view. The Party speaks not to understanding but to the heart. At one point he admits:

> We could never persuade the German people by rational arguments; things always worked out badly with that approach. The people were won by the man who struck the chord with the people's feelings, the sentiment, the heart.

We see here spelled out clearly all the ingredients for rhetorical persuasion necessary in order to elevate a prejudice to a delusional conviction. Most central in this advice is the detachment of the person from his/her individual experience by spectacle, theater and argument. The primary given (Nazi) inference has no truth value, but nonetheless connects the listener comfortably to a bigger story where he can position himself. Over and over, the Nazi rhetoric begins with a given unsupported but authoritatively delivered (hence inducing mindlessness) premises, then uses deductive logic to infer the logical course of action. 'As is well known...'. 'There can no longer be any doubt that...', 'Even the Archbishop in England will need now to admit that...'. Ontologically distinct categories (for example, people and rats) are matched up with the intent that distinct experiences become blended and mislabeled. The use of spectacle and theater to stimulate emotional engagement was of course a hallmark of Nazi rallies. Although the Nazi rhetoric drew on pre-existing consensually and culturally active prejudices (e.g. anti-Semitism), it reframed such prejudice as heroic by blending it with well-rehearsed

German myths. It drew, in other words, on fantasy and imagination and gave these great play in the Party rhetoric in place of current senses. The rhetoric consequently was also able to make remote and even symbolic events feel immediately lived in.

Conclusion

Narrative gains its power not from the sum of its parts but from the dynamic of its form, structure and delivery. It contextualizes thoughts spatially and temporally in terms of experience as a personal unit but it also positions the person in their space. Various narrative devices such as miscategorization and blending can confuse the impact of language on experience and lead people to react in inappropriate ways. But the reaction is not a result of a cognitive process of exaggeration, overdramatization or other sensitivities, it is simply a natural result of reasoning in this way. In addition, what is not said or said ambiguously can exert a powerful experience on inductive inference, since it leaves gaps to be filled in by experience. Narratives convince and beliefs may be formed by routinely performing the same narratives. So beliefs are not necessarily enduring hypothetical cognitive products, just well-rehearsed stories. Narratives not only convince but transport through the use of rhetorical techniques, from the present to the more remote and imbue self-stories with a sense of a wider inflated worth.

The persuasive power of rhetoric highlights a crucial dynamic within stories, namely the tension between actual and remote experience, between what is and what might be. This point leads us on to discuss the role of possibility and the imagination in inference.

INFERENCE AND IMAGINATION

Inferring Possibilities

We noted in the last section the importance of experience as a source of reference for reasoning. Also that experience fills in or bridges connections by appealing to all its modalities. In the present section we underline the importance of drawing on possible experience in induction. Making inferences in the context of possibility is essential to understanding not only the temporal continuity of inference but also the way in which imagined inferences can trump reality-based inferences. Leibniz (1682) was one of the earliest thinkers to introduce the importance of considering 'things that are possible but yet not necessary and which do not really exist'.

Dretske (1981) extended Leibniz's concept to talk of 'possible worlds', worlds similar to ours that could exist but do not, yet whose characteristics serve to reveal essential referent qualities of our own world. More recently, artificial intelligence has also employed the mathematical construction of possible worlds as a way of reasoning about changes in expected actions (Ginsberg & Smith, 1988).

Possibility covers what might be, what might come later, what might constitute a tolerable variation of what already exists, how my changing position might modify my future perception. However, the notion of possibility does not just apply to what might be, it applies also to what is here now since what exists now equally contains possibility. The intentional nature of my projects in the world makes them directed but also directed into the future, ahead of themselves. In other words, their possibility in some way defines their intentions. Since everything I see, I see inside a project, so the 'seen' too is defined by its possibility for my project. What I see about a telephone or a lamp or a door depends very much on what I intend to do with it. When I hold a knife in my hand, it is just a sharp steel object, but its potential to harm scares me. We are constantly surprised to detect new physical attributes in familiar objects which we never noticed before, but notice now because our project dictates a possible relevance. Equally, as noted earlier in Chapter 2, the physical attributes of a visible object are never sufficient to define its possible use, so objects are frequently inferred as complete despite the absence of their complete physicalness (e.g. the corner of the table I cannot see but whose absence from view does not deter my belief in the table's solidity). Clearly, however, the leg of a table I cannot see momentarily due to the perspectival limitations of my position has a different possibilistic status to the object not yet at all in view, or the scene around a corner I have not yet turned, or the possible use for an object not yet conceived. Although there are as many possibilities for an object as there are projects, it seems nonetheless feasible to quantify possibility dimensionally in terms of a maximum and a minimum within any one project.

The philosopher Martin Heidegger (1987) pointed to the many forms possibility could take and how these possibilities influence the present. His oft-quoted phrase, 'the past comes towards the present from the future', encapsulates the important role that 'what might happen' plays in how we react in the present. If I think a charging herd of wildebeest is just around the corner, I will act and feel very different in the here and now than if I anticipate seeing a mouse, even though these are presently just future possibilities and hence have equal status. If I am parched with thirst and I know I will get a drink in two minutes, my experience of the same thirst will differ if I don't know when I will get a drink. Rachman (1984) has noted that perceived access and speed of return to safety is a primary determinant of discomfort in agoraphobic anxiety disorder. John Riskind and colleagues (1997) have demonstrated the importance of the sense of 'looming vulnerability' in OCD, and how perceived degree and speed of contamination spread is critical to obsessional fears.

The dilemma, then, is that although our senses tell us what is there, we must also make inferences about what might be there later, and our experience of current reality is thus, in part, constructed by possibility. In our everyday routine, we have a tight set of possibilities which carries us through the day. The bus may be late or early. It may be crowded or empty. The weather may be sunny or stormy. It's when we are in less predictable situations that we realize how crucial constructed possibilities are to our sense of reality. Indeed, it is not too strong to say that available possibilities dictate our sense of reality. Is that shadow a murderer, a dog, a woman, or the light cast by the lamp against the door? Even in a benign way, a rich array of available possibilities can change our experience. Think of an activity you are planning tomorrow, then think of three or four alternatives you would rather do. How have thoughts of these alternatives influenced your reaction to the first activity? As Johnson-Laird (2001) has noted, where there are less possibilities, the speed of decision on a suitable mental model will be quicker.

In the same way, when we don't yet have a sense of reality, thinking of alternative scenarios can help us arrive at a sense of reality. Conversely, where we already possess a strong sense of reality, alternative scenarios can increase doubt rather than certainty. Pick up a pen that you know is just a pen and rate your confidence in the fact that is a pen. Now, using the narrative devices we mentioned earlier, tell yourself alternative stories about it being a camera; a gun; a microphone. Obviously, since your investment in the alternatives is likely to be minimal, your confidence in the original assertion about the pen is likely to remain high, but perhaps slightly less certain.

We have operationalized this doubting effect of alternative possibilities on initial levels of confidence in a series of experiments where inferences arrived at by logical normal inferential processes can be doubted by either given or self-generated alternative inferences. Under certain conditions people with OCD seem more susceptible to this doubting effect. The experiments are described in Chapter 5.

As we've noted, what is seen is necessarily also defined by what is not seen. In addition, it is defined by what could be. If possibility is a defining dimension of thinking, then imagination must play an important role in thinking since we conceive the possible through the imagination. Perception operates outwards, and deals with what is there, while imagination is inward-looking and deals with what is not there.

However, we can switch between imagination and perception, and replace one with the other. In fact, within the structure of consciousness itself, there are always aspects of the real, which we assume are there, but which present themselves by their absence (the back of a chair I cannot see). So any 'real' object is always part of a larger unseen context of which I have only marginal awareness, where imagination helps to form the perceived event and is part of it. Hence, both perception and imagination are in different ways part of the same inferential context. At the margins of consciousness are always unseen possibilities (e.g., the corner I haven't yet turned; the variation I haven't yet experienced). An integral part of my knowing is inferring what is not there, hence in inference, reality and possibility also go hand in hand. It may seem then more reasonable to see imagination and perception not as distinct cognitive functions but rather as operating together within the same cognitive functions (O'Connor & Aardema, in press). Three separate claims support the role of the imagination in sensing reality: (1) What I am doing always exists alongside what I am intending to do – my projects on the world; (2) imagination as the 'art of the possible' is a creative aspect of thinking, and fills up the gap between what is and what is not; and (3) living in reality is a matter of degree, and I exist in a gradient of awareness where the plausibility of different possibilities is associated with distinct senses of reality.

• *Imagining and doing.* On the one hand, everything which is real in the here and now must, in order to be so real, already be, with its history before and beyond me. But it only has this real property or 'facticity' in the first instance because it has a future, and this future primarily determines its existence as real. This future for the object always, of course, ties in closely with my projects for my future. So, for example, if my intention is to make a cup of tea, everything I see, all attributes, fit into my tea-making enterprise, and their ordering on the center or on the margins of consciousness is decided on the basis of their relevance to my tea-making. Of course, I want to make my tea in a 'real' teapot, not one I'm just imagining. A real teapot is one that stands before me, beyond me, with its own 'factual history' as a teapot capable of holding scalding hot water and pouring a good cuppa. If my project changes to clearing out old chinaware, a whole new structure of past and future attributes of the same objects comes into being. The real teapot now becomes an 'old-out-of-date-stained-to-be-thrown-out-teapot', whereas previously it was a 'solid-capable-of-holding-hot-water-teapot'. A counter argument might be that even though I may not notice all attributes of an object at one time, they nonetheless exist independently of me. But if someone points out attributes of objects I hadn't previously noticed and I go back and see them, my seeing is still intricately tied up with my being and my projects (in this case a 'going-back-to-see-missed-attributes'-project). When I am seeing, I am always doing. Seeing and doing are inseparable. I can of course become absorbed in a memory or recall an activity at a different place and time. But memory access depends nonetheless on my current mood and project. Elements of the past become important as they fit into future projects. Clinically speaking, the future also looms large as in the importance of 'looming vulnerability' in anxiety (Riskind, 1997); anticipation is the hallmark of anxiety (e.g. what might occur, what if the worst happens) while in depression it seems the absence of hope which conditions past and present ruminations.

- *Imagination as the art of the possible.* We exist alongside emergent events, as about-to-be events, events not yet emerged, or completed events that cannot be seen. They emerge into full consciousness as I switch my head to a different position or my intention to a different project. Gibson (1979), in his direct realist approach, locates these emergent properties invariantly within the objects themselves. So the use of an object is reflected in its about-to-be-used attributes. Its use affords its existence for me in a certain way. But the Gibsonian account cannot explain how all possible uses of an object emerge. Many possibilities are due to conceptual, not physical, attributes and so can be triggered by meta-suggestion. There is a creative aspect to seeing, which is embodied in imaginal possibility. I may use a book as a wedge or a hammer or for other uses not solely dictated by its singular attributes. In other words, imagination can be concerned with possibilities which are not uniquely afforded physically by the object.

- *Absorption in degrees of reality.* Sense of reality does not suddenly collapse in the absence of sense information. It comes not from what is 'out there' but from our level of relative absorption in what is most possible. Such a degree of absorption implies logically a comparable lack of absorption in a range of alternative possibilities. What is seen arises against a background of not-seens, what was there, what can never be there, what might be there later, what is yet to come into view, all on the margins of consciousness. There is a clear distinction between supposing and imagining. Imagining always takes place in a lived-in context, just as perception, otherwise we are supposing and not imagining. So although I may suppose a possibility as an abstract idea, it is absorption in maximal possibility which gives me the sense of reality in which I live, and so conditions what is there (what I know I see) and what I know is not there.

The Possibility Distribution

The idea of a personalized possibility distribution may be heuristically compared to a likelihood distribution where the maximum possibility is a maximum likelihood (Edwards, 1972). In its simplest form the possibilistic model proposes that what we take as our reality is arrived at as the most possible world in the context of other possible worlds. So this world is never a stand-alone reality, rather, it is only ever constructed as a maximum possibility relative to other possibilities. Hence, it forms the maximum of a special distribution of alternative possibilities, some likely, some remote, given the maximum. The possibility distribution may be skewed, it may be irregular, it may be sharp or flat. If flat, this would mean that in the face of certain alternatives, the person would be more vulnerable to transition from one reality to another. The person might tolerate more deviation in one direction or another. The maximum possibility may then easily shift among closely competing possibilities and may be constantly modified or updated in continuity with minor adaptation on the basis of interactive experience with the world. Choosing between the possibility that a roaring noise outside my apartment door represents a pack of wild wolves, or the caretaker hoovering the hall floor, may not be difficult; everything about my current horizons, history, and projects supports the caretaker as maximum possibility. There are other likely possibilities, it may not be the caretaker who is hoovering, but his assistant, or someone else. These possibilities are likewise well tolerated by my distribution and do not require re-orienting my projects in which both the noise and the caretaker were in any case on the margins.

Of course if my current project involved the caretaker and hoovering, the possibility distribution would be more focused on the nuances of hoovering and could be sharpened by resolving these possibilities, through opening the door, updating experience, and gaining perceptual fit. This is the normal way to pursue perceptual fit and refine a possibility distribution by testing the extent to which possibilities thrown up by my project in the world coincide with the figure ground relationships of pre-existing self–world horizons: my wider sense of reality. The more remote the possibilities from my current intended project, the more they form the tail end of the possibility distribution and the flatness of the tail end of the possibility distribution means I have more tolerance for a variety of possible outcomes. But the maximum can also be modified by changing the personal context of comparable alternative possibilities, forming around the margins of the distribution. In other words, a change in the conception of what could be there (but isn't) could change inferences about what is there. A good example here is waking up the first night in a strange hotel room, forgetting you are not in your own bedroom at home, and being disoriented by your perception of objects in apparently strange places, a perception rapidly normalized by contextualizing the space as a hotel room.

The margins and the peak of the distribution are inter-dependent. Obviously change in one will affect the form of the other. A bad fit between my intentions and my possibilities will shift the peak possibility of the distribution, as may a change in the alternatives on the margins. However, the point is that both are at the mercy of the possibility distribution. We interact with an object and a possibility distribution immediately forms, which defines my field of operation, but imagining other forms of possibility can easily change the distribution. Suppose, for example, I am looking at a photograph of a man standing on a bridge. I know nothing of the context of the photograph. But in my imagination I conjure up different contexts. If I imagine that he is about to be shot and the photograph is taken by one of his executioners, the way I 'look at the photograph' will be distinct from if I imagine he is a tourist ambling by a historic bridge. Of course perception could be influenced by information about, say, the age of the man or his achievements which might also guide my focus. But the point here is that even without such cognitive information, the imaginal context can also change my inferential focus.

Technically, to be absorbed in possibility X implies not being absorbed in possibility Y yet the level of absorption in Y may affect the level of absorption in X. Thus, absorption always exists in relation to other possibilities where the degree of absorption in a particular scenario would be viewed as the result of the *relative* degree of absorption in possibility X *given* the degree of absorption into competing possibilities Y1, Y2, Y3 ... etc. If there is a displacement from what is possible to what is not possible, then this could likely be due to perceptual error, but also due to shifts in the imagined context. So the reality value of possibility X is defined by the reality value of alternative possibilities.

Meta-Cognitive Absorption in Different Possibilities

Absorption at any moment for any project then is defined by the maximum possibility distribution. It follows that one could be absorbed in two maximum possibilities while still perceiving only one reality, since an absorption in a maximum possibility is a combination of alternative possibilities and intentional project in the world. My project is always in the process of becoming and so the object(s) towards which it is directed are also in the process of becoming. Since at any one time an object may have two or more equivalent possibilities, so I could be equally absorbed in both possibilities. Also, a maximum possibility distribution, and a sense of absorption, can exist for something totally unrelated to information coming through the senses, because an imminent attribute could have a possibility value even though it is not real. A possibility distribution could for instance involve a sense of realness towards the idea of invisible contaminants on a doorknob, which may be unrelated to actual perception.

A visibly clean object could *become* dirty if touched or knocked over in the dust, but these possibilities also relate to the past. It could possibly also have been dirty, or dirty and not washed properly, or be dirty while not appearing so. The fact that I do not see any dirt does not challenge the sense of reality attached to the possibility that it could be dirty. As we noted, physical 'thereness' is not a criterion for sense of reality and anyway our physical scene is always partly unseen. So it would be feasible for me to, at the same time, know that a door is locked but at the same time entertain the possibility it is not and accord both a 'sense of reality'. Or to know on the one hand I have my hat and gloves in my hand, but to feel a strong sense on the other hand that I could have left them behind in a café. Entertaining two competing possible worlds at the same time is entirely possible and even in some situations desirable. The problem is the degree of absorption in both possible worlds. Although there are several possible worlds, there is only one reality for any given project. But the same reality can spawn distinct and contrasting possibility distributions. Absorption in this case is not a question of project–world fit, but of how my project, by my intentional self–world relation, maintains a remotely possible world in preference to a more plausible world with better fit. Although from one position we can be conscious of the imaginary part of a possibility and consciously know that we are living 'as if' or seeing 'as if' something is there, in a more absorbed position, the metaphorical stance may be forgotten and we may become confused as to the reality value of the imaginal possibilities. We can consider three stages of absorption: (1) Detachment – an attitude of intellectual curiosity; (2) a metaphorical stance – acting 'as if'; and (3) living 'as if' – complete absorption.

I may consider the lamp in front of me has several possibilities. It could change angle, go off, flutter, perhaps change color slightly, it could even perhaps explode, all of which would maintain its perceptual fit as a lamp. However, if it started flying around the room, my normal attitude towards it, as a lamp, would be very disrupted. As a consequence, I would likely in the process revise my possibilities and projects towards it and my other self–world horizons would change dramatically. Supposing, however, I felt that a lamp which performed all the normal functions of a lamp could at the same time also be a latent bird. So that the light was its eye, the stem its neck, the position its perch. In this circumstance, all the normal features of the lamp would stay identical but with the additional possibility that they might develop into bird features. Now in some sense my project towards the lamp and its operation would retain the normal possibilities and perceptual fit of the lamp and treat the lamp as a lamp. If its bulb fails, I replace it, I change its height or position for better light, but at the same time I can act towards it as a bird, occasionally stroking it, talking to it, making it more comfortable. In this case I am not at all surprised if it squawks or flies around the room, as well as shining light on the table. In one view I am treating a lamp 'as if' it were a bird, but from another view I'm treating a bird 'as if' it were a lamp. Both positions could be supported by appeal to the same reality. I could point to the switch or the metal cover of the lamp and without denying anything about their metallic properties, I could consider them bird-like. To say in the cognitive sense that I have interpreted or attributed bird features to a lamp, is to add an unhelpful layer of cognitive process onto reality which does not reflect the seemless way in which I alternate and integrate the two possible forms (one near, the other remote) of the lamp *within* the same reality. In fact, 'seeing' the same physical reality is at the root of the two distinct (bird/lamp) possibility distributions, and only because they both 'fit' real 'seen' features could they be held simultaneously to both be possibilities. Real information, for example, about birds is more likely to fuel my lamp-as-bird possibilities since in any case the reality of birds or lamps is not in question and real information, as noted, is the starting point for both competing distributions. If the lamp were to physically mutate into a chair, it would no longer be seen either as a lamp or a bird. It is only, in this instance, by changing my imaginative degree of absorption that I am likely to change my lamp-as-bird possibility.

Hence a person could legitimately be absorbed in two possible worlds at the same time, as, for example, in states of dissociation, or flip alternately from one to the other, with a very small perceived change in context. For example, a client could alternate between a strong sense of possibility that a purse could be left in a restaurant and knowledge that it is certainly with its owner. However, if there is a pathological dissociation from reality, it may not be a problem of perception but of absorption in the imagination.

So why would people construct and absorb themselves in different competing possibility distributions? It seems compelling, personal and cultural narratives may fuel the necessity to find alternatives, and fill up a self-created possibility space.

How 'Believed-In' Imaginings Become 'Lived-In'

Imaginary beliefs, in order to be lived in as well as believed in, must be convincingly placed in the world. De Rivera and Sarbin (1998) have suggested that the background for such beliefs must be a strongly identifiable cultural framework. The lived-in world must have a familiar past and a future, and an ecologically coherent history that creates a credible current environment and a future horizon.

The process of lived-in imagination could be viewed as a kind of hypnosis. During hypnotic suggestion, the person is led to believe in a story-line, and respond and feel appropriately. The induction techniques restrict the influence of the senses on experience, and attentional focus on internal experience positions the person as a passive recipient of possible experience where hypnotic induced images may be experienced as vividly as a real one (Bryant & Mallard, 2003), and invoke similar physiological reactions (Kosslyn et al., 2000). As several authors have pointed out, the absorption in hypnosis loses its role-playing 'as if' qualities and becomes a lived-in experience.

The enhancement of the sense of reality towards inner experience is the result of a person's ability to impose familiar and personally meaningful attributes on suggestions. The inductive narrative and procedure works best, however, if it is familiar and culturally credible in order to be trusted and believed in. In this context, it is interesting to note that in a sample of people with delusional beliefs cultural familiarity within the context of delusional narratives mediated estimates of their probability (McGuire et al., 2001). Lynn et al. (1996) report that hypnosis depends more on a person's ability to absorb themselves in suggestions through imaginative and dissociative abilities than on induction technique or trance-like states. Green and Brock (2000) stress the importance of the *transportation* quality of a narrative to influence belief. Elevated hypnotizability is associated with increased levels of absorption, and other traits and cognitive styles (Bryant & Mallard, 2003). Others report a close relation between imagination inflation and hypnotic suggestibility and dissociativity (Heaps & Nash, 1999).

However, people under hypnosis often report a meta-cognitive aspect as part of their experience, unlike, for example, during hypnagogic imagery where sense of self is often compromised. Thus, people under hypnosis can observe and report on their state (e.g. hidden observer technique) as well as sometimes be partially aware of the environment and the hypnotic illusion/ delusion. The experience of hypnosis then, rather like obsessional preoccupation, does not necessarily change perception and can be viewed as a way of modifying degrees of absorption in imagined possibilities. Similarly, in both mime and magic, the spectator can be aware of the environment and of the illusion. The magician's patter and misdirection or a mime's actions lead us to believe that what is not there is real, even in the absence of proof. In all cases, we are aware of the illusion, and meta-cognitively aware that we are aware of the illusion, but are nevertheless content to be absorbed in it, since the metaphorical 'as if' is maintained.

Part of knowing I am in the here and now is knowledge of how I got here, what is beyond here, what is inside, outside, what is me/not me. It is when this narrative about our immediate environment is temporarily supplemented with a more remote but convincing one that we 'knowingly' see illusions. We act 'as if' they were real, even though we may know differently, because to question the reality of an illusion puts into question our normal way of arriving at the real. So we accept two competing narratives with a meta-cognitive awareness that our sense of reality has been tricked.

Clinical Implications of Absorption

Sense of reality can change, then, not only due to problems of project–world 'fit' in either stimuli or consequences, but also due to absorption in a possible world through transportation by an imaginary narrative. Furthermore, such absorption is a logical consequence of being led to see competing narratives as less likely either by experience or narrative. It follows, then, in the evaluation and understanding of altered states of consciousness, that the background distribution of other possible states should also be explored. The cognitive tendency has been to assume that in states of delusion or hallucination, data gathering or perceptual processing is biased (Garety & Freeman, 1999), whereas, as we have seen, it may be an imaginary possibility, not perception, that maintains an abnormal sense of reality. In this case, what might be required is a therapy to change the parameters of the imagination. This would include operationalizing a possibility distribution, and manipulating alternatives on the margins of consciousness, in order to shift absorption through proposing a narrative context to introduce new credible alternatives. Meta-cognitively, the imagination can challenge the sense of reality, providing it can give a coherent and detailed story of the historical, spatial, biographic, material context necessary for an alternative possibility to generate a sense of reality. For example, if I stated that the walls in my house have microphones in them, there would probably be a little shift in the maximum possibility that the wall is simply a wall. If I embellished the story with details of its past, present and future as a repository of microphones, accompanied by my acting as if there were microphones in the walls of my house, the possibility might be more marked. For example, I could add the following factual elements: that my house was recently visited by a person from a telephone company, during which visit I could not be present, and that since then several people have telephoned but hung up on me; also that several suspicious-looking cars have been parked in front of my house. The story would require spatial and temporal depth plus a repositioning of my project towards the wall in order for me to be better absorbed in the wall-with-microphones sense of reality. If we apply this insight clinically, it provides a different viewpoint on distorted perceptions.

The clinical message is that when people enter states of absorption in unreality, they may not be suffering from distortions of reality but from over-reliance on meta-cognitive use of the imagination when making inferences. In this case, the top-down approach of attempting perceptual 'fit' through information seeking is inappropriate. As an example, people with obsessional contamination fears are frequently convinced of the existence of 'unseen' dirt, despite the presence of an intact and accurate perceptual system which 'sees' no dirt. Further exploration reveals absorption on the basis of a convincing narrative in the possibility of what might be there *despite* proof to the contrary. The therapeutic approach proposed here is to work on constructing alternative imaginary scenarios in an attempt to dislodge the maximum possibility from the bottom (i.e. margins) upwards. A cognitive focus on perception of reality will not be helpful if reality is not the problem.

Although there is only one world or 'reality structure', our meta-cognitive ability permits us to be absorbed in several possible worlds at the same time, and to experience a sense of reality in relation to worlds which do not (and which we sometimes know do not) exist but which nonetheless, by their non-existence, inform perception. The same perceived attributes may be seen inside distinct and possibly opposing intentional contexts and projects, thus feeding distinct senses of reality.

Intricately wound up with absorption is the intent of the person as personified by projects, positioning and doings in the world. This link is inescapable and nothing can be seen or imagined unless the person acts towards the world to bring out its promise and possibility. Hence change in intentional context can change possibilistic context and vice versa.

Sense of reality can be changed from the margins upwards, as well as by perceptual 'fit' downwards. Imaginal illusions can lead us to see conflicting or paradoxical information because narrative cues create a competing context to perception. It is normal on such occasions to 'see' imaginary events and hence experience conflicting senses of reality, while, however, 'knowing' only one reality.

It may even be desirable on occasion to be metaphorically absorbed in two senses of reality, for example, when watching a magician's or a mime's illusion. The cognitive explanation here is that we 'suspend our disbelief' on such occasions. Alternatively, we may be transported by a convincing visual or verbal narrative to construct a maximum possibility distribution and believe in it accordingly, without in any way compromising our wider perceptual sense of what is 'really' there.

Meta-cognitively the person can adopt one of three levels of absorption with respect to possibility: detached; metaphorical; or living-as. The problem, clinically speaking, occurs when the metaphorical stance is dropped and the temporarily 'believed-in' becomes 'lived-in'. Psychopathological distortions of reality where the person enters a state of dissociation, and appears absorbed in unreality, may not signal cognitive distortions, but rather meta-cognitive shift of the imagination. Absorption occurs on the basis of a good story line which limits plausible alternatives not on the basis of facts. Facts are unlikely to influence absorption.

In the case of delusional disorder, a person may function well in everyday reality. The person will see the walls in their house for exactly what they are, plastered, painted, 10 feet by 8 feet. The person is, however, convinced that the neighbors have installed microphones in the walls to monitor and spy on them. There is no proof of the microphones, only ambiguities, hearsay and stories, but for the person the presence of microphones represents the maximum possibility. In fact, the delusional belief will often circumvent any direct reality testing of the belief ('we can't test it out because if we drill holes in the wall to find microphones, the neighbors will know'). Or in the event of dramatic evidence against the belief (e.g. the wall collapses revealing no microphones), the belief will negotiate a way around the fact ('they must have removed the microphones beforehand').

Here again, the therapeutic strategy may be more profitable if the imagination is addressed. Exploring the margins of the possibility distribution where it is flatter, more flexible and less certain, will reveal the remoter possibilities of what is not there, what certainly cannot exist inside the walls. For example, the person, although believing microphones a possibility, may not accord radio transmitters a high possibility. Looking at what is more or less possible helps contextualize the significance of the microphones and why these and not anything else (loudspeakers, cameras, CD players) are most likely. Revealing the remoter context surrounding the belief will also reveal the intentional context and project the person has towards the neighbors which accords microphones but not, say, radio transmitters to be a maximum possibility. The belief then may be seen as an imaginative creation of an intentional context rather than a stand-alone delusion, and the person may understand the confusion between a maximum possibility and the inference of real microphones, and hence how delusional belief is a maximum possibility within a certain possibilistic context, but never a certain fact.

CONCLUSION

In this chapter, we have discussed a model which accounted for the role of the imagination in inference. Essentially, inference involves possibility and imagination represents possibility to us in the form of narratives about what might happen. Since narrative, as we discussed in previous sections, can elicit different degrees of absorption, so a person could be absorbed in two or more possible states of affairs. Possible states could be represented as a possibility distribution with the most likely possibility being inferred on the basis of intentionality of the project in hand and perceptual fit. But imagination could be influenced by competing narratives on the margins of the distribution, which could make remote imagined possibilities not just believed in but lived in.

We now return to psychopathology to see how reasoning research has addressed thinking disorders and to what extent modifying inferential processes can form the basis of therapy.

CHAPTER 4

REASONING AND PSYCHOPATHOLOGY

REASONING IN CLINICAL POPULATIONS

In their numerous studies on reasoning, Wason and Johnson-Laird (1972) came across instances where participants reacted in non-habitual ways during deductive and inductive tasks. In fact, pathological expressions such as repetitiveness, self-contradiction and denial of facts were observed. The authors suggested that this may be caused by the demands of the tasks and certain people's reasoning processes, together creating a stressful condition inhibiting the task's resolution. The authors hinted at a link between these observations and pathology.

For example, in a hypothetico-deductive task called the 2-4-6 Problem (described earlier), Wason and Johnson-Laird observed that participants' reasoning processes became rigid where they had difficulty discarding their own hypotheses once they had asserted and confirmed these. The authors go on to present the case of a participant persisting in this manner which to them expressed 'strong obsessional features', that is 'his [the participant's] fertile imagination, and intense preoccupation with original hypotheses, has narrowed his field of appreciation to the point where he has become blind to the obvious' (ibid. p. 233).

Previous Research into Clinical Populations

As Johnson-Laird (1999) pointed out, in deductive reasoning, theories are derived from two types of experimental paradigms. That is, measures of performance: exploring *mechanisms* of thoughts and measures of competence: exploring the *content* of reasoning.

Similarly, in regards to reasoning and pathologies, two major currents emerge:

1 *Reasoning processes in pathology*: how reasoning performance can inform us about the mechanisms of pathology.
2 *The effect of content on reasoning competence*: how manipulating content with characteristics of a pathology can influence reasoning competence.

The following section reviews the current state of research into reasoning and pathology, looking at it from these two perspectives: studies that inform us about certain pathologies by using reasoning paradigms and studies that manipulate content in order to understand reasoning processes in pathology.

Reasoning Processes in Pathology: Mechanisms of Pathology

In hopes of explaining how psychological disorders are developed and maintained, researchers have used well-established reasoning tasks. To use reasoning paradigms as a means of understanding mechanisms of pathology is to consider that reasoning in itself plays a determinant role in human behavior. Therefore, observing its variations can inform us about the processes that guide behavior. The advantages of working with such paradigms are that the tasks used are well documented and have been tested in a variety of conditions in the general population. These findings serve as an anchor for estimating differences. However, there are limits as to the implications of such differences because a 'deficit' or 'bias' in one's performance may not necessarily explain the 'mechanisms' of this particular disorder but simply reflect the impact of pathology on reasoning performance. We will discuss the point further, however, as reasoning paradigms have been very useful in pointing out the important aspects of pathology. Hence, the following section describes one of the commonest tasks administered in clinical populations, that is, a Bayesian probabilistic task which tells us about the ability of individuals to estimate the likelihood of an event and about their decision-making style.

A Probabilistic Reasoning Paradigm

In 1966, Phillips and Edwards developed a probability inference task to examine the effects of probability estimates on different variables such as prior probabilities, amount of data gathered before making a decision, diagnostic impact of data, payoffs and response modes. The task involved imagining 10 bags containing 100 poker chips each, while manipulating the ratio of red to blue chips in each condition. Participants estimated how likely it was that a bag containing predominantly red or blue chips would be chosen, on the basis of the experimenter's draws of chips from a (presumably) randomly chosen bag.

Volans (1976), Huq et al. (1988) and Garety et al. (1991) used modified versions of this probabilistic task in a series of studies with people suffering from diverse clinical disorders. The probability task described here is that of Garety et al. (1991) and is administered as follows: Participants are presented with two jars (A and B) and told that they each contain 100 colored beads. Jar A contains a greater proportion of colored beads 'A' to colored beads 'B' (85:15) and jar B contains the inverse ratio of color B to color A (85B:15A). Once the jars are hidden from the participant, jar A is picked by E who begins to draw beads out of this jar only. Participants are told that the jar is picked at random and that draws are random as well. However, the order of appearance of the colored beads is predetermined.

Condition 1: Decision-making: participants first estimate how likely it is that a particular color of bead will be chosen (i.e. 'How likely is it that an A bead will be picked first?'). Then, E starts drawing beads out of the (A) jar and participants use a 'go' or 'stop' card to indicate if they need more draws before making a decision about which jar has been picked. Measures are: (1) initial certainty: the *a priori* probability that colored bead A would be drawn first; (2) draws to decision: the number of draws made before making a decision on the chosen jar; and (3) error in decision-making: concluding that the wrong jar has been chosen.

The following shows the predetermined sequence of beads for condition 1:

A A A B A A A A A B B A A A A A A A A B

Notice that A beads are the predominant ones to be drawn so the correct choice is that jar 'A' has been chosen.

Condition 2: probability estimates: Here, the participants estimate how likely it is that jar A has been chosen. The measures are: the initial posterior estimate (that jar A has been chosen); draws to certainty (estimate of $\geqslant 85\%$); effect of confirmatory evidence on judgement; effect of disconfirmatory evidence on judgement; errors of decision; draws to change; size of change. The effects of evidence and size of change measures are calculated on the normative Bayesian estimate (see Huq *et al.*, 1988).

The following illustrates the predetermined sequence of beads for condition 2:

A A A B A A A A B A B B B A B B B B A B

Note in this sequence, more A beads are drawn in the first set of 10 which should lead to ratings that A is more likely to have been chosen (confirmatory evidence) and in the second set of 10 beads, more B beads are drawn to measure the effect of disconfirmatory evidence.

The task used by Phillips and Edwards (1966) showed that when confronted with this task, people in the general population were conservative in comparison to a more normative way of estimating likelihood ratios, calculated on the basis of what is called Bayes' theorem. This means people had a tendency to request more information to come to a decision than logical probability calculus would predict.

Reasoning Mechanisms in Thought Disorders: Delusions and Schizophrenia

Given the reasoning deviations found in the normal population and the hypothesis that delusions follow a continuum from normal beliefs, Huq *et al.* (1988) decided to test groups of deluded, psychiatric and normal controls on the Bayesian probabilistic task just described. The authors' clinical observations of delusional patients led them to hypothesize that fixity of belief and intensity of conviction would lead this group of participants to be less conservative than the other two groups, that is, require less information before making a decision and be over-confident about these choices compared to normal controls or other psychiatric participants. Their hypotheses were confirmed on both accounts: results suggested deluded participants showed a significant higher level of conviction on their 'initial certainty' estimates, which demonstrated they were over-confident compared to the two other groups. Also, deluded participants requested less evidence before making a decision (requesting 1.22 draws) compared to normal controls (a request of 2.6 draws) and to the psychiatric group (a request of 3.58 draws). The finding shows how, in a laboratory task, people with delusions react to decision-making. However, it remains to be understood how this translates into everyday decision-making and if this reasoning 'bias' means that people with delusions jump to a conclusion about any information that is presented to them. The fact that the task is neutral would indicate that such is the case but the study lacks ecological validity, that is, a more realistic context.

Nevertheless, the findings needed to be replicated since the previous study had included a group of people diagnosed with schizophrenia without distinction of deluded participants without hallucinations. Hence, Garety *et al.* (1991) extended their work using the probabilistic reasoning task with better defined diagnostic groups. Effectively, in addition to a group diagnosed with schizophrenia, a 'pure delusional' group was included, that is, people diagnosed with DSM-III-R (American Psychiatric Association) criteria for delusional disorder (paranoia type). An anxious control group and a non-psychiatric control group served as comparisons. The hypothesis was that delusional disordered patients would show a greater bias in probabilistic reasoning than schizophrenic patients since their abnormal beliefs were more subtle, they suffered no hallucinations. All groups completed the Bayesian probability task and measures of initial certainty and draws to decision were collected. No significant differences were found between schizophrenic patients and paranoid delusional patients on their responses of the probabilistic task. Effectively, both these groups were over-confident and required less evidence before making a decision than the anxious and normal control group, which replicated the previous results of Huq *et al.* (1988). Again, we are faced with results which describe a particular way of reacting by people with thought disorders but it is not clear whether this reasoning bias is present in all facets of life and whether or not it preceded the onset of psychopathology. Also, more was needed in order to differentiate between a possible task effect or a genuine different reasoning style. Effectively, research has been conducted in order to test this idea, by using a different probabilistic task and seeing if this would lead to variations in style of reasoning. For example, Dudley *et al.* (1997a) devised two separate experiments to examine whether people with delusions exhibited a general deficit in reasoning, when using different probabilistic material and by varying the ratio of beads from the standard probabilistic task. The first experiment verified performance on a 'biased coin task'. People with delusions, depressed controls and non-psychiatric controls needed to estimate the chance that a coin was biased to 'heads' when presented with a set of results from throwing the coin. Bayes' theorem is used to assess performance. The results on this task showed there were no differences in probabilistic estimates between the three groups. This finding is important because it indicates that people with delusions do not have any problems with estimating probabilities.

However, the second experiment tested decision-making and with variations in the ratio of beads the replication of the "jumping to conclusion" (JTC) bias was apparent. Here, two versions of the probabilistic task were used where ratios of beads were manipulated: a proportion of 85:15 condition and a 60:40 condition. As mentioned, the manipulation aimed to test whether a different base rate would yield a more cautious strategy from the delusional participants. Results showed that, indeed, delusional patients took notice of the different base rate and were more cautious but still required less evidence than the two control groups for the same condition. Thus, it transpires that people with delusional disorder use the same reasoning process as normal controls but that they require less evidence to do so. It becomes clearer from these experiments that people with delusions do appear to have a different reasoning style. However, the question remains on how this translates into reality.

In their critical review of cognitive approaches to delusions, Garety and Freeman (1999) compare three main theories of development and maintenance of delusional disorder. Their own theory is the only one where reasoning is considered to play a part in delusions although they specify that this applies only to certain delusional types. Effectively, Garety (1991) and Garety and Hemsley (1994) propose a multifactorial model that includes past experience, affect, self-esteem and motivation as having a role in some delusions while biases in perception and judgement would be more crucial to other types. As described previously, the series of experiments using the Bayesian probabilistic task have been quite consistent in demonstrating a 'data-gathering deficit' (gathering less evidence to form a hypothesis) in people with delusions. The authors conclude that although erroneous conclusions are not always the result of this 'data-gathering deficit', it does predispose individuals to accept incorrect hypotheses. In a wider perspective, it also implies that people who suffer from delusions show this style of reasoning when faced with neutral material and that both diagnostic groups, delusional and schizophrenic, are prone to reason in this manner. Further experiments using emotionally salient content confirmed these findings (see Dudley *et al.*, 1997a, 1997b) and are described later.

Reasoning Mechanisms and Anxiety Disorders

Reasoning mechanisms in anxiety disorders have been relatively less investigated than in thought disorders. One of the reasons may be that thought disorders are more readily associated with the hypothesis that 'faulty reasoning' plays a key role in bizarre idea formation. Nevertheless, in the cognitive era where terms like 'irrational thinking', 'cognitive errors' and 'irrational beliefs', etc., are regularly used, it is surprising how little information we have about the mechanisms in the development of such pathological irrationality. The traditional classical conditioning behavioral theory of the fear response developing in association with a catastrophic thought offers an explanation of the development of anxiety, but what of the formation of the 'catastrophic' thought in the first place? Reasoning performance on neutral tasks can be informative if they yield observations of diverse reasoning strategies for pathological groups.

However, two questions are worth keeping in mind. First, the question of causality: does pathology influence reasoning performance? Or do reasoning strategies cause pathology? Second, the question of the implications of results: how does reasoning performance inform us of a particular pathology? As Garety and Freeman (1999) have suggested, longitudinal studies are needed to answer the first question and it's up to researchers to translate reasoning findings into clinical applications which can sometimes become quite a challenge! For example, among the first attempts in testing reasoning processes in clinical populations was a study by Milner *et al.* (1971) examining decision-making in obsessive-compulsive disorder (OCD). They compared the performance of a group of people with OCD and a control group on an auditory signal detection task. A faint tone embedded in white noise was presented and participants had to decide whether they needed additional trials before stating if the tone was present. The results suggested that before making a decision, OCD participants requested a higher number of trials than people in the control group. It was hypothesized that 'in obsessional disorder decisions may be deferred (in favour of gathering further relevant information) to an abnormal extent'

(Milner *et al.*, 1971, p. 88). This finding marked the beginning of a series of experiments yielding consistent results about people with OCD needing more information before being certain of their decision. Unfortunately, none of the research proposed explanations on how this contributed to the development or maintenance of OCD.

For example, Volans (1976) investigated reasoning in OCD using the standard Bayesian probabilistic task (described earlier). The participants were tested over four different conditions: the first required a YES–NO response as to which jar (A or B), was chosen. In the second condition, the same YES–NO response was required with the addition of probability estimates of the next color of bead to be drawn. The other two conditions measured predicted probability estimates based on the evidence of a previous draw without a YES–NO response mode. Three groups participated in the experiment: patients with OCD, patients with phobias, and a non-psychiatric control group. The probability estimates of the obsessional group deviated significantly more from the Bayesian norm than did the phobic and non-psychiatric group. In effect, draws to decision for the normal control group was a mean of 4.8 draws, while the OCD group requested 8.86 draws and the phobic group 5.28 draws. These significant results were replicated by Fear and Healy (1997) who tested probabilistic reasoning in both OCD and DD groups as well as a 'mixed' group (people with both delusional and obsessional beliefs) in comparison to a normal control group. Results echoed those of Volans (1976), where the OCD group differed in their reasoning style from the DD and the mixed group by requesting more evidence before making a decision. So where people with DD seem to exhibit a 'data-gathering deficit' by requiring less evidence than normal control, they are still much closer to the Bayesian norm than people with OCD. It would appear, then, that people with OCD exhibit a 'data-gathering excess', because of their extreme deviation from the norm. Again, a clear explanation is lacking in terms of how this contributes to the conceptualization of OCD. What kind of decisions in everyday life would be affected by this bias?

One study actually seemed to contradict the 'data-gathering excess' style of reasoning found in OCD. In effect, Rhéaume *et al.* (2000) used a modified version of the probabilistic task with people who showed pathological perfectionism, a symptom which has been linked with OCD. Here, the ratio of beads that was used was a proportion of 60:40, which raises the ambiguity or difficulty of the task because of almost equal proportions of each color of beads. Rhéaume and colleagues measured functional and dysfunctional perfectionism to form two separate groups. People with dysfunctional perfectionism (which is hypothesized to be linked to OCD) required less draws before making a decision when compared to people with functional perfectionism. Although the authors found a relationship between dysfunctional perfectionism and an obsessive-compulsive behavior scale, at the moment, the concept of perfectionism is not considered a predictor of OCD (Frost *et al.*, 2002) so it may be premature to draw any conclusions.

It seems that results obtained from sub-clinical populations lead to contradicting conclusions. For example, the probabilistic reasoning paradigm was used in a non-clinical sample of people scoring high on the Intolerance of Uncertainty Questionnaire (IUQ) which distinguishes worriers meeting GAD criteria from those who do not. Ladouceur *et al.* (1997) used a modified version of the Bayesian probabilistic task. However, in order to operationalize the concept of 'intolerance to uncertainty' (IU), two levels of ambiguity, moderate and high, were created by varying the ratio of the colored beads (moderate ambiguity = 85:15 and high ambiguity = 60:40), and then having people decide from which bag the individual beads had been picked. Their results suggested that under the moderate level of ambiguity condition, more people characterized with IU required a greater number of draws before making a decision. However, the effect disappeared in the high ambiguity condition and the authors explain the finding by postulating a lower threshold of perception of ambiguity by people with IU, which creates a need to precipitate a decision. The modification by the authors of the original probabilistic task meant that the order of appearance of the color of the beads was undetermined. Therefore, the number of draws requested by the participants was confounded with the order of appearance of the color of the beads (determined by chance). Consequently, it is difficult to compare these results with previous probabilistic reasoning studies.

Probabilistic reasoning informs us of people's abilities to estimate the occurrence of an event drawn from base rate information which, as we saw in Chapter 2, constitutes only one aspect of reasoning. Other types of reasoning have been investigated in psychopathology such as deductive and inductive reasoning processes. Effectively, Reed (1977; 1991) initiated such formal investigation with participants who were diagnosed with what was formerly called 'anankastic' personality disorder, the equivalent of obsessive-compulsive personality disorder (OCPD). In his study, he compared an OCPD group to psychiatric controls on a deductive reasoning arithmetic task and an inductive task requiring participants to infer a rule about a series of numbers. Results showed that the OCPD group performed better on the deductive task but that their results on the inductive task were inferior to that of the psychiatric control group. The extent to which the results are representative is unclear in the absence of a non-psychiatric control group and a better diagnostic definition. However, Reed's research pinpointed the relevance of examining inductive and deductive reasoning in the obsessional population and prompted further investigation of such processes.

Effectively, Pélissier and O'Connor (2002a) examined formal deductive and inductive reasoning in OCD and to our knowledge, the study constitutes the only research to have extensively examined such processes in OCD. A group of 12 people with OCD was compared to 10 people with GAD and a normal control group of 10 other participants, on a series of six inductive and deductive tasks. The deductive tasks involved were: the Wason Selection Task, the 2-4-6 problem and a deductive exercise designed by the authors. Essentially, no significant differences were found between groups on either of these measures. The inductive tasks were three exercises designed by the authors based on reasoning literature: estimating plausibility of 40 different given inferences ('Finding the evidence'), linking two separate, unrelated premises ('Bridging') and estimating the validity of an arbitrary statement before and after supplying arguments to support it ('Supporting an arbitrary statement'). The results in the inductive tasks suggest group differences in two of the three exercises. Effectively, the OCD group takes longer to initiate their inference process than the two control groups. Also, they seem to doubt an arbitrary statement in a higher proportion than the two other groups, even after generating supporting evidence for this particular statement. Drawing on Johnson-Laird's mental model theory, we hypothesized that these findings were due to an excessive production of alternative mental models on the part of people with OCD which may have both slowed down the process of generating inferences as well as created excessive doubting by multiplying cognitive loading on the inductive reasoning process. The implications of these results are fully discussed in Chapter 5.

Effect of Content on Reasoning Competence

The following section deals with studies that have modified diverse reasoning paradigms by including themes that were relevant to the pathology they were testing. This line of research is intended to find out whether reasoning patterns persist or diverge when pathological relevant content is introduced into the reasoning paradigm. If the patterns of reasoning are more pronounced than those observed in the neutral condition, it is possible to hypothesize that this particular reasoning style plays a role in the maintenance of the pathological symptoms, while not being a causal factor. However, if the reasoning style is different in the pathological relevant content condition, then it would be hypothesized that a special case of reasoning is employed in that particular condition. More still, the studies that have used these modified paradigms also manipulate variables other than reasoning and which have already been hypothesized to play a role in diverse pathologies (i.e. perfectionism). So the reasoning paradigms may serve only as a template to verify whether these other variables are relevant.

Effects of Content in Affective and Thought Disorder

One of the first experiments introducing content in a reasoning paradigm was that of Young and Bentall (1997) who modified the Bayesian probabilistic task and replaced beads by descriptions of people (a person who was liked and a person who was disliked) to create a 'personality' condition. So, for example, participants would hear the description of 'what has been said about a person' from a pool of 100 people and they needed to assess whether this was the description of a person who was liked or unliked. The condition was designed to test whether the meaning of the material would influence the groups' probabilistic estimates and decision-making style. Three groups were tested: deluded patients, depressed patients and normal controls. A standard version (85:15 ratio condition) was also administered, serving as an anchor. Results showed that, overall, the three groups reached an initial level of certainty and revised these certainty levels more rapidly in the personality condition than in the neutral condition. However, this effect was more pronounced in the clinical groups compared to the normal control group. Young and Bentall concluded that emotionally salient themes may produce 'abnormalities' of probabilistic reasoning which would be expected if such a factor played a role in the development and maintenance of delusions. So here we are presented with the case of an increased reasoning bias. However, these results tell us that the normal control group also showed a quicker decision-making strategy. So the reasoning style seems to be the same for everyone but people with psychopathology exhibit a stronger bias. These results were replicated by subsequent research. For example, Dudley et al. (1997b) tested whether the JTC bias was observed when using realistic material versus abstract material and also whether reasoning with emotionally relevant material would increase the rapidity with which delusional patients seemed to make a decision. Three groups were tested: people with delusions; people who were depressed; and normal controls. The participants were presented with two versions of the Bayesian probabilistic task where both versions used realistic material but one of them had emotionally neutral content and the other used emotionally salient themes. Results of these two experiments show that people with delusions request less evidence before coming to a conclusion when presented with realistic content, so the JTC bias is generalized to realistic content. The second finding was that all groups request less evidence when the material is more salient. Therefore, emotionally relevant material increases the JTC reasoning style for everyone, although the authors underline the tendency for people with delusions to require even less evidence than the two other groups but this was not statistically significant.

Drawing on the previous results, it seemed important to find out if the JTC bias using salient material was present in other forms of reasoning in order to rule out a task effect. To do that, Dudley *et al.* (1998) modified the Wason Selection Task by manipulating the content, going from neutral to being more realistic. Hence, conditional reasoning performance of people with delusional disorder was compared to a non-deluded and normal control group. Four versions of the Wason Selection Task (WST) were devised to vary in content of realism. Results showed that people with delusional disorder reasoned in the same manner as the two control groups on all but one of the four versions. In fact, the difference in reasoning was found in the most realistic version of the WST where people in the delusional group solved the task in a less efficient manner than the normal control and depressed group. The results were perplexing since increased realism usually increases the WST performance so the authors proposed that people with delusions may have a working memory deficit not permitting them to manipulate all the necessary elements. The authors caution that this remains to be determined in future studies but it appears that a more realistic context leads clinical groups to a stronger bias. The results underline the importance of tailoring reasoning tasks to particular psychopathologies since it may be much closer to everyday reasoning and thus, much closer to clinical reality.

Effects of Content in Anxiety Disorders

Research into reasoning and anxious clinical populations seems to have moved much closer to clinical reality than reasoning studies of thought disorders. Essentially, this line of research has mainly involved the modification of the Wason Selection Task by replacing the symbols with anxious content or simply using anxiety-tailored scripts as the basis for requesting inferential performance. For example, Arntz *et al.* (1995) investigated inductive reasoning processes biased towards danger and subjective anxiety in a population of anxious participants compared to non-anxious controls. Their study involved four groups of anxious patients (52 spider phobics, 41 panic patients, 38 social phobics, and 31 other anxiety patients) compared to 24 normal control participants. All participants had to rate the perceived danger in anxiety-tailored scripts, where objective danger vs objective safety as well as objective anxiety vs objective non-anxiety information were varied. It was hypothesized that anxious patients would not only infer danger on the basis of objective danger cues but also infer danger on the basis of subjective anxiety information where normal controls would not. The hypothesis was confirmed and the authors concluded that a process termed 'ex-consequentia reasoning' was responsible, where anxious participants conclude that feeling anxious implies danger. One possible limit to the implications of these results is the fact that the task requires all participants to infer either 'danger' or 'not-danger'. This dichotomous choice may lead anxious participants to consistently infer danger, not necessarily because they have faulty reasoning strategies but precisely because they have no experiences that yield conclusions of safety. The results then seem to underline the difference between being anxious and not being anxious. In other words, it is unclear if the inability to conclude 'if I feel anxious, then I am not in danger' (presumably the reasoning of normal controls), is based on faulty reasoning on the part of anxious participants. So although this would also need to be tested, it should not be ruled out that the inference of danger may simply be the absence of sufficient premises to permit a safety conclusion.

The previous results prompted De Jong et al. (1997) to devise two separate experiments: the first tested phobic participants on a conditional reasoning task where they had to assess the validity of conditional statements in the context of general threats or phobic specific threats. Modified versions of the Wason Selection Task (WST) were used where danger rules (if p, then danger) and safety rules (if p, then safety) were proposed. The two groups tested were high and low spider-fearful students. In the second experiment, the same material was used but was administered to three groups: treated and untreated spider phobic women, and a group of non-fearful control participants. The results of these two experiments showed that in the general threat condition, reasoning strategies were guided by utility judgement, that is, all participants in all groups relied on confirming evidence when faced with a danger rule (selecting the q card) and relied on disconfirming information when given a safety rule (selecting the not-q card). In the phobic threat condition, this pattern was even more pronounced especially in the non-treated spider phobic group. What these results seem to show is that the more salient the content for phobic participants, the more they use a reasoning strategy that the authors call 'fear-confirming reasoning' and which seems to be the natural flow on a continuum of this reasoning strategy. However, presumably the normal control participants did not respond to the anxiety-salient condition because the content was irrelevant to them. This makes sense since they do not suffer from the specific phobia. This 'fear-confirming pattern' needed to be replicated and a good way of finding out about its consistency was to test it in other anxiety disorders, which is precisely what these authors did in a subsequent study.

Effectively, De Jong et al. (1998) examined performance of hypochondriacal patients on a series of modified versions of the Wason Selection Task (WST) to verify if these participants used 'fear-confirming reasoning'. Recall that fear-confirming reasoning describes the strategy of trying to confirm danger rules and disconfirm safety rules in the context of objective as well as phobic threats. As in previous results with spider phobics, hypochondriacal patients did use fear-confirming strategies but this was not significantly different from the control group. The authors conclude that the threat of health problems would be more prone to make even non-hypochondriacal people search for disconfirmation whereas spider information would be neutral to non-spider phobics. However, a later study by Smeets *et al.* (2000) found a significant difference between a group of hypochondriacal patients and controls using the same modified WST, but this time they deleted a worry statement that may have influenced normal controls in the previous study. The results of this later study confirmed a fear-confirming reasoning style that is more pronounced in the health threat condition for hypochondriacal patients. So although it is not a specific trait of hypochondriasis to reason in a 'better safe than sorry' manner, this fear-confirming reasoning pattern may serve to maintain the health fears in place.

In an attempt to expand on the concept of 'ex-consequentia reasoning' (Arntz *et al.*, 1995), a recent study by Engelhard *et al.* (2001) examined 'emotion-based reasoning' (ER) and compared it to what is called 'intrusion-based reasoning' (IR), a process where danger is inferred on the basis of the occurrence of an intrusion (an upsetting thought about an anxiety-related stimulus). The study verified whether a population of Vietnam combat veterans suffering from posttraumatic stress disorder (PTSD) compared to those not diagnosed with PTSD, inferred danger on the basis of anxiety responses (emotion-based reasoning) and on the basis of intrusions (intrusions-based reasoning) when presented with objective danger information and objective safety information. All participants were presented with scenarios that varied in content with objective danger/ safety information and anxiety/no anxiety response for the ER condition and with objective danger/safety information and intrusions/no intrusions for the IR condition. The inference of danger was measured by asking people to estimate how dangerous each scenario was, by scoring a visual analogue scale for each of them. Results showed that all participants inferred more danger on the basis of objective danger information compared to objective safety information. However, combat veterans with PTSD rated the scenarios as being significantly more dangerous on the basis of both anxiety responses and intrusions where non-PTSD veterans did not show such a significant difference. Engelhard and colleagues conclude that ER and IR are linked to PTSD and may serve to maintain PTSD symptoms. As previously mentioned in reference to the Arntz *et al.* (1995) study, the maintenance of pathological symptoms may be characterized by the tendency for anxious people to infer danger on the basis of anxious symptoms and here, on the basis of anxious thoughts, not so much because they use a faulty reasoning strategy ('if I feel anxious and think about scary events, then there must be danger'), but more because the induction process itself involves providing additional information to the premises, from which one infers conclusions. So the additional information may be different for PTSD sufferers than for non-PTSD sufferers because presumably they have a richer experience of anxiety and of intrusions. A further attempt was made to establish a causal link between ER/IR and the development of PTSD in a subsequent study.

Essentially, Engelhard *et al.* (2002) tested the IR condition (dropping the ER condition) to establish whether IR predicted PTSD symptoms, following a train disaster. Participants were 29 directly exposed witnesses of a train crash compared to 14 non-witness villagers from the small Belgium town where this disaster occurred. The task used to assess the inference of danger was similar to Engelhard *et al.*'s (2001) previous study, where scenarios were devised to manipulate objective danger/safety information with intrusions/no intrusions segments. Participants needed to rate how dangerous each scenario was, using the visual analogue scale. Results showed that the group of direct witnesses rated the scenarios with intrusion segments as more dangerous than the scenarios without such intrusions and this was significantly different than the control group (non-witnesses). Also, participants within the directly exposed group who showed higher ratings in IR reported higher levels of chronic PTSD symptoms at 3.5 months. This study raises an important point about how intrusions can predict PTSD symptoms. However, the authors mention that one of the limits to this conclusion is that completing a task involving intrusions may have prompted the witnesses to experience similar intrusions. Also, the non-witnesses may have found the intrusion segments irrelevant, not having been exposed to the trauma.

Conclusion

This section has made an attempt to outline a novel line of research in clinical psychopathology. Effectively, research into reasoning and pathology is twofold: studies that manipulate content in order to understand reasoning processes in particular psychological disorders; and studies that inform us about psychopathology by using reasoning paradigms to show how reasoning performance can inform us about the mechanisms of pathology.

So to answer the question about how reasoning performance informs us of a particular pathology, one example can be drawn from the extensive work of Garety and collaborators (Garety & Freeman, 1999; Garety & Hemsley, 1994; Garety *et al.*, 1991; Huq *et al.*, 1988) and Dudley and colleagues (1997a, 1997b, 1998, 2003) where consistent results have been found about delusional disorder and other thought disorders. As Garety and Freeman

(1999) point out in their review of research in delusional disorders, most of the studies are not longitudinal and do not lead to any causal explanation of the disorders. However, the implication of their findings can be translated into clinical applications. For example, the 'data-gathering deficit' seen in thought-disorder patients could be addressed by developing an intervention that would teach patients to amass greater evidence before concluding or hypothesizing about events surrounding their delusional themes.

In anxiety disorders, the consistent results about people with OCD exhibiting a 'data-gathering excess' would seem to logically involve the clinical application of having people reduce the amount of information they require before making a decision. However, this is basically what exposure and response prevention asks of a patient (i.e. inhibiting repetitive checking before leaving the house). So, in terms of the impact of these results, it becomes apparent that the mechanisms of pathology are not necessarily explained but more or less described by the reasoning paradigm. The clinical and theoretical implications of the results remain unclear.

Concerning the effect of content on reasoning, that is, how manipulating content with characteristics of a pathology can influence reasoning competence, the results of most probabilistic studies show that emotionally salient themes increase the reasoning patterns already observed when using neutral content. What this tells us is that when it comes to salient themes, people increase the bias in their reasoning pattern but it is not clear how this applies to everyday life. Reasoning research in anxiety has focused largely on the idea that anxious people infer danger on the basis of feeling anxious. We have underlined how the implication of these results presents its difficulties: inferring danger may not necessarily be because anxious people have faulty reasoning strategies but precisely because they have no experiences that would help them to infer 'no danger'. So the inability to conclude 'if I feel anxious, then I am not in danger' (presumably the reasoning of normal controls) may be that the inference of danger may simply be the absence of adequate experience which would permit a safety conclusion. The induction process itself involves providing additional qualifiers to the premises, from which one infers conclusions. So the additional qualifiers (rules) may be different for anxiety sufferers than for non-anxious sufferers.

Studies using pathology-relevant content seem a promising avenue to understanding specific aspects of pathologies. How people reason within the pathology should be observed but we are lacking in empirical measures. Creative use of reasoning paradigms helps entertain the idea that logical abilities are standard but what is becoming clear from this review is that reasoning paradigms have difficulty informing us about the mechanisms of psychopathology. Hence, it may be preferable to observe reasoning strategies in their context, using tailored scripts or narratives taken from people suffering from psychological disorders and drawing conclusions from the reasoning processes involved within these narratives. Essentially, reasoning may not follow from fragmented premises and the combination of such propositions but constitute the end point of a complex script which is hardly accessible through the actual standard reasoning paradigms. The following section reviews attempts to influence pathological inferences through addressing the language of reasoning as embedded in narrative units and how this approach can influence the aims of therapy.

REASONING THERAPY

Cognitive Approaches to Modifying Reasoning

The first level of reasoning intervention is simply the use of retraining techniques, which might come under the term cognitive remediation. Reasoning training then follows the same course as that of other approaches to cognitive remediation. Wykes and van der Gaag (2001) see a close relationship between cognitive therapy and cognitive remediation. For example, studies have shown that schizophrenic patients can learn through practice to improve attentional allocation, strategies for organization and memory, and formulate reasonable associations. Evans (1989), in his review of attempts to remove reasoning biases by 'debias' training, reports mixed results. He suggests that verbal instruction does little to remove deductive reasoning biases. However, either rule-based or example-based training does improve probabilistic reasoning. Evans (1989) points to experience-based approaches as more beneficial for replacing faulty intuitions and implicit thought processes, and has himself developed software aimed at building up mental models through immersing the person in the stage-by-stage process of reasoning using graphical display and feedback. Evans (1989) also emphasizes the importance of language and semantic content in removing biases and considers that good reasoning results from drawing analogies between current and past situations. The analogies stem from experience, and the language of reasoning instruction is best related to the person's experience. Since people reason for pragmatic and concrete purposes, Evans concludes that education in general abstract principles of reason may not be helpful. Wells et al.'s (1997) and others' (Teasdale et al., 1995) attempts at attention training to limit input of self-conscious or threatening information, or thoughts, have also impacted on reasoning biases and this also falls within the cognitive remediation bracket.

Wells (2000) suggests targeting and modifying meta-cognitive beliefs as well as internal criteria for regulating behavior (positive and negative beliefs about performing rituals) to change the mechanism of processing obsessional thoughts. Clinical application involves eliciting key meta-cognitions, reviewing advantages and disadvantages for holding these beliefs, practicing detachment from thoughts and the meaning of thoughts by not acting on them. Finally, the model involves reassessment of the criteria for knowing when to start/stop a ritual. Essentially, Wells (2000) refers to 'inverted reasoning' where the OCD patient's failure to remember particular events is interpreted as proof that unwanted behavior has occurred. Wells proposes training patients in using a different attention strategy, that is, learning to stop monitoring threat in the obsessive situation, and replace it with focusing on what is actually evident, in reality. This replacement strategy is designed to let disconfirmatory information be processed. However, the thrust of other cognitive therapy is to point out errors of reasoning rather than assume the person needs training in such reasoning. As Ellis (1962) puts it, the question is why potentially logical people are thinking illogically.

Albert Ellis (1962), more than any other cognitive therapist, draws on the foundations of reasoning research for his rational-emotive-therapy (RET), which arose, according to Ellis, through realizing the pitfalls of previous psychoanalytical and behavioral approaches. Essentially, Ellis realized that the difference between animals and humans was language, and that many of the maintained dysfunctional behaviors or blockages and resistances were not extinguished naturally in humans due to human language's symbol-producing facility, in particular, the self-signalling processes which produce self-conscious thoughts about thoughts and actions. Humans just need to be told about something in order to develop a fear of it. People develop imagined or defined fears which have no basis in physical or sensory reality, and such fears persist because people keep talking to themselves about the fear. But the same language facility also enables people to talk nonsense. In particular, by telling themselves so, people define things as terrible when, at worst, things are inconvenient and annoying. This definitional sleight of hand allows people to translate psychological desires into definitional needs. Ellis represents this faulty thinking in terms of conditional clauses such as: In order to be good, I must be perfect. If people judge me badly then that is the most terrible event. Although Beck or other cognitive thinkers also use conditional if-then clauses to frame irrational thinking: 'If X doesn't happen, then I'm no good', RET explicitly employs reasoning to challenge such thinking. The RET therapy in this case resolves around not confirming (if A, B, by *modus tolens*) but disconfirming the premise (if not B, then not A). As one of Ellis' early patients put it: 'I need to catch and change sentences which say if . . . then it would be awful, by questioning why would it be so awful?'

Ellis was also pioneering in his approach to linking up emotion and belief. He realized that much inference was on the basis of 'feeling', but that behind feeling is belief, and he drew on philosophers such as McGill (1954) and Rokeach (1960) to conclude that appraisal and judgement always involve emotion. However, such judgements are not innate and the values and emotions are the product of conclusions drawn from basic premises. The RET therapist believes that sustained negative emotions, such as intense depression, anxiety, anger and guilt, are almost always unnecessary to living and can be corrected through 'straight thinking' and linking effective action to such thinking. Emotion, according to Ellis, does not exist in its own right, it is an essential part of the sensing–moving–thinking–emotive complex. What we label as thinking is just a calm dispassionate end of an evaluation continuum with strong emotional evaluation at the other passionate end. Patients then need to be shown that their internalized sentences are illogical and unrealistic and that they have the ability to change their emotions by telling themselves or convincing themselves of the truth of more rational and less self-defeating sentences.

Ellis is unabashed in claiming illogical thinking as the sole source for emotional disturbance, and claims therapy should focus exclusively on converting thinking to the exclusion of other non-specific factors. Unfortunately, unlike Beck, Ellis did not focus on content specificity, nor did he develop and test a model of OCD. Recently, although espousing a postmodernist framework, Ellis (1991) has reiterated more general therapeutic themes of disputing absolutist 'shoulds' and 'musts', and emphasizes tolerance and self-acceptance as a means to full functioning rather than striving to be fully adjusted and problem-solving-oriented.

Donald Meichenbaum (2001, p. 102) has consistently noted that 'it is what people say to themselves which is critical'. The collaborative process of therapy, according to Meichenbaum, is designed to help the client 'say' different things to herself and others. Improvement comes when there is a process of ownership evident in new narratives emphasizing the 'I' and integrating a powerful voice into their experience. Langer and Abelson's (1972) work on mindfulness has highlighted how language delivery can manipulate emotion and behavior. These authors conducted a series of experiments showing that when narratives are presented in an absolute form given by an authority, there tends to be greater acceptance of the account than if this is presented in conditional language. In conditional language, the message is considered more reflectively and flexibly. Langer and Abelson, however, view this as one defining characteristic of the mindfulness–mindlessness dimension which they see as underlining distinct phases of conscious behavior.

One attempt to accord a greater role of language in cognitive therapy is Isabel Caro's (1991) introduction of semantic theory into cognitive therapy as a way of explaining cognitive evaluation. Essentially, semantic theory strives to separate the world of words from the world of facts. Caro draws on Korzybski's (1994) theory of general semantics. A psychotherapeutic system based on general semantics seeks to change the clients' evaluation by teaching the clients the right order of identification, first 'facts', then 'words', so patients learn to label just what is there and no more. Caro distinguishes her therapy of evaluation from other cognitive therapies on the basis that semantic therapy encourages clients to speak correctly rather than think correctly. In this therapy the client does not bias 'reality' with cognitive errors, rather, the client adjusts language to facts. Techniques include securing insights into the fact that we live in the world of words and we see the world through what we say about it. A key element of Caro's approach is 'extensionalization' where a person learns to adapt the structure of language to the structure of the world. This is done by understanding that there is an initial 'unspeakable' level of contact with an object, followed by a labeling level by which one describes what is experienced, followed by an inferring level by which we infer what comes next.

Perhaps the most direct application of thinking processes to psychopathology is Serban's (1974) short paper on the process of neurotic thinking. In this paper, delivered to the Piagettian Society in 1973, Serban foresaw many of the links between thinking inference and conscious narrative. He suggests at the outset that we need to return to the neurotic's own thinking processes to understand neurotic conflict. At the same time he links thinking to consciousness, saying in effect that experience in the mind is linked to continual conscious flow and the stream of life and thus projects itself into the future. We start with an abstract premise and work logically through an existential premise to a conclusion and this reasoning underlies all patterns of behavior.

Serban then applies this reasoning template to anxiety disorders. He cites the case of a woman too anxious to cross the road and notes she is unable to join up acceptable observed circumstances for crossing with actually crossing the road, because she introduces an unrelated sub-proposition about the possibility of untoward events occurring, 'I can cross the road but maybe I'll be run down', which negates the logical conclusion that she can cross safely. Serban notes that the broken logic disallows her from seeing herself successfully crossing and so this judgement introduces a high degree of ambiguity towards herself and her competence. She is unable to profit from past successful experiences in the same situation because the current situation is always qualified to appear unique and dangerous. Serban also cites an obsessional case where a lady feels compelled to repeatedly check her oven. She formulates the logic for checking in syllogistic terms where the existential premise is modified from a descriptive factual one to a conditional one which leads to a tentative conclusion. Gas ovens which are not turned off properly will explode. In order for the oven to be turned off properly, I need to check it again and again. Otherwise the stove will explode. The process of OCD thinking is hence characterized by false syllogistic terms and equates completion of the act with an irrelevant perfectionist standard.

Serban also applies the logical template to the misattribution of bodily symptom in panic attack. Shortness of breath is a sign of death. I have shortness of breath, therefore I could die. He also notes how fixed beliefs can become the only referential framework for any judgement, thus leading the neurotic to associate irrelevant judgements with neutral outcomes. Further, Serban anticipates the role of superstitious thinking in obsession, particularly thought action fusion, and notes how superstition replaces logic, particularly in the child when logic is not available. Magical expectations creep into logical process when an individual has no logical solution. The syllogistic thinking about an intentional act is thus distorted by magical assumptions.

Constructionist Therapies and Reasoning

The constructionist movement has of course thrown up a range of expressive, verbal and non-verbal, idiographic, therapeutic approaches. The hallmark of these approaches is to place emphasis on idiographic rather than normative aspects of the person's communication. One approach increasingly central to these therapies is Kelly's (1955) personal construct psychology. Although cognitive therapy explicitly recognizes Kelly as an influence, his construct approach has not found wide application among cognitive clinicians. Essentially it is an idiosyncratic way of eliciting the terms by which people construct the world. Based on the linguistic principle that each language term which has meaning must imply a term with an opposite meaning, Kelly's repertory grid technique permits teasing out the semantic boundaries which enclose a person's evaluative world and define both the significant elements in that world and the relationship between the elements.

Phenomenological approaches such as Georgi's (1985) also rely on common language description of conversations as made by the people themselves. Descriptive phenomenology aims to stay as close as possible to the words and language of the person, extracting themes from the regularity and repetition of words and phrases in conversation. These themes are then reduced to essential idiosyncratic concepts in one or two further stages of reduction by the experimenter. Georgi encourages a variety of techniques to slow the person down and ensure that the person avoids the use of stereotypic or alien terms in their description to short-hand or short-cut experience.

Smith *et al.* (1999) have also suggested that interpretative phenomenology can help explore a participant's world-view. Like Georgi, Smith and collaborators record natural talk and then reduce the language to themes and superordinate themes. The experimenter then attempts later to connect the themes of several people into a comprehensible whole. One way of ensuring such themes rest with the person's definition is to combine phenomenological analysis with personal construct psychology, whereby the themes become identified with explicit and implicit constructs (Blowers & O'Connor, 1996). However, there is always the danger that superordinate themes become more and more remote from the narrative and end up reflecting an abstract pattern level where communalities of experiences become reduced further to generic statements.

A mention here is merited for Guidano (1991) and Guidano and Liotti's (1983) attempts towards a post-rationalist cognitive therapy. Effectively, these authors suggest that the only adequate etiological understanding of thinking is that of a developmental psychopathology whereby the multi-level reconstruction of life-span transformational experiences brings about the present patterns of meaning coherence. They note that psychopathological episodes, far from striking the person from without, are intrinsically bound up with his or her way of assimilating experience within the coherence of personal meaning. For example, worries or obsessions always touch personal themes. They challenge the rationalist attitude that assumes the existence of logical axioms by which to objectively evaluate rationality of a belief or attitude. Each individual belief has a personal meaning organization which brings forth a world with distinct tonality and with its own self-referential ordering logic. However, contrary to Caro, Guidano (1991) holds that process gains coherence from the formal structural properties, not from the semantic aspects of knowledge.

According to Guidano (1991), a key structural property of meaning organization is a tension between the immediately experiencing 'I' and the 'me' which reflectively scaffolds and appraises experience. Thus, experience is made understandable through selective appraisal of sensory-affective-motor features already recognized by the current self-image. Memory, then, is at the mercy of experience, although language gives memory the ability to abstract from experience. However, because of this 'me'-centered selectivity, prejudices rather than judgements constitute the historical reality of being. The selective abstracting from experience also gives us the capacity for conscious self-deceptions about our image.

Guidano highlights the importance of persuasion in therapy. Persuasion technically consists of intervening at a surface level directed at modifying the semantic aspects of explicit cognitive processes, while neglecting the tacit syntactic rules. If the intervention is limited to a modification of cognitive appraisal, the critical emotions, although better controlled, remain alien and controlled from the outside, as a mere semantic change inside the same meaning tonality rather than a reorganization of personal meaning.

As Guidano notes, if rationality is interwoven with the experience of acting, it cannot refer solely to the logical abstract (true–false) categories employed in recording such experience semantically. In other words, the use of personal rationality merely highlights the self-referentiality of adaptive processes in pursuing a useful aim. Rationality is hence intrinsically relativistic and should be judged according to its adequacy referred to personal meaning rather than to an absolute criterion.

The aim of post-rational therapy is not to make the client fit a rational axiom but rather to increase self-awareness and comprehension of his or her way of experiencing and explaining self and reality. The basic procedure consists of training clients through self-observation to differentiate between immediate perception and experience and conscious beliefs and attitudes, and then see how it is coherent and personally logical for them to act in accord with beliefs. The therapy has to trigger affective change and thus it has to address real living interaction to facilitate new experiences and the reframing of existing ones. Successful therapy requires that the therapist him/herself can distinguish fact from theory since, often, technological and scientific jargon is mere theory, whereas the accompanying unscientific experience is actually fact. The client also learns to distinguish between direct and indirect experience in the way they are reporting on an event. What happened is said now, but what is said now influences what happened in the past. Clients are trained to focus on the structure of the immediate experience that occurred in the course of a situation. The person uses the 'cinematographic (moviola) techniques' of panning in and out of experienced scenes in order to clarify their temporal and sequential structure.

Linguistic Experiential Therapy

One of the most elaborate attempts to base a therapy on language as experience is Linguistic-Experiential phenomenology. Owen (1996) draws on the work of David Groves (1991) which seeks to explore subjective experiences in a descriptive manner by attending to specific phrases and making them less abstract. Groves' method is termed 'clean language' and seeks to elicit the relations between speech and lived experience. In particular, the method reveals the place of metaphor and metonym in connecting spatially and temporally language and lived experience. Owen attempts to integrate this clean language into phenomenological principles. The aim is to de-intellectualize language away from signifiers and signified, and repatriate meaning and abstract semantics to experiential self-evident truths held in specific times and places. Clean language is dedicated to eliciting metaphors and metonyms in language use and deducing from these descriptions the cognitive and experiential process normally out of reach of awareness. A process of questioning is used to elicit how the person imposes their representations in language and lived experience. The speech is accepted as pure verbal representations and no attempt is made to interpret or to abstract from the metaphoric terms.

Since ordinary language use often takes the speaker away from the lived aspects of experience, the clean language questioner does not use complex terms likely to activate rational intellectualizing processes. The questioning focuses the person on the experience following from the language use. Ordinary speech is dissociative because in speaking 'about' something, one becomes separated from what is being described. Clean language re-associates speakers with experiences, especially 'felt' speech, which is represented figuratively in metaphors (for example, comparing anxiety to a drum). In fact, the metaphor may be expanded and elaborated to help the person connect with the important way the image of a drum guides their experience. Clean language also looks at the flow of language to help the person see how accounts are qualified by what happened in the past and what might happen in the future (e.g. if it was not for that memory, I would not feel so hopeless now). Reference points are highlighted as historic accounts in order to illustrate past influences on current inferences. The therapy insists that the person explores (by use of minimal prompting) the time and place ordering within the person's speech and also connects words, feelings and experience. For example, the phrase 'talk of my father' becomes located in the top half of the body and as a feeling that is 'like a ball which won't move'. Clean language presupposes none of the five senses as predominant and tries to link language with all experiences.

In a sense, experiential linguistics is an extension of the Sapir and Whorf hypothesis that language shapes thought (Owen, 1996). Certainly restrictions and formal constraints on language can determine experience. If we only have certain metaphors or connections available (e.g. I exploded with rage), then this metaphor limits our experience. Similarly, metaphysical problems such as mind and body dualism may signify the language limitations on ways to describe our habitual integrated mind–body rather than identify real experiential problems of a separate mind–body.

Lakoff and Johnson (1980) likewise relate metaphor to cultural and bodily experience. Metaphors compare something unknown to something known. They conceptualize the non-physical in terms of the physical and the vague in terms of the precise. Their cognitive linguistics places its definition of metaphor as central to the way language does its work of producing meaning. Thinking must follow the constraints of acceptable metaphor. Metaphors and metonyms are spatial and temporal ordering principles for our self–world, self–society relationship. They color our intentional experience and bring our language alive as an existential lived-in project. Consequently, we draw inferences, set goals, make commitments and act on the basis of metaphors. Several clinicians independent of linguistic philosophy have pointed strongly to the power of metaphor in therapy (Berlin *et al.*, 1991; Zimmerman & Dickerson, 1994).

Discursive Therapy

A postmodern approach which explores narrative and language in the construction of psychopathology is the discursive approach or discourse analysis. The assumption of discourse analysis is that the person's narrative contains received meanings which immediately position the person in a power relationship to their own thought and the world. The meaning of our talk comes from institutional or dominant interests and the goal of therapy is to deconstruct such meanings and reinstate or reascribe personal meaning. As Terry Eagleton (1983) puts it, 'to deconstruct is to reverse the imposing tapestry of thought in order to expose in all its unglamorously dishevelled tangle the threads constituting the well heeled image it presents to the world'. Discursive approaches insist not that thought is illusory, but that it is institutional. Often politically motivated, discourse analysts adopt what Chia (2002) terms the hermeneutics of suspicion, whereby language is suspect as a personal medium for conveying ideas, when really it maintains power and ideology. So language always needs to be seen against wider social practices that position the speaker. Most discursive approaches draw on Foucauldian analyses of the powerful institutional influences that underpin the individual's everyday experience, to the extent that the individual speaker is de-authored of his/her talk and left on a crossroads between the history and politics of a dominant culture which defines individuality and self-hood and so even defies a person's ownership of the self. Psychopathology then arises from the way conflicting received terms and discourses position a person away from their authentic self-voice, and therapy aims to deconstruct such unhelpful ways of talking.

Deconstruction is a term first employed by Derrida (1994) as a performative activity centered around questions of practice, justice and ethics. As a textual intervention, deconstruction articulates the paradoxes and double binds inherent in discourses of power and institution in order to minimize their violent repression of personal difference and the other. Discursive therapies accept that narrative is also a dialogic position which emphasizes meaning as created by conversational interchange, but they criticize narrative approaches which confine themselves to an individual-based text, since such interchanges could not take place outside of culturally available symbols and constructs. Hence the world of language cannot be separated from the relevant social and political realm.

Unsurprisingly, postmodern discursive therapy no longer pursues a modernist repertoire focusing on internalized individual experience but pursues a relational engagement and focuses on the processes by which people come to create their language use by particular modes of understanding and acting. Thus, rather than be concerned with dysfunction, psychotherapy becomes a space for conversational opportunities, inviting an array of voices and relationships rather than one dominant therapeutic discourse. Rather than pathologizing individual behavior, normality is left indeterminate and problems are retalked rather than solved. Such lack of resolution is encouraged, since today's problem may be tomorrow's normal performance, and psychotherapy needs to respond to the multiple personalities, shifting identities and changing cultural standards of a postmodern age. Roger Lowe (1999) considers that postmodern therapy is currently in transition and between the 'no longer' and the 'not yet'.

The impact of such postmodern therapies is unclear, but there seems a risk of imposing a blanket political agenda over personal nuance. It's not clear either how individual inferences about the person's immediate ecological setting are alleviated by open-ended conversations. Although all postmodern therapies would agree on the power of language, their technical analysis is limited to viewing language's effect through one sole rhetorical device, i.e. discourse. In this sense, they overlook other experiences that narrative might represent and reduce it to 'political' textual analysis. Narrative texts may be multi-authored and dialogical, but, for discourse analysts, they gain meaning through social practices and ways of talking. As a consequence, it is difficult for social constructivists to stick with the experience of language because the basic premise is at an ideological level. But people first of all experience their narrative as a story, not as a political discourse.

Narrative Therapies

However, other non-discursive narrative therapies have taken root, which although espousing many aspects of social constructionism, still practice within an individualistic therapy context. Although in such therapies place is given to the socially constructed use of terms and understanding and the distrust of objective fact or truth, emphasis is put on the individuals' perspective and beliefs in constructing their personal world so that 'believing is seeing'. Although people's actions may be guided by culturally derived meanings and stories, these are continuously being reconstructed depending on the individuals' context and interactions. In this narrative context, the practice of re-authoring dialogue takes on a more individualistic turn, with the aim of repositioning the person individually in relation to their talk. The therapist may externalize conversations so the clients' identity is no longer mixed up with the person's self. In this way the client may also free themselves from an oppressive story by contrasting it with another story in which they are repositioned differently and more positively. So instead of 'I'm an OCD person', a re-authored text might be 'I'm a person who happens to have OCD'. One of the tasks of narrative therapists is to create an environment in which the client's stories can be unraveled often from abbreviated calcified short-hand descriptions, snap judgements and unhelpful nuances.

Sometimes we do not have an adequate story to account for a problem, or we work with unsatisfactory, incomplete narratives. We feel then that things are beyond our grasp and out of control since we are unstoried. People can become stuck in monologues that prevent a satisfying outcome because they unwillingly perpetuate old static cultural myths. An inferential template becomes accorded a finality 'she does that because she's lazy'. Often monologues conflict with each other because one monologue (valid) cannot include another monologue (valid) due to competing concerns. A 'he's lazy' monologue could have difficulty accepting a 'he's doing his best' monologue. An important concern of narrative therapists therefore is to learn accounts of what led the person to the inference that, for example, coming to therapy was a good idea. The emphasis is on how stories get told, who can talk to whom about what, and who is the author. The person can also adopt different reflecting positions to their discourse, shifting back and forth between a talking, listening, eavesdropping, credulous position, rather like linguistic role-playing.

Anderson and Goolishian (1996) propose that the therapist adopts a 'not knowing' stance to all conversation which decreases the suggestibility associated with authority. Anderson (1997) emphasizes the importance of 'conversational partnership' since meaning in an encounter is generated in and through language, not in the mind of any one speaker. The emphasis is on the contextual nature of meaning and its negotiation over time as a product of social exchange or joint action. Shotter (1994) defines joint action as dialogically and responsively linked to previous action and anticipated actions. In Gadamer's (1975) 'fusion of horizon', an understanding emerges in an encounter that cannot be attributed to either participant. It is never exhaustive or complete and is limited to the encounter and hence non-renewable. In a sense, the talking person is always in a hermeneutic circle since the terms of reference are already known and must refer to a closed circle of experience which can, however, infinitely be re-talked. Hence in this type of narrative therapy, overcoming miscommunication just requires a long and flexible enough dialogue to cover enough horizons or until the terms of references or metaphors allow for a compatible story, and one can construct a story of someone who is both lazy and good.

Georgaca (2003) draws on Lacan's (1977) and Bakhtin's (1929/1973) notions of social and linguistic construction of subjectivity to understand that conscious and unconscious processes are interlinked semiotic signs, a thought presupposes a dialogue and utterances are always in a social context. Part of therapy is about tracing the origin of the clients' discourse to its constitutive parts, revisiting the specific history of words, phrases, styles and speech. Therapy provides a space in which positions can be voiced and counter-positions assigned without consideration of how realistic they are. The client and therapist take up and voice each other's positions. They recontextualize and reframe each other's speech, so authorship becomes shared and distributed. There is reflexive recognition in the intersubjective space and the transsubjective space of language to create a jointly authored ambience which allows the client to distance him or herself from threatening statements and at the same time intellectually address through a joint language issues of transference and resistance to change, and recognize certain habitual themes which are repeated in conversation.

In the more hermeneutic/dialogic narrative approach, emphasis is not only placed on recognizing the contextual nature of language. There is recognition that it's fine to have conflicting monologues in different contexts, since our stories are always multivoiced, and also dialogical in that they are one-sided conversations.

The Dialogical Approach

The dialogical approach employs metaphors of voice and conversation (dialogue) to understand a person's self-positioning. The dialogical concept derives from Bakhtin's (1929/1973) writings on literature, where a single author can possess several 'voices' and identities in a novel. Hermans (1966), transposing this idea to the everyday self, viewed identity as a series of distinct 'I' positions without any enduring entity behind them. Rather, the 'I' in a grammatical artifact indexes a speaker and his/her voice in a particular context rather than a finite-self. In support of this point, Harré

(1991) points to the ability of one self-voice (Self 1) to refer to another self-voice (Self 2) and even draw comparisons about attributes across contexts (for example: now I feel stupid but then I feel I was right).

A dialogical approach, then, necessarily places the self-voice inside a scripted narrative rather than a self-schema or mental representation. Hermans (1996) contrasts the implications of viewing a unitary self as stable with the idea of being positioned within a dialogue. Obviously in the latter case the self is a function of the interpersonal constraints of the dialogue, not an internal disposition.

Hallam and O'Connor (2002) have proposed that a dialogical approach may help understand some anomalies in the clinical presentation of obsessions. Obsessions could be viewed in unresolved dialogue. In other words the contrary modes of thoughts present in obsessions, for example, the thought of harming combined with the strong desire not to harm, could be treated as a problematic and unresolved dialogue. The dialogue may need to be reformulated or answered to bring it to resolution. But, most likely, the person may need to reposition themselves in the conversation to counter the pervasive influence of a dominant voice.

As Hallam and O'Connor (2002, p. 338) put it:

> A dialogical approach sees the issue of designating an obsessional thought, image, or impulse as consistent or inconsistent with the 'self' in a contextual and dialogical manner. In the context of formal psychological assessment, anomalous phenomena are likely to be viewed by the client from a unitary rational standpoint, even though, in certain provoking situations, the phenomena define reality and self at that moment. For example, a belief that burglars will break into the house if the front door lock is not checked several times may be held with utter conviction at one moment and regarded as silly the next. The dialogical approach conceptualizes these context-dependent changes as the expression of different voices speaking from different discursive positions and not as the varying attributes (e.g. degree of conviction or degree of ego-consistency) of a single self. The analogue here would be a 'role-play' in which eliciting opposing characterizations of the situation would be enacted according to the role that is played.

Dialogical Therapy

A dialogical approach would initially seek to normalize a person's experience of conflicting aversive thoughts and preoccupations with alien intrusions through education about the transituational variation in self-position and self-expressions and show how, of necessity, self-awareness adapts to context on a normal process. This adaptation could be illustrated by examples of how perceived boundaries of self change depending on task and context, and how we act differently with different people. The co-existence of different self-positions and voices simply expresses the dynamics of the role-playing requirements in different contexts. The dialogical approach would then call upon dramaturgy and conversation as speech metaphors to help the person rescript the obsessional dialogue in a more empowering way. The person might redefine their relationship with the intrusive voice from one of passive listening to active response. The person might distance themselves from the voice, deciding to treat it as an immature and irrelevant voice. The idea is for the person to feel empowered to engage with and respond to the obsessional voice, rather than feeling overwhelmed and helpless before it. The person then realizes that the way she/he interacts with the voice determines its potency. Hence the person has the liberty to create different dialogues with the voice and elicit different emotions, and so counteract ideas that obsessions are fixed and signs of madness and lack of control. Although Hallam and O'Connor (2002) report some case illustrations of the dialogical approach, it clearly requires further elaboration.

Narrative Therapy and Inferential Therapy

We have dwelt here on postmodern hermeneutics because it is clearly an extension of language philosophy and overlaps with narrative methods. It is situated at the far end of an approach which sees narrative as a unit of reasoning and inference and language as the representation of experience. Although social constructive approaches are theoretically and ideologically well grounded, in fact, they do not stick well to the phenomenological experience of the narrative which is first and foremost a thinking device and later an interpretation of social practice. Such sensitivity to the structural features of a narrative allows the therapist to assess the complexity of the narrative and hence plan a way by which another narrative may place the old narrative in a newly intelligible light.

Conclusion

A therapy targeting inductive reasoning then needs to consider that thinking takes the form of a narrative. The internal structure of such a narrative needs to be understood holistically, in terms of its temporal dimension, and its connected dynamic quality. The persuasive elements of language such as metaphor and metonym bring it alive. Narrative language leads to conviction through its persuasive ability to immerse the person in its story so that the person experiences only within the bounds of the narrative structure. In particular, narrative connectivity (and devices which trick connectivity) and relatedness are particularly important for inference processes. Stories lead onto other stories, they also support or undercut other stories. In particular, stories which place the person in all their self-referent attributes at the scene are likely to be well rehearsed and well invested with inferential meaning.

Narrative therapy then largely involves increasing insight into the role of narrative and language in creating emotion. In particular, the dialogical nature of language can explain how different monologues drawn from different sources may conflict or overlap, and that such polyphonic events are normal. People can learn that creating or continuing their own stories, using narrative devices to modify terms of reference, can accommodate apparently conflicting beliefs or identities. Thinking and inferring, then, are always a product of 'joint action' in relation to another person or activity: thinking does not speak for an inner self but for a social self.

GENERAL CONCLUSION

We began in Chapter 2 reviewing research into formal reasoning which showed that people apply personal mental models to reason about everyday life, rather than follow logical rules, and that acquired heuristics determine inferences, perhaps more adaptively than logic. We then discussed the crucial role of experience in induction. Experience is what we feel we should be certain of, and the appeal to experience explains why paradigmatic logic sometimes goes awry in everyday situations, because the contextual framing of the problem may condition inference. The creative aspect of induction means adding information to original premises. So there is always a tension between knowledge from our senses and what we infer from more remote experience. In addition, inductive thinking always has content and direction. It is always about something and it always goes somewhere, even if round in a circle. So our inferring is closely linked with our doing in the world and the 'intentionality' of our projects. Intentionality is a kind of theme, thread or plot line which connects our doing, sensing, inferring and being seemlessly from moment to moment and connects what would otherwise be a very fractionated and disjointed world.

We connect experience through language, and the way we talk influences our reasoning. Language devices allow us to articulate the multi-layered meanings of experience, and also allow us through the use of metaphors, metonym, blending and categorization to recontextualize immediate experiences 'as if' they were remoter, bigger, more dramatic. Also, what is not said is not silent and we are adept at filling in gaps to infer personalized contexts around otherwise isolated thoughts. In order to be fully understood, isolated propositions or descriptions of human experience need to be placed within a wider context extending horizontally and vertically, to reveal the breadth and depth of surrounding thought. This wider context is the narrative unit. Narrative gives a spatial and temporal continuity and a human dimension to our talk, but it also positions us. When we narrate, we narrate from a position, and the endpoint of the narrative will reflect this position. The more we tell the same story, the more we may invest in it and believe in it. Indeed, what we term 'belief' may be no more than the result of relating mutually supporting narratives about ourselves and our relationship in the world; our self-themes run through our stories and our self-attributes are elaborated through stories of what we do. The more coherently these stories feature our actions, the more they reinforce self-themes. Narrative can, however, transport us away from our everyday selves through the use of rhetoric, and transform the mundane into the magical, by replacing immediate personal sense experience within a more remote symbolic context. The power of narrative is such that a rhetorically presented remote myth or story can become not only believed-in, but lived-in in the here and now.

Because we live in time, narrated experience has a temporal dimension and our projects are always directed to the future. Hence what *will* happen forms an essential part in making inferences about the present. When we reason about the world, we consider not only what is, but what this 'is' might become. In other words, possibility exists alongside actuality, and both influence our immediate sense of reality. But whereas immediate sense information reveals one version of the here and now and only one reality, possibility is in the realm of the imagination and has no perceptual constraints: although there may only be one reality, the same reality could spawn several competing possibilities. We generally have a range of plausible possible worlds available at one time. This array of possibilities can be conceptualized as a likelihood distribution with an empirically derived maximum possibility surrounded by less likely possibilities in the margins of the distribution. The maximum likelihood can thus be updated on the basis of its 'aboutness' and how this fits with projects in hand, but also by changes in the distribution of competing possibilities.

Problems arise when there is excessive absorption in a possibility remote from experience, perhaps due to a convincing narrative which transports the person away from sense information into the imagination. Hence, while perception of reality remains intact, it may be imagination which is dictating inferences about what might be there. Clinically speaking, then, some states of dissociation might be viewed more as disorders of the imagination than distortions of perception. If so, then modifying the role of imagination in inductive reasoning might be an optimal target for therapy. Research into reasoning in clinical populations has shown that people with OCD and other disorders do show particular reasoning styles. People with

OCD are more cautious in reaching decisions. They also seem less confident about their inferences. This doubt may be because they are generating more possibilities, or inferring not on the basis of objective information but subjective emotional cues. Or their distrust of safety information may lead them to disconfirm rather than confirm (better safe than sorry). However, there has been no comprehensive characterization of OCD in the literature as a reasoning disorder. Current cognitive models now emphasize the role of more remote cognitive structures such as schema in psychopathology. But narrative therapies have recognized and targeted the role of language and language devices in guiding inductive inference, and the role of narrative in positioning the person psychopathologically.

In particular, narrative approaches have generally been concerned to deconstruct the multi-authored, storied nature of thought and reveal its discursive nature as a dominant discourse, and thus reposition the person away from their problematic voice into a safer space. But, with the exception of the dialogical approach, none of these therapies has explicitly addressed obsessional content. A dialogical approach has, however, proposed that obsessions may be conceptualized as one-sided conversations and that a conversational metaphor viewing thought as dialogue, rather than the usual information processing metaphor, may better explain the nature of obsessional thoughts; in particular it explains their ego-dystonic and persistent nature and so draws on narrative and role-playing techniques to aid resolution.

In the next chapter, we present a tentative model of OCD as an inductive reasoning disorder. We first review the clinical evidence that initially led us to look to reasoning research as a model of OCD. Phenomenologically speaking, obsessional intrusions resemble inferences and are produced by a characteristic reasoning style, which appeals more to subjective experience than to logic. This appeal to experience connects with remote possibilities, themselves generated by an imaginary narrative which employs narrative and rhetorical devices (blending miscategorization, misplaced correctness, emotional self-reference). The narrative convincingly trumps sense information through inverse inference and leads the person with OCD to live and experience a remote possibility 'as if' it were reality. So OCD is an inferential confusion.

Therapy, then (within such a reasoning model), should address obsessional thoughts as inferences. And an inference-based intervention aims primarily to identify obsessional inferences and unravel the narrative context, content and form that have trapped the person within their obsessional cycle.

CHAPTER 5

AN INFERENCE-BASED APPROACH TO OBSESSIVE-COMPULSIVE DISORDER

CLINICAL AND PHENOMENOLOGICAL INVESTIGATIONS INTO INFERENTIAL CONFUSION

OCD seems at first sight to be a phobic disorder. The person is afraid of something: harm, dirt, negative outcomes. Phenomenologically speaking, the OCD client is not anxious about what is but what 'might' be, hence, the standard epithet attached to OCD is the pathology of doubt. It is almost exclusively what is not physically apparent which is feared, and this fear is not simply in anticipation of what might happen but of what might be there now and cannot be seen or detected in the normal way. OCD clients have no problems perceiving reality (Brown *et al.*, 1994) (although they may be less confident about what is seen), and, in any case, it is not just perceived attributes that trigger OCD behavior. Although, at first glance, it may appear that the OCD client fears dirt, disorder, etc., the fear is largely of what this state symbolizes, either overtly as in the case of mental pollution (Rachman, 1994) where moral or other symbolism is clear (e.g., cleanliness is next to godliness) or more subtly, where the obsessional behavior is conditional on non-physical qualities (e.g., the person fears microbes emanating from one group of people or situations but not another).

The person with OCD is not consistently preoccupied in a uniform way with objects or events. A client who meticulously orders books in her bookcase according to neat criteria doesn't use the same criteria when dressing. The neatness criteria itself is also very subjective and requires ordering books by descending size or thickness rather than a criteria perhaps more appropriate for ordering books (e.g., by topic or authors). People with contamination rituals are often less troubled by contact with some objects compared with others, despite similar dangers. A woman will under no circumstances touch the pole in the metro or the door knobs in a public building, but if need be she can place her hand into mud or dirt to retrieve objects. It would be accurate to say that any given obsessional content is an instance of a theme extending beyond the physical situation and calling on other associations for its aversive meaning.

In fact, people with OCD tend not to be overly preoccupied with the physical characteristics of the target of obsessional preoccupation for the very reason that the interest is thematic, not physical. People afraid of dirt on their hands will often not even look at their hands since they are convinced that they are dirty. A man currently checking for ants in his clothes, or on chairs, cannot describe an ant physically except to say that it is a small insect. Sometimes people may feel contaminated without any physical contact at all, just by being in the vicinity. The thematic association is supported by a narrative which explicitly trumps physical evidence from the here and now in favor of irrelevant facts, memories that conspire to impose an imaginary aversive value on reality.

In other words, imaginary associations are imposed on reality and the person then reacts as if this imaginary story were true. As O'Connor and Robillard (1995, p. 890) note:

> Our hypothesis is that the 'doubt', 'ambivalence' and 'maybe's' that provoke repetitive rituals form part of the confusion the Obsessive-Compulsive experiences when trying to treat imaginary associations as though they were current reality. In other words, those people who check and recheck locks, or clean and reclean the floor for hours, and say they do so just in case something may be there, are confusing a *remote probability* with a *completely fictional narrative*. Unfortunately, in performing the ritual they are attempting to change an imaginary image by modifying reality, which is akin to attempting to erase a cinema image by wiping clean the cinema screen rather than changing the film in the projector. As a result the person never succeeds in satisfactorily completing the ritual, since it is impossible to do so. But as long as they continue under the impression that they are acting on a real not an imaginary probability, they will not realize that they are attempting the impossible and hence they will persist, stopping finally only through fatigue or for superstitious reasons (e.g. 'I've done it 15 times, that must be enough').

OCD can be reconceptualized as a disorder of the imagination rather than perception in the sense that the client imagines a state of affairs which is then taken 'as if' it were a reality. The person then acts in accordance with the dictates of the imagination rather than the perceived demands of the real world. The OCD person is perfectly able to perceive reality and to distinguish between what is or is not real. But imagination imposes on this reality a preoccupation with what might also be there, or with what this 'reality' might signify.

This conceptualization of OCD as a disorder of the 'imagination', has some heuristic value in accounting for the 'may be' quality of OCD doubt. The OCD 'belief' is usually always about a possibility, not a certainty. In this sense, as the Obsessive Compulsive Cognitions Working Group (1997) has noted, the word belief may be a misnomer, since beliefs are usually always certain. In fact, the OCD person 'infers' a state of affairs rather than 'believes' in it.

Perception deals with what is there, imagination with what could be there. The OCD client could have no problems perceiving reality and yet 'know' at the same time that something other than the evidence of his or her senses might be present. Equally, the model would predict that in carrying out the ritual, the client would not be attentive to reality but to the imagined reality, and that performing the ritual would be antagonistic to taking in new perceptual information. Doubt is likely to be maintained through enacting the compulsive action since by such action the person is rehearsing the imaginary possibility. The OCD client does not confuse a perceived event *per se* with an imagined event, since the OCD client has no difficulty in perceiving what 'is' there or 'is not' there, but with imagining what 'might' be there as well.

CRITICAL CONCEPTS IN AN INFERENCE-BASED MODEL

An inference is essentially a plausible proposition about a possible state of affairs, itself arrived at by reasoning but which forms the premise for further deductive/inductive reasoning (O'Connor, 2002). The inference is logically implied by the compulsive acts characterizing OCD, and even though some have reported difficulties in identifying obsessions associated with certain compulsions, an appropriate logical template inevitably leads to uncovering the obsessional inference (O'Connor & Robillard, 1999). That is, if the person washes his/her hands, then the action implies that the person must have inferred that there might be something on his/her hands. If the person checks whether or not the door is locked, then there must be an inference with respect to the possibility that the door is left open. The inference of doubt is already emotionally charged and leads to a spiraling chain of second possibilities, all of course negative. In fact, we can quite distinctly identify two thought components to the doubt: the primary inference of doubt 'maybe the stove is on' and its consequences or the secondary inference 'if the stove is on, the house will catch fire, I'll lose everything', etc. It is this latter secondary inference that contemporary appraisal models of OCD tend to focus on rather than on the original primary inference of doubt.

In sum, a conceptualization of obsessions as inferences leads to a different set of questions than those posed by an appraisal model, which locates the genesis of obsessions in intrusive thoughts. In fact, if obsessions develop from the appraisal of intrusive cognitions then the obsessions themselves require no explanation, and the focus would be solely on their appraisal. In contrast, a conceptualization of obsessions as problematic inferences would raise questions as to how these inferences come about in order to explain their persistence and intrusive character. Thus, in the inference model there is no such thing as an intrusion (O'Connor, 2002). Rather, an 'intrusion' is an inferred state of affairs that comes about through specific reasoning processes. The main differences in conceptualization between an inference- and appraisal-based model can be schematically represented in the following way (O'Connor, 2002):

Intrusion → Evaluation → Reactions to the evaluation

(Salkovskis, 1999)

Internal/external percept → Primary inference →

Secondary consequences and evaluations

(O'Connor, 2002)

Figure 5.1   Schematic representation of the appraisal- and inference-based model

Clinical evidence suggests that these initial inferences are supported by an inductively generated idiosyncratic narrative which employs one or several rhetorical devices to strengthen the obsessional doubt. These reasoning processes can be viewed as cognitive distortions, similar to the cognitive distortions proposed by Beck *et al.* (1979), but with hypothesized unique relevancy to OCD. An example of such an idiosyncratic narrative which convinces the person that her hands are dirty is the following:

> So I say to myself, well, my kids were playing outside and, like, I know it's dirty outside (*selective use of fact*). I've seen the dirt on the pavement and I think they may have touched something dirty (*category error*), like, picked up something from the street, dirty paper or dog shit, and then I say, well, if they're dirty, then I'm going to be dirty (*apparently comparable events*) and I'm going to make the house dirty, and I imagine the house dirty and me with my dirty hands, so I start to feel dirty (*imaginary sequence*). So I go in and wash and I can't stop, you know, it's like a voice in my head, saying over and over again, you're dirty, even though you're washing and see nothing (*distrust of normal senses*), you could still be dirty (*inverse inference*).
>
> (O'Connor *et al.*, 2003)

This confusion of a subjective discourse with reality, complete with some or all of the above reasoning devices, we term *inferential confusion*. Such people

Table 5.1 Overview of inference processes in OCD

Inference processes	Examples
Category errors – confusing two logical or ontologically distinct properties or objects	'If this white table is dirty, it means the other needs cleaning.'
Apparently comparable events – confusing two distinct events separated by time, place and/or causal agency	'My friend often leaves the garage door open, so mine could be left open.'
Selective use of out-of-context facts – abstract facts are inappropriately applied to specific personal contexts	'Microbes do exist so therefore there might be microbes on my hand.'
Purely imaginary sequences – making up convincing stories and living them	'I imagine the waves entering my head and I can feel them infecting my brain.'
Idiosyncratic associational networks – creating chains of arbitrary associations or rules	'If I count to 6, this means I'm safe, unless someone passes by.'
Distrust of normal perception – disregarding the senses in favour of going deeper into reality	'Even though my senses tell me nothing is there, I know by my intelligence that there is.'
Inverse inference – inferences about reality precede reality rather than follow from observation of reality	'A lot of people must have walked on this floor, therefore it's certainly dirty.'

Source: From O'Connor *et al.* (2003a)

with OCD, however, do not appear to have any problems perceiving or sensing reality, it seems rather that the certainty of correctly perceived information is replaced by doubt generated through 'inferential confusion', so resulting in the belief that 'maybe' a state of affairs is possible despite contradictory evidence from the senses. Clinically, such a conceptualization highlights the persistent character of the obsession as an essential feature in OCD. In contrast to normal doubts, which are generated by reality-based information, obsessional doubts are not readily resolved because they are generated more subjectively. For example, the person who washes his/her hands continuously on the basis of a doubt that invisible dirt may be present, will have difficulty deciding whether or not his/her hands are clean if this washing was initiated on the basis of purely subjective information to begin with.

Clearly, the reasoning devices outlined above show common overlap, since they all share the common element of going beyond reality, which leads to inferential confusion. Thus, an essential feature of inferential confusion is the *distrust of the senses* and *inverse inference* – an inverse type of reasoning where the person does not start out with the senses in reaching an obsessional inference or doubt, but instead comes to infer this doubt without any actual indication of it being present or even in contradiction to what is seen or sensed. That is, the obsessional inference does not come about as the result of entertaining a particular possibility (example: 'maybe my hands are contaminated'; 'maybe I drove over someone with my car') that has any basis in reality or the senses, but instead, this doubt is generated as the result of purely subjective reasoning. As such, O'Connor & Robillard (1995) propose OCD does not follow a phobic model of development where the person exaggerates that which is seen or felt (for example, spider phobia), but that the person with OCD fears exactly those things which cannot be seen or sensed.

Intrusions as Primary Inferences

Intrusions do not occur in a vacuum, but, as Rachman (1998) and O'Connor (2002) have argued, are preceded by a stimulus or percept, which initiates the obsessional narrative. Initial thoughts of 'God', 'sex', or 'violence' may be internal percepts forming part of an internal context triggering the 'intrusion' or 'inference'. The internal context may be something said, a feeling, a memory, or any other current event, which provokes the worrying intrusion/inference.

This was apparent in one of our patients who suffered from blasphemous obsessions. He recently moved from the USA to Quebec, which meant moving from a largely English-speaking community to a largely French-speaking community. Further, at the same time he moved in with his Greek grandfather who was in the habit of cursing in Greek. Both new experiences provided him with a whole new obsessional repertoire and often more colorful blasphemy than in English. It was quite clear that these new obsessions did not come out of the blue without a specific situation preceding them. It also seems very unlikely that this OCD patient actually experienced these new thoughts (i.e., actually cursing whether out loud or in one's mind). Instead, the development of such new obsessions more likely took the form of thoughts such as 'What other terrible things can I think of?' This was confirmed by the patient. Another of our patients put it quite clearly: 'When my obsessions get very severe, I imagine what could be worse than this obsession and then something worse always comes along.'

Another example was a man who had once imagined that a woman could read his sexual thoughts and be shocked by this and reject him. The fear was based on a particular abstract conversation about women's reactions to men. So every time he was in a particular situation with a woman, he became preoccupied with the idea that he might have sexual thoughts which could be read by the woman. He didn't have the sexual thoughts, but imagined having such thoughts and reacted 'as if' he had. As such, his reaction to his thoughts about the sexual thoughts was incited by the story of what might happen rather than any moralistic motive. The maintaining factor here was not some static, moral appraisal but a replaying of the imagined possibility. In other words, acting 'as if' there were sexual thoughts and 'as if' his thoughts could be read.

How does the OCD patient come to infer the presence of a thought that is, in fact, an imaginary thought? In the case of obsessional ruminations, the question is what convinces the person to confuse thinking about having the thought with the thought. In our clinical work, it appears so far that a highly charged narrative about what the person might be or might become dictates the confusion. These narratives appear similar to the narrative supporting inferential confusion in obsessions with overt compulsions and includes irrelevant associations, a dismissal of actual evidence in support of a hypothetical reality, and mistaking a far-fetched narrative with an actual probability (O'Connor & Robillard, 1995). The following is a paraphrased narrative of a patient explaining the origin of one of her obsessions:

> I dreamt of stabbing someone and enjoying it, which means I have the hidden desire to actually stab someone (going deeper into reality). The dream felt so real that I might be able to do this in real life also (irrelevant association). I know I never really hurt anyone in real life since these obsessions have started, but there always might be the possibility that I could (mistaking a far-fetched narrative with an actual probability). Even though I read about similar obsessions of other people and I know that people with OCD are not dangerous, their obsessions were never totally the same, which means I still might be dangerous (dismissal of actual evidence in favor of a hypothetical reality).

What is striking in the above account is that stabbing someone was experienced in a dream and not actually experienced as part of the normal stream of consciousness. Having the impulse is confused with dreaming of having an impulse. Even though the origin of the obsessions is not exactly an imagined impulse in the normal sense, it certainly cannot be traced back to intrusive thoughts.

For some OCD patients, the tendency to engage in imaginary scenarios is especially clear. Examination of the particular sequence in which thoughts evolve is especially helpful in determining how the obsessional inference comes into existence. For example, in one instance (when listening to music) the sequence of thought was the following: (1) 'Maybe other people are bothered by it.' (2) 'I want to listen to it anyway.' (3) 'Maybe I'm putting on music to bother other people.'

The inference that 'maybe I'm putting on music to bother other people' points towards an irrelevant association being made between the thought 'I want to listen to music' and 'maybe other people will be bothered by it'. More specifically, the motivational component of wanting to listen to music is transfused into the idea that other people might be bothered by it. Further, the thought that 'I want to listen to it anyway' was suspect in the mind of this patient because it might indicate that she would listen to music whether people are bothered by it or not. Obviously, the whole thought sequence starts out with a simple wish to listen to music, which evidently is not the same as purposely putting on music to bother people. Yet, this fact is lost when the context motivating the initial thought of wanting to listen to music is swapped for an imaginary scenario producing a possible motivation (putting on music to bother people).

Examples of Narratives Illustrating Inferential Confusion

> Narrative 1: I sometimes feel angry and depressed, and these are not the right feelings to have. I do not want such negativity inside of myself. These feelings are a bad thing to have and who knows how deep they go? They are the kind of feelings that the devil would have all the time. Having these kind of feelings is like thinking of the devil. I don't want to have these feelings or ever think about the devil, because it is a negative thing to do. If I try as hard as I can not to think about the devil, then it's like getting rid of all negativity inside of me.

In this narrative, an actual internal modality (feelings of anger and depression) becomes associated with thinking about the devil to the degree that having negative feelings inside of oneself is synonymous with thinking about the devil. The association is formed through 'likeness' where having negative feelings is 'like' thinking about the devil. However, an association based on likeness does not make negative feelings and thinking about the devil the same thing, but they are in fact two different types of internal modalities. However, the person in the above narrative acts as if modifying an irrelevant internal modality (thinking of the devil) would result in a change in a relevant internal modality (negative feelings).

The narrative proposes a strategy to get rid of negative feelings by banishing any thoughts of the devil from one's mind. This strategy would make sense if indeed thinking about the devil is the same as having negative feelings. However, the strategy is bound to fail even if the person were to successfully banish the image of the devil from his/her mind because the association between negative feelings and the devil is irrelevant. Instead, the person becomes preoccupied with the 'possibility' of thoughts of the devil occurring. The normal stream of consciousness never was and never will be preoccupied with thoughts of the devil but the person acts 'as if' it is by mixing up negative feelings with thoughts of the devil. However, since the person is unaware of this categorizing error, the person will engage in the meta-cognition goal 'not to think about the devil' 'as if' such thoughts are actually there (thought–thought fusion). The meta-cognitive thought 'not to think about the devil' has the paradoxical effect of bringing the 'to be avoided' within awareness, but in essence continues to refer to the imagined state of affairs, since thoughts of the devil are not actually what is preoccupying the normal stream of consciousness of this person.

> Narrative 2: I can't go too far from home, or the city that I live in, because I don't know how panicky I might get. I might go really crazy and do something to myself. Who knows what is really wrong with me? One of my family members has schizophrenia, and I might have some serious disturbance also. I could be crazy enough to cut out my tongue. When I'm anxious, I can 'see' myself doing it, using a knife to cut it off. It feels I could actually do it. Then I'll be in the middle of nowhere without help. Then when I'm found, I'll be sent off to a psychiatric hospital somewhere that I don't know, and they'll lock me up.

In this impulse phobia client, the obsessions are about cutting off the tongue, and fearing going too far out of the city, and are built up to a crescendo with a dramatic narrative.

PSYCHOMETRIC MEASUREMENT OF INFERENTIAL CONFUSION

What are the prospects of identifying central cognitive markers in OCD through self-report, in particular, the inference processes as described by O'Connor and colleagues (O'Connor & Robillard, 1995; O'Connor et al., 2004)? According to Taylor (2002a), despite difficulties in the assessment of cognitions through psychometric means, these methods should not be under-valued either. In an insightful review on cognitive variables in OCD, he draws a parallel with research on cognitive factors in panic disorder where the construct of anxiety sensitivity has been proposed as central to this disorder, and recent evidence suggests that a combination of learning experiences and genetic factors influences the level of anxiety sensitivity. However, the particular types of obsessive-compulsive beliefs that play a central role in OCD have yet to be established, and it remains to be seen whether appraisals and beliefs identified so far are not epiphenomena of more central cognitive characteristics of this disorder. Thus, despite advances in measurement research into cognitive variables, OCD still presents an enormous challenge.

One particular complicating factor in identifying central cognitive markers for OCD is the overlap between these measures, which represents a difficult challenge for researchers carrying out multidimensional investigations (Clark, 2002). Even if cognitive measures show adequate differential validity by conventional standards, they leave open alternative hypotheses of findings that reflect more central cognitive markers. Since the relationship between cognitive measures and OCD tends to be rather modest, there is little leeway to establish unique variance while controlling for other measures. However, due to the overlap between cognitive variables and other measures, cognitive markers of OCD cannot be introduced without controlling for mood states and other cognitive measures. New and existing cognitive measures need to establish their differential validity and unique contribution to obsessive-compulsive symptoms as compared to other cognitive measures, mood states, and perhaps even personality traits. This places a considerable burden of proof on researchers who wish to introduce new cognitive concepts that may be relevant to obsessive-compulsive disorder, or those who wish to continue investigating existing measures of cognitions and determine their unique relevancy to OCD. However, this requirement may eventually clarify which markers are fundamental and specific to OCD, and which cognitive variables are epiphenomena of these central cognitive markers. In particular, this would open the doorway to experimental studies that can specifically target the cognitive variables in question (Rachman, 2001), and eventually reveal learning experiences and genetic factors involved in OCD (Taylor, 2002a).

Inferential confusion is one such relatively new cognitive concept with several ambitious claims. Not only is this concept introduced as a central process characteristic of OCD, it would locate these processes before the formation of cognitive beliefs and appraisals. In particular, an inference-based approach would argue that the 'intrusion' and appraisal are inherently linked and the obsessional sequence begins with the intrusions (O'Connor, 2002). In other words, certain beliefs and appraisals may follow logically and naturally from the intensity and reality value of the primary obsessional inference, which inherits its persistence and strong reality value from the reasoning processes associated with its occurrence (O'Connor & Aardema, 2003). For example, a thought such as 'I might have driven over someone with my car' would logically result in a need for certainty, elevated responsibility, attempts to control, and giving the thought importance if this thought is experienced as realistic due to a confusion between reality and possibility (i.e. inferential confusion). It then naturally follows that some beliefs and appraisals are elevated in a person suffering from OCD, but these cognitive elaborations do not represent causal factors in the development of OCD, since the obsessional sequence begins with the doubt.

In recent years several of these claims have been systematically investigated in a series of studies through psychometric means, which can be broadly divided into the following sections: (1) the measurement of inferential confusion; (2) inferential confusion and obsessive-compulsive symptoms; (3) inferential confusion as a construct in obsessive-compulsive disorder and other disorders; (4) inferential confusion as a non-phobic characteristic of OCD; (5) inferential confusion and obsessive-compulsive beliefs; and (6) inferential confusion and treatment outcome.

The Measurement of Inferential Confusion

The initial measurement of inferential confusion was carried out in a study by Emmelkamp and Aardema (1999), comparing the predictive validity of cognitive variables in obsessive-compulsive symptoms. In this study, items were written to capture crucial aspects of inferential confusion where most of the items reflected inverse inference and a tendency to distrust the senses, which led to the first version of the Inferential Confusion Questionnaire (ICQ). A significant portion of the items revolved around inferential confusion pertaining to threat-related information (i.e. 'Even if I have all sorts of evidence against the occurrence of a certain danger, I still feel it will occur'), since obsessions often refer to threat in one way or another, and as noted by Clark (2002), 'it is difficult, if not impossible, to define or measure other cognitive domains in isolation from threat'. An alternative solution to avoid any reference to threat in the items would have been to specifically refer to obsessions in the questionnaire, or prime the person in the instruction towards linking the items in the questionnaire to inferences or 'intrusions' as has been done in other cognitive measures (Salkovskis et al., 2000), but this would likely have led to an artificial inflation of the importance of inferential confusion in OCD. Thus, while the inference processes such as those reflected in the initial item set of the ICQ are associated with threat, they contain the element of inferential confusion that leads the person to persist in his/her preoccupation despite contradictory evidence coming through the senses.

The reliability of the initial version of the ICQ was adequate in the study of Emmelkamp and Aardema (1999), but no efforts were made to investigate the dimensional structure of the questionnaire and the scale only contained eight items. Therefore, 11 additional items were conceived to capture the construct of inferential confusion for a second study in another community sample ($n = 108$) (Aardema et al., 2004e). Factor analyses followed by oblique rotation revealed one large first factor explaining 30.1% of the variance with an eigenvalue of 5.9. This result was consistent with current conceptualizations, since the questionnaire attempted to measure a crucial sub-aspect of inferential confusion (i.e. 'inverse inference'), which was expected to be a unidimensional construct. A total of four items were removed with the lowest factor loadings, resulting in a unidimensional questionnaire of 15 items. In particular, as compared to the previous version the reliability improved with the addition of new items (Cronbach's alpha = 0.85). However, a limitation of these studies was the use of a normal population, and further steps were taken to investigate the ICQ in a clinical OCD sample.

The final study investigating the psychometric properties of the ICQ was carried out in a clinical OCD sample (Aardema *et al.*, 2004f). In order to further improve the psychometric properties of the ICQ an additional five items were written, and five items with the lowest factor loadings in the previous study were removed. Factor analyses with oblique rotation on this latest item set once again revealed one large factor explaining 41.5% with an eigenvalue of 5.8, which confirmed the unidimensional structure of the Inferential Confusion Questionnaire in a clinical OCD sample. No items were removed, which resulted in the final 15-item version of the Inferential Confusion Questionnaire (see Table 5.2). The final version showed an excellent internal reliability of 0.90 (Cronbach's alpha). In conclusion, the

Table 5.2 Inferential Confusion Questionnaire Items

Items

1. I am sometimes more convinced by what might be there than by what I actually see.
2. I sometimes invent stories about certain dangers that might be there without paying attention to what I actually see.
3. I sometimes know there is a danger solely on the basis of my understanding of something and so there is no need to look.
4. No matter where you are, you can never be sure whether you are safe.
5. As soon as I think there might be danger, I immediately take precautions to avoid it.
6. I often cannot tell whether something is safe, because things are not what they appear to be.
7. Sometimes I have the idea that danger is near even though there is no obvious reason.
8. Even if I don't have any actual proof of a certain danger, my imagination can convince me otherwise.
9. There are many invisible dangers.
10. Just the thought that there could be danger is proof enough for me that there is.
11. I often know a problem exists even though I don't have visible proof.
12. My imagination can make me lose confidence in what I actually perceive.
13. Even if I have all sorts of visible evidence against the existence of a certain danger, I still feel that it will occur.
14. I am more often afraid of something that I cannot see than something I can see.
15. I often react to a scenario that might happen as if it is actually happening.

Inferential Confusion Questionnaire is a reliable, unidimensional measure of inferential confusion as established in two community samples and one clinical OCD sample. High scores indicate a reasoning process where the person persists in the possibility of threat or danger, despite evidence to the contrary, or without actual proof for its occurrence, and, indeed, explictly recognizes the imagination as a source of inference.

Inferential Confusion as a Construct in Obsessive-Compulsive Disorder

The relevance of inferential confusion to obsessive-compulsive behavior was established in several studies with both non-clinical and clinical samples that have consistently found moderate to strong relationships with obsessive-compulsive symptoms (Emmelkamp & Aardema, 1999; Aardema *et al.*, 2004e, 2004f). However, relationships between cognitive measures and obsessive-compulsive symptoms have been found to be closely associated with negative mood states, and zero-order correlations may misrepresent the actual relationship (OCCWG, 2003). Indeed, inferential confusion was found to have moderate relationships with neuroticism, anxiety and depression in both the non-clinical and clinical samples.

Another issue is the potential overlap among cognitive measures, which complicates the interpretation of results. However, the initial study carried out by Emmelkamp & Aardema (1999) in a non-clinical sample showed inferential confusion to be related to most forms of obsessive-compulsive behaviors while controlling for depression and 13 competing cognitive domains. In particular, inferential confusion was found to be independently related to the impulses, rumination, checking subscales of the Padua-Revised Inventory. In another study in a non-clinical sample (Aardema *et al.*, 2004e) inferential confusion was found to be related to all subscales of the Padua-Revised Inventory (van Oppen *et al.*, 1995b) while controlling for neuroticism – a personality variable that has been found to be strongly associated with other cognitive measures (Aardema, 1996). While no other cognitive measures were included in this study as controls, the study emphasizes the resilience of the inferential confusion using a personality variable such as neuroticism as control rather than anxiety and depression. The final study in a clinical OCD sample using the Padua Washington State Inventory (Burns *et al.*, 1996) showed inferential confusion to be significantly related to obsessive-compulsive symptoms, while controlling for anxiety, depression *and* six belief domains as measured by the OBQ, thereby further confirming its relevance to OCD independently of negative mood states and other cognitive measures. With these controls, inferential confusion was related to obsessive-compulsive symptoms overall as measured by the Padua Revised total score, obsessions about harm and washing compulsions. In particular, the relationship with obsessions remained quite substantial.

However, comparing all the studies carried out with the ICQ reveals some inconsistencies in the relationship between inferential confusion and specific obsessive-compulsive symptoms. While the initial studies with non-clinical samples found inferential confusion to be related to checking compulsions after controlling for other variables (Emmelkamp & Aardema, 1999; Aardema et al., 2004e), no relationship was found with checking compulsions in the clinical OCD sample using similar controls (Aardema et al., 2004f). Similarly, there was a relationship between inferential confusion and washing compulsions in the clinical OCD sample while controlling for negative mood states and other cognitive measures, while no such independent relationship was found in the study of Emmelkamp and Aardema (1999). This points towards some inconsistencies as to the role of inferential confusion in the area of compulsive behaviors.

Obsessional impulses is another area of specific obsessive-compulsive symptoms where we find some inconsistencies in the relationship with inferential confusion. Inferential confusion was moderately related to obsessional impulses in the studies using the Padua-Revised Inventory (van Oppen et al., 1995b) in the non-clinical samples, while no relationship was found with the impulses scale of the Padua Revised (Burns et al., 1996) in the clinical samples. However, this subgroup of OCD patients may be under-represented in general samples of OCD patients, which may have attenuated results. Also, inspection of the items in the PI-WSUR impulse scale showed that they do not seem to reflect obsessional impulses or thoughts, but rather seem to represent a generalized type of impulsivity. This is corroborated by the finding that the obsessional impulses scale in the Padua Revised Inventory shows the least amount of specificity in differentiating OCD patients from anxious controls (Aardema et al., 2004f).

In sum, it appears that inferential confusion is related to most obsessive-compulsive symptoms while controlling for a wide variety of other cognitive measures and negative mood states. In particular, inferential confusion is strongly related to obsessions, which is consistent with an inference-based approach that primarily attempts to account for the occurrence and persistence of obsessions.

Inferential Confusion as a Construct in OCD and Other Disorders

What evidence is there that inferential confusion is specific to OCD? The only study that has addressed this question so far found that OCD patients score significantly higher on inferential confusion than anxious and non-clinical controls (Aardema *et al.*, 2004f). The inclusion of a delusional disorder sample in this study showed this group scored as high on inferential confusion as the OCD group. This finding is consistent with a conceptualization of OCD as a type of belief disorder, which locates OCD on a different spectrum of disorders from the anxiety disorders. However, people with anxiety disorders also score higher on inferential confusion than non-clinical controls, and this suggests that inferential confusion may operate to different degrees in a variety of disorders, even though it is more prominently present in OCD.

Inferential Confusion as a Non-Phobic Characteristic of OCD

According to the IBA model, OCD primarily follows a non-phobic model of development. The tendency to remove oneself from the senses, and reach inferences on the basis of purely subjective information, may be a characteristic that is shared among OCD patients and the schizotypal disorders. This is corroborated by the finding that individuals with Delusional Disorder score as high or higher on inferential confusion (Aardema *et al.*, 2004f). Also, inferential confusion was found to be related to several schizotypal symptoms, including perceptual disturbances and delusional thinking (Aardema *et al.*, 2004e). However, inferential confusion is not necessarily related to obsessional conviction even though particularly relevant to treatment outcome (Aardema *et al.*, 2004a). Instead, it appears that inferential confusion represents a separate dimension from obsessional conviction. Although inferential confusion as a process may account for the development of obsessional conviction, degree of belief in the obsession may also depend on insight or vulnerability towards specific content.

While the relationship between obsessive-compulsive and schizotypal symptoms has been noted before (Enright & Beech, 1990; O'Dwyer & Marks, 2000), there is currently no coherent conceptualization of these relationships. In particular, it is unclear how to conceptualize the relationship between perceptual disturbances and obsessive-compulsive symptoms, especially since OCD patients appear to have no problems with perceiving reality (Brown *et al.*, 1994). The role of perceptual disturbances is, however, consistent with inferential confusion characteristics of OCD where the person removes him/herself from reality to such an extent, that although reality continues to be perceived correctly, certain disturbances in reality perception may start to occur as the person removes him/herself from it. This has been identified by O'Connor and Aardema (2003) as a cross-over point from reality into the imagination where the person starts to rely solely on imaginary criteria to determine a state of affairs in reality. It is particularly noteworthy that where inferential confusion occurs with perceptual disturbances, OCD symptoms tend to be more severe (Aardema *et al.*, 2004e). This result can be viewed as the point where the obsessional inference starts to be 'lived' as real accompanied by high degrees of absorption into an imaginary reality, and as the endpoint of the inferential confusion process where the person confuses an imaginary possibility.

Inferential Confusion and Obsessive-Compulsive Beliefs

The relationship between inferential confusion and obsessive-compulsive beliefs is a complicated issue that has been specifically addressed in one study investigating whether inferential confusion could account for most of the relationships between beliefs and obsessive-compulsive symptoms (Aardema *et al.*, 2004b). According to the inference-based model, some appraisals and beliefs may follow logically from the obsessional primary inference. It would then be naturally expected that inferential confusion would show a relationship with these obsessive-compulsive beliefs and appraisals. Indeed, inferential confusion is quite strongly related to some obsessive-compulsive beliefs (over-estimation of threat and responsibility), and shows moderate correlations with other beliefs. However, at the same time, some of these relationships threaten the divergent validity of inferential confusion, in particular with respect to over-estimation of threat, which showed the strongest relationship with inferential confusion. Yet, clearly, inferential confusion remains significantly related to several forms of obsessive-compulsive symptoms when controlling for these other cognitive domains (Emmelkamp & Aardema, 1999; Aardema *et al.*, 2004f), and thus we can surmise that inferential confusion is a process that operates independently from other cognitive domains despite its relationship with these domains. However, most crucially, the hypothesis that inferential confusion is a marker of OCD that takes *precedence* over obsessive-compulsive beliefs, needs not only to show its independent relationship with obsessive-compulsive symptoms, but an ability to accommodate the relationships between beliefs and obsessive-compulsive symptoms. Indeed, the relationships between obsessive-compulsive beliefs and obsessive-compulsive symptoms, as measured by the OBQ-44, almost completely disappear when controlling for inferential confusion (see Table 5.3). This provides strong evidence as to the unique role of inferential confusion in the development of obsessive-compulsive symptoms and its precedence over belief domains.

In the same study that found inferential confusion could largely account for the variance between obsessive-compulsive beliefs and obsessive-compulsive symptoms, a competing hypothesis was proposed that argued

Table 5.3 Zero-order correlations and partial correlations: OBQ belief domains and ICQ with obsessive-compulsive symptoms in an OCD group ($n = 85$)

	OBQ-44 (controlled for ICQ)	ICQ (controlled for OBQ-44)
Padua Revised – Total		
Zero-order correlation	0.48***	0.52***
Partial correlation	0.18	0.41***
Padua Revised – Obsessions		
Zero-order correlation	0.57***	0.72***
Partial correlation	0.24*	0.50***
Padua Revised – Impulses		
Zero-order correlation	0.25*	0.20
Partial correlation	0.11	0.05
Padua Revised – Checking		
Zero-order correlation	0.32**	0.26*
Partial correlation	0.03	0.08
Padua Revised – Contamination		
Zero-order correlation	0.28*	0.38***
Partial correlation	0.01	0.26*
Padua Revised – Dressing		
Zero-order correlation	0.19	0.12
Partial correlation	−0.09	−0.02

$*p < 0.05$, $**p < 0.01$, $***p < 0.001$
OBQ-44-T = Obsessional Beliefs Questionaire-44 total score; ICQ = Inferential Confusion Questionnaire

that the overlap between over-estimation of threat and inferential confusion could account for these findings (Aardema *et al.*, 2004b). The overlap between inferential confusion and over-estimation of threat may indicate that controlling for inferential confusion means controlling for over-estimation of threat as well. However, factor analyses with varimax rotation on the item set of the ICQ and the scale over-estimation of threat appeared to indicate otherwise. Results indicated that over-estimation of threat and inferential confusion were distinct factorial domains, and the relationship of the ICQ score with obsessive-compulsive symptoms, while controlling for anxiety and depression, showed inferential confusion significantly related to obsessive-compulsive symptoms. No significant relationships were found between over-estimation of threat and obsessive-compulsive symptoms when controlling for these negative mood states. In sum, the results of these studies appear to indicate that inferential confusion is an independent process that accommodates the relationships between belief domains and obsessive-compulsive symptoms.

Is Inferential Confusion a Central Marker in OCD?

The studies discussed in the previous section strongly suggest that inferential confusion plays an important role in OCD. However, what is the evidence in support of the notion that inferential confusion is a *central* cognitive marker in OCD? There are a number of findings that appear to point in this direction, while some other findings indicate the need for further work. These can be briefly summarized as follows:

(1) Inferential confusion is a cognitive variable that is related to most forms of obsessive-compulsive behaviors as compared to other cognitive variables (Aardema *et al.*, 2004f; Emmelkamp & Aardema, 1999). In particular, inferential confusion is related to obsessive-compulsive symptoms overall as measured by the Padua Revised total score, and has a relatively strong relationship with obsessions. Both findings are consistent with an inference-based approach that locates the focal point of the obsessional sequence in obsessions rather than its aftermath. However, the relationship of inferential confusion to other forms of OCD symptoms has shown some conflicting findings, in particular the relationship with compulsive behaviors. Thus, while the current results look promising with respect to obsessive-compulsive symptoms in general and the occurrence of obsessions about harm to self or others, further work may be needed to establish the relevancy of inferential confusion for all compulsions.

(2) The concept of inferential confusion is surprisingly resilient to controls including a variety of cognitive variables and negative mood states. These results confirm the role of inferential confusion as an independent process operating in OCD. In addition, inferential confusion is able to accommodate the variance of other cognitive markers shared with obsessive-compulsive symptoms. The latter is perhaps one of the strongest research findings so far with the Inferential Confusion Questionnaire. However, given the important implications of these findings, replication of these results is needed before more conclusive statements can be made.

(3) Inferential confusion shows specificity to OCD and related disorders. The current findings indicate that OCD patients score significantly higher than those with other anxiety disorders (Aardema *et al.*, 2004f), while individuals with delusional disorder score as high as OCD

patients. However, anxious controls also score higher than non-clinical controls on inferential confusion, and classification of these groups on the basis of scores on the Inferential Confusion Questionnaire is not recommended at this point. Thus, while the finding that OCD patients score higher than anxious controls is promising, further work may be needed to better distinguish OCD patients from anxious groups.

(4) Therapy specifically targeting inferential confusion has been found to be particularly beneficial for a subgroup of OCD patients where obsessional conviction is high (O'Connor *et al.*, 2004). However, change in inferential confusion as measured by the Inferential Confusion Questionnaire is associated with change in obsessive-compulsive symptoms in a general sample of OCD patients receiving standard CBT. It may be that change in inferential confusion as measured by the Inferential Confusion Questionnaire will have a greater impact on symptoms for those with higher obsessional conviction than for those with lower conviction levels, but so far inferential confusion appears an important cognitive variable associated with change in symptoms for the majority of OCD patients receiving therapy (see p. 144).

Conclusion

In sum, while results appear very promising in many regards, it may be too soon to tell whether or not inferential confusion is a central marker in OCD. First and foremost, current results require replication, and further work is needed in several areas, as described above. More importantly, there are certain limitations to psychometric research, and for any cognitive marker to be considered central to OCD, experimental data is required to support this position. However, as far as psychometric methods permit, the current results strongly support inferential confusion as an independent process, and perhaps as a central marker in OCD.

EXPERIMENTAL STUDIES OF INFERENTIAL CONFUSION

In order to better understand the reasoning styles of people with OCD and whether or not inferential confusion was involved in OCD, we developed two separate paradigms empirically testing reasoning. Our initial study explored inductive and deductive reasoning, using six different reasoning tasks (Pélissier & O'Connor, 2002a). As described earlier (Chapter 4), our initial aim was to determine if any particularities existed in the reasoning processes of people with OCD. One of our main conclusions concerned the fact that people with OCD performed similarly to the control groups on deductive measures, which was an interesting result in itself since it showed no apparent difficulty was present in standard logical abilities of people with OCD. However, one of the results taken from 'supporting an arbitrary statement' task revealed that people with OCD doubted an initial statement much more after having produced several alternative possibilities supporting that statement. The task stated that participants had to generate possibilities themselves and at that point, we had not considered whether people with OCD would have reacted differently if they had been given alternative arguments by the experimenter.

Thus, a pilot study was conducted where we devised a task to test the condition of self-generated versus given inferences in people with OCD compared to a non-OCD control group (Pélissier & O'Connor, 2001). We also compared whether there was a difference in response when the content material was relevant to OCD symptomatology (OCD-relevant themes) versus non-OCD-relevant examples (neutral themes). The task was adapted from a probabilistic inference task developed by Johnson-Laird (1994b). In our version, two premises are supplied and participants (Ps) are instructed to generate an inductive conclusion or they are given such a conclusion by the experimenter (E). Then, Ps need to estimate how confident they are about the plausibility of the initial conclusion (whether or not it was given or self-generated). The E then instructs Ps to generate more plausible conclusions or the E provides at least three alternative conclusions. Finally, the Ps need to estimate the initial conclusion again. Of the 11 examples, 4 are neutral and 7 are OCD related. Four examples illustrating the various possible conditions are presented here:

Example of Neutral Condition with 'Given' Conclusions

It rained a lot since the beginning of the day.
Jenny planned a picnic this afternoon.
Possibility: The picnic will be cancelled.

What is your degree of confidence about this conclusion?
_____%

Let me suggest other possibilities:

Jenny will go ahead with the picnic even if it rains.
Picnics can be held under tents.
Jenny will invite everybody into her home.

Now, tell me what your degree of confidence is, about the initial conclusion. _____%

Example of OCD-Related Condition with 'Given' conclusions

Mark arranged his living room just as he likes it.
He had his friends over with their children.
Possibility: Maybe the children moved the objects around in the living room.

What is your degree of confidence about this possibility?
_____%

Let me suggest other possibilities:

> Maybe Mark asked the children to play in another room.
> Parents often ask their children to be careful when in other people's homes.
> It is possible that Mark replaced each object as it was moved around.

Now, tell me what your degree of confidence is, about the initial possibility. _____%

Example of a Neutral Condition with Self-Generated Conclusions

The old man was bitten by a poisonous snake.
There was no known antidote.
According to you, what happened?

Maybe . . . _____

What is your degree of confidence about this possibility?
_____%

Are there any other possibilities?
Maybe . . . _____
Maybe . . . _____
Maybe . . . _____
Maybe . . . _____

Now, tell me what your degree of confidence is, about the initial possibility. _____%

Example of an OCD-related Condition with Self-Generated Conclusions

A client is about to eat a meal in a restaurant.
He just noticed greasy fingerprints on his drinking glass.
According to you, what happened?

Maybe . . . _____

What is your degree of confidence about this possibility?
_____%

Are there any other possibilities?

Maybe . . . _____
Maybe . . . _____
Maybe . . . _____
Maybe . . . _____

Now, tell me what your degree of confidence is, about the initial possibility. _____%

At the end of the inference task, Ps were asked to fill out a form where all the examples were listed and each set of premises was rated in terms of how anxious people would feel if they heard of such a situation in reality. The scale ranged from 0 (No anxiety) to 4 (Extreme anxiety). This extra measure was meant to ensure that OCD-relevant examples were in fact provoking anxiety in people with OCD compared to control participants and also, that neutral examples did not provoke such anxiety in either group.

In a pilot study conducted with 10 people with OCD and 10 normal controls (Pélissier & O'Connor, 2002b), we found that both groups doubted the initial conclusion after considering or generating alternative conclusions in all conditions. Also, results suggest that both groups doubted more in the 'given' condition. However, there was a tendency for these effects to be more pronounced in the OCD group so the study needed replication. Before administering the task to a subsequent sample, we refined certain examples to ensure internal validity. For example, some of the items were producing floor effects where both groups did not endorse the initial conclusion as being highly probable in the first place, so subsequent ratings did not change that much after being given other possibilities. These questions were revised to produce higher base rates.

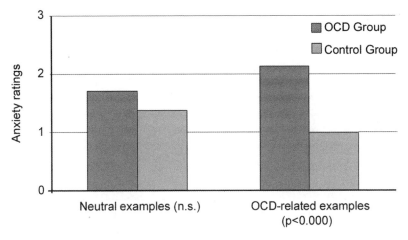

Figure 5.2   Measures of associated anxiety

The second study tested 20 people with OCD and 19 non-anxious controls who presented no significant differences on demographic variables but varied in degree of psychopathology symptoms. The inference task described earlier was given and t-tests were used to compare the two groups. The first analysis consisted of two t-tests to verify that the examples were either actually neutral or OCD related. Figure 5.2 shows how there was no significant difference between the two groups for neutral examples and that, effectively, the OCD-related examples discriminated between the two groups, where the OCD group rated the examples as being more anxiety-provoking than the control group did.

Second, we did two paired t-tests within each group to identify if neutral and OCD-relevant conditions were considered differently by each group (see Figure 5.3). Analysis revealed that, in the OCD group, there was no significant difference between their ratings of anxiety of neutral versus OCD-relevant examples. This was surprising since the anxiety ratings did discriminate between the OCD and control group. However, it seems that both OCD-relevant examples and neutral examples were just as anxiety-provoking for the OCD group. The same analysis in the control group showed that the neutral examples were rated as being more anxiety-provoking than the OCD-relevant examples. We hypothesized that the OCD-relevant examples may have seemed irrelevant to the control group, while the neutral conditions were situations more likely to preoccupy them.

Third, we looked at overall pre- and post-measures in all conditions by performing an ANOVA for repeated measures. Both groups equally doubted the initial conclusion after considering alternative conclusions in

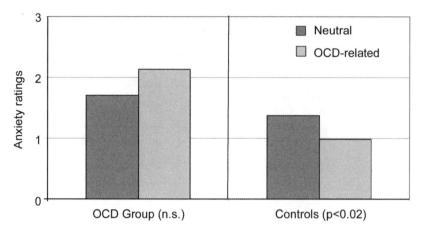

Figure 5.3   Anxiety ratings within groups

ALL conditions: that is, whether or not the examples were neutral or OCD-related and whether or not the conclusions were given or self-generated ($F(1,37) = 68.6$; $p < 0.000$). This supports the results of the pilot study but also establishes this task as a good analogue for creating inferential doubt. Figure 5.4 shows that both groups reduced their degree of certainty in all conditions.

Fourth, we compared the OCD-relevant condition versus the neutral condition and found that both groups significantly lowered their degree of confidence more in the neutral condition than in the OCD-relevant

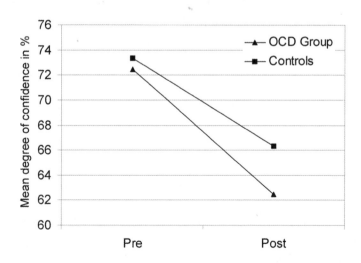

Figure 5.4   Overall pre- and post-measures in all conditions

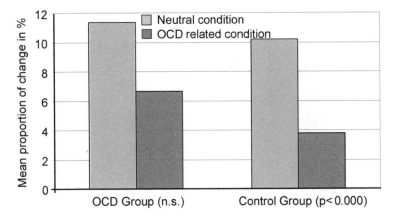

Figure 5.5   Neutral vs OCD-related conditions

examples (F(1,37) = 12.8; $p < 0.001$). To further understand the previous result, we performed a repeated measure analysis within each group which revealed that within the OCD group, there was no significant difference between the neutral and the OCD-relevant examples. This makes sense: recall there were no significant difference between their rating of anxiety versus neutral examples. In other words, they reacted similarly to both conditions whereas normal controls did not. In fact, there was a significant difference (F(1,37) = 26.5; $p < 0.000$) within the control group between neutral and OCD-related examples where they seemed to doubt the initial conclusions more in the neutral examples. This different reaction is not surprising, considering they were more preoccupied with the neutral examples than with the OCD-relevant ones on the anxiety rating scale (see Figure 5.5).

When we compared the given versus the self-generated conditions, it appeared that both groups significantly lowered their degree of confidence more in the given examples than in the self-generated ones (F(1,37) = 8.2; $p < 0.007$). Again, this result was further explored by verifying within each group what influence each condition was operating on each group. The results show that there are no differences within the control group but that, this time, the people in the OCD group doubt the initial conclusions significantly more in the given conditions than in the self-generated examples (F(1,37) = 7.79; $p < 0.012$). Results are presented here in Figure 5.6.

Discussion

To summarize the results, it seems that people with OCD doubt an initial conclusion much more when this conclusion, given by the experimenter, is

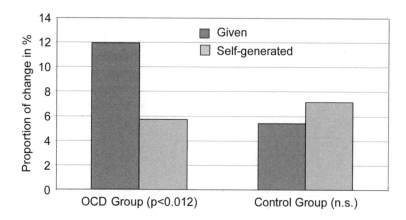

Figure 5.6   Given vs self-generated conditions

followed by other possibilities, also given by the experimenter. They do not show such a great amount of doubting when they infer conclusions themselves. This result needs to be explained since such doubting is not found in the control group: non-OCD sufferers are not particularly influenced by whether or not conclusions are inferred by themselves or given by the experimenter. So what is different about inductive reasoning when people with OCD are given conclusions?

In our previous study (Pélissier & O'Connor, 2002a), we had used Johnson-Laird's theory of mental models to explain how people with OCD seemed to doubt more in the 'supporting an arbitrary statement' inductive task. In effect, in a situation of being given a conclusion and having to assess if this conclusion was plausible after inferring other possible alternatives, people with OCD doubted the initial given statement more than the two control groups. We proposed that people with OCD may have been producing too many alternative models before coming to a conclusion which made them uncertain of the initial statement for having brought up a complex array of models (recall, models are structures of possibilities illustrated by images, words, sentences, etc.). We also hypothesized that the production of too many inferences may have led the person with OCD to qualify the premise with irrelevant elements of doubt. In mental model (MM) theory, one searches for alternative models to find out if a conclusion is valid. The OCD group may be searching through too many mental models and not reaching a resolution as to whether a conclusion is valid, so they end up doubting the conclusion rather than reaching certainty.

Recall that the MM theory suggests that there are three levels of thinking that people go through when they infer conclusions. They first try to understand the premises by using what they know in general and according to their level of language as well. Then, they will construct models about what has been understood from these premises and, finally, they will combine the models in order to draw a description of the state of affairs they are trying to compose. So if we hypothesize that people use MM to draw a conclusion, it would be possible that in the self-generated condition, where people are requested to generate their own inferences, that people with OCD are generating alternative conclusions which illustrate their own mental models. These may not be revised for possible falsification. Recall, when a person finds a conclusion, they will search for alternative models that would be coherent with the premises but where the supposed conclusion would be false. This last level involves validating that no falsifying model compromises the conclusion, that is, that the conclusion is valid. If alternative models do falsify the conclusion, then it is false and the reasoner must search for a new conclusion that no alternative model does falsify.

So, for example, results of our preliminary study could be explained in the following manner. The fact that conclusions are *given* may be asking the person with OCD to search for models in which the conclusion would be valid. In doing so, they would be trying to find a model in which the conclusion would be false. Supposing people with OCD have a tendency to produce more alternative models, reviewing the complex array of models may create too many possibilities which would create doubt in terms of knowing which model yields a valid conclusion. Into this cognitive explanation we can introduce the role of possibility. The person with OCD is drawing on possibilities remote from current experience. In fact, the maximum possibility is generated only by an imaginary narrative. Each time, then, that people with OCD consider alternatives, they are going further away from their senses. Whereas normally a person might draw on a model to test a conclusion, in OCD the premise is always faulty, so all models lead to faulty conclusions. Faced with this confusion, people with OCD would become less certain of initial conclusions. In other words, rather than trying to validate the evidence through existing mental models, people with OCD would be creating additional alternative mental models which would create cognitive overloading. This would be reflected by not concluding with more certainty but with more doubt (hence significantly reducing their level of confidence in the 'given' condition).

These findings need to be replicated and the possibility model hypothesis explored further. The question of doubting could be addressed by developing a task which would create certainty. Our prediction would be that people with OCD would be less certain of their inferences than the control group in the face of increased certainty because of the tendency to invoke more alternative mental models.

CLINICAL TRIALS OF AN INFERENCE-BASED APPROACH TO THERAPY (IBA)

The treatment resistance, of those with over-investment in their obsessional ideas, to behavioral treatments was noted early on in clinical trials (Foa *et al.*, 1983; Rachman, 1983) and still poses problems (O'Dwyer & Marks, 2000). This treatment-resistant category of OCD has been linked with over-valued ideation (OVI) which is currently ill-defined (Veale, 2002) but is generally characterized by a strong intellectual investment in a fixed idea not shared by others, where the content of the idea does not arise from everyday life experiences. Fixity of ideas occurs across diverse psychiatric complaints (e.g., depression, mania, schizophrenia) but OVI is generally located by psychiatric authors (Jaspers, 1913, 1963; Spitzer *et al.*, 1991) on a dimension between obsessions and delusional disorder.

There are clearly reasons why those with OVI might not respond to the behavioral treatment of choice for OCD. First, it would be difficult for the person with OVI to accept the habituation model, inherent in exposure *in vivo* and response prevention (ERP). As noted previously, in OVI there is a conviction in the logic of the belief in and out of the OCD situation. There is a risk also during exposure that the belief or some modification of it will maintain anxiety by covert neutralization (Trinder & Salkovskis, 1994). The problems with OVI hold equally for CBT centered around modifying appraisals (the cognitive appraisal model (CAM)) (OCCWG, 1997). This model proposes that unwanted intrusive thoughts are a universal experience, but if they are appraised as holding negative implications for the person (e.g., having this thought means I'm a bad person), the person will become preoccupied and try to 'neutralize' (i.e. alleviate the threat) or otherwise suppress the thought, thus maintaining the preoccupation with the thought. However, in OVI, the content of the initial intrusion may hold an intrinsic meaning reflected in a higher than normal conviction which will dictate the strength of subsequent reactions. Hence, in OVI the intrusion and the appraisal are inherently linked and the obsessional sequence begins with the intrusions. This latter point has important implications for the clinical management of OVI.

The remedy recommended for OVI by different authors has included more of the same (Salkovskis *et al.*, 1998). Others have suggested a creative use of educational strategies (Bouman, 2002; Zucker *et al.*, 2002). However, an inference-based approach (IBA) considers that in OVI the initial intrusion is actually a faulty inference, hence it is part of the obsession. The initial doubt or inference (example: 'maybe I am contaminated') is maintained by an idiosyncratic reasoning process which invests meaning in the initial thought (primary inference; PI), and subsequently spirals off to secondary aversive consequences (secondary inferences; SI) leading to appraisals of the obsessional thoughts ('this is terrible to have such thoughts') and perhaps further coping appraisals ('I can't deal with this problem, I'm out of control').

A recent treatment outcome attempted to establish the efficacy of an inference-based approach to the treatment of OCD as compared to ERP and CAM. A total of 44 participants were randomly allocated to each treatment modality (O'Connor et al., 2004). The main distinctions between the three modalities were that in ERP obsessional beliefs of any kind were not addressed, and the focus was on behavioral exposure and response prevention. CAM addressed only appraisals and SI, by use of cognitive challenges and reality testing, and treated PI as normal, near universal experiences. IBA exclusively addressed the PI as an obsessional doubt and focused on reasoning patterns which led to the doubt with no reference to exposure, or to challenging SI or appraisals. So, in the case of a person with contamination obsessions and washing compulsions, the thought–action sequence might be: 'I touched a door knob (trigger) – maybe there was unseen dirt which contaminated my hand (PI) – if my hand is dirty, I'll infect others and cause harm (SI) – that's terrible, I would be irresponsible (appraisal) – just thinking about all this makes me feel ill and tired, I can't cope (further appraisal).' Obsessional conviction was represented by the client's rating (0–100) in terms of the degree of probability of the primary inference (e.g. my hands could be dirty) (e.g. how probable is it that your hands might be dirty?). Secondary inferences (e.g. if my hands are dirty, I'll contaminate my whole family) were rated (0–100) according to how realistic were the consequences. One representative relevant OBQ appraisal item (chosen in collaboration with the participant from high scoring items on the OBQ-87) was also monitored daily.

Results of this study indicated that three treatments were equally effective in reducing symptomatology as measured by the Yale-Brown Obsessive Compulsive Scale (Y-BOCS) (Goodman et al., 1989a,b) and Padua Revised Inventory. Thus, while IBA was originally developed for OCD with over-valued ideation (see O'Connor & Robillard, 1999) it appears IBA is a viable alternative to CAM and ERP for all types of OCD. This is consistent with questionnaire and experimental findings which suggested 'inferential confusion' may be to different degrees a characteristic of all OCD, whether OVI or non-OVI (Aardema et al., 2004f; Pélissier & O'Connor, 2002c).

The particular relevance of inference-based therapy for those participants who show strong conviction levels is highlighted by the finding that IBA was *more* effective than CAM for these participants. This confirmed expectations that participants with higher conviction levels in primary

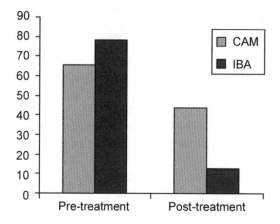

Figure 5.7   Pre- and post-treatment change in probability of primary inferences

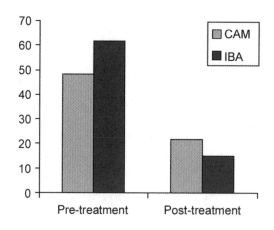

Figure 5.8   Pre- and post-treatment change in how realistic the secondary inferences are

inference show a greater clinical improvement with IBA than with CAM. The IBA group showed a greater decrease in PI post treatment than the CAM group, but both groups showed a decrease in SI (see Figures 5.7 and 5.8).

Interestingly, all three treatments affected the key OBQ appraisal item targeted in conjunction with the participant and monitored in the daily diary, which suggests the appraisal was related to change in symptomatology.

Table 5.4 Differences between non-responders and responders on change in process variables during treatment

	Responders (n = 26)	SD	Non-Responders (n = 14)	SD	t	p
Primary Inference	−37.6	22.1	−16.4	37.1	2.27	0.03
IF PI > 50	−52.5	36.2	−23.3	24.4	2.14	0.04
IF PI < 50	−14.0	25.0	−4.0	8.9	0.85	0.41
Secondary inference	−41.1	23.8	−17.3	23.2	2.88	0.007
IF PI > 50	−40.1	25.0	−21.1	23.6	1.91	0.07
IF PI < 50	−41.9	26.3	−8.7	25.2	2.28	0.04
OBQ Belief Item	−44.4	25.6	−14.3	24.8	3.46	0.001
IF PI > 50	−46.2	25.8	−16.3	26.5	2.51	0.02
IF PI < 50	−41.5	26.3	−12.0	24.9	2.17	0.05

At baseline, strength of PI did not correlate with strength of the OBQ appraisal item. Conversely, strength of SI was highly correlated with strength of the OBQ appraisal item, which would concur with the notion that SI represents a type of appraisal or consequence of the PI. Post treatment, as noted earlier, all measures tended to relate significantly.

In terms of relationships between change in appraisal, inferences, and clinical symptoms, there was a significant difference between non-responders and responders in SI change if PI was low (< 50), but change in SI did not differentiate non-responders and responders if PI was high. Conversely, changes in PI were significantly different for responders and non-responders if PI was high, but not when PI was low. This finding suggests that, except in the high PI group, the PI are independent of symptom levels. The independence of PI from both SI and appraisals would suggest that where there is a low strength of conviction, the PI may be a separate process not tied to symptomatology (see Table 5.4).

The findings of this study may have implications for treatment-matching in OCD with high and low PI respectively. The current results would suggest that high PI regardless of SI would indicate IBA (see Figure 5.9), but otherwise all modalities are equal. However, limitations of this study were that no standardized experimental or questionnaire measures of inferential confusion or over-valued ideation were taken pre- and post-treatment to better identify baseline predictors of therapy outcome. Measures such as the Inferential Confusion Questionnaire (Emmelkamp & Aardema, 1999) or the Over-Valued Ideas Scale (OVIS) (Neziroglu *et al.*, 1999) did not exist or were not in the public domain at the start of the study (1998). There was however

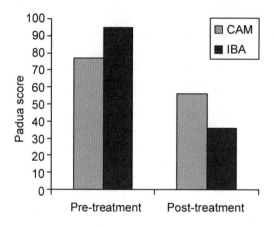

Figure 5.9   Pre- and post-treatment Padua scores (if PI > 50)

a significant correlation of strength of PI with the Y-BOCS insight scale that adds support to the claim that high investment in the initial doubt can be linked to over-valued ideation. Interestingly, other authors have linked over-valued ideation with degree of conviction in secondary consequences of obsessions (Tolin *et al.*, 2001).

More recently, the particular relevance of the inferential confusion process in terms of treatment outcome was investigated using the Inferential Confusion Questionnaire in a sample of 35 participants receiving standard cognitive-behavioural therapy (Aardema *et al.*, 2004a). Results of that study indicated that changes in inferential confusion as measured by the ICQ represent an important cognitive factor for treatment success for all of those undergoing cognitive-behavioral therapy where changes in inferential confusion were significantly higher for responders than non-responders. Inferential confusion was not related to SI and PI both pre- and post-treatment. However, it seems with high scores of PI the relationship between symptomatology may differ from low PI scores (O'Connor et al., 2003a). Although current conceptualizations of inferential confusion locate the concept within a wide spectrum of schizotypal characteristics that have been noted in OCD, it is conceptually and empirically distinct from these schizotypal characteristics (Aardema *et al.*, 2004e).

Inferential Confusion and Treatment Outcome

Therapy specifically targeting inferential confusion has been shown to enhance treatment outcome for those individuals with a high obsessional conviction (O'Connor *et al.*, 2004). In particular, such individuals benefit more from inference-based therapy than conventional cognitive-behavioral therapy. More recently, a study by Aardema *et al.* (2004c) found that changes in inferential confusion as measured by the Inferential Confusion Questionnaire were significantly related to treatment outcome in a sample of OCD patients receiving cognitive-behavioral therapy. Thus, it appears that changes in inferential confusion may be an important cognitive ingredient for treatment success for all of those undergoing cognitive-behavioral therapy. Thus, it appears that changes in inferential confusion may be an important cognitive ingredient for treatment success for all those undergoing cognitive-behavioural therapy even if PI is not specifically targeted in treatment. This is not entirely surprising, since conviction levels as measured by the primary inference have been proposed to operate independently from the severity of obsessive-compulsive symptoms, and largely comes into play when obsessional conviction is high and where primary inferences dictate subsequent reactions to the obsession in terms of secondary inferences and symptomatology.

Inferential confusion also appears to have unique relevance to obsessive-compulsive symptoms rather than being a general measure for treatment outcome, since change in inferential confusion is not associated with change in anxiety and depression during treatment. This is important, since the relationship of other cognitive measures with treatment outcome have been called into question with respect to their specificity in detecting change in obsessive compulsive symptoms, and changes in these measures may merely reflect changes in mood states (Emmelkamp, 2002).

Strength of obsessional conviction as measured by PI did not discriminate between non-responders and responders. This is not surprising, since this variable has been proposed to operate independently of obsessive-compulsive symptoms, but largely comes into play when obsessional conviction is high and where PI dictates subsequent reactions to the obsession in terms of SI (O'Connor *et al.*, 2004). As expected, SI did significantly discriminate between responders and non-responders.

It is questionable whether a one-dimensional measure as represented by conviction levels in PI sufficiently captures those with over-valued ideation. Also, the concept of over-valued ideation and insight is currently ill defined (Neziroglu & Stevens, 2002; Veale, 2002). However, the measurement of obsessional conviction in terms of PI has been found to be empirically meaningful in that those who have high obsessional conviction benefit more from an inference-based approach than standard cognitive-behavioral therapy (O'Connor *et al.*, 2004). Further research needs to establish the importance of this particular sub-aspect of over-valued ideation, or whether other dimensions of over-valued ideation are also important in terms of treatment outcome. Also, further refinement of the measurement of conviction levels in PI may be necessary, in particular with regard to the systematization of the obsessional belief by including measurements of PI both in and outside of the OCD situation. This may lead to more refined measurements as to the degree of ego-dystonic and ego-syntonic experience of obsessions.

So far, it appears the investigation of OCD from a non-phobic type of development benefits the identification of cognitive markers that play an important role in this disorder. In this respect, it is important to note that cognitive distortions and beliefs that focus on OCD from a phobic perspective by emphasizing the exaggerated interpretation of intrusive cognitions, have been faced with several difficulties with respect to their modest relationship with treatment outcome, and it has been suggested that changes in current measures of cognitive beliefs and appraisals may be epiphenomena of changes in mood states (Emmelkamp, 2002; Emmelkamp *et al.*, 2002). Such changes in cognition as artifacts of successful treatment may indicate a need to focus on cognitive measures, which are able to show differential relationships with treatment outcome variables rather than global indicators of successful treatment.

Inferential confusion appears to qualify as a cognitive characteristic in OCD that is able to show differential relationships in terms of treatment outcome. In particular, it is noteworthy that, in the study of Aardema *et al.* (2004a), changes in inferential confusion were not related to changes in anxiety and depression. Further research in this area is important, since cognitive measures that are able to show differential effects on treatment outcome rather than general indicators for successful treatment outcome represent the next evolution in the measurement of cognitive markers considered to be relevant to OCD.

CONCLUSION

The findings from the foregoing studies testing aspects of the inferential confusion model are supportive but not conclusive.

Phenomenologically speaking, obsessional preoccupations do take the form of an inference of doubt about a state of affairs, even if the doubts are accompanied by images, flashes and other ideas. Narratives justify the inferences with reference to remote events and associations that go against perceived information in the here and now. In effect, remote imagined possibilities are confused with reality, so leading to inferential confusion.

The initial doubt can be measured clinically as a primary inference. The probability accorded to the primary inference varies across clients and is distinct from the degree of conviction in secondary inferences and subsequent cognitive appraisals.

Inferential confusion can be operationalized in the form of an Inferential Confusion Questionnaire which shows excellent psychometric properties and distinguishes OCD from other anxiety groups but not DD. It also contributes variance to OCD symptom scales not explained by other cognitive domains.

People with OCD do show characteristic inductive reasoning styles and seem particularly susceptible to accord given possibilities greater credibility than non-OCD controls and other anxiety groups. They are more likely to modify confidence in an initial reasonable conclusion on the basis of further possibilities.

Finally, a therapy aimed at modifying primary inferences does reduce OCD symptomatology and does so as effectively as other cognitive behavioral approaches based on exposure and appraisal models. The IBA approach seems particularly useful for those people with high levels of obsessional conviction.

The exact relationship between experimental, psychometric and clinical indices of inferential confusion, as well as their relationship with types of OCD, remains to be clarified.

Final IBA Model

- People in general are influenced by the presence of alternative possibilities. So when faced with more possibilities, they are likely to doubt an initial decision more than when faced with fewer possibilities. This seems to support both Johnson-Laird's (1991) assertion that less possibilities make inferences easier, and the possibilistic model given earlier in Chapter 3.

- However, people with OCD seem more likely to doubt under conditions of increased possibility to the extent of not only changing their level of confidence but reversing their confidence in favor of alternative choices.

- This seems particularly potent when the reasoning involves OCD-related examples and alternatives are given to the person rather than self-generated.

- These findings are consistent with the clinical finding that people with OCD arrive at their primary obsessional inferences on the basis of inductive narratives.

- These narratives seem to generate a range of reasoning devices which cause the person to mix up near and remote events, misclassifying events from different categories, and transfer irrelevant facts inappropriately into the context here and now.

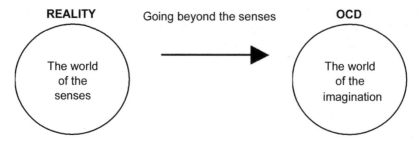

Figure 5.10   Going beyond the senses

- These narratives effectively convince the person that they must distrust their senses by constantly qualifying the factual premise of the senses with doubting inferences derived from the inductive narrative. In effect, this inductive narrative is purely subjective, the person crosses over from reality into the imagination (Figure 5.10).

- Effectively, the end point is inverse inference where the person invalidly accords a hypothetical possibility the status of a real probability. Inverse inference is an inductive illusion equivalent to the deductive illusions of reverse and converse inference in that all produce invalid conclusions.

- The doubting possibility is generated by the imagination which generates a pool of possible states, and possibility trumps the senses.

- This reliance on imagination in preference to certain sense information is operationalized and validated as a key characteristic of OCD versus anxiety but not delusional disorder. Thus suggesting that all belief disorders may contain elements of inferential confusion.

- The involvement of imagination explains how patients can become immersed in OCD, doubting possibilities to the extent of living-in the imagining, even while they are still grounded otherwise in reality. Imagination and perception are separate but complementary faculties.

- The thematic nature of the OCD is likely to relate the doubt to a wider self-doubt about being able to perform the action or task which elicits the OCD doubt. A strong investment in an OCD belief probably means a strong investment of the self in a related self-referent theme. This self-doubt is also imaginary and a product of inferential confusion.

The task of IBA therapy is hence to target inferential confusion by modifying the inference processes and hence narrative leading up to the primary inference.

CHAPTER 6

USING THE IBA TREATMENT MANUAL

INTRODUCTION TO TREATMENT

Following the evaluation process the therapist describes the general treatment model to the client using the information contained in the 'Overview of our Treatment Program for Obsessive-Compulsive Disorder', which is provided for comment to the client (Appendix 1). The main message to the client at this point is that the compulsions, anxiety and discomfort are driven by initial doubt. The person may locate the source of the problem in a particular feeling, compulsion or urge, but it is argued that these follow directly from the doubt. Use the diagrams in the treatment overview (p. 215) to explain the obsessional sequence. In addition, emphasis is made that this doubt comes about as the result of a certain type of reasoning behind the doubt. The doubt does not appear out of the blue, but it seems reasonable because it has a story of doubt behind it. The story goes against the senses and makes the person unsure, which leads the client to act upon the doubt as if it were real. The story has a personal theme plotline present throughout, and this theme accounts for why the person does not feel confident in certain OCD situations. After the basic tenets of the therapy model have been explained to the client, the therapist uses Box 6.1 to show how therapy will progress through the successive steps, addressing all the elements of the doubt. Any outright objections or questions should be dealt with (see p. 170).

At the end of the session, the collaborative nature of therapy is emphasized, as is the client's active participation during therapy through exercises to be carried out at home. The overview of treatment package is then given to the client. This may be read at home, and contains several exercises to be completed at home.

STEP-BY-STEP PROGRAM

Step 1 Obsessional and Normal Doubt

The therapist invites feedback from the client on the information given to the client in the session in order to establish adherence to the model. Any

Box 6.1 General outline of therapy

IBA Focus	Appraisal Focus
Obsessional → Primary ⇥ Secondary → Appraisals → Further	
Doubt Inference Inference Coping	
Appraisals	
↑ ↑	
Narrative Construction Assumptions	
↑ ↑	
Reasoning Devices Schema	
↑	
Self-Theme	
↑	
Distrust of Self	

difficulties with filling in the diagrams and open-ended questions of the overview package are addressed. Common difficulties usually revolve around difficulties conceptualizing the obsessional preoccupation in the form of a particular doubt. To identify the doubts, the therapist and client need to keep in mind that the presence of a neutralization or ritual *always* implies the person's attempts to change *something*. The presence of a compulsion, or any covert type of neutralization, implies that the person must have come to the conclusion that there is something not quite right, and this can always be traced back to a doubt. For example, the client preoccupied with contamination infers they may be contaminated, and further questioning generally quickly reveals the primary doubt that precedes the preoccupation with contamination such as 'there might be germs on the doorknob' or 'the person seemed dirty'. In most cases, obsessional preoccupation can be simplified tremendously by tracing it back to a few single doubts, and it is important to convey this notion to the client. As overwhelming, detailed, and intricate as the OCD may seem to the client, usually there are only a few doubts by which most of the obsessional preoccupation stands or falls. The consequences of the primary inference can often be used as a springboard to trace back to the primary inference by using a logical template of the form 'if...then'. For example: 'If my hat blows off in the wind, *then* I will be exposed to ridicule.' Here, in logic, the first clause after *if* is the primary inference, the clauses after *then* are the secondary inferences (or corollary). If the primary inference is not clear, it is possible to work back from the consequences and ask: 'And what will happen if what state of affairs is [true], or [happens]?' So in the following example, the client spontaneously volunteers a consequence to the therapist (O'Connor & Robillard, 1999):

(C):   If I don't check the cooker, the house will burn down.
(T):   And the house will burn down if what state of affairs is true?
(C):   Well, if the cooker is left on and catches alight.
(T):   So you are checking the cooker for what?
(C):   Well, to make sure the plates are not left on. Of course, I know they aren't really, but I just want to be sure.
(T):   So, when you go to check, precisely what thought comes into your head?
(C):   That the plates may still be on.

The primary inference in this instance is *'The plates may still be on'* followed by the secondary inference *'(Then) the cooker will catch alight and burn the house.'*

Once the main obsessional doubts have been identified, the client should be able to fluently recount the obsessional sequence as described in diagram 3 of the information package (p. 218), including the trigger for the doubt, the doubt itself, its emotional consequences, and compulsive behaviors. It is important that the client realizes that without the initial doubt he/she would experience no discomfort nor would feel the need to engage in compulsive behaviors. For example, the person who thinks 'maybe the stove is still on' may focus on the consequence that if the stove is still on, the house may catch fire. However, without the initial doubt about whether the stove is still on, the person would feel no need to check the stove nor worry about a subsequent fire. Thus, doubt is the source of the problem and without the initial doubt, there would be no consequences or rituals. Likewise, if a person did not doubt whether his/her hands are clean, then there would be no further consequences of any form. The person would not feel discomfort, nor any need to take corrective measures through washing.

The therapist continues to explore with the client the primacy of its nature as obsessional doubt compared to normal doubts, as described in Worksheet 1 (pp. 228–229). The therapist gives a quick résumé of the worksheet after which the client can pick a non-obsessional doubt that has recently occurred to him/her, and comparisons can be made with the obsessional doubt. An important aspect of this difference between normal and obsessional doubts that needs to be highlighted is the context in which obsessional doubts occur as compared to normal doubts. Normal doubts occur in an appropriate context and/or with sense information that provides some justification for the doubt. Obsessional doubts always occur without such direct information. Of course, there are triggers for the doubt (for example, seeing a stove), but there was no sense information that supported the obsessional doubt.

After the identification of the major differences between obsessional and normal doubts, the therapist highlights the sensory certainty present before the occurrence of the doubt. In other words, sense information already provided certainty regarding a state of affairs in reality before the doubt arose. For example, the person has just locked the door and sees the door is locked. The trick of the OCD is to infuse doubt in this situation even though the senses tell the person all is fine. The obsessional doubt may be so pervasive that the person is never aware of this moment of certainty before the doubt, in which case, this phenomenon can be rephrased as 'the certainty exists with the senses'. In other words, all the doubt takes the client away from certainty, and makes the person cross over into doubt. Once the person has crossed over into doubt, any attempts to obtain certainty will be counter-productive, unless the person returns to the certainty of the senses. Clearly, the aim here is to help the person to start distancing him/herself from the doubt as a valid doubt, but rather than expecting the client to find a resolution to his/her obsessions, the therapist should maintain a non-confrontational approach. In other words, the obsessions are not 'challenged', since even querying whether the doubt should be considered could already mark the start of the OCD. Once the person has embarked on querying the obsession, it is difficult 'to think one's way out'. In fact, the client is discouraged from trying to 'solve' or analyse the OCD and take this information too far in terms of its *implications* for the obsessional doubt.

At the end of the session the accompanying worksheet for this first stage of therapy is handed out to the client, accompanied by an exercise sheet to reinforce what has been learned (see Appendix 1). Also, the client is given a training card with the most important learning points and exercises to be carried out several times per day. These exercises are intended to help the

Box 6.2

Criteria for progressing to the next stage

Client is aware that:
    (a) the obsession begins with doubt;
    (b) doubt is the start of the obsessional chain;
    (c) he/she crosses over from certainty to doubt;
    (d) compulsions and appraisals follow from the doubt;
    (e) obsessional doubt differs from normal doubt.

client make a start in changing his/her approach towards the obsessions and become more aware of the source of the problem instead of getting caught up in the emotional consequences. At the same time, the client is learning to identify differences in the way that normal and obsessional doubts come about, which will form a springboard for future sessions. The therapist may wish to discuss with the client a practice schedule during the day.

Step 2   The 'Logic' of OCD

The main goal of the next stage of therapy is to familiarize the client with his/her reasoning behind the doubt. This should be carried out in an exploratory fashion without neccesarily identifying the justification behind the doubt as the *cause* of the problem. In fact, it is emphasized to the client that the justification can appear quite logical. The main reason for this apparent 'logicity' behind the obsessional doubt is that the arguments supporting the doubt are not necessarily incorrect in isolation from the context in which they occur ('People do die from infections', 'There is always the possibility of doors being left open'). In other words, it is often not the content but the context of the justification which renders the doubt 'illogical'. Emphasizing to the client that the justification behind the doubt often presents itself in a logical fashion avoids unhelpful debates between the client and therapist regarding the justification behind the obsessional doubts. Moreover, it removes the client from the assumption that the obsession can be resolved through internal dialogue by recounting arguments for and against whether or not the doubt is valid. Thus, it puts the client and the therapist on the same footing in that it raises the question: *if* the justification behind the obsessional doubt presents itself in a credible fashion, then *what is* the source of the problem? Up till now, this issue has not yet been addressed, except that the client can already be made aware that it is not the particular content of the justification behind the obsessional doubt that is important here, but, rather, its relevance and that there are some peculiarities that have to do with reasoning *processes* that bring about obsessional doubts.

Of course, at times, the client may already be aware of some of the peculiarities in the reasoning *process* behind the obsession, in particular with respect to several category errors that may be evident in the rationale (e.g. the client may be aware that he/she is jumping to conclusions). However, identification of the reasoning behind the primary doubt functions to help the client become familiar with the idea that obsessions do not come out of the blue, but have a certain type of misguided rationale behind them. Also, there appears to be some clinical evidence that an awareness of the reasoning behind the obsessions has an immediate positive effect on the reality value of the obsession for those clients with over-valued ideation where the doubt is a taken-for-granted reality. A partial realization by the client that the obsession is not completely factual, but, at least in part, originates from him/herself, can already have beneficial consequences for these clients.

In order to illuminate the reasoning behind the doubt the client is invited to generate reasons as to why his/her doubt might be valid. The use of the categories as provided on the accompanying worksheet (Worksheet 2) may help facilitate this process by assigning the reasons within the categories 'authority', 'common knowledge', 'hearsay', 'previous experience' and 'logical calculation'. In addition, the client is invited to repeat the same exercise with an obsessional doubt that is neutral to him/her. Thus, the point can be made that all obsessions contain a certain reasoning, and that the client's doubts are no different from other people's obsessional doubts.

At the end of the session the client is asked to complete the exercise sheet using the information in the worksheet, as well as to familiarize him/herself with the reasoning behind the obsessional doubt through the use of the training card. In addition, the client is asked to think about how the reasoning behind their obsessional doubts makes these doubts different from normal doubts.

Box 6.3

Criteria for progressing to the next stage

Client is aware that: (a) doubt does not appear out of the blue;
(b) there is always a justification behind the doubt;
(c) the justification behind the doubt *seems* very logical.

Step 3   OCD Doubt is 100% Irrelevant to the Here and Now

The most important element in therapy is to establish with the client the imaginary status of the doubt. When we use the word 'imaginary', we mean the realm of subjectively generated possibility, which goes against the senses and perceptual data. That is, the doubt and the justification behind it arise 100% subjectively, while the client continues to treat the doubt as an objective plausible probability. This is the essence of the inferential confusion process where the person confuses an imagined possibility

with a probability based in the senses. T............................... n
introducing the idea that the obsessional .... ıe
basis of imaginary criteria and not from c .... ıe
here and now, but often, the implicat....... .. ..y
understood. The client might argue: 'Yes, I realize it's imaginary, but it is possible.'

Of course, a lot of things are possible. Stoves are indeed left on, and fires do start as a result. Doorknobs sometimes do have germs on them, and people do get sick. It would be hard to argue against this, and the therapist is wise not to do so if he or she doesn't want to lose credibility. However, the term 'imagined' does not refer to *impossibility*, but instead, it highlights the 100% lack of sense data in the *here and now* that could possibly justify the obsessional inference, and, in the absence of sense data, the obsessional doubt is completely arbitrary and irrelevant to the situation at hand in spite of its 'possibility'. In other words, IBA does not rely on convincing the client of the unlikelihood of the obsessional inference (whether 0.01%, 0.001%, or 0.0001%), but proposes its irrelevance to the situation in which the obsession arises. If the client continues to focus on the fact that the doubt is possible, it could be argued by the therapist that just because something is possible does not explain why the client has OCD. It does not explain the particular preoccupation of the client, since the therapist would readily agree that the doubt may be possible, yet it does not cause him or her any problems. Thus, obsessional doubts are possible, but accepting the mere possibility of something bad happening never caused anyone to have OCD. It can be shown to the client that he/she believes many other harmful things to be possible yet the client does not obsess about these things.

The main criterion for progressing to the next stage is a recognition on the part of the client that the doubt originates from him/her rather than from the senses. If the client at this stage in therapy does not agree that the imaginary status of the doubt renders it arbitrary or irrelevant, the therapist can still progress to the next stage of therapy as long as the client agrees the doubt originates from within rather than from the outside.

Box 6.4

Criteria for progressing to the next stage

Client is aware that: (a) the doubt originates from within rather than outside;
(b) the reasoning behind the doubt is 100% subjective in the here and now.

Step 4   The Narrative

The next step in therapy is geared towards highlighting the power of the imagination, and explaining how the obsessional doubt obtains its strength and reality value from a convincing story which leads the person logically to the doubt. The isolation of primary and secondary inferences provides a systematic unit for evaluating treatment progress. In practice, however, the power of the primary inference only makes sense in relation to the narrative context around it. The narrative provides the internal monologue behind the primary inference and endows the primary inference with a reality value. The therapist should already have identified several elements in the narrative from previous discussions with the client (i.e. the justification behind the obsessional doubt), but care must be taken to identify genuine elements behind the obsessional doubt, and not solely those that have been primed in the context of an exercise.

Questions like 'What makes you think your hands are dirty?' or 'Why do you think the door could have been left unlocked?' often quickly reveal the narrative behind the doubt. Sometimes the story is volunteered spontaneously (O'Connor & Robillard, 1999).

The following narrative is from a woman convinced for several years that her house was contaminated by urine:

> I use the toilet at work and as I am wiping myself, I feel that my fingers are wet. I conclude that I have urine on my fingers (on the side of my index finger). I wipe my finger with more toilet paper. Since there are no washbowls, I cannot wash my hands and the urine stays on my finger all day. For me, if something is there, it stays there until you wash it. I arrange it so I don't touch things at work with my index finger to avoid contaminating things. If I touch something with that finger, a part of what is on my finger will find itself on that particular object. When I get home, I open the patio door with both my hands while trying to avoid touching the door with that part of my finger that touched urine. If that part touches the door, a part of the urine on my finger will find itself on the door. What is on the door stays on the door because I have not washed my finger. The next day, I suddenly realise that other people have touched the door. So now they have urine on their fingers. Because those people touched objects in my home, there is urine here and there in my home.

After the obsessional narrative has been identified by the therapist, it can be read out to the client in its entirety, and comments from the client are invited. Next, the therapist introduces the client to an alternative non-obsessional story phrased in opposition to the obsessional story and doubt. This should be introduced to the client as merely an attempt to come up with an alternative rather than to cognitively challenge or attempt to 'disprove' the obsessional story. The basic requirement for the alternative story is that the story is *in line* with the senses although differences between both stories are generally not yet addressed in detail at this point. Thus, the non-obsessional story may contain a lot of subjective, even imaginary, information as long as it is meaningful and it does not conflict with the senses. Once again, after the non-obsessional story has been established, the therapist reads it out aloud to the client and invites comments. It should be kept in mind that both stories are likely to be in short-hand form at this point, to be filled in with more and more details in the course of therapy.

In the case of the woman above, an alternative narrative is:

> When I wiped myself with toilet paper, I removed the bit of urine I had on my fingers. If I wipe water on the counter, I trust my senses in order to know if there is still water or not (by looking or by touching). I have no reason to behave otherwise with urine. If I have cola on my fingers, it is the sticky sensation that will indicate if there is more. If I don't feel anything or see anything, then I will believe that there is nothing on my hands. The fact that I consider urine dirty is not proof that I have some on my fingers but simply a way of removing myself from my senses. When I feel dirty, it is simply because of things I imagine, so the fact that I feel dirty is not proof that I am dirty. Even if I had urine on my fingers, it must have evaporated during the day, since it was not long after that I didn't feel it on my fingers anymore. If I wash my hands and do not wipe them afterwards, water will end up evaporating by itself and I will feel nothing on my hands. There is no reason for this to be different for urine. It is also possible that the urine dries up. When something is dry, it becomes impossible to transmit it from one thing to another.

Next, the therapist contrasts both stories with a simple question to the client. The therapist asks the client whether he/she agrees with the idea that both stories are equally plausible. Usually, the client will agree that both stories are equally possible. Sometimes the client will remark that he/she finds the obsessional story more convincing, which should come as no surprise, but the question pertains to both stories being equally plausible. Hence, the client should agree that there is no basis in reason to assume that the obsessional story is any more valid than the non-obsessional story.

The therapist then explains why the obsessional doubt has such an impact on the client while referring to the particular way we all are absorbed in certain types of ideas based on the stories we tell ourselves. Basically, the obsessional story is a very good story that leads the person to quickly doubt or dismiss any alternative stories. One of the ways to lessen the strength of the obsessional story and the ensuing doubt is to actively engage in alternatives. The engagement is not an intellectual process where the non-obsessional story is contrasted hypothetically with the obsessional story, but by an engagement in the non-obsessional story 'as if' it were the only reality. Obviously, the non-OCD story cannot start to function as another cognitive ritual in the OCD situations.

As emphasized in the exercise sheet for the client (pp. 245–246), the therapist addresses the importance of the active engagement of the client in developing the alternative story. The alternative story is something that the client will work on throughout therapy, and it will be up to the client to make this story as real as possible as an exercise of the imagination rather than an intellectual exercise. Clearly, according to IBA the obsessional story is wrong, since it is not grounded in the senses, and consists of several reasoning devices that lead the person to go beyond the senses. However, these aspects of the obsessional story are only addressed in subsequent stages of the therapy.

Criteria for proceeding to the next stage depend on the individual client. For example, some clients prefer to leave the obsessional story and its characteristics behind for a while, and solely focus on developing and exploring the alternative narrative. Others may prefer to continue to rehearse the alternative narrative while at the same time working on deconstructing the obsessional narrative. How to proceed can be discussed with the client, but in general it is often best to allow the client to work on the alternative story for a couple of sessions until he/she feels the alternative story is starting to get into shape. The ultimate goal is to create a truly convincing non-OCD story that can be lived as real by the OCD client.

As the non-OCD story starts to get into shape, there may be some OCD situations that the client is able to go into without engaging in compulsive rituals. However, our advice to the client is to only practice the non-obsessional story outside of OCD situations, and once the client is progressing, to only invoke the non-obsessional story in OCD situations when the client is relatively certain that the non-obsessional story is able to over-ride the obsessional story rather than the opposite.

Use the accompanying worksheet, exercise sheet and training card as part of step 4 (pp. 243–247).

Step 5   Crossing Over

Crossing over refers to the idea that people with OCD leave reality behind as soon as they engage in obsessional doubt. People sometimes identify this as being in the OCD 'bubble' or 'circle'. In other words, they enter unreality on the basis of a purely subjective narrative that has nothing to with the here and now. This cross-over point can be identified, as it is initiated by thoughts that lead the client away from reality and remove themselves from

Box 6.5

Criteria for progressing to the next stage

Client is aware that:
    (a) the obsessional story is as plausible as the non-obsessional story with regard to the rationale behind them;

    (b) engaging in the non-obsessional story should be carried out without continually contrasting it rationally with the obsessional story;

    (c) trying to 'solve' the OCD by finding the 'right' story is not the way to go. Rather, the solution is to be able to live an alternative story as real.

---

what they can actually see or sense. Often this cross-over point can be identified by thoughts that take the client beyond the senses such as 'I see it's clean, but maybe . . .'. Crossing over into the imagination may sometimes be accompanied by varying degrees of derealization and a mild perceptual disturbance when the person removes him/herself from the senses.

The goal is to help the client create distance from the obsession by learning to identify this cross-over point, through the completion of several exercises that create a moment of reflection in the OCD sequence. This includes identification of the thoughts or narrative that initially take the client beyond the senses, to hold still without acting upon the doubt in between reality and non-reality, and reflect on the certainty that was already available before the OCD took hold. During the session the therapist should help the client identify the thoughts and sensations that lead him/her to cross over in order for the client to be able to become aware in detail of the inferential confusion process. Next, the therapist tries to determine the exact point at which the client will have difficulty returning to the world of the senses, which usually occurs at the exact moment the person starts to distrust the senses and starts to feel an urge to engage in the compulsive behaviors. The therapist has to explain to the client that compulsive behaviors will not provide a resolution, since they have come forth from an imaginary doubt, and thus all compulsive behaviors are no more than attempts to change an imaginary reality. This can be likened metaphorically to an attempt to manipulate events in a movie by touching the movie screen when, in fact, the film must be changed. There will be no effect since the doubt was imaginary to begin with. In fact, performing the compulsive behaviors will only reinforce the notion that there is a problem in reality, since the person acts 'as if' the problem exists in reality and the person will find it more and more difficult to return to the world of the senses. Finally, the therapist practices the exercise with the client as described on the exercise sheet (pp. 250–251). The training card contains the same exercise to be completed at home. Remind the client to continue with developing the non-OCD story, to be practiced daily in non-obsessional situations.

Box 6.6

Criteria for progressing to the next stage

Client is aware that: (a) they have crossed over into the OCD doubt as soon as they yield to the initial doubt;
(b) OCD takes them away from reality – not further into it.

Step 6   The Reasoning 'Devices' of OCD: Part I

The reasoning devices that lead up to obsessional doubt should be understood as particular process characteristics operating in OCD that are challenged on the basis of irrelevance to the OCD situation rather than on the basis of their content. In other words, the therapist does not challenge specific beliefs or thoughts that are contained in the narrative leading up to the obsessional doubt, but instead attempts to convey to the client how the reasoning devices of the OCD which are part of the narrative make an unreal doubt experienced as though it were a real doubt. In other words, if the OCD story is generated purely subjectively and in contradiction or in the absence of sense information, it is not relevant to the OCD situation. The particular rhetorical elements that lead the person to believe that the OCD stories actually do not have something to do with reality in the here and now and can be subdivided into several reasoning devices leading to inferential confusion and to confusing an imaginary reality with a real probability based in the senses. Worksheet 6 (pp. 253–254) contains the most common reasoning devices that lead the person to consider the obsession to be a realistic probability.

During the session, the therapist explains with examples the most common reasoning devices and how they lead to inferential confusion. Generally, it is advisable to first use an OCD story that is neutral to the client since it is less likely to provoke 'buts' and 'what ifs' from the client. Afterwards, the therapist can show how some of these reasoning devices also apply to the client's story. If there are objections, it is important to view these objections as an opportunity rather than label them as argumentative, controlling, or as a 'need for certainty' on the part of the client. OCD requires only the smallest percentage of doubt to persist, and the inferential confusion model attempts to provide OCD clients with a complete resolution of the obsessional doubt in the sense that all questions and objections from the client need to be answered and addressed for the client to find such a resolution. A partial agreement as to the imaginary nature of the doubt and its justification will invariably still leave room for the OCD to operate. However, the main aim at this stage in therapy is for the client to identify the most common reasoning devices behind the obsessional doubt. Any 'buts' and 'what ifs' usually relate to one of these devices, which render the person unable to find resolution to the obsessional doubt. The exercise sheet and training card are meant to resolve any further lingering questions from the client when he/she attempts to identify the reasoning devices operating behind the obsessional doubt.

Box 6.7

Criteria for progressing to the next stage

Client is aware that: (a) reasoning devices maintain credibility in the OCD narrative;

(b) personally relevant reasoning devices can be identified.

Step 7   The Reasoning 'Devices' of OCD: Part II

The second part of addressing the reasoning devices emphasizes the implications of the reasoning devices. That is, the reasoning devices render the obsessional doubt unfounded. Although the person may readily agree with the therapist as to the subjective nature of the obsessional story, the person has yet to come to a full realization of the implications. Therefore, it is important that the therapist discusses any questions raised by the exercises of the previous steps. It is possible that the client might say: 'I know it's all senseless, but I still doubt.' However, this type of response should warn the therapist that the client only has a partial understanding of the inferential confusion process, and indicates the client still has some objections to the model. If the client is less than forthcoming with objections, the client can be invited to act 'as if' speaking for the OCD. The therapist describes an obsessional situation and the obsessional doubt, and then using the model shows why the obsessional doubt is unfounded. The therapist then asks the person what the OCD would say is wrong with this argument. Usually, some type of reasoning device will surface that has been overlooked, or it will become clear the person only has a partial understanding of the reasoning devices operating in OCD.

The therapist may continue to the next stage if the doubt still has an impact on the person, but the person should at least intellectually agree that the obsessional doubt is wrong, and all arguments against that idea should have been identified and addressed.

Box 6.8

Criteria for progressing to the next stage

Client is aware that: (a) the reasoning devices render the OCD doubt invalid;

(b) even if the person *feels* the OCD doubt is valid *intellectually*, they should be certain it is not valid.

Step 8   The Selective Nature of the Doubt

Recognizing the selective nature of the doubt builds upon previous arguments against treating obsessional doubts as normal doubts, and is geared towards diminishing the reality value attached to the obsessional doubt by the client. If the client can become increasingly aware of other situations where he/she adopts a 'normal' type of reasoning, this will highlight the irrelevance of obsessional doubts in the situations where they occur. The selectivity also leads to realization of the thematic nature of the obsession where personal themes, and not reality, dictate the OCD.

The therapist introduces the client to the selectivity of the obsessional doubt by exploring situations where he/she does not experience doubts. There should be quite a few situations where the person does not experience any obsessional doubts, and it can be pointed out to the client that in most areas of his/her life there are no obsessional doubts. Clients may find this a trivial observation, but the therapist should point out that this is important, since there is no difference between obsessional situations and the situations where the client experiences no obsessional doubts. If there are indeed no differences, then why treat the obsessional situation any differently?

The client and the therapist proceed to look closely at a situation where the client experiences no problem. A good example where few OCD patients have doubts (although not invariably) is crossing the street. What does the client do differently in that situation as compared to the obsessional situation? The answer obviously is the use and trust of the senses in those situations, whereas the obsessional reasoning bypasses the senses. Next, the client is invited to describe his/her obsessional situation as if it were like crossing the street where the person trusts the senses (looking left and right; seeing no traffic; crossing the street).

During the session the client may come up with reasons why the obsessional situation is different. For example, he/she may argue that germs are invisible whereas seeing cars is not. It should be pointed out that these arguments form part of the reasoning devices of the OCD, and, in fact, can also be applied to the example of crossing the street. For example, even if you don't see a car, an OCD narrative can always justify that there is a car by applying the same kind of reasoning ('a car may turn the corner suddenly' or 'I heard of a person who was blinded by the sunlight'). The therapist may have to backtrack to the inferential confusion process and reasoning devices of the OCD to make these points, but it can be a very helpful exercise, since if applied correctly, and if the client understands the argument, the selectivity of obsessional doubt very clearly illuminates the inferential confusion process and how the reasoning devices of the OCD bypass the senses in the here and now.

In preparation for the exercise sheet, the therapist and client together choose a situation that is neutral for the client. Next, the client will be asked to create a doubt in this situation by going beyond the senses. In other words, the client is asked to write an obsessional story different from his/her own. The client's own obsessional doubts should not be part of this story, although they will of course share the same type of reasoning devices

Box 6.9

Criteria for progressing to the next stage

Client is aware that: (a) obsessional doubt is selective reasoning;
(b) the client reasons differently in non-OCD situations;
(c) the difference lies in the use of the senses in non-OCD situations and the use of OCD reasoning devices in OCD situations.

as the OCD. In the next session this exercise is addressed, and the client often will readily volunteer that the story is flawed. Next, the therapist should point out that the neutral story is no different from the client's own story, and so why continue to treat obsessional situations differently if the reasoning behind them is flawed? The training card contains similar exercises to reinforce the notion of selective reasoning in obsessional situations (p. 267).

Step 9   The Vulnerable Self-Theme in Obsessional Stories

In addressing the vulnerable self-theme the therapist attempts to delve deeper into the selective nature of the obsessional doubt. Why does the person with OCD experience doubts in one area, but not in others? Often, there appears to be a self-referent theme running through the narratives behind obsessional doubts which renders the person vulnerable to particular types of obsessions. It is as yet unclear whether these self-themes are causal factors in the development of OCD, especially since personal investment in specific areas of life do not invariably seem to lead to OCD. However, problems may arise if these self-referent themes lead to imaginary doubts due to ambivalent self-identity, perhaps due to their interaction with inferential confusion.

The self-referent theme can be pursued initially through logic, where the doubt is linked to the person's self-view. For example, if the person has obsessions about contamination, then he/she must consider him/herself as a person who could be contaminated. Or, if the person has blasphemous obsessions, or engages in frequent attempts not to have blasphemous obsessions, he/she must consider him/herself to be a person who could be a blasphemer. Thus, the self-referent nature of the doubt provides the first step in identifying the self-theme. It should be noted that this self-theme in one way or another is often linked to 'doing'. That is, the person feels he or she has to do more than necessary in this area of his/her life. In a sense, the self-theme functions as a self-doubt in that the person feels that they might be, for example, 'careless', and so act to prevent this through precautions.

After the main elements that make up the self-referent theme have been identified the therapist explores with the client how the theme links up with the client's obsessional theme, and whether this self-referent theme is really founded in reality. Next, an alternative, more reality-based, self-view is explored together with the client.

In the course of the week the client is required to write out both the reasons as to why he/she feels the self-referent obsessional theme is correct, and in addition, write out the reasons why it may be at variance with established biographical fact. In this way the client establishes whether perhaps a different view of him/herself would be more realistic and appropriate, and so repositions him/herself with regard to the self-doubt.

Box 6.10

Criteria for progressing to the next stage

Client is aware that: (a) his/her self-referent theme creates a vulnerability to certain types of obsessions;
(b) the difference lies in the use of the senses in non-OCD situations and use of OCD reasoning devices in OCD situations.

Step 10   Reality Sensing – Tolerating the Void

The last stage of therapy consists of training the client in the proper trust of the senses in obsessional situations. The particular way the client uses the senses in obsessional situations should be explored in detail, and often one will find several self-perpetuating strategies in this area. Due to the nature of inferential confusion, it is not uncommon for OCD clients to take no note whatsoever of the senses, since the OCD has rendered the senses irrelevant. At other times, using the senses may consist of 'staring' or 'looking very hard', which in effect is the opposite of using the senses normally, but rather signifies distrust of the senses by going beyond normal sensing. Next, the therapist educates the client in the proper use of the senses. It may help to compare the proper use of the senses to a non-obsessional situation for the client to get a feel for what it means to use the senses in obsessional situations. Even the client reminding him/herself to use the senses implies a distrust of the senses.

The therapist proceeds to question the client on what it would feel like if the client used the senses in a normal way. Often, the answer will consist of the client feeling he/she has not done enough. This feeling should be explained in terms of the client having invested a lot of effort in OCD situations for so long that he/she will now feel that using the senses is insufficient. Typically, using the senses will feel sloppy or inadequate to the person with OCD. In other words, trusting the senses leaves a void as if the client is forgetting something, not doing enough, or not giving the situation proper attention. It should be explained to the client that this feeling is temporary, and that by his/her learning how to use and trust the senses again, this feeling will disappear over time.

The therapist continues to explain that the coming sessions will consist of reinforcing the natural use of the senses, and will address any problem areas that come up in the meantime. The client is asked to use the senses in some OCD situations, and act on the information he/she receives from the senses. The goal is to feel as little as possible anxiety or discomfort in these situations using the strategies of previous exercises by keeping the OCD story and initial doubt at bay. Generally, entering OCD situations where the client will be overwhelmed by the OCD should be discouraged; rather, choose situations which the client can handle and where the confidence of the client can gradually increase. The exercise sheet contains the different steps the client can use to reinforce non-obsessional thinking and behavior in OCD situations (pp. 270–271).

Future sessions include discussion of these exercises, and address any problems that arise. It may be necessary to reinforce or repeat certain exercises and worksheets in this process. At the same time, there may be other obsessions that have not yet been addressed. Depending on the degree of generalization across obsession in the course of treatment so far, it may be necessary to repeat the entire cycle of therapy, or parts thereof, while going through the different stages of treatment for these other obsessions. The length of therapy varies from client to client, ranging from as few as 8–12 therapy sessions to a slow progression through the various stages taking up an entire year of weekly meetings.

COMMON QUERIES FROM CLIENTS

The following queries and statements often arise in the course of treatment.

What is meant exactly by direct information or evidence for the doubt?

There are usually all kinds of triggers outside you that may provoke an obsessional doubt. So obviously, there is information around you when you doubt. For example, you may just leave the house, see the door, and then doubt whether the door has been locked properly. However, what is meant by no direct information or evidence for the doubt is that there is no information in reality around you that supports the obsessional doubt. For example, while locking the door, you may sense or feel something out of the ordinary, like not being able to turn the key as far as usual. In that case, there is specific direct information or evidence for a doubt such as 'The door may not have been locked properly.' Obviously, this information is not conclusive, but it is sufficient to call the doubt a normal doubt. Obsessional doubts, however, occur without this type of information or evidence, and this is an important aspect of being able to tell the difference between obsessional and normal doubt.

I never really have certainty before the doubt occurs. I doubt all the time. So where is this certainty before the doubt?

There is some variation among people with OCD as to how generalized their doubt is. Some people only doubt in particular situations they encounter during the day, and in calmer moments wonder why they were so upset, or started to doubt anything at all. Others have doubts that persist all day, and continue to experience the doubt as a valid concern, no matter what situation they are in. In those cases, the certainty may not be apparent, but there is always certainty 'before' the doubt, which exists in that your senses have told you by default that everything is okay.

I do not doubt. I am certain that my obsessional concerns are real.

Sometimes people with OCD are convinced that their particular obsessional concerns are the only possibility that exists. Then it seems as if there is no doubt. For example, you may be utterly convinced that there are dangerous germs on your hands, or that you do have a serious illness. However, what you are not certain of is the opposite of your own concern, and this is the kind of doubt we are talking about (that there are no dangerous germs, and that you are healthy). So, instead of saying that you do not doubt, it would be more accurate to say that you doubt so much, that you are certain of your doubt.

My doubts are more like a feeling. There is no particular thought going through my mind.

The OCD cycle can become automatic, with thought becoming lost in feelings, which makes it seem there are no thoughts related to your compulsions or discomfort. However, behind this OCD feeling there always is a doubt. You can ask yourself a series of questions to uncover the doubt. First, ask yourself: 'What would happen if I did not carry out the ritual?' This question usually uncovers the first layer of thoughts that have to do with your primary doubt. However, continue to trace these thoughts back to the primary doubt. For example, with washing compulsions, the immediate concern might be that you will be contaminated, or for checking compulsions you may have thoughts like 'the house will burn down if I don't check'. Ask yourself 'How will I be contaminated?' or 'How will the house burn down?' The answer might be something like: 'The doorknob might be dirty' or 'I might have left the stove on.' These are so-called primary doubts that give rise to everything else. Without them, you would feel no need to check or wash. Remember, your therapist can help you in identifying your primary doubts.

My doubts seem to come out of the blue. I do not think about anything in particular, and they suddenly appear. So are my doubts different from those of other people with OCD?

It's not uncommon that there appear to be no immediate thoughts associated with the doubt. For example, think about driving. As you learned how to drive, every action required a particular thought. Look in the mirror, change the gear, accelerate, brake, etc. As you became more practiced, these actions no longer required any conscious thought. OCD is no different, where with continued practice, your rituals, and even doubts, no longer seem to require any justification, since they have become largely automatic. However, that does not mean that there was no justification initially. More importantly, you can still trace the justification behind these doubts with some creativity. Act as if the doubts you wrote down are someone else's. Then, try to imagine the justification this 'other person' could have for such doubts.

My doubts are totally senseless. I can't think of any justification for them.

Obsessional doubts often appear 'unreasonable' even to the person experiencing them. However, do you feel the same way inside the situation where you doubt? Most people with OCD find their doubts absurd, yet feel differently inside the situation where the obsessional doubt occurs when, suddenly, there are all kinds of thoughts that seem to support the doubt. So try to go back to the last time that you had an obsessional doubt, and how you justified it back then.

Isn't my doubt possible even if the chances of it being true are very small?

A lot of things are possible, but in no way does that account for your OCD. Let's say, for example, that you doubt whether or not there is a dog sitting behind you right now. It is easy to come up with all sorts of ideas and facts that could support the doubt ('Dogs do exist', 'I have heard of dogs entering neighbors' houses', 'It is always possible', etc.). However, you do not doubt that there is in fact no dog behind you. The doubt doesn't even enter your mind, and even though you may consider it to be possible, you very quickly dismiss this doubt as a very arbitrary and irrelevant doubt. So we are not arguing that the doubt is impossible, but what we argue is that the doubt is *irrelevant* to reality in the here and now.

If you truly believe that the obsessional doubt is not relevant, then the doubt will not even occur, in very much the same way that you don't consider worrying about dogs behind you now to be relevant, even though you have conjured up the possibility in your mind. And the fact of the matter is that obsessional doubts are not really different from the above example. However, OCD has a great number of tricks up its sleeve to make it seem as if obsessional doubts are different, and actually do have something to do with reality around you. However, if you look closely, you will always find that obsessional doubt occurs without direct evidence in the here and now. There is nothing in reality around you to support the doubt. Since there is nothing around you, not even 0.0001%, the doubt can only be 100% imaginary.

So my doubts are simply imaginary? It's all in my imagination?

The word 'imagination' is sometimes used in this kind of dismissive way where it refers to things like: 'It's just your imagination', 'You're imagining things', or 'You're making up things.' However, imagination is much more than that, and in no way do we use the word 'imagination' dismissively. In fact, it is a faculty similar to other faculties like perception. In other words, we all rely on our imagination to make sense of the world around us, and it can help us to perceive better, particularly in ambiguous situations. As shown in Worksheet 3 (Figure 1), the imagination is an important part of having normal doubts, and plays a role in how we come to believe in things generally. The difference for people with OCD is that there is a confusion, which makes it seem as if the doubt has something to do with reality or perception, while in fact the obsessional doubt is in no way related to the world around you. In other words, there is no overlap between perception and imagination, and the two faculties operate independently of each other (see Worksheet 3, Figure 2). This is a rather more complicated process than simply saying, 'It's all in your imagination.'

How can my doubt be 100% irrelevant if I can justify it with all kinds of facts that come from reality?

The OCD story can contain elements that originate in reality, but as we said earlier, it has come about on a purely imaginary basis in that there is nothing in the here and now to support the obsessional doubt. Of course, there may be all kinds of facts 'wheeled' into the story that make the doubt seem more plausible and probable. However, you will need to ask yourself whether these facts serve reality or whether they serve your imagination. If the doubt was provoked by nothing that was actually around you that supported the doubt, then how do these facts have anything to do with reality? In other words, the facts have become part of a 100% imaginary process. Remember, no one ever got OCD from the fact that something is possible, or that it has happened before to someone else. People with contamination concerns, for example, will frequently cite the existence of SARS as a 'fact' supporting their concern. But neither SARS nor any real event elicited their OCD; rather, such facts are produced to confirm the already existing fear. These facts or possibilities are merely rhetorical devices by which you come to feel your doubt as real. They are rhetorical, because you apply them in a situation where they are irrelevant, since they are provoked solely by your imagination and not by reality around you.

So if I trust my senses, all will be fine? Are the senses never fallible?

This argument, where one might say 'senses can be wrong', is of course quite true, but again irrelevant. First, as we have said before, the senses are indeed fallible – but OCD does not help you guard against this fallibility. In fact, it is likely to make it worse, since in the OCD bubble you are disconnected from reality and *less* aware of what is going on around you. Having confidence in yourself does not mean assuming your senses aren't always right. It means accepting that your senses are all you've got to connect to reality. So OCD is no substitute for any fallibility of the senses. All it does is take you even further from the senses.

TROUBLESHOOTING GUIDE

Co-morbidity

It is important to distinguish OCD from other anxiety disorders, and in particular, tic disorders. Certain repetitive thoughts (replaying a song in one's head) are often better conceptualized as mental tics with a distinct etiology (see O'Connor, 2002). Personality disorders may interfere with treatment, but differ in terms of treatment compliance. In our experience, narcissistic personality disorder is particularly problematic. However, mild personality disorders do not merit exclusion from IBA. The anxiety may sometimes be worse if the person has co-morbid generalized anxiety disorder, since they will begin to anticipate problems, and become anxious beforehand.

The Client is Lost in the Emotion of the Obsession

Usually, when the patient is overwhelmed or sunk into the power of the emotion, this will impede progress in therapy. However, this problem often has little to do with the OCD itself, but how the client thinks about it – their reaction to it, their idea of how it reflects on the future, or on themselves, or their family. Of course, the anxiety may spring from the OCD directly rather than reactions essentially unrelated to the OCD. However, if the reactions do not directly spring from the OCD, it will be necessary to address them in therapy, since these clients will nurture the anxiety and not permit the therapy to work. In effect, dealing with the OCD under these circumstances may feed into the exaggerated reactions and anxiety, with the client focusing even more on the symptoms. Effectively, emotional reactions to the OCD are dealing with a problem other than OCD.

Cognitive Ritualizing

A general risk of cognitive interventions in the treatment of OCD is that they may become a neutralization tactic. For example, in appraisal therapy an instruction such as asking the person to ignore the obsessions or intrusion may lead to obsessive attempts to ignore the thought. Peculiar to IBA may be that the person starts to contrast non-obsessional narratives with obsessional narratives 'to think' one's way out of the OCD. Similarly, the person may obsessively attempt to use the senses to counter obsessional doubt. The safeguard against this is that the person understands the model before cognitive interventions. The person needs to use their senses naturally without extra effort and learn not to give the OCD situation any special status as compared to other situations.

Narrative Construction

Although the OCD narrative can usually be fully accessed, there may be difficulties collaboratively constructing an alternative narrative with the client. The narrative is best not forced or imposed but built up gradually with the client, by a continual process of creating extra elements. The clients may also be discouraged because they feel that they should believe in the alternative non-OCD narrative straight away, since otherwise it is not going to help. In fact, the opposite is the case, and the expectation is rather that credibility of the non-OCD narrative will initially be low but will increase in strength with time as details are added (see Case Study 1, pp. 178–183). Finally, one client, instead of rehearsing the alternative narrative and becoming immersed in it, spent her time arguing against it and finding fault with it. Obviously the person must feel comfortable enough with the alternative story to be able to engage in it as a possibility.

See-sawing Comprehension

It has been noted that some people have comprehension in the sessions, but relapse between sessions. This is a natural consequence of learning and should not be alarming to either the client or therapist. The client will have good days and bad days. It should be explained to the client that this is a normal process in the way we overcome habits, and that the person will eventually make progress.

Combining IBA with Standard CBT

In principle, IBA can be combined with standard CBT as long as the models do not conflict. So there is no inherent reason not to address reactions to the intrusions or doubt in IBA, and this may be useful with clients caught up more in reactions to the emotional consequences of the OCD. However, IBA would not locate the origin of obsessions in normal intrusions, nor send the message to the client to treat the occurrence of these thoughts as normal universal experiences even though the content might be normal. Also, there is the risk of 'challenging' the narrative behind the obsessional doubt on the basis of its content if the therapist is too entrenched in standard CBT. Thus, care should be taken to distinguish reactions from obsessions, and the reasoning processes leading up to the obsessional doubt when combining both approaches.

Similarly, IBA may be combined with exposure *in vivo* and response prevention, but not doing the ritual in IBA involves a distinct rationale. In general, IBA would ask the person to only stop the ritual if the person is able to overcome it through the cognitive method proposed in IBA where the person is able to keep the OCD story at bay. As such, IBA is highly cognitively oriented where preference is given to changing cognitions before engaging in behavior rather than the other way round. However, in our clinical experience, clients who progress with IBA sometimes need to be reminded not to do the ritual, since they may continue to do the ritual out of habit rather than a compulsive urge. In those cases, giving up the ritual is a painless process and easily accomplished by the client. Thus, combining IBA with exposure in terms of temporarily increasing anxiety and discomfort in order to achieve habituation is generally avoided in IBA.

However, combining IBA with exposure *in vivo* in separate stages of treatment where, for example, the person initially starts out with weakening obsessional conviction through IBA, followed by exposure *in vivo* and response prevention, may be indicated for some individuals who find themselves able and willing to do the exposure exercises after IBA.

Generalizing over Obsessions

In some cases, IBA generalizes to types of OCD situations and obsessions other than those specifically addressed in therapy. However, in other cases, obsessions may have to be addressed separately in treatment. The therapist may need to repeat some worksheets and go through the various steps in therapy tailored to the obsessions that have not been addressed previously in treatment.

Jumping ahead too fast

The major problem likely to arise in the early stages is the tendency for both client and therapist to jump ahead to confronting the validity or verity of the doubt. The first few stages are non-confrontational and simply seek to establish a logical fact. *Either* the source of the doubt is from the senses in the here and now, *or* it comes from within (i.e. from the person). There are logically only two options for the source of conviction. The word 'imagination' is best avoided initially, since until the person is more familiar with the model, it may be understood pejoratively (i.e. it's all in my head – I'm imagining it all). It will usually be immediately obvious to the client that the source of the obsession is not in the senses, since, of course, a key aspect of inferential confusion is that the person cannot trust their senses and the person will immediately start to contest the distinction between real versus non-real on the basis of the senses by producing one of the inferential confusion reasoning devices such as: 'Yes, but just because you can't see it – doesn't mean it is not real' ('out of place facts'). During the first stages of therapy the client can be reassured that for the moment we are not contesting the validity of the argument. We are not asking them to disbelieve the reasoning, but simply to recognize that the 'proof' for the doubt nonetheless comes from the person – not from the senses. In this way, to ensure errorless learning, it is important to program stage by stage and not jump ahead, because the client (often compulsively) wants to go as fast as possible.

Themes Precede Facts

The main argument against the reasoning errors and the narrative behind the doubt at later stages in the therapy is their selectivity and incoherence.

The best example here is 'microbes'. Microbes, of course, do exist – but why is the person using this fact in some situations, but not in others? The person is not afraid of breathing in microbes in the air. When comparing the obsessional doubt to other situations where the person uses the senses normally, the response might be: 'Well, it's not the same. My doubt is important and different.' Usually, however, other situations are equally dangerous. The aim here is to let the person understand that the facts do not cause the fear, the fear precedes the facts, and the facts are there just to confirm the fear. The person can be led to understand that the vulnerable self-theme guides selectivity of the obsessional conviction.

Importance of Meeting Criteria for Each Step before Progressing

Each of the different stages in therapy builds upon previous stages. Therefore, it is important the therapist ensures the client meets all criteria before progressing through the various stages in therapy. Partial understanding of one stage in therapy will lead to problems in successive stages. Conversely, in clients with excellent insight, therapy may progress faster if they meet the criteria. In general, however, it is better to err on the side of caution, and proceed through each successive stage slowly while taking care its main points have been understood.

OCD Controlling the Therapy

A problem may arise where OCD controls the therapy. Most obviously, OCD may have set an implicit barrier which says 'you can't go any further than so far'. Typically, at this point, the person with OCD will only improve so far. Maybe the OCD will impose a meta-cognitive belief such as 'If I improve, I will actually get worse.' Another form of OCD controlling the therapy is the person engaging in preparation 'not to do the OCD'. In fact, the person uses the OCD *not* to do the OCD in an OCD way. The therapist should identify the point where therapy is stagnating and should be sensitive to factors that can impede further progress in order to address these problems in terms of any other OCD impediment for a successful treatment outcome.

The Power of Metaphor: Language in Therapy

Metaphors tend to be very powerful in organizing people's experiences. It is important to use metaphors that explain progress rather than use self-defeating metaphors clients already use. Terms such as 'fighting the OCD' need to be avoided since this sets the person up for treating the OCD situations differently from other situations; the metaphor is one of enlightenment rather than conflict.

Competing Messages from Outside Authorities

Competing messages from outside authorities may include adverts or scary news stories. For example, the person may have seen on television that he/ she needs to wash their hands several times per day. Similarly, news stories such as those on SARS may be mentioned by the client as proof of his/her obsessional doubts. It should be explained to the client that this information is not a cause for OCD, but is wheeled into the OCD selectively to support the OCD. As such, this reference to authorities can be treated like any other reasoning device of the OCD that makes the OCD seem plausible. Other competing messages may come from mental health professionals in different models. In these cases, the client needs to be reassured and told that if he/she feels comfortable with the IBA model, it probably applies to him/her and the client should not be discouraged.

Challenging Beliefs and Values

The use of exercises and collaboration is useful at all times to avoid any confrontation. The team is the person and the therapist against the OCD and the therapy progresses largely by the client's recognizing the nature of the OCD and how it detracts from functioning and destroys confidence. In this case, it is especially important that the client's values are not inadvertently challenged in the guise of confronting the OCD. As we have seen earlier, people with OCD tend to confuse perfectly acceptable expectations with OCD, and may use these terms to explain the OCD. The client may wish to have things 'well done' or even 'perfectly done'. Normal values of perfectionism or even rigid codes are often blended into OCD. There is a temptation for the therapist to locate harsh moral codes in the client, or rigid thinking as a factor in the appraisal of events to be challenged in therapy. People may be inadvertently told to be more flexible in their thinking, to tolerate uncertainty, to be less perfectionistic, or to abandon notions of responsibility. Where there is a semantic confusion between these normal terms and OCD, it is simply a case of realizing the confusion, since it is not personal beliefs that are the target of therapy, but inferential confusion.

Another mistake is inadvertently attacking the person's values. This is sometimes seemingly encouraged by the person who believes they are too perfect, too religious, too hard-working, too honest, too responsible. In all cases, even though the person may adhere to these values, it is never the values which cause the problem. It is the idiosyncratic application of inferential confusion which the person then labels as part of his/her values, and which seems at the same time to justify the values and appeals to the person.

The therapy is not intended, then, to change moral values or beliefs, but to overcome inferential confusion and label it differently than in terms of value. In the same way as one cannot end up arguing facts, so one does not end up arguing values.

Contra-indications for Therapy

Contra-indications for therapy occur where the person is strongly opposed to the IBA model. Secondary gains or dynamics maintaining the OCD that lead the person to state he or she is unable to dedicate time and energy to the program are further contra-indications for therapy. Also, clients following other therapies simultaneously with IBA is discouraged. Finally, contra-indications for IBA treatment may include cost-effectiveness considerations.

Problems Identifying Primary Inferences

Problems can sometimes be encountered in the unravelling of the primary inference or doubt in OCD. Frequently, the primary doubt is self-evident – 'well, maybe I left the stove on', 'I thought my hands could still be dirty', 'maybe I'd need it one day.' But sometimes the person will be at a loss or draw a blank when asked to identify the doubt.

It might be tempting here to say simply, well, there's no primary inference and that's that, and feel understandably that to persist in trying to find a primary inference is only going to put words in the client's mouth. But the logic of OCD is that there must always be a primary inference if the action is a compulsive ritual, since the aim of the ritual is to neutralize obsessional anxiety or discomfort and the anxiety must spring from a doubt of some kind. Of course, it is possible that the action is a stereotypical gesture or a tic, in which case it is not OCD. But one way to establish the presence of the primary inference is just to pursue logic. Why this action – tidying the room, smoothing the cover and not something else? All that is required is a logical premise, for example, 'I'm cleaning the table, because maybe it needs cleaning.' The type and style of this compulsive action will mostly be due to the primary inference, which may relate directly to the type of person the client feels they may be.

It should be recognized that if there are no obvious rituals, some experience in IBA is required from the therapist, often because the therapist is required to establish the whole context of the obsessional preoccupation in order to understand it in terms of a primary inference. In fact, the therapist may need to adopt an inductive approach, where all elements of the obsessional preoccupation fit with one particular primary inference that resonates with the client as the main problem. For example, one of our clients had difficulty following suggestions made by others. Even trivial situations such as a friend suggesting going to the movies led her to feel paralyzed and unable to act. It would be inappropriate to start guessing the doubt such as 'maybe the suggestion is the wrong suggestion' and leave it at that. Rather, identifying the doubt in this case requires the therapist to explore the invested meaning of the client in following suggestions. Further probing regarding the difficulty with following suggestions originated in the client's self-referent theme where she had blamed herself for too easily following suggestions by others and trying to be a good girl. In her mind, this self-perceived character flaw had led to problems in the past, and was heavily emotionally charged due to events that were associated with this flaw. After the client had identified 'following suggestions' as 'her major problem', even the most trivial situations and suggestions started to lead to problems with the client unable to act upon them. Within this context, the primary inference was able to account for the totality of the obsessional experience took the form of 'It might be wrong to follow suggestions' as part of a self-referent theme where she considered herself to be a person who too easily follows suggestions made by others.

The Inferentially Confused Therapist

One problem that may arise in therapy is inferential confusion on the part of the therapist. As noted earlier, inferential confusion probably exists on a continuum in the population, so we all react in a small way to some aspect of inferential confusion as heuristic devices. The degree of absorption of course is distinct, but this can still lead to inferential confusion. As a result, the therapist may be inclined to agree with some of the client's arguments as valid reasons behind the obsessional doubt (for example that because microbes exist, so the client's hands could be contaminated), while forgetting that these reasons are selective and arise in inappropriate idiosyncratic situational contexts and without sense information that would justify the doubts they lead up to.

There is also the problem of unfamiliarity with the technique, with most therapists trained in standard CBT or other techniques and feeling uncomfortable if they are not challenging the content of the reasoning directly or not doing anything behavioral with the client. IBA of course does involve doing, but the doing follows from the cognitive method. The method tends to be client-friendly – clients click well with the initial exercises – but the therapist may need to master the model completely before application.

CASE STUDIES

Case 1

The following ongoing case is a good illustration on the use and impact of rehearsing alternative narratives in the course of IBA. The client (R.M.) is a 40-year-old woman, who was diagnosed with severe OCD. The obsessions and compulsions occupy almost the entire day and provoke an extreme state of distress. The client also exhibits varying degrees of derealization during severe obsessional episodes, and has been diagnosed with co-morbid hypochondria and agoraphobia.

A pervasive theme throughout all the obsessions is a constant concern about dying, which provokes an extreme state of distress. In particular, R.M. has frequent obsessions about the possibility of her food being poisoned. In order to reassure herself about the safety of food, she requires family members to eat everything first, in order to see their reaction and reassure herself that the food is safe to eat. Other obsessions R.M. has revolve around the fear that she has a serious illness. She is unable to leave the house unless accompanied by family members for fear of becoming ill or dizzy, or fainting. During her worst obsessional episodes she is unable to leave the couch for fear of 'moving too much' and straining herself.

There are many other fears, all revolving around the possibility of death, such as reading certain words related to death, and she performs numerous rituals to prevent potentially lethal accidents and events from happening. The severity of R.M.'s symptoms is evidenced by her inability to discuss her problem and where anything reminiscent of death is avoided in conversation. The obsessions cause extreme anxiety and most of the information gained regarding her obsessions about death was obtained in the form of yes/no answers. However, R.M. allowed herself to talk more freely about the other predominant obsessions of poisoning and having a serious illness.

R.M. has received extensive cognitive-behavioral therapy in the past for a total period of around five years from several different qualified psychologists. Therapy involved both exposure *in vivo* with response prevention as well as cognitive therapy where beliefs were challenged. In some instances, therapy had been successful in partially reducing symptoms, but invariably the symptoms returned. In R.M.'s words: 'I can do some of the exercises, and things get a little better for a while, but I never stop believing in the obsessions.'

The presence of over-valued ideation may have contributed to the lack of success in previous treatments. Although exposure exercises helped reduce symptoms to a certain extent in the past, her obsessional belief never wavered, even though specifically addressed in previous therapy through the use of cognitive techniques. At the start of therapy, R.M. was 95% convinced that she could be poisoned or that she might have a serious illness as evaluated on clinical rating scales.

Clearly, the obsessional doubt was all-pervasive across a wide variety of situations, and it was impossible to deal with all the obsessions at the same time. Therefore, the most debilitating obsession regarding poisoning, both in terms of psychological and health impact, was addressed first in therapy. The obsessions were phrased in terms of a doubt, which consisted of the fairly straightforward doubt 'that her food could have been poisoned'. R.M. progressed through the various first stages of therapy in differentiating normal doubts from obsessional doubts, raising awareness of the thoughts and justification behind the doubt, and identifying the reasoning devices that led her to believe that her food might be poisoned. In R.M.'s case, the unabbreviated narrative behind the doubt took the following form:

> It's not safe to eat food or drink liquids, because someone may have tried to poison it. I heard a long time ago about someone with a grudge against a pharmaceutical company who poisoned their medicine and several people died because of that. Even though I have never heard of anyone poisoning food, it is always possible that someone could do the same with food or liquids. Someone could add the poison in the grocery store, or during the manufacturing process. Someone with a grudge against a certain company, or any other unstable person. The same could happen for make-up, conditioner, dental floss or any other product that I come into contact with. Even if the grocery store foods are fine, someone could break into my house and poison my food, drinks, or my toothpaste. Especially if I left food unattended, then I am no longer able to tell in any way whether someone got to it. Liquids are especially dangerous since it's hard to tell if anyone has poisoned it. Someone could have injected something in the drink and you would never know. All it takes is to go into a store and inject some cyanide or other poison. It all seems very unsafe to me. Walking into a grocery store is like walking into a chemical laboratory for me. If I look at the vegetables and see spots on them, it bothers me. It might indicate that someone has tampered with it. For the same reason I have difficulty with eating anything that comes from an opened package, since I can no longer determine if it was without marks when it was bought. So I always look carefully at my food. If I see anything that is out of the ordinary I have difficulty eating it. Like small unidentified pieces in a cookie, or anything else that I can isolate, but not identify. Since there might be poison on the food, I wash it with hot water so that maybe I can get rid of the poison. Maybe the hot water will help neutralize it. Then, I ask my boyfriend to taste the food first to make sure it is safe to eat.

It quickly became clear that for R.M. there existed no alternative as to the safety of food, or at least, not an alternative that R.M. was able to experience as a realistic possibility. That is, besides the convincing power of the obsessional narrative, R.M. was unable to come up with any reasons or ideas as to why food was safe. The inability of OCD clients to come up with alternatives is often overlooked, because the non-obsessional alternative is so self-evident for those not experiencing the obsessions. Since R.M. had great difficulty in coming up with alternatives for herself, she was given an initial outline of an alternative story that was phrased in opposition to the obsessional story. Over the next few weeks R.M. was required to add to the alternative story, and rehearse the non-obsessional story several times per day without contrasting it with the OCD story. Care was taken to ensure the alternative narrative matched or exceeded the detail of the obsessional story, and R.M. was required to immerse herself in it, add detail to it, and act for a while in her imagination as if the idea that her food was safe was completely realistic. Frequent checks were performed to ensure R.M. followed the spirit of the exercise rather than her rehearsing the non-obsessional story as a form of neutralization. It should be noted here that the risk of rehearsing the non-obsessional story as a form of neutralization is rather low, *but only if* the therapist ensures the client understands the purpose of the exercise, since any OCD patient will instinctively make any new information part of the obsessional doubt.

After the initial story was formed, subsequent sessions focused on identifying those elements that could make up an alternative story with the greatest likelihood of success. For this purpose, an attempt was made to locate those elements in close proximity to the OCD story but those, as yet, were elements that had been untouched by the OCD. In the case of R.M., further probing revealed some interesting inconsistencies in her belief that foods could be poisoned. It turned out that bread was the least likely food to be poisoned. R.M. justified these inconsistencies by saying that it was not an intellectual judgement, just simply she could not believe that anything as delicious as bread could be poisoned. It was decided simply to add these associative elements to the alternative story because, after all, these associations are in line with the senses, and thus lead away from inferential confusion.

In the course of 10 weeks, the alternative story took the following form:

> There is no need for me to worry about drink or food being poisoned. A cookie, meal or juice is just that – a cookie, meal or juice, nothing more. Drink and food are something that is enjoyable. It is natural, life-sustaining and, most importantly, tasty and wonderful. What can be better than warm bread with melted butter and sweet jam in the morning? What is nicer than a hot caramel soy drink with tons of whipped cream and extra caramel toppings on a cold day? And how good is an icy glass of water on a hot day? All drink and

food is healthy and nourishing and great holidays and social events are made better by meals. Sitting over hot teas and coffees with friends and family over the holidays and sharing warm and inviting food are times when I can really enjoy drinking and eating. Christmas dinners, birthdays, and beautiful weddings are all times when really lovely drink and food are shared, making the moment more special.

There are all kinds of preventative measures that are put in place to prevent poisoning from happening. Companies that sell well-known drinks and food products take precautions against accidents. Machines do all the bottling and packing, and once again, there are usually cameras in these factories to catch any mistakes or foul play. These companies don't want anything showing up in their drink or food that doesn't belong there, and thus are willing to invest considerable amounts of money to prevent anything happening to their products. Fish that is bought and stored correctly is just as safe to eat as bread. You are not more likely to get food-poisoned by fish than other food just by virtue of the fact that it is fish.

Bottled or cartoned drinks and food on the shelves of grocery stores are not highly susceptible to poisoning. There are always people around and then someone would have to remove the safety seal, tamper with the product and somehow re-seal the container, then put it back on the shelf without any hint of foul play (mess, leaking, damage to container, etc.) and without anyone seeing. If fruit were injected with some poison, then wouldn't the fruit show signs of the poison?

Spots on apples and fruits are natural. Bugs, wind, rain and fruit falling all cause the imperfections you find on the skin or bruising in the inside of the fruit. The variety of texture and taste that drinks and some foods have can cause a variety of feelings in the mouth. Crunching on something or something tasting bitter or sour does not mean that food is poisoned or dangerous.

People who work for beverage and food companies are just the same as people I know. They are most likely caring, considerate individuals with families of their own who are very interested in assuring that the drink and food they make are safe and healthy. Employees of these drink and food companies probably eat a great deal of the food that they make, either for enjoyment or quality insurance and therefore would want the food to be safe and, more importantly, know if it is not. Just like small bakeries and small food and drink distributors, large manufacturers apply the same healthful and caring philosophical values to their companies. Like when I watched *Unwrapped* on FOODTV I saw the production line of many mid/large-sized companies and they all seem to have the same commitment to providing good drink and food products.

For 15 weeks R.M. was asked to rate each of the elements in both stories in terms of their convincing power on either 'that food might be poisoned' and 'that food might be safe to eat'. The average score on both stories has evolved as represented in Figure 6.1.

In addition to rehearsing the alternative story, R.M. was asked to perform other imagination exercises that involved watching herself eating at various exotic locations in the world and slowly build up to more difficult foods and liquids in her imagination. R.M. soon started to enjoy her extensive

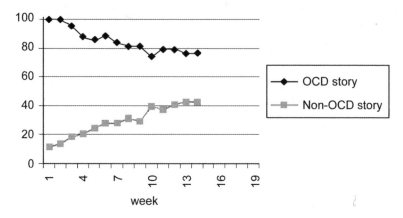

Figure 6.1   Conviction levels of OCD and non-OCD food story

meals at a romantic terrace in Paris without anxiety. Once the alternative narratives started to take hold on R.M., she was asked to start rehearsing the alternative narrative in some OCD situations, but only if she was relatively certain beforehand that she would be able to stop the rituals without anxiety, and be able to dismiss the obsessional doubt on the basis of the alternative story.

The exercises soon started to have an effect on R.M.'s obsessions and compulsions in real life. She started to learn to eat food without other people pre-tasting it and without anxiety or rituals. Recently, she started to eat with no one present. Liquids still remain a problem due to the obsessional reasoning that 'you would be less able to see poison in liquids than in solid foods'. However, R.M. has started to drink some types of liquids on her own without others being present. It is important to note here that this approach has been completely cognitive and painless with none of the exercises having produced any anxiety or discomfort.

Further work is clearly needed with this client, but so far, there are some promising indications that R.M. is responding to treatment. Most importantly, for the first time the ideas behind her compulsive rituals are starting to waver. Currently, her belief that her solid food might be poisoned has reduced to 50%. Particularly encouraging is her under-standing of the inferential confusion process as therapy starts to address the reasoning errors that lead up to obsessional doubts. In her own words: 'I feel like I'm reaching a point that my doubts are incorrect. And if they are incorrect, then what else can I do but give up my rituals?'

Another encouraging sign is that R.M. is starting to fear getting better and all it may entail, which is a normal response to having lived with a particularly debilitating OCD for so long. She is currently making plans to go back to university. However, clearly, R.M. still has a long way to go. Only recently has she found herself able to discuss the topic of death in therapy, and long-term success will likely be dependent on overcoming the self-referent vulnerability surrounding death. However, this challenge has come into full view now that R.M. is able to dismiss at least some of the obsessions that have convinced her for such a long time that she could die at any time.

Case 2

In the following case report, IBA was successfully applied to the treatment of a 28-year-old Canadian female (L.J.) diagnosed with OCD, with a combination of OVI and non-OVI obsessions. L.J. initially received a CBT for 20 weeks, followed by IBA for a further 20 weeks. Each therapy lasted 20 weekly sessions with a baseline period of one month. Since both therapies were given within the same clinical research infrastructure at the research center (but within different programs and with different therapists), the outcome measures of each treatment are comparable and both are reported. At the time of referral, L.J. was a widow with a daughter aged 6 and working full-time as an administrator. She was initially assessed by a psychiatrist on DSM-IV criteria, and subsequently assessed by an independent clinician on the Anxiety Disorders Schedule-IV and the Yale–Brown Obsessive-Compulsive Scale (Y-BOCS). Both clinicians rated her OCD in the moderate-to-severe range and this was reflected in her initial Y-BOCS score of 26; both also agreed that there was a co-morbid avoidant personality and some generalized anxiety with no other axis 1 or 2 disorder.

Assessment and case formulation

L.J.'s list of obsessions and compulsions involved both OVI and non-OVI obsessions. A non-OVI ritual involved a 'hit and run' ritual: returning to check if she had hit someone while driving her car. She would return along her route to check that there were no accidents or signs of injured cyclists. Her primary inference was that maybe she had struck a cyclist without her knowledge and consequently she would be blamed and imprisoned despite her innocence. This compulsion then took a more classic non-OVI form. Top of the list for OVI was a fear of contamination 'at a distance' (both in time and space). She feared being contaminated by people or things even if they were remotely in the vicinity. Additionally, she was strongly convinced that even if an object had been dirty or 'contaminated at a distance' in the past, it maintained this 'power' for ever, and could never be used again. Her insight into her OCD was poor (but not zero) in the sense that although she recognized the bizarreness of the behavior and that the contamination she imagined might not occur, yet she remained 100% convinced that she was correct to take what she termed 'precautions', and that others who did not do so were incorrect. She also adhered strongly to the belief in the plausibility of the means of contamination. She also described the thoughts about contamination 'as if' they were a voice speaking to her. The theme or 'plot' of her obsessional thinking about contamination was that she would become 'infected' because she didn't know enough, that as a consequence she would infect others including her daughter and start an epidemic. She frequently stated that she viewed her hands as potential murderers.

Her fear of contamination touched every aspect of her life and she made a list dividing mortal outcomes from dangerous outcomes. Passing near trash cans, tramps, sprinklers, dirty water and traveling could kill her, whereas being near contaminated food, furniture and clothes would make her ill. For example, a chair on which a 'dirty' cat had once been placed was permanently contaminated and had been kept locked in the basement for several years. Certain corners of her house had become infected by virtue of their position as 'receptacles' for a contamination wind blowing infection through the house. She had been unable to use her swimming pool in the garden for several years, since she felt it was possible that animals had once come into it at night, or birds flew over it, so contaminating it. She had drained and refilled it several times and had even paid for a sanitary inspection, but remained unconvinced of its cleanliness. She was unable to eat out in restaurants since she was uncertain about the food. She had recently returned from a vacation in the South early and at great expense, because she had overheard a conversation at another table about someone on the island catching hepatitis, and had assumed she would be contaminated next.

She was unable to wash her laundry for fear of contamination and she had collected clothes over a number of weeks, unable to wash them or throw them out, although the compulsions were slightly less pronounced in the presence of real dirt. She was unable to dust or pick up objects in the house, and was unable to visit other people's houses for fear of unseen contamination. However, she did, sometimes under great duress, manage some washing and cleaning in her house. If she did manage to wash something, she would subsequently wash herself compulsively for several hours. But her principal coping strategy was avoidance. She avoided social contact, visits, dating, leisure activity, eating out. She was preoccupied with the obsession and with the fact that she had the obsession, and this qualified all social, interpersonal possibilities.

She had been without a partner for four years since the death of her husband. She felt alien, handicapped and unable to enter into any viable personal or social relations. She felt she could never attract a partner, had little to offer as a person in a relationship in terms of personal attributes. She considered she had no positive characteristics. Her only socialization was with colleagues at work who were either married or in couples, which reinforced her alienation. At the same time she refused to undertake social activities for fear of exposing her OCD. Effectively there was no element of her life not touched by OCD. Her daughter also suffered OCD by proxy, in that she did not allow her daughter to play outside, swim in the pool, touch objects, or eat out. Her daughter was experiencing a lot of distress and anxiety on this account, which further distressed the mother, frequently to the point of tears. She fell in the mildly depressed range of the Beck Depression Inventory, and although no suicidal tendency was present, there was a feeling that her life had no meaning except to care for her daughter.

History

She had been raised by a mother (widowed) who herself had suffered from a variety of phobias, including probably agoraphobia. Her mother had been very protective of her and prone to warn her constantly of every conceivable danger lurking beyond the home. The mother would discourage her from any outside activity. For example, if she were going out for the night, her mother would immediately relate all the potential negative events that might occur and how any harm befalling her would reflect on the mother. The mother was very critical of her daughter's abilities to cope. The client felt this was part of the mother's strategy to discourage her from leaving home and not looking after the mother. She eventually left her mother's house at age 20 to live with the first man with whom she had had a serious relationship. Soon afterwards the client developed a form of limited symptom panic with agoraphobia. She would experience vague feelings of insecurity and being trapped in public places. However, there were clearly obsessional preoccupations at this point masked by the more general avoidance due to agoraphobia. The 'agoraphobia' had a spontaneous remission two years later, following her pregnancy. She had been in two other of what she termed 'destructive relationships', one with a fellow lodger in her apartment building, the other with a minor criminal, who was subsequently killed and who was the father of her daughter. Both partners tended to be very critical of her and to publicly criticize her, so reinforcing her low self-esteem. She felt, however, that she gained protection from the relationships and used the partners to accommodate her fears. On the other hand, her fears were accepted by the partners since it enabled them to play assertive roles in the relationship. The OCD had developed to a significant disabling degree about the time her 'agoraphobia' had subsided. She had been diagnosed and treated by a psychoanalytically oriented psychiatrist, which she felt had helped her to understand personal relations, but had not touched her OCD symptoms.

Treatment

She was inducted into our research program and allocated randomly to CBT. The initial CBT based on the appraisal model was carried out by a qualified psychologist with previous experience in CBT for OCD and who was supervised by two senior clinicians. The CBT followed the appraisal model, where calculation of probabilities of consequences and appraisals of responsibility were targeted along the lines outlined by van Oppen and Arntz (1994) and Salkovskis (1996). As part of the research evaluations, treatment integrity and therapist competence were evaluated. This therapist was competent and had in previous clinical work in the program achieved significant clinical improvement in eight diverse cases of OCD using CBT.

The CBT challenged the likelihood of her imagined consequences if she was contaminated. The fear of the excessive consequences of contamination dictated her belief that she could not take the risk of not neutralizing. Information on how performing the rituals encouraged the doubt, and disallowed proof of their utility, was combined with reality-testing procedures. The work on appraisals of danger and responsibility addressed the dramatization of consequences by probability and pie charts methods. She was also encouraged to confront and tolerate certain beliefs, e.g. that there should never be any danger whatsoever, that anything less than complete safety was intolerable. Her appraisals of her OCD as being prudent and responsible were targeted as an instance of unhelpful binary thinking. Prudence, as normally understood, had become synonymous with obsessional precautions ('either I am excessively cautious or I am irresponsible'). The over-importance of thoughts was also addressed. Experiencing a thought or feeling was just that, an experience. Thoughts were not necessarily significant in themselves, and might reflect mood rather than reality. A program of graded exposure and reality testing was implemented over 20 weekly sessions whereby the client exposed herself to washing glasses, cupboards, throwing out rubbish, washing her laundry, letting her daughter play, not checking if she had hit someone in her car and finally taking a holiday.

Her main problems in response to the CBT program were that her anxiety would initially lessen and then be refueled by thoughts of new consequences. The belief in contamination never disappeared and she continued to feel edgy when not neutralizing and felt she was constantly fighting and repressing OCD rather than coping with it. But she made progress. Her efficacy ratings improved and she reported a greater understanding of how her appraisals and reactions strengthened her obsessional behavior. Her Y-BOCS total score decreased to 21 post treatment.

The outcome of CBT in this case was very similar to the outcome found in our larger study of CBT in OVI and non-OVI cases (O'Connor *et al.*, 2003a). The frequency of non-OVI compulsive behavior (returning to verify if a person has been hit by the car) had reduced considerably. There was considerable reduction in strength of secondary consequences and appraisals foreseen in relation to hitting someone in a car. There was an increase in the ability to resist some of the touching and washing rituals, mainly due to an increased ability to tolerate anxiety and danger. However, in the client's words 'the stories remained' and even where there was a reduction in consequences and appraisals and an increase in resistance, there was little drop in strength of primary conviction concerning contamination (see Figures 6.2 and 6.3 on p. 195).

Inference-based therapy

Eliciting the narrative. After further evaluation and a break of eight weeks, the client received IBA. The first step was to examine in more detail the narrative supporting the strong conviction in the primary inference. The nature of the primary inference was ill-served by the summary statement, 'I may be contaminated', and its force was far better captured by the narrative justifying and thus perpetuating the conviction. If we take one such narrative concerning the swimming pool, we can see clearly how the imagination worked to trump the senses, by adding in possible (imaginary) states of affairs, derived on the basis mainly of inductive non-pertinent associations.

> But I look at the pool and it's surrounded by trees and the garden backs onto a field. Animals could get in during the night. I've heard noises, they could swim in the pool, or do things in it. It's disgusting, I've seen the mess dogs make, they have fleas and germs on them. The more I think about it, the more it disgusts me to even look at the pool. How can I know it's ever clean? Once the germs are there, they have the power to infect anything.

It might be tempting to say that the story was simply based on ignorance of how contamination is spread. But this client, an otherwise intelligent woman, had made no attempt to seek out relevant knowledge or information to confirm or disconfirm the OCD narrative. In fact, the client later agreed that more knowledge or objective information would not be helpful in alleviating the fear. In a narrative with such a highly charged premise, the issue was not really the degree of probability of the event occurring, but whether it might or might not to any degree. As long as she thought there was even a slight chance of an animal having been near the tank or pool, then it was infected and the scene was set for imagining any variety of catastrophic consequences. She might accept that the more exaggerated consequences were unrealistic but the thought of any infection rendered her so uncomfortable that whatever consequences followed seemed superfluous. The primary inference itself then produced much of the discomfort. Her favorite expression when thinking of the pool or other infected objects was a grimace and an exclamation 'Oh! It's disgusting' (*C'est dégueulasse*) without articulation of any consequences. Since the discomfort began at this primary stage, the OCD train of thought was likely to evolve into and accept any coherent consequence. So, if one consequence was accepted as irrational, another equally confirmatory of her primary impression could take its place. It might be argued that the initial strong reaction to the premise was an over-learned response originally conditioned by consideration of the consequences. But, in fact, while the initial response to the primary idea was spontaneous, soliciting the exact consequences was more labored.

Clarifying the source of the narrative. The next stage after eliciting the narratives associated with key premises was to examine the source of information in the narratives. Generally the source of 'knowledge' in the narrative comes from unreliable remote sources (hearsay, memory, irrelevant facts, non-pertinent associations, imaginary sequences, apparently similar events), but never from actual experience or proof. In this client's case, stories and news items heard about animals biting children and infecting them or children touching animal faeces and catching eye infections justified the idea that animals could permanently infect her swimming pool. The remoteness of these sources to the actual here and now was emphasized by her recalling that her mother's 'voice' or words sometimes featured prominently within the narrative. The client had already located her mother's continual worry as a 'source' of her OCD fears. After examining the narrative in detail, the client agreed that the stories were subjective and largely imaginary and her specific assertions in the specific situation were not based on actual proof, but she maintained that even if infection was unlikely to occur, she could not take the risk. It was better to act 'as if' the infection were real than 'as if' it were not likely, since in precautionary terms and cost–benefit ratio, the former choice made more sense.

Highlighting discrepancies between OCD risk perception and normal risk perception. At this point we looked more intensively at how she made inferences in non-OCD domains of life and how she dealt with risk in these areas. The aim was to highlight discrepancies in the extent to which information from the senses was credited in OCD and non-OCD situations, thus highlighting the subjective and imaginary nature of OCD inferences and the inverse inference process. Two non-OCD situations were examined in detail: crossing the road, and dealing with routine enquiries in her job. In both cases, she used her senses (sight, touch, smell, hearing, taste) to determine what was there, and then subsequently drew inferences about meaning. This was not only distinct from, but opposed to, what she did in the OCD situation, where her 'senses' informed her that nothing was there but she nevertheless inferred there must be something there on the basis of her narrative. She was perfectly able to see dirt and marks on clothes or packaging and trusted her senses when she saw it. But she did not trust her senses to see no dirt in the OCD situation.

We also established that the recital of the story about possible contamination was 'antagonistic' to using her senses. When gripped with the OCD fear of contamination, she would not dare, for example, to look at her hands to see if the 'imaginary dirt' was there because it was too odious for her to do so. So she never tried to verify if her hands looked or smelled dirty, rather, she relied entirely on her OCD story to convince her. Likewise, she would not visually examine her pool or objects or a tramp in the street since she found this, also, too aversive. She had not previously been aware that she did *not* use her senses in the OCD situation and this new awareness highlighted for her the discrepancy between recounting her OCD story and sensing reality. Along with this realization came the realization that authoritative objective evidence which contradicted the story would *never* be accepted by her as invalidating the OCD story. For the client this explained why repeated attempts to drain and redrain her pool had not in the long run alleviated her anxiety.

Refining the OCD narrative 'plot'. We also examined variations in severity of anxiety *within* OCD situations. For example, the client was unhappy eating out anywhere, but considerably unhappier in restaurants where the food was unfamiliar, unknown and where the cooking was out of view. The aim of comparing the high and low variations within an obsessional theme was to highlight and refine again the subjective theme or 'plot' which allowed otherwise disparate hearsay memories, associations, to stick together as a narrative. The plot in this lady's case contained two or three key elements and is captured best in her own words: 'Despite my good intentions, I could be implicated in something bad, because I'm ignorant about lots of facts, there's dangers out there and I'm not aware all the time. I mean, I'm unaware of unknown dangers, so I have to take precautions because I don't know enough.' At another point she said: 'The unknown, what you can't see, has powers to harm you. The world is a dangerous place, I feel insecure most of the time.' Some elements of this 'plot' could be traced, according to the client, to her mother's admonitions, that despite appearances, bad things could happen to her, plus the 'double blind' constantly reiterated by her mother that she was not competent enough to deal with problems, but that no one would help her if she didn't, and it would be her fault.

Illustrating respective roles of imagination and perception. At this point we broached more formally the distinction between the imagination and reality, and the respective role of each function: the latter to gather information; the former to envisage possibilities not already existing in reality. The explanation of the 'normal' role of imagination can help to clarify why inferences are at times imaginary, and at other times realistic. Approaching the distinction through a formal model limits the chance of misinterpreting the argument, since there is a danger that the person may believe the therapist is saying 'your problem is in your imagination' rather than 'the problem is with your imaginative faculty'.

The role of the imagination, both constructive and destructive, was illustrated from the client's use of imagination in other aspects of her life. For example, imagining the possible events that might unravel on a journey elicits a variety of emotions, but purely in the realm of possibility; conversely, on an actual journey the experiences are drawn from the senses. The important aspect of the imaginary process is the chaining or spiraling of possibilities, one after the other, whereas, in contrast, perception leads to realistic deductions on the basis of what is there, it does not add to what is seen as there.

We next re-examined situations where she gathered information in everyday life (crossing the road, and dealing with files and phone calls at work). We established that in these situations she did not rely on imaginary stories to decide on what was there and what needed to be done. We then analyzed the components of her narrative and their relationship to the *actual* context to which they supposedly applied. This is important since much of the meat of the narrative is contained in associations and generalities drawn from another time and place. Example:

L.J.:   But squirrels are disgusting, I've seen them in the park running in and out of mud, if you touched one you'd be dirty, and there are cases of children being infected by dogs.

T.:   So, how is this relevant to your pool?

L.J.:   Well, imagine if an animal had come into the pool, and all their germs would be in the pool and the water would become infected.

T.:   Yes, but has this ever happened?

L.J.:   Not to my knowledge, I mean, I've never seen it, but you never know.

T.:   But the story about it happening then is not based on direct evidence or experience?

L.J.: No, that's true, but it could happen. It could spread, I mean look at radioactivity, they have to bury it because it lasts so long, for thousands of years.

It is important to illustrate how the power of the imagination can elicit strong emotions and behavior, and how imaginary beliefs can be gripping even when we know they are imaginary, and even more so when we don't know. In this client's case, we played through the scenes of an imagined holiday in the Caribbean, and showed how images of what she might do on the beach produced parallel sensations (of heat) in the here and now. The power of the imagination can also be demonstrated by taking narratives using the habitual OCD 'plots' pertinent to the client, and then recounting an alternative narrative with an alternative plot to see how the narrative influences emotions (as described in detail later).

A sticking point with this client, and this is not unusual, was the continued belief in the small probability of the imagined event occurring. She had accepted that the imagined story was not drawn from real information, that it was maintained by her imagination. But even if it were only a possibility, it could still happen. After all, anything can happen. It was this element of the small risk involved which still gripped her. This problem of the 1% risk has to be dealt with both at an intellectual and lived-in experience level. Intellectually, it is important to restate the distinction between an imagined possibility and a remote but real probability, since the latter, but not the former, is based on real observation of the event's albeit rare occurrence. It was also important to emphasize that the estimation of risk was a function of her subjective state and thinking, not a product of anything objective. In other words, the 'plot' of the narrative, not external objective factors, decided the severity of her OCD reaction. For example, the risk seemed greater when she felt more uncomfortable, and when the key elements of her 'plot' were present. Conversely, objective risk factors (e.g., observable environmental aspects) did not seem to play a role in her risk assessment. Put another way, the idea of a remote risk ('it might *just* happen') was itself part of the OCD narrative, and her belief in the remote possibility was grounded in the persuasive power of the narrative. This was demonstrated by carefully modifying the narrative to counter every supportive piece of inductive associations and reasoning with a counter-proposal (i.e. no squirrels had come into her garden, contamination was dispersed in the wind, germs have no power to live on their own), and then arriving at the conclusion that there was now zero likelihood of the 'rare' event occurring. Why? Because now all the imaginary preconditions and associations leading to her inference had been countered, there was no coherent justification for belief in the remote probability of the obsession. Her OCD narrative had led her up to the conclusion that contamination could either happen or not happen, in the same way as it could rain or not rain on any day. But the presence or absence of contamination were not equiprobable events where perhaps the relative cost of each alternative might determine the utility of preparing for one or the other event. In fact, the odds of being contaminated were analogous to the odds of a kettle boiling when it hadn't even been switched on, or a car running without a motor. The probability was not 50/50 or 99.99/0.01 but zero, since the preconditions necessary for actual contamination existed only in the imagination.

Using the imagination to reduce anxiety and conviction. We now rehearsed, within sessions, modification of the OCD narrative by replacing it with an alternative narrative for each of the OCD situations. The aim was to give further insight and credibility into the idea that the OCD inferential confusion stemmed from the influence of the narrative, and could only be changed by treating the imaginary inference as imaginary. In order for this exercise to work, the alternative narratives have to be detailed and match every aspect of the OCD narratives. Of course, the alternative narratives take a lot more effort to construct than the OCD narratives, since they are not automatic.

> *OCD narrative.* The tramp is sitting in the road, in his own filth, he hasn't washed and he's dirty and he's probably got infected spots and fleas and then he's going to be surrounded by bacteria which is going to drift into the air and fly over to me and stick on me and contaminate me, and then I'll contaminate what I touch, etc.

> *Alternative narrative.* The tramp is sitting in a cleanly swept part of the road, he washed himself in his hostel, and wears old but clean clothes from the Salvation Army. He is young and healthy and has a good complexion, and just finds himself temporarily down on his luck. His hands and fingernails are spotless. There is no bacteria and any particles in the air pass by in the wind and cannot cling on, so she cannot be contaminated.

It is important also that the alternative narrative begins at the primary source of the OCD inference, since a typical problem is that, unless challenged at source, the OCD story tends to take off automatically by itself and spirals up to its convincing conclusion, without the client being able to stop it. Once all the associated OCD emotions are elicited, it is then difficult for the person to resist the logic of 'not taking the risk'. The aim of the alternative scenario exercise is not to create an alternative narrative, nor to give 'correct' information to counter the OCD narrative. This narrative exercise is introduced only after the person is aware that both the OCD and alternative narrative are imaginary, and intellectually understands the distinction between the imaginary possibility and the real evidence-based probability. The aim of the exercise is to demonstrate the potential of the imagination to increase and then decrease anxiety, and so increase awareness that the OCD anxiety arises in the imagination and is best dealt with in the imagination, not by trying to change anything in reality.

Reality 'sensing'. This occurs when in the OCD situation the person does not recount any narratives but resists onset of the initial OCD inference on the basis that it is 100% irrelevant to the here and now and replaces it with sense information drawn from the here and now. In the case of this lady, it was a revelation to her to actually look at what was there and see it was *less* shocking to her than not looking. She related, 'It's true the tramp was youngish and not at all bad looking and although I'm not sure his clothes were clean, he wasn't obviously dirty or covered in sores.'

Some alternating between success and failure in resisting inferential confusion is to be expected at this stage, with the client sometimes being able, sometimes unable, to dismiss the initial inference in favor of a real sense appreciation of the situation. The particular conditions surrounding any failure need to be analyzed in order for the client to learn and prevent any repetition. Most frequently in this client's case, the reason for failure was that the original inference kept creeping back into her head and taking hold, thus corrupting her attempts to use and rely on her senses. Once this process was understood, she prepared herself to expect the OCD inference to return three or four times before the alternative non-OCD information from her senses could be installed.

The rationale behind reality sensing is different from exposure and reality testing in CBT. In reality 'sensing' the person employs an antagonistic logic, whereby instead of avoiding the situation or adding doubt to it by going off into the imagination, the person defines reality by relying entirely on information from their five senses. This anchoring of coping strategies as a reaction to *either* imagination *or* reality helps identify otherwise small and difficult-to-identify neutralizations and avoidance, since the behavior is readily identified by its source in OCD or in reality. As with other cognitive behavior therapies, it was very important to eliminate all avoidance and neutralization rituals, large and small, which impair using the senses, or whose rationale was justified by any aspect of the imaginary narrative.

A particularly strong motivation to eliminate avoidance for this lady was the realization that her narrative took her away from looking at the real situation and thus actually exposed her to more danger. An illustration of this was when she instinctively gave a wide margin to a tramp slumped on the pavement and consequently nearly got knocked down by a car. Conversely, when she used her senses, she was more often pleasantly surprised to see that nothing was as bad as she had imagined. As noted, when actually looking at a tramp in the street, she realized the person was disheveled but not actually dirty or contaminated. The irony was that even if she did see 'real' dirt or came into contact with 'real' dirt, this was not as disturbing as the imaginary contamination and all its powers.

End of treatment. During the final stages of the therapy, she also moved house. This meant exposing herself to many of the 'contaminated' objects she had locked in the cellar, plus attending to other aspects of her house which she had previously avoided. She imagined the removal men being dirty, and contaminating her things. She had even thought of arranging for her sister to oversee the move so she wouldn't see anything 'dégueulasse'. However, she realized this would only reinforce her imagination, and in the end the move went well under her direct supervision.

In principle, once the person understands the inverse inference process and how it produces reliance on OCD narratives, generalization to other OCD situations should be easier. However, this is not always the case, and it is important to spend time with the person elaborating ground rules for knowing what counts as OCD and what does not, and illustrating this distinction in future situations. In general, a reality rule is helpful: if my actions are directed to what is there, then my actions are normal; if I imagine 'maybe' it's there, 'acting as if it were' is OCD generated. Using this 'reality rule' we eliminated any vestigial rituals, and also looked to see if any minor habits or automated actions could be traced to an original OCD belief which could be dismissed as 100% irrelevant. She consciously implemented the antagonist logic of relying on her senses in any situation where she felt the urge to avoid or neutralize.

Outcome. At the end of 20 weeks of IBA therapy, her principal primary and secondary inferences had become negligible (see Figures 6.2 and 6.3). She had started to see herself as non-OCD and her confidence in herself had also increased. She had less preoccupations with her self-worth and felt more sure of herself at work. She had also started a relationship for the first time in four years and was comfortable in her new house, which was a non-OCD zone. Her Y-BOCS total score of 4 was in the non-clinical range for both obsessions and compulsions. The gains were maintained at nine months follow-up.

Discussion

Essentially this case report has discussed the cognitive treatment through use of IBA of a lady diagnosed with severe OCD with OVI. The ideation consisted of a firm conviction in a bizarre mode of contamination and in the power of objects, animals and people to contaminate and be contaminated at a distance, and stay contaminated for years afterwards. The 'precautionary' measures she took to neutralize the contamination were often dictated to her by a 'voice', so there was also an element of dissociation.

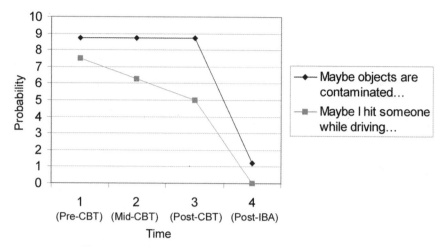

Figure 6.2   Case study 2 – primary inferences (0–10)

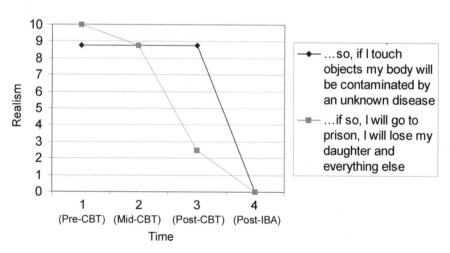

Figure 6.3   Case study 2 – secondary inferences (0–10)

There is controversy over the classification of OVI and certainly the more psychotic features present in other cases presented in the literature were not present in this lady's case. The labeling of obsessional thoughts as 'like a voice' is not uncommon even in non-OVI OCD and in this case there was insight that it was like a voice rather than actually a voice from an external source.

However, there was a very strong primary conviction that invisible dirt could have the power to contaminate and an equally strong belief in the correctness of her 'precautions'. This conviction was supported by a convincing narrative which had remained unquestioned until IBA therapy. Effectively, the primary intrusion was an inference based on imaginary premises, but taken 'as if' it was reality. Although such inferential confusion may also exist in non-OVI OCD, it is rare that the conviction level is so strong in non-OVI OCD either in primary or secondary appraisals. In fact, in non-OVI OCD, conviction in the correctness of the secondary appraisals is usually stronger than the conviction about primary inferences. In this case, the more usual CBT focusing on restructuring appraisals seems appropriate, whereby reducing over-reaction to the thought may modify obsessional preoccupation as well as strength of the primary inference (O'Connor et al., 2000). However, in OCD with OVI, the primary inference needs to be directly addressed as the source of, rather than just the occasion for, obsessional thinking.

The inferences in OVI are not interpretations in the hermeneutic sense of conscious interpretations made about an event, since the narrative essentially constructs a parallel imaginary world. What is seen is not 'seen' intrinsically but symbolically in terms of how it relates to a plot. In this case, it makes more sense to directly address the narrative plot rather than attempt a discrete reinterpretation of events. A story convinces the person that there is more there than can be seen, and learned physiological and emotional support systems reinforce the motivation to act 'as if' the imagined is real. Starting with the narrative as a unit is simply more descriptive of how clients themselves report their experience. It captures the lived-in quality of the experience and highlights the associated historical context in the past in which the inference may have developed and might have been adaptive. The narrative also reveals the dynamic theme or 'plot' which threads disparate associations into a credible story. The notion of 'plot' could be construed as a more dynamic version of 'a schema'. However, whereas schemas such as 'over-responsibility' take the form of top-down generalities, plots are rather bottom-up, idiopathic and complex. Typically, they contain several key elements and are best captured as complex themes rather than categories or summary statements.

The key elements of IBA are eliciting the narrative; producing awareness that the narrative incites the inference; giving insight into the subjective and 100% imaginary status of the narrative and inference; establishing that rehearsal of the narrative and rituals is antagonistic to using the senses; seeing what is there and making appropriate inferences; demonstrating that the small risk of things not being correct is itself an imaginary inference. The turning point in therapy for this lady was clearly the realization that her primary and secondary inferences formed part of a narrative that was 100%

imaginary, and was not even a little bit realistic. This intellectual insight was enacted emotionally by manipulating imaginary scenarios to reduce and augment her anxiety, and reinforce her awareness that imagination, not reality, controlled her OCD state, and so there was no point in trying to modify her anxiety by changing reality through rituals. Since the narrative was a product of the imagination, changing the imagination should be the goal. The task then became a question of building on this realization of the antagonism between belief in the imagination and confidence in her senses, by supplanting, through regular practice, the inverse inference of OCD by normal inference based on the senses.

IBA concentrates on revealing the processes by which inferences are built up and letting the person understand, play with and ultimately manage the workings of the narrative and its build-up towards the primary inference. Having obtained this insight, the person decides what is imaginary and what is real and then distances themselves from the imaginary convictions. IBA seems preferable also to questioning the veracity and implications of the primary inference itself. In such an approach, the therapist is in danger of colluding with the OVI by becoming a co-authority on the interpretation of the fundamental delusion-like belief.

The application of IBA within a relatively short time span requires at least some insight into the distress associated with the belief, motivated cooperation and the lack of ego-syntonic maintaining factors. The IBA uses awareness of the selective nature of OCD, plus awareness of discrepancies in inference processes used in and out of OCD situations in the therapy. The generally ego-dystonic quality of OCD is one element distinguishing OVI from DD. It has been hypothesized that delusions may serve the purpose of guarding the person from low self-esteem in an otherwise ordinary and depressing situation in life (Bentall et al., 1994). Although low self-esteem and low self-confidence may be hallmarks of OCD (Salkovskis, 1999), the person with OCD generally considers that the OCD exacerbates rather than relieves self-doubt. IBA pinpoints this unhealthy antagonism whereby acting on the basis of an imaginary narrative prevents development of confidence in the senses.

CHAPTER 7

FUTURE DIRECTIONS

IBA AND OTHER COGNITIVE THERAPY

IBA and Cognitive Appraisal Model

The inference-based approach (IBA) is a cognitive therapy and so shares the therapeutic aims and rationale of mainstream cognitive therapy (CT) for OCD. The aim in both cases is to reveal to the person how their thinking patterns lead them away from adaptive behavior towards performing acts that involve unnecessary effort and stress and that are self-sabotaging. As Paul Salkovskis (1999, p. 334) neatly puts it, 'How can people be helped to try to stop trying too hard', and we would add, 'and feel confident in using their senses in a normal way (as they do in other walks of life)?' The end point of therapy is that the person feels distanced enough from their obsessional thoughts not to dwell on them, analyze them, or try to think a way out of them, or react to them at all abnormally, but rather to dismiss them from the start as obsessional.

In the cognitive appraisal model, therapy targets the person's interpretation of intrusions that makes them important and compelling. There is evidence that OCD-specific beliefs about responsibility or risk of danger sensitize the person to react abnormally to otherwise normal intrusions, although there is controversy over whether these beliefs are primarily rooted in assumptions or deeper level schemata (Clark, 2002).

The IBA therapy targets the initial inference which sets the person off on an unnecessary doubting expedition which has no relevance in the here and now and leads usually to more doubt. The person learns at an early stage in the IBA program how to distinguish between genuine and obsessional doubt and how not to get drawn into and trapped in the web of doubt. Since the IBA and CBT approaches seem to target different stages in the obsessional process, Clark and O'Connor (2004) have suggested an upstream/downstream analogy to explain their complementarity. Although differing in terminology, both approaches would broadly agree on the mechanics of OCD maintenance. The more the person performs the compulsive ritualization, neutralization or avoidance, the more they are likely to continue in OCD performing mode. CBT draws on learning theory notions of reinforcement and insufficient exposure to permit habituation of anxiety and extinction of the ritual coupled with a lack of reality testing to allow falsification of OCD-specific beliefs.

Cognitive thinkers like Beck (1976) have also emphasized how pathological beliefs can take the person away from registering reality (and equating hypothesis with fact). The IBA model explicitly sets up a dialectic in inductive reasoning between certain experience coming through the senses and more remote experience, which can create doubt where there should be certainty.

From the IBA perspective, going into the doubting or questioning spiral only takes the person away from reality and the senses into possibilities. In doing so, there can never be resolution of the doubt since the more the person goes into the imaginary doubt, the further they remove themselves from the only source of certain information about current reality, namely sensory experience and knowledge related to the here and now. In extreme cases the person can enter a state of complete dissociation, an OCD bubble, where the person is completely unaware of real events around them (for example, their baby crying, traffic passing by). The person turns away from the senses by reasoning that the senses cannot be trusted, that what looks locked, clean, well placed, orderly, rubbish to be thrown out, is not as it appears. The IBA model also links the obsessional content of the unnecessary doubt firmly with a more pervasive insecurity manifested in self-doubt and lack of self-confidence in intentional self-world relations (e.g., 'I need to make extra effort to check for mistakes because I could be the kind of person who could make mistakes').

Discovering the self-theme is placed at the end of the program since there may not be a sufficient level of awareness until other stages have been covered. It could be that at the end of IBA therapy, despite clinical improvement, the repositioning of the self-theme is still a work-in-progress. However, where it is possible to access the self-theme, application and generalization of IBA strategies across different obsessions can be facilitated. In a recent case study by Guay et al. (2004), the self-theme, 'I could be like my father', was linked at the assessment stage to a range of OCD doubts and compulsions and at eight weeks of treatment there was complete remission of OCD symptoms. Cognitive researchers have also pointed to lack of self-confidence and self-ambivalence (Bhar & Kyrios, 2001) and self-fragility (Clark, 2004) as markers in OCD, but so far such insights have not been linked functionally to other OCD symptoms, although Sookman et al. (2001) proposed that vulnerable self-concept may exacerbate perception of threat.

In the IBA model, doubt is imposed on certainty. This doubt can lead to people feeling incompetent to perform the simplest act independent of OCD. Clients ask how they can know that their hands are clean, the doors are locked, that nothing is left behind. Such doubt can usually be dispelled by asking them to explain the know-how of actions, which they are inevitably able to do.

Although attempts have been undertaken to render cognitive and behavioral strategies seamless in CBT practice, they remain distinct; joined by a common rationale but applied at different moments in therapy. Cognitive processes do not replace behavioral strategies although they may enable them. The cognitive challenge addresses beliefs, which then enables the person to expose themselves and reality test further assumptions. Individual case studies using predominantly CT for OCD have shown some success, as Freeston et al. (2001) noted, and the person realizes that there is just no point in doing the OCD ritual. This cognitive focus holds true of IBA where the behavior is modified on the basis of a realization that the thinking producing the doubt is baseless, hence action on the grounds of the doubt is equally pointless. This approach avoids the need for the person to tolerate high levels of distress and arousal and replaces understanding of general processes of habituation with understanding of how idiosyncratic logic leads to a related action.

IBA can be applied clinically in conjunction with behavioral and appraisal strategies. It may be necessary at the beginning of therapy to address the person's evaluation of their OCD or their ability to cope in order to unlock a lack of motivation to participate in therapy. At the end of treatment, sometimes principles of habituation can aid understanding of a lingering emotional pull to do a ritual despite the intellectual realization of its irrelevance.

The IBA model would, however, make a distinction between appraisal, occurring as part of or as a direct result of the inductive narrative, and other appraisals independent of the OCD process, such as those termed by Clark (2004) as 'coping appraisals'. Appraisals involving, for example, exaggeration of danger and, possibly, responsibility and intolerance of uncertainty, would be viewed in IBA as the end result of the narrative recounting the secondary inferences following on from the primary inference. If I was really convinced that, because I left my light on, the apartment block would burn down and everybody's belongings and lodgings destroyed, it would seem realistic to feel anxious, guilty and responsible.

A similar convincing absorbing story could also account for other cognitive biases such as omission bias, and misperception and thought–action fusion. Walking past someone lying down on the pavement is not the same as injuring the person, but if in your imagination you are the only person in the vicinity and the person's life depends on immediate treatment, the allusion to complicity in manslaughter is not completely outlandish. The narrative approach shifts focus from cognitive structure, whether beliefs or traits, to cognitive process. It hence moves away from notions of distorted perceptions, or sensitized predispositions, towards understanding maladaptive inferences as a product of an observable, accessible reasoning process whose path can be traced in detail back from the initial problematic doubt.

A narrative approach then emphasizes idiosyncratic case formulation in OCD, linking the inference within a wider adaptational psychosocial perspective and targeting the evolution of the inductive reasoning process through a variety of devices in therapy. People do not have propensities to overgeneralize, catastrophize or feel unduly responsible, feelings that are located within them in a kind of contextless, no man's land. Rather, the dynamic interplay of inductive reasoning and behavior lead up to an obsessional narrative–action coupling, where action follows narrative conviction and self-construal.

As noted in the introduction, the concern here with reasoning ties in with work in delusional disorder (DD), and begs questions of whether a continuum model of OCD and DD as belief disorders is feasible, and also the extent to which the current IBA might be specifically tailored to DD as well as to other anxious beliefs. The continuum idea in its simplest form suggests that DD and OCD differ in degree on a number of dimensions defining belief, such as preoccupation, conviction level, emotion and insight. Insel and Askiskal (1986) proposed that even obsessions may become delusions as a consequence of learning resistance, poor insight and negative humor. But insight itself is not defined easily or uniformly (Marazziti et al., 2002) and is probably multidimensional (Grenier et al., 2004). Some authors argue that obsessional ideas cannot be satisfactorily dichotomized by insight and that a continuum model of fixity–flexibility of belief may have more clinical utility (Coles et al., 1996).

One could, from a conceptual point of view, characterize delusions at one extreme of a dimension characterized by certain conviction, poor insight, strong systematization with OVI and OCD on a scale characterized progressively with less of each by degrees. However, empirical support for this view is mixed. First, obsessional convictions can be strong, while delusional conviction can wax and wane. Second, the ways of defining insight vary and the evidence tying OCD subtypes to poor or good insight and tying insight to prognosis is equivocal.

Whereas some authors (e.g., Foa & Kozak, 1995) measure insight as a function of belief into secondary inference, our current research would tie insight to strength of primary inference. There is some evidence that PI is independent of SI and cognitive appraisal and is related to the Y-BOCS insight item number 11 (O'Connor *et al.*, 2003a). Clearly, the exact relationship of PI to obsessional content and other belief domains requires clarification.

Interestingly, clients with DD, unlike anxiety groups, score high on the Padua Inventory (Aardema *et al.*, 2004f). But items may be interpreted in a more paranoid than obsessional way. Furthermore, clients with DD also score high on the ICQ, suggesting that they share a high degree of inferential confusion. However, clearly they are not worried by it. Distrust of the senses and investment in subjective monologue may be seen as a conscious strategy to counteract a malevolent world, rather than a source of doubt and loss of self-confidence. Whereas in OCD the person may feel the need to go beyond their own sense of reality simply to be sure of what is there, in DD the person may feel the need to go beyond reality in order to feel important. In either case, confidence in self, senses and self-esteem might be underlying issues to pursue in explaining inferential confusion in OCD, OVI and DD.

In addition, there is clear use of the imagination in DD and the same reasoning devices seem present. It may be present to a greater degree in delusional patients. There is a tendency to categorize everything within a single homogenous menacing category. Beck and Rector (2002) have noted the crucial role of extended fantasy, and daydreaming as a predictive and activating factor in delusions. The extensive systematization could signify an increased level of assumption of living 'as if' in the imaginary world.

As in the case of OCD, there is also a pre-morbid self-theme linked closely with the content of the delusion. A cognitive therapy of the imagination would then seem appropriate to DD, addressing imaginary possibilities and modifying the possibility distribution from the margins upwards rather than attempting to challenge perceptual fit.

The worry characteristics of generalized anxiety disorder, on the other hand, form perhaps the opposite end of a belief spectrum to DD. Worries also take the form of an internal monologue, but several features of the narrative are distinct from OCD. The narrative addresses the future: it is occupied by real events, and is not necessarily intrinsically ego-dystonic. The monologue builds up to a worse-case scenario, and leaves the person stranded there, remote from coping resources. The monologue also counteracts any positive sense of outcome for the person and in some cases can spiral off to completely hypothetical concerns. The themes of worry are person-specific and also tend to relate strongly to a vulnerable self-theme related to coping ability: 'I'm likely to be exploited', 'I'm not able to cope'. In the case of worry, there is less absorption in 'as if' and more in 'what if', so already there is less inferential confusion since the worry relates to the future not the present, with the insight that it is not yet reality.

Cognitive Therapy and Narrative

We noted in Chapter 4 that Cognitive Therapy (CT) could offer an obvious clinical home for reasoning models, using reasoning paradigms as an anchor for cognitive theory. CT recognizes the importance of language use and ways of talking in therapy (Barnard, 1985).

Yet, the clinical interest of CT is not within the structure of reasoning or language, but with the cognitive structure of beliefs behind the reasoning. Beck's (1976) original cognitive formulation of psychological problems was in terms of 'incorrect premises and a proneness to distorted imaginal experiences' (p. 19). He noted the importance of 'common place experiences such as ... making incorrect inferences on the basis of ... not distinguishing adequately between imagination and reality' (pp. 19–20). Later in the same text he emphasizes that it may not be the patient's appraisal of reality that is distorted but 'his system of making inferences and drawing conclusions' (p. 219). However, the concern of cognitive therapy is with the rules and beliefs which code experience and guide automatic thoughts and irrational ideas. There is no attempt to explore a reasoning template further in terms of deductive/inductive processes. On the other hand, cognitive theorists may feel quite justifiably that reliance on belief has been extremely fruitful and has already characterized a range of psychiatric disorders.

A recent example of how reasoning becomes embedded in schema in CT appears in Beck's reworking of his original schema model. Beck (1996) begins by acknowledging thinking researchers (Kelly, Bartlett, Piaget) as his inspiration. He notes the need to address discrepancies within cognitive theory, particularly the apparent multi-modal inter-action of affective, physiological and thinking systems in dysfunctional responses. He attempts to reconcile such interactions within a modal theory. He begins with the case history of Bob, who is afraid to use an elevator. Beck analyses Bob's fear sequence as comprising an activating circumstance around the anticipation of the event, followed by an orienting schema which signals alarm and in turn activates all systems in this mode whether affect, motivational, attentional or physiological. However, this activation is controlled by the cognitive system as the principal system for the assignment of meaning through control of selection of data, attention, interpretation, memory and recall. Other separate cognitive structures represent goals and expectations. Yet more remote structures are involved in the secondary elaboration of more abstract themes such as social desirability and self-worth. Experiences are abstracted and organized around specific themes and it is the cognitive schemas which are involved in inferences and interpretations.

Here, the conscious control system can over-ride automated impulses by setting controls on primal systems and applying logic to evaluate the products of the primal system as irrational. We know biased cognitive processing is underway by its products, namely the cognitive distortions. Attentional and thinking processes are then locked into the specific content of any one activated mode. A key metaphor in the modal theory is 'energetics', since such activation stays 'charged' or 'energized' for some time until it is de-energized or discharged.

Core beliefs, according to Beck (1996), consist of the most sensitive components linked to self-concept. Conditional rules are embedded in orienting schema and stipulate under which conditions beliefs are applicable. They take the form of 'if–then' clauses, and the rules can be conditional, compensatory, or imperative. If I mingle with others, I will be rejected (conditional rule) but if I avoid others, I avoid rejection (compensatory rule). I must not be rejected (imperative rule). The particular conditional rules for OCD, according to Beck, are: (1) conditional: If I'm exposed to danger, grave consequences will occur. If I do not act to prevent harm, I am responsible; (2) compensatory: If I take appropriate measures, I can prevent harm; (3) imperative: I must do everything to prevent harm.

One cognitive approach to representing the complexity of experience is given in Barnard (1985) and Teasdale's (1996) interacting cognitive subsystem (ICS) analysis. According to ICS, different codes represent different experiences. Certain codes represent raw sensory experience, others represent regular patterns of experience. Information processing can, however, transform experiences from one code to another. In addition, there are also two basic levels of meaning. There is propositional specific meaning which relates to discrete concepts such as 'Roger has brown hair'. There is also an implication level which represents a more general holistic level of meaning as in poems, parables, stories. Such synthesized general meanings can cause holistic generalization which can have great impact and explain, for example, the greater emotional impact of a poem versus text. Coherent patterns of implication code represent schematic models of experience whereas, according to Teasdale (1996), Johnson-Laird-type mental models represent only semantic relations. Schema models represent interrelations between high level patterns which are implicit, not explicit. Teasdale suggests that change at the implicational level is necessary to change emotion reliably. Teasdale also feels that schematic processing should proceed at the holistic level, modifying whole experiences of, say, failure rather than individual elements. The implicational code deals with how meanings are generated by different contexts and the strategies suggested to effect holistic change resemble narrative approaches. Altering coherent packages of meaning and sense may be achieved through replaying scenes and using guided discovery techniques.

In fact, the essence of the ICS model is quite compatible with a narrative approach, where narratives necessarily make references to near and remote events within the same text.

Interestingly, CT prefers Socratic dialogue (SD) to narrative technique as a means of persuasion, which, as Socrates himself realized, was inherently the more argumentative rhetorical form. The aim of SD is not to look at how a person's position makes sense to them but, by repeated questioning, to expose the fallacies, or incoherence in the argument. In CT, language is just a sign pointing somewhere else for the source of the error, often to hypothetical higher order cognitive products. The unproblematic use of contracted language terms as a medium for representing beliefs and thoughts, as isolated stand-alone units, reflects the view of language as a means of communication, not as a formative influence. CT's neglect of language can in part be attributed to the distinction between the mediational realist model adopted implicitly by CT and the constructionist model of reasoning.

A problem with the current CT neglect of the important role of language devices in the construction of problems, is that CT inadvertently reinforces the misleading use of language devices by the client. One example here is the use of the word 'perfectionism' to describe some compulsive motivations. Clients with OCD frequently justify their compulsive action in terms of perfectionism: 'I'm just an extreme perfectionist, I can't be satisfied until it's absolutely well done'. Clinicians dealing with pathological perfectionism (PP) have underlined how indeed PP can undermine performance. However, PP is generally characterized by an inability to tolerate mistakes, placing a high performance as an obligation, having unrealistic expectation of self and others, over-identification of self with good performance, and so on (Basco, 2000).

In OCD, the so called 'perfectionist' action is in no way related even to PP, since it is actually performance of a task totally unrelated and irrelevant to the task the person wishes to perform. But the unnecessary task becomes confused with perfection and is even conceptually blended as the perfect job.

A client spends two hours every evening hanging his trousers exactly symmetrically on the hanger and spacing all trousers 3 cm apart. He justifies his actions by saying he wishes to keep his clothes 'perfectly well hung, well kept and organized, nothing less'. But where is the tailor's manual which says clothes are well kept if they are always hanging symmetrically? Do people working in clothes shops who depend on keeping clothes well for their livelihood hang clothes in this way? In fact, such counsel is likely to have the adverse effect of creasing the trousers repeatedly in one place.

A similar confusion is present in a man who spends 1½ hours to fill out a cheque because all the letters must be equidistant from each other and above the line in order for him to do a perfect job. But he is not doing a perfect job, he is doing another irrelevant job, rather than perfectly doing the real job of legibly writing a cheque. The remoteness of the second job from any perfection of the main job is only evident from the narrative supporting the inference that 'maybe it's not perfect'. The narrative reveals the subjective nature of the performance criteria.

In the case of the cheque writer, he was confusing an aesthetic with a functional criteria: 'Well, sign writers take all sorts of measurements before they paint their signs and the evenness and spacing are beautiful and look so good, so it applies to my writing as well.' But the person is not sign writing, he is filling in a cheque to be cashed. The allusion to sign writing is irrelevant. Accepting these conceptually blended actions at face value as a form of PP may encourage inferential confusion since the term suggests a continuity between real and OCD driven tasks; one is an extreme of the other when really the tasks are completely discontinuous.

Other limiting features of CT theory concern: (1) reliance on information-processing metaphors to explain constructivist cognitive operations; (2) ill-defined and poorly validated constructs; (3) the growing divorce between cognitive theory and practice; (4) the failure of CT to be self-reflexive about its own metaphors and language use, in particular its reliance on common-sense terms and metaphors; (5) the failure to see thinking 'errors' or 'biases' as adaptive thinking within a specific life story; (6) the effectiveness of CT independent of behavior therapy; (7) the uncertain status of foundational theoretical claims; (8) the shift away from early idiopathic content-specific cognitive formulation towards broader and broader schema to account for cognitive distortions; and (9) problems with the reliance on introspection as a means of accessing cognition or meta-cognition.

Christine Lee (1992) has addressed several of these problems in her critique of cognitive therapy. She notes a great deal of research seems to be no more than correlations between the self-reports of hypothetical constructs. She quotes Skinner (1977), 'Cognitive psychologists invent internal surrogates which become the subject matter of their science.' Cognitive constructs are particularly good at reifying metaphor. She notes that models which deal entirely with hypothetical constructs complicate rather than simplify, since everything hypothetical is in mid-air, not grounded. The lack of clarity in defining unobservable variables simply leads to a proliferation of theories.

Such is the case with schema theory and Russell and van den Broek (1992) make the point that the proliferation of schema is likely to undermine their explanatory value. McGinn and Young (1996) consider there are 18 schemas which guide different types of interpersonal behavior, but the schemas seem a mix of motivation, attitude, distorted belief. Indeed, for every micro-part of life, there seems to be a schema which fits areas of interpersonal, social, affective, attachment activity. One solution to this proliferation, as we saw with Beck (1996), is to move towards multi-modal schema. The definition and operationalization of a schema vary greatly (Williams, 1996). A schema is a regrouping of knowledge and experience deposited in long-term memory. However, the influence of a schema is more measured by its effect than by direct access to its content, whereas people produce narratives all the time.

Clinical insights of CT have generally proved correct, for example, in linking negative thoughts to mood states; in actively involving the person in conscious change through thought modification; in showing that resilient thought patterns lie behind fixed behavior patterns. However, tests of the predictions of cognitive theory have not been so supportive. Bieling and Kuyken (2003) remark that although descriptive elements of cognitive theory seem upheld, explanatory theory has lent support and this has a negative impact on cognitive case formulation.

As Beck (1996) noted, there have been several discrepancies. In general, the causal direction of thoughts to emotions has not been supported. There is little systematic evidence that cognitive therapy adds effectively to behavior therapy, and currently no CT is 'purely' cognitive although there have been tentative case studies. A key prediction of the cognitive model is that different disorders have high content specificity, but although this appeared the case initially and the cognitive content seemed to differ between depression and anxiety, increasingly, belief models and meta-cognitive approaches are emphasizing general similarities in appraisals (Clark & Steer, 1996). We have noted earlier the overlap between OCD relevant appraisals such as threat and responsibility. Others such as intolerance of uncertainty cut across different disorders such as OCD and GAD. At a meta-cognitive level, the coping appraisals of the thoughts about thoughts may be even more general.

Meta-Cognitive Model and Obsessive Compulsive Disorder

Recent theoretical and clinical applications of the meta-cognitive model have been developed by Wells and Matthews (1994) and Wells (1997). In this model, obsessive thoughts are considered to trigger meta-cognitive beliefs of three sorts: thought–event fusion (TEF), thought–action fusion (TAF), and thought–object fusion (TOF). These meta-cognitive beliefs are defined as believing that thoughts mean an event or an action will occur on the basis of having a thought in itself. In the case of object fusion, it is about believing that objects carry memories, thoughts or feelings. The meta-cognitive beliefs also include negative and positive beliefs about performing compulsive rituals, that is, the meaning of the compulsions. For example, a negative meaning about a compulsion would be that the rituals will take over forever. A positive belief about the rituals would be that they keep you safe. An alternative explanation of meta-cognitive beliefs about TAF and TOF has been proposed by O'Connor and Aardema (2003).

There is debate over the processes producing fusion experiences. TAF has been linked to appraisals of over-responsibility (Thodarson & Shafran, 2002) or to a meta-belief which gives priority to internally generated thoughts (Wells, 2000). However, inferential confusion is a process which could account for TAF, particularly where imagination plays a role in rendering remote events more probable, for example imagining my mother falling ill makes another event more probable.

As part of an absorption in an imaginary story, a person may experience physical sensations of events 'as if' they are occurring. The person starts with the possibility, 'What if my thoughts make an accident more likely?', 'What if thinking of illness makes me ill?', and then lives 'as if' the possibility were plausible.

TAF and other fusion experiences reflect a greater degree of absorption in imaginary possibilities than non-fusion experiences. Indeed, when looking at the narratives associated with fusion experiences, one finds the thinker more likely to produce inferential confusion. Experimental paradigms, which elicit fusion experiences, explicitly use imagination as in the instructional set (e.g. Radomsky et al., 2002). The following thought-shape narrative is taken from O'Connor and Aardema (2003, p. 231).

> I was feeling comfortable like I'd lost some weight, my jeans and pullover felt loose, then I weighed myself and saw on the scale I'd gained two pounds, so I began to think I can't feel OK since I must look really fat (dismissing sensory evidence in favour of a hypothetical reality). I thought about a pizza slice I'd eaten earlier in the week and had the same sense of fullness (purely imaginary sequence) so I thought if my stomach is sticking out, people will look and point at me as well (misapplying facts to personal context); I felt I'd better hide my stomach, so I ended up feeling really fat and hating myself.

Accessing Cognitions

In her critique, Lee (1992) notes that it is unclear how cognitive variables arise from external events; it is unclear how cognitive variables interact with each other. So the exact predictions of cognition on behavior are unclear. Furthermore, cognitive assessment techniques require consistency and accuracy at the descriptive level if they are to give credibility to hypothetical entities. Hence it may be better for cognitive theory to become less abstract and more grounded in experience. Otherwise it remains at the level of common-sense metaphor. Even its main means of evaluation of cognition is problematic, since self-report relies on a facility of introspection which is doubtful. The classic methods for assessing cognitions all involve different degrees of self-report, either by cognitive listing, speaking aloud, or questionnaire methods.

Wilson and Dunn (2003) note that there may be motivational constraints on the recall of memories, but a more persuasive limit on self-knowledge is that much of the mind is inaccessible to conscious awareness. When people are asked to introspect about their performance or on how they arrived implicitly at judgements, they are unable to do so.

As McClelland et al. (1989) have argued, implicit motives 'automatically influence behavior without conscious effort', whereas self-attributed motives need more deliberative effortful behaviors. This also applies to comparisons between implicit and explicit personality traits which seem to be dissociated. People often disguise automated implicit attitudes to appear in a better light.

As Wilson and Dunn (2003) note, there is considerable evidence, however, that people have limited access to the reasons for their evaluations and that the process of generating reasons can have negative consequences. When people analyze, they become less satisfied with their choices (Wilson et al., 1993), and introspect poorly about predictions of their own behavior (Wilson & LaFleur, 1995), and they actually reduce the correlation between their expressed feelings and their later behavior (Wilson & Dunn, 1986; Wilson et al., 1984). There is a discrepancy between people's evaluation of a product and expert evaluations of it (Wilson & Schooler, 1991).

Why does analyzing reasons have these effects? Consistent with the idea that introspection is often a constructive process, people do not have complete access to the actual reasons behind their feelings, attitudes, and judgements and thus generate reasons that are consistent with cultural and personal theories and are accessible in memory (Nisbett & Wilson, 1977). But, people do not recognize that the reasons they have just generated are incomplete or inaccurate, and thus assume that their attitude is the one implied by these reasons. Put differently, people construct a new attitude, at least temporarily, that is consistent with the reasons that happen to come to mind, but which might not correspond to their implicit attitudes (Wilson et al., 1989, 1995, 2000).

People seem particularly bad at revealing and explaining their reasons for actions or thoughts or other implicit information. Most studies on self-perception theory involve self-fabrication, not self-revelation. There may of course also be a healthy side to deceptive self-knowledge since its lack of insight may speed up some performance. Dretske (1981) has noted that introspection is inferential. It requires a connecting inference between observing an experience and talking of that experience. In other words, introspection is a separate behavior in its own right, not a faithful observation of experience. Wilson and Dunn (1986) suggest that rather than searching for reasons, people should focus on the act itself, and maybe use visualization to gain more insight. Vividly imagining an upcoming scene allows someone to sample the feelings directly rather than passing through another behavior such as introspection. In other words, sticking close to the lived-in narrative of the experience is more likely to capture the cognitive process than attempting to access the process via contextless thoughts which involve an additional level of behavior.

In order to accept a narrative turn, CT would need to accept that knowledge is conveyed in narrative form, so that the narrative is the unit of representing experience not reducible to word choice, stereotypic statement or logical proposition, and that events, people, emotions, acquire significance within the telling of the emotion. Narrative organizes and constructs. The narrative unit becomes the initial primordial unit of cognitive analysis. Its richness, irregularity, multi-level reference points are accepted as they appear. This contextualist view, as Russell (1991) notes, is fully consistent with the guiding principles of CBT. In fact, many CT techniques verge already on constructionist approaches, and there have already been valiant efforts to integrate CT and constructionism (Mahoney, 2003).

FUTURE DEVELOPMENT IN IBA

The IBA program here has been validated on adult OCD and people with over-invested ideas. It has not been systematically investigated as an intervention for children or groups with special difficulties. However, narrative approaches have proved useful in reducing anxiety in children (Smith & Nylund, 1997).

Do all obsessions contain doubt? Some intrusions are reported as images, but as Beck and Emery (1985) note, images usually dwell on the consequence of the initial thought, and are not primary. A doubting inference such as, 'I could have an accident', might lead to vivid images of injury, which then become a principal source of distress.

The concept of inferential confusion needs further work in a number of areas, such as its relationship with compulsive behaviors, and enhancing the specificity of the concept of inferential confusion to obsessive-compulsive symptoms. In this regard, it should be noted that the current measurement of inferential confusion with the Inferential Confusion Questionnaire focuses on one sub-aspect of inferential confusion, namely a distrust of the senses and inverse inference, while there may be other processes that lead to inferential confusion as identified by O'Connor and colleagues, in particular the roles of irrelevant associations, category errors, selective use of acts, and individual levels in absorption that lead the person to live the obsessions as a reality (imaginary sequences). Further work is currently ongoing in an expansion of the Inferential Confusion Question-naire to include these concepts in the questionnaire in order to identify other underlying dimensions of inferential confusion. This may also aid in further differentiating the Inferential Confusion Questionnaire from the concept of over-estimation of threat, and while these constructs can be empirically distinguished, it would be preferable to also separate both concepts in questionnaires. Similarly, experimental studies examining the impact of reasoning in both increasing and decreasing doubt may yield more specific targets for therapy.

The multidimensional investigation of cognitive variables in OCD remains a challenge even with the use of partial correlations to establish the unique variance of cognitive measures with obsessive-compulsive symptoms, which do not completely eliminate competing hypotheses. In this regard, some of the methods used in the study of Aardema et al. (2004c) may be promising. In this study, the item set of the ICQ and over-estimation of threat scale (OBQ) were subjected to factor analyses with varimax rotation, which produces independent constructs. The benefit of generating psychometrically unrelated constructs is that it allows for more conclusive statements as to the unique variance that these constructs share with obsessive-compulsive symptoms. However, a drawback of this research may be that a considerable amount of power is needed if one wishes to include the item sets of a large number of cognitive domains.

Another important area for future research is to link psychometric data to experimental methods investigating the concept of inferential confusion. In this respect, it is encouraging to report that there have been some important advances in the operationalization of doubt and the experimental manipulation of inferential confusion (Aardema et al., 2004d, ongoing project). Primarily inferential confusion deals with a confusion between reality and possibility, which would dictate conviction levels in a possible state of affairs. Therefore, OCD patients, as compared to other clinical populations, would be expected to react in different proportions to reality and possibility-based information in reaching a conclusion about a probable state of affairs. In particular, it would be expected that OCD patients would be particularly susceptible to the negating influence of possibility-based information in inferring a state of affairs in reality. Experimental manipulations by introducing reality and possibility-based information to participants may reveal important differences in how a person comes to doubt reality and believe in a probable state of affairs that negates reality.

A FINAL COMMENT

Several authors agree that specificity of cognitive domains is key to an understanding of obsessive-compulsive disorder, and it has been suggested that further work is needed in identifying specific obsessive-compulsive beliefs (Steketee *et al.*, 2002; Taylor, 2002a). If the cognitive specificity hypothesis of Beck in terms of specific dysfunctional beliefs is correct, then indeed we would be wise to continue searching for beliefs that are specifically relevant to OCD.

The inferential confusion model provides an alternative cognitive approach to OCD that accommodates idiosyncratic mental content in OCD, yet, at the same time, identifies common characteristics in this disorder in terms of cognitive processes. Inferential confusion has been subjected to a large number of systematic controls in several psychometric and experimental studies while controlling for other cognitive variables proposed to be relevant to OCD. However, it is too soon for any conclusive statements, and, in particular, there is a need to replicate current findings. Whatever the merits of an inference-based approach, the current results suggest that there are important processes operating in OCD not fully recognized by other cognitive models of OCD, and that an approach focusing on these processes may lead to a greater specificity in cognitive interventions.

APPENDIX 1

OVERVIEW OF OUR TREATMENT PROGRAM FOR OBSESSIVE-COMPULSIVE DISORDER

OVERVIEW OF HOW YOUR OCD WORKS AND HOW WE WILL TREAT IT

Obsessive-compulsive disorder, as the name implies, has two components: obsession and compulsion. The obsession drives the compulsion and the aim of the compulsion is to reduce or neutralize the anxiety associated with the doubt. Let's see exactly how obsessions lead to compulsions.

The OCD sequence is as follows:

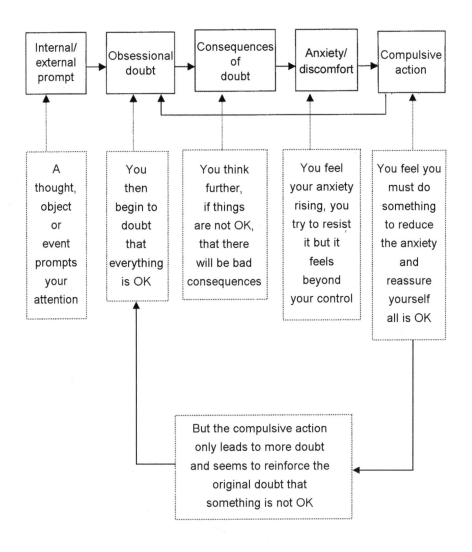

Examples

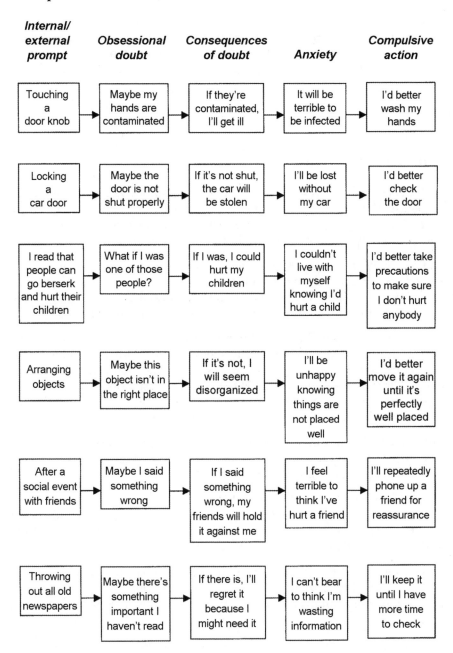

Now fill in the sequence of your obsession.

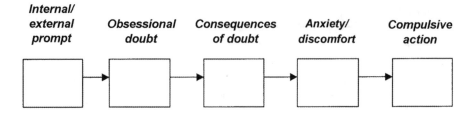

THE DOUBT

So, OCD begins with your doubt. It is the doubt that leads you into the OCD sequence. If you did not experience the doubt, you would stay firmly grounded in the reality, in the here and now. You would not get anxious and you would not feel forced to do the compulsion.

Notice *everything* in the OCD sequence follows from the initial doubt. All the consequences and anxiety, plus the need to do the ritual. You may sometimes feel a little better when you have done the ritual, but of course giving in to the obsession reinforces the credibility of the initial doubt.

The first point you will learn in the program is that OCD doubt is not the same as normal doubt. In normal questioning, you instinctively look for an answer from reality using your senses. Example: Was that bang the window closing? Is the coffee still warm? The doubts are easily resolved by seeking evidence in the here and now, you look at the window, you feel the coffee cup. Also you accept this sense information as final.

But in OCD doubt, the opposite is the case and the questioning leads you away from reality and your senses into OCD-land where doubt only leads to more doubt, not to a resolution.

So now you might say, why does the OCD doubt lead to more doubt and not to a resolution, since I perform my ritual precisely in order to reduce the doubt and feel more certain? But of course you never feel certain about the doubt, even if you do the ritual several times – why so?

The reason is that the OCD doubt is based on a subjective story which has no basis in reality. Usually what happens is that just as your senses are telling you everything is OK, in jumps the doubting story with...yes, but maybe...

In the program you will learn to distinguish between real sense information and stories, which can sometimes be difficult. Doubting stories usually begin with a 'yes, but maybe...'

Examples of doubting stories:

Sense information:
> The door looks firmly closed...but...maybe...

Story:
> There is dust inside the lock which I can't see which makes it not shut properly and I remember reading about a person who thought the door was locked but then got robbed, so I'd better go back and check because...

Obsessional doubt:
> Maybe the door isn't shut, even if I know I closed it.

Sense information:
> My hands look perfectly clean...but...maybe...

Story:
> There were invisible germs on the pole I touched and the invisible germs might have jumped onto my skin because microbes exist and the microbes might be capable of burrowing into my skin.

Obsessional doubt:
> So maybe my hands are really contaminated even if I see nothing.

The story leads you to believe that maybe there is something wrong in reality and that therefore you should act in reality to overcome it. But the doubt is only a story. So when you give in to the story, you are only encouraging more doubt. Which is why the more you perform the ritual, the deeper you go into OCD, the less you are in touch with reality and so the more you doubt. Ironically, in going into OCD-land, you sometimes feel you are getting deeper into reality, but it's exactly the opposite: the more you go into OCD-land, the further away you go from reality.

The sequences are as follows:

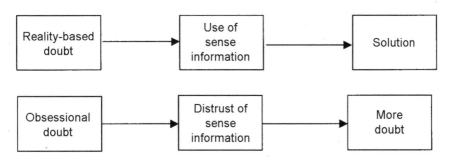

You might argue that it is exactly because you are unsure of your senses that you doubt. But our research shows it is exactly the opposite. You will learn in the program that it is only when you are certain according to your senses, that the obsessional doubt then takes over, and tells you *not* to be sure of your sense information. It trumps the senses and creates doubt on the basis of a good story, not on the basis of sense information.

How it seems:

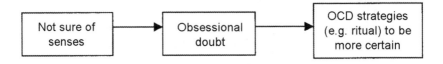

How it is:

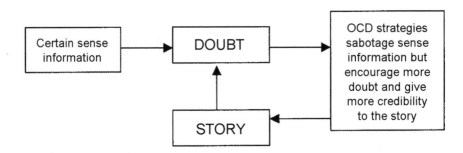

Now as we have said, you are obviously convinced that your OCD story, even though it is triggered inside your head, has a basis. If not, you would not give it credibility and you would not get anxious about it and act on it. For example, you are not afraid that a bear will attack you now. Because you do not believe there is a bear here, so you are not afraid. Your degree of belief in the story influences your level of anxiety. If you didn't believe in the story, you would not be anxious. So we need to show you how the story is really baseless and constructed on faulty logic.

In fact, the OCD is a bit like a magician leading you to believe things which are not real. Except with magicians you suspect this, but with OCD you are unsuspecting.

Please write down your story behind your obsession. It will begin with:

Maybe... _____

_____

_____

In the program we will look one by one at the reasoning errors in the OCD story which lead you to believe the obsessional story is possible, when actually it is baseless, in the context in which it arrives.

In the program we compare the way you reason in OCD situations with the way you reason in other comparable situations. You will see that the big difference is the way you ground your reasoning in the senses in the here and now in non-OCD situations. You don't run off with stories which import facts from elsewhere as though they are happening now. YOU TRUST YOUR SENSES.

In the program, we compare in detail how you deal with danger in non-OCD situations (example: crossing the road) and how this differs from OCD coping with danger because you are using your senses. So OCD takes you away from reality. You lose touch with the here and now and enter a 'bubble'.

But you may say ...

... DOING THE RITUAL MAKES ME FEEL BETTER

You feel better because you have given in to the OCD. It's like giving in to someone shouting orders at you. Initially you feel less stressed. But one thing should be clear, doing the action does not make you more secure, IT MAKES YOU LESS SECURE. Also giving in does not make you less stressed, IT MAKES YOU MORE STRESSED.

OCD makes you more stressed because you are constantly putting in more effort than necessary and doing irrelevant actions to make yourself feel secure. But effectively, you are working overtime for nothing and worse, all your effort is sabotaging your security, and at the end of all this, you are more anxious then when you started. That's why people often end up avoiding OCD situations. It all seems so stressful. Anticipating, preparing, all that extra attention, muscle tension, you're worn out after OCD, and yet you think OCD makes you less stressed? OCD is some salesman!

Extra efforts I make in OCD situations:

_____

_____

_____

You only feel better because you have given in to a screaming bully and if you do as the bully says, s/he stops screaming for a short while, but of course in the long run you reinforce the bully.

How can OCD make you more secure when OCD takes you away from reality? Remember, you go into the OCD spiral on the basis of a subjective doubt which is generated by a story. The more you go into OCD, the more you generate doubt, since this is the only outcome. OCD peddles doubt so it cannot give you anything else. You think you will find a solution in continuing the questioning, but mostly you just doubt more. Sometimes a rule will let you out of the spiral. Example: I've done this five times or I've put a lot of effort in so it must be done. But you are NEVER more certain of real information than when you started the doubt, you are always LESS certain. The reason is because you were certain before the OCD doubt came along, but the OCD made you doubt your sense of certainty with its story. So now you are not focused on reality at all but on a story. So actually OCD is exposing you to more danger while you are absorbed in its story. We have met people who have ignored real dangers and been hurt because they were too absorbed in their OCD spiral.

BUT EVEN IF MY DOUBT IS NOT BASED IN REALITY, IT STILL COULD BE CORRECT

We have said that OCD is an imaginary story, now we add another claim: the OCD doubt is ALWAYS SENSE-less.

Now that sounds a brazen claim, after all you might say, OK, it may be imaginary but even imaginary ideas can come true, or just be true by coincidence. However, in the case of OCD, we know it is always unfounded again by logic because of the way the OCD story is constructed. The doubting takes you away from the here and now by making you believe a story that has nothing to do with the current context. It tells you to ignore your senses. So it is *against* reality from the start.

Your senses have already told you that all is correct. In fact, your senses have given you CERTAIN information as they always do on the current state of affairs. The OCD then goes against this certainty by creating an imaginary story. But since the original sense information was correct, it came from your senses and is real, then the OCD must always be unreal.

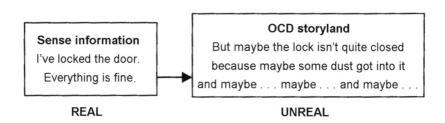

The doubt of course jumps in so quickly you don't realize that you were certain before it arrived. This is why in the program we get you to slow down, break up the sequence and create distance between your senses and the doubt.

The proof that the OCD story is false is that never once, in our experience, has an OCD 'maybe' turned out to be true.

How often has your OCD story been correct?

_____

_____

_____

What proof have you ever had that your OCD story is correct?

_____

_____

_____

OCD SABOTAGE

However, not only is the OCD always wrong, it's even worse, since it sabotages the very action it is supposed to make secure.

First of all, people with OCD are often so caught up in the OCD bubble they are not aware of what is going on around them. They may not hear their baby cry. They may not notice a car looming up. They may not realize they are being pick-pocketed.

But OCD actions can also directly sabotage the aim of being secure. For example, testing a door several times per day will make it loose. Asking people if you said the right thing because you are afraid to upset them eventually will make them upset. Staring at a locker to make sure it is closed properly so you won't be robbed will draw the attention of thieves. Scrubbing your hands to remove invisible infections will eventually destroy protective skin.

List some examples of how your OCD sabotages your security:

_____

_____

_____

SO WHY DO I HAVE MY OCD?

You are probably asking why you have one or several subtype(s) of OCD but not others. Please fill in your subtype(s) here: _____. As you know, there are other subtypes which you do not experience. The answer is simply that you have a theme of vulnerability which makes you more likely to respond to some prompts than others with an imaginary story. This is something you have learned usually in childhood. To discover your theme, we start again with logic. If you are afraid that 'maybe' you have made an error, then clearly you consider yourself the type of person who could make an error. At the same time a strong part of your image is that you do not wish to be seen as someone who could make an error. As we shall see in the program, this negative self-conception, like the doubt it drives, is also baseless. But of course you treat it as a real possibility – you have to guard against it – and because it itself is imaginary, so it further incites the imagination. So what is your theme? To discover your theme: (1) take the content of your doubt, it always begins with a maybe; (2) if you have this 'maybe', it means you consider yourself the kind of person to whom this maybe could happen. So your self-referent theme is:

I am the kind of person who could maybe ...

_____

_____

_____

So we now have a complete picture of how your doubt is produced (by the story) and maintained (by your acting as if the story were true).

The end-point of therapy is that you are able to carry out actions using just your senses. No stories and no extra efforts or strategies. So, in other words, our end-point in your case is:

I am able to: _____

_____

without doing: _____

In order to get to this point, we need to go through several steps in the program.

First, you learn to recognize the doubt for what it is, an obsessional doubt not to be taken seriously.

Next, we teach you to distance yourself from the doubt by pausing when it comes along and reflecting on where it comes from.

The *third step* is gaining the ability to distance yourself from the power of the OCD story by recognizing the reasoning errors which convince you it is possible, and recounting an alternative, more reality-based story. This new story also helps the *fourth step* which is to confront your vulnerability theme and see that there is no evidence for you not to have confidence in yourself. Gaining confidence is an important part of the program.

Finally, you learn through practice using only your senses, feeling confident in your senses and not putting in any extra effort than you do in normal non-OCD actions. We apply these strategies one by one to your obsessions, arranged in order of difficulty so we start with the easier and progress to the more difficult.

You should cover all the steps at your own pace. Although the treatment follows a pattern, it is always individually tailored to your needs.

So in conclusion, our program emphasizes:

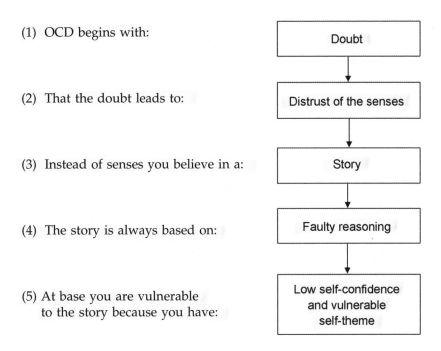

(1) OCD begins with: Doubt

(2) That the doubt leads to: Distrust of the senses

(3) Instead of senses you believe in a: Story

(4) The story is always based on: Faulty reasoning

(5) At base you are vulnerable   Low self-confidence
    to the story because you have: and vulnerable
                                              self-theme

In the program, we address all aspects of this model step by step in order to eliminate the doubt and restore confidence in your self and your senses.

If you have any queries about this brief overview, please ask your therapist and answer the following queries:

- Did you understand this text?   ☐ Yes   ☐ No

- Did it tell you new things about OCD?   ☐ Yes   ☐ No

- Do you find the model credible?   ☐ Yes   ☐ No
- Are you willing to be open-minded and give the program a try?
                                                          ☐ Yes   ☐ No
- Do you have any major objections to the program?   ☐ Yes   ☐ No
  If so, what? _____
  _____
  _____

APPENDIX 2

WORKSHEETS, EXERCISE SHEETS AND TRAINING CARDS

WORKSHEET 1
OBSESSIONAL AND NORMAL DOUBT

In many ways Obsessive-Compulsive Disorder (OCD) begins with doubt. Doubt occurs whenever you are not sure of something, or when you have the feeling that things might not be 'quite right'. By definition, when you doubt you are uncertain. There is also the feeling that you could be more certain. These experiences happen to everyone with OCD, no matter which particular form your OCD might take. Whether you compulsively check, wash, order, hoard or otherwise, you would feel no need to do so if you didn't start to doubt in the first place. For example, the person who repeatedly checks the door is motivated to do so because he/she doubts it is closed. The person who washes constantly feels the urge to wash, because there is doubt that his/her hands are clean. Without the doubt there is no compulsion. Likewise, without the doubt about contamination you would not worry about possible consequences like getting ill or if you doubt you left the door unlocked, you would not worry about the house being robbed. In other words, not only is doubt the cause of the compulsions, it is also responsible for a lot of discomfort and anxiety that would not be there if there was no doubt. However, what makes these persistent obsessional doubts different from normal doubts? Some of the characteristics and differences between obsessional and normal doubts are listed below:

(a) Normal doubt or questioning occurs with *direct* evidence from your senses and in an appropriate context.
(b) Normal doubt is resolved quickly once the proper information or evidence is obtained.
(c) Obsessional doubt occurs when you are already certain from a common-sense point of view that all has been done.
(d) Obsessional doubt excludes evidence since it is trying to go beyond the senses.
(e) Obsessional doubt increases the more you think about it.
(f) In obsessional doubt you never know exactly what you are looking for. It's always a general 'maybe'.

Examples of normal doubt or questioning:

(1) Will it rain tomorrow?
(2) How long will the journey take?

Such normal doubts occur with specific evidence or information for the doubt. They occur in an appropriate *context*. For example, you may have plans to spend the next day outside, or you noticed you were running late for an appointment. Also, these doubts are quickly resolved (check the weather report, or do a simple calculation on how much longer the journey will take), and from a common-sense point of view, you would be convinced all had been done.

Examples of OCD doubt or questioning:

(1) Did I shut the stove?
(2) Did I read that word correctly?

These doubts, if they are indeed obsessional, occur without specific evidence or information. You would check without having direct evidence or information that the stove was still on, or that you didn't read the word correctly. The doubt would arise in a situation without having any real indication that the stove is left on. Even if from a common-sense point of view you know you have checked enough, the compulsive urge would continue, and you would doubt more, the more you think about it.

EXERCISE 1
OBSESSIONAL AND NORMAL DOUBT

As discussed on the worksheet, there are several important differences between obsessional and normal doubts. The exercise on this page is intended to help you to better differentiate your particular obsessional doubts and the type of normal doubts that occasionally occur to everyone yet create no problems. For example, you may experience obsessional doubts after having touched something you think is dirty. In that case, the doubt could be something like 'I may have dirt on my hands', or, for example, if you experience doubts while reading, the doubt could be 'Did I understand that sentence correctly?' Doubt often takes the form of 'perhaps', 'maybe', 'could be' or 'I wonder if'. Try to identify the main areas in your life where you experience obsessional doubts and write them down here:

Obsessional doubts

(1) ....
(2) ....
(3) ....
(4) ....

Try to realize that the doubts you have written down are responsible for almost all of your OCD symptoms. Imagine for a moment that you do not have any doubts in the above areas. Allow yourself for a moment to look at these doubts from a distance without making immediate demands on yourself to stop your rituals, or trying to 'fix' the problem. Ask yourself quietly, how many of your symptoms would remain without the above doubts? Looking at it this way, with a little bit more distance while tracing your symptoms back to a few basic doubts, makes the OCD seem less overpowering.

Now write down four normal doubts, which occasionally occur to everyone in non-OCD-affected walks of life, yet do not cause any problems:

Normal doubts

(1) ....
(2) ....
(3) ....
(4) ....

Identify the differences between each obsessional doubt and normal doubt that you have written down by using what you have learned from worksheet 1. Ask yourself the following questions: (1) Does the doubt occur with *direct* evidence or information and in an appropriate context? (2) Would the doubt be resolved quickly once the proper information is obtained? (3) Is the doubt based on common sense? (4) Does the doubt exclude the senses? (5) Does the doubt increase the more you think about it? (6) Do you know exactly what you are looking for when you doubt?

You should now be able to get an idea of the differences between an obsessional doubt and a normal doubt. Try to reinforce what you have learned by regularly using the training card that you can carry around with you at all times.

TRAINING CARD 1
Front

Obsessional and Normal Doubt
Major Learning Points

(a) Normal doubt or questioning occurs with *direct* evidence or information from your senses and in an appropriate context.
(b) Normal doubt is resolved quickly once the proper information or evidence is obtained.
(c) Obsessional doubt occurs when you are already certain from a common-sense point of view that all has been done.
(d) Obsessional doubt excludes evidence since it is trying to go beyond the senses.
(e) Obsessional doubt increases the more you think about it.
(f) In obsessional doubt you never know exactly what you are looking for.

Back

Obsessional and Normal Doubt
Exercise

Step 1
Ask yourself at least four times per day whenever you are anxious or upset about something, or engaged in some kind of compulsion like checking, washing or ordering, what the specific doubt was that preceded these symptoms.

Step 2
After you have identified the doubt, ask yourself the following questions to determine whether it is a normal or obsessional doubt:

(1) Is there any direct evidence or information that justifies the doubt?
(2) Would the doubt disappear with more information?
(3) Is the doubt based on common sense?
(4) Does the doubt lead to more doubt?
(5) Does the doubt go beyond the senses?

Beyond Reasonable Doubt by K. O'Connor, F. Aardema and M.-C. Pélissier.
Copyright © 2005 John Wiley & Sons, Ltd.

WORKSHEET 2
THE 'LOGIC' OF OCD

The exercises of last week were intended to help you develop 'a feel' for the difference between normal and obsessional doubts, and you should now be able to identify your initial doubt behind your worries and actions. But, of course, even though you know they are not normal doubts, they still have credibility. We will now look at the reasons why you believe to a certain extent in your doubts. That is, what is the reasoning behind the doubt?

Both normal and obsessional doubts are particular statements about people, events or objects, which you (reasonably) believe to be probable. They are all those things that *could be* or *might be*. These statements do not come out of the blue. Instead, they have a certain kind of logic and reasoning behind them, even if your doubts may sometimes *seem* unreasonable or illogical to you. In other words, obsessional doubts are *inferred* in one way or another with a reasoning process behind them. So OCD is much more than 'just' a feeling. This is good news, because if obsessional doubts appeared out of nowhere, there would be little you could do about them. However, do not confuse reasoning with thinking like a computer. Reasoning involves far more than just thinking 'logically'. Below you see some of the categories that may be part of the reasoning by which any of us arrives at a doubt (obsessional or not):

(1) Common knowledge
(2) Authority
(3) Hearsay
(4) Previous experience
(5) Logical calculation

Now let's say, for example, a person has inferred that he/she might have been contaminated with dangerous germs, and consequently washes his/her hands for long periods of time. What type of information could justify such a doubt? It may look something like the following:

(1) Germs exist. (Common knowledge)
(2) Surgeons wash their hands too. (Authority)
(3) I heard of someone getting ill after visiting a bathroom. (Hearsay)
(4) I once got ill. (Previous experience)
(5) There is always a chance of contracting infections. (Logical calculation)

As you can see, the elements that make up the reasoning in the above example sort of 'make sense'. So in fact, your doubt seems on the surface to be reasonable, since there is reasoning behind it. This is why your doubts can present themselves to you in a quite 'sensical' and 'logical' fashion that is based on elements (common knowledge, authority, etc.) all of us use in reasoning. However, there are some peculiarities in the reasoning *process* that lead you to have *obsessional* doubts. You may already have some idea of what these peculiarities are if you think of the exercises of the previous week. However, for now, learn to think of your obsessional doubts as a particular statement about what might be or could be.

EXERCISE 2
THE 'LOGIC' OF OCD

As discussed on the worksheet, a doubt is a statement that you consider to be a valid possibility with a particular reasoning process behind it. However, often the reasoning that accompanies these doubts gets lost over time because of habit or we get caught up in the emotional consequences of the doubt and react automatically. It helps to start thinking of your obsessional doubts as a statement of what could be or might be, and increase your awareness of the particular way you justify these doubts. Some examples of the form obsessional doubts take are given below:

(1) I might have left the door unlocked.
(2) I might have been contaminated.
(3) I might think something terrible.
(4) I may have contracted a dangerous disease.
(5) I may have run over someone with my car.
(6) I could harm my children.

Go back to exercise 1 and rewrite the two obsessional doubts that bother you the most in the form of a statement of what could be or might be (if you haven't done so already):

(1) ....
(2) ....

Now as discussed on worksheet 1, there are several types of justification that we use to justify our doubts. Try to determine for the two obsessional statements that you have written down the particular justification that makes sense to you within each corresponding category (common knowledge, hearsay, previous experience, etc.).

(A) Common knowledge
    (1) ....
    (2) ....

(B) Authority
    (1) ....
    (2) ....

(C) Hearsay
    (1) ....
    (2) ....

(D) Previous experience
    (1) ....
    (2) ....

(E) Logical calculation
    (1) ....
    (2) ....

You may now begin to understand why your obsessional doubts are not so easily dismissed, and can present themselves to you as very real doubts.

TRAINING CARD 2

Front

The 'Logic' of OCD

Major Learning Points

(1) A doubt is a statement about what *could* be or *might* be.

(2) Obsessional doubts do not come out of the blue.

(3) There is a reasoning process behind obsessional doubts.

(4) OCD is not the result of not being 'logical' enough.

Back

The 'Logic' of OCD

Exercise

Step 1
At least four times per day, try to identify the doubt that motivated you to carry out compulsions or made you feel anxious, and rephrase the doubt in the form of a statement of what could be or might be.

Step 2
Next, identify the reasoning you have applied to justify the doubt or statement. Be specific, since the reasoning behind the doubt may be different for each situation. If you are not immediately aware of any thoughts that preceded the doubt, then ask yourself, why does the doubt seem real? Or use the categories of common knowledge, hearsay, authority, previous experience, or logical calculation, to help you identify the justification behind the doubt.

WORKSHEET 3
OCD DOUBT IS 100% IRRELEVANT TO THE HERE AND NOW

Although the justification behind the obsessional doubt may make 'sense', there is a very important difference between the reasoning that characterizes obsessional doubts and normal doubts. The most important difference between the reasoning that characterizes normal and obsessional doubt is not so much a matter of the *content* of the information that justifies the doubt, but *how* and *when* this information is applied. Consider the following examples of obsessional doubts: 'The door might be unlocked' or 'I might have been contaminated with something dirty'. You may have just stepped outside on your way to work and locked the door, or you may have just touched a metal pole in the metro or bus. But was there anything in the here and now that justified these particular doubts? Did you actually sense anything that supported the doubt? For obsessions, the answer to this question is always no.

Obsessional doubt *always* comes from you and never from the outside. It is almost impossible to over-estimate the significance of this fact. It is *the* basis for all of your OCD symptoms. Ask yourself the following questions for your own obsessional doubts:

(1) Was there any information in the here and now to justify the doubt?
(2) Did the doubt go beyond objective sense information?

You may readily agree that your doubts have no basis in reality, yet you may wonder why this is so important. The reason why this is so important is because it implies that the obsessional doubt is 100% irrelevant to current reality. It makes obsessional doubts as irrelevant as having doubts about the ceiling collapsing down on you right now.

Like your obsessional doubts, it is easy to back up the *possibility* of the ceiling coming down with all kinds of reasoning. Yet, ask yourself, why *don't* you worry about it? You may say: 'Well, the chances are small, it's unlikely.' However, that is also the case for your obsessional doubts, and yet you take them seriously. The *real* reason why you don't worry about the ceiling coming down is because there is nothing in the *here and now* that supports this idea.

For example, if you see sudden cracks in the wall, and hear noises coming from above you, then the doubt about the ceiling coming down would be relevant to the situation you are in. Yet, with obsessional doubts you have an exception to this rule. You have convinced yourself to doubt without any such evidence. So it is never a matter of the facts or logical calculation that is of any importance in obsessional doubts, but *how* and *when* these things are applied. Instead of saying that the obsessional doubt is 0.0001% possible, it would be far more accurate to say that it is 100.0000% imaginary, since the doubt has no basis whatsoever in reality, in the here and now.

Reality   Imagination

Figure 1.   Normal doubt   **Figure 2.**   Obsessional doubt

The difference between obsessional and normal doubt is that normal doubt always has *some* basis in reality. This may be very little or a lot, but it continues to be a *normal* doubt. However, in obsessional doubt (Figure 2), it is almost as if the doubt comes out of nowhere. It may not always *feel* that way, but there is no overlap at all between reality and the doubt. That is, it always comes from you and never from outside of you.

EXERCISE 3
OCD DOUBT IS 100% IRRELEVANT TO THE HERE AND NOW

Perhaps with the information on the accompanying worksheet you may now intellectually accept the idea that your obsessional doubts originate 100% from you. However, it is only by applying this information to your obsessional doubts that you can make a difference. In other words, you need to be able to tell whether the *reasoning elements* that make the obsessional doubt seem realistic have anything to do with the here and now. Some examples of the thoughts and ideas which form part of the reasoning process that convinces people with OCD their doubts are relevant are the following: 'I can't remember if I closed the door'; 'There could be a terrible fire here if the stove caught light'; 'I don't feel comfortable not checking the money again'; 'I could have made a mistake'; 'I've read about so many accidents I'd better be sure'; 'What if there was even a small risk?'

It may not be immediately clear that these ideas have nothing to do with reality. Obviously, they are *about* reality. But, if these ideas have nothing to do with the here and now, then these considerations are completely irrelevant. As you begin to question your obsessional doubts you will find that OCD is a very creative disorder, and will come up with an infinite amount of information to keep the doubt alive. You may say: 'OK, maybe it's 100% imaginary – but it's still possible.' But actually, at the moment you conceive the idea, it is not possible, because it goes against reality, and so this consideration is irrelevant.

In the hundreds of people we've seen with OCD, never once did someone have their OCD doubt proved correct. But, of course, the OCD says, 'Yes, but maybe this time it could happen.' To become aware of the impossibility of OCD, let's apply your OCD reasoning to a non-OCD situation. Let's say you want to cross the road. You look and see no traffic and you cross the road. But if you were using OCD logic you would look – see nothing – yet still doubt against your senses and think, 'maybe there is a car I can't see'. So the OCD doubt always goes against objective reality – hence the moment it comes along, it is always unfounded.

To start to put this into practice, pick one of your doubts, and try to remember the last time that this doubt really bothered you. Or perhaps choose a doubt that bothers you right now. Then, question this doubt by asking yourself calmly whether there is or was any basis in reality for the doubt. Do *not* try to *convince* yourself of anything, since that is not the goal

---

of this exercise. As you question the doubt, take a note of all the thoughts that go through your mind that 'argue' with your questioning, and make it seem the doubt is a valid doubt. Write them down. Take your time with this.

After you have completed the above, take a closer look at all the thoughts that you wrote down that made the doubt seem real and 'reasonable'. Take a look at each thought individually, and try to determine whether these considerations had anything to do with the here and now (or there and then).

Now, repeat the same exercise, and once again start to question the doubt. However, this time, dismiss each of the thoughts you have identified earlier as not relevant to the here and now as it comes up during your questioning. Write down any considerations that you are unable to dismiss as irrelevant, and write them down on the obsessional story page using the entries. Bring this with you to the next session.

TRAINING CARD 3

Front

OCD Doubt is 100% Irrelevant
to the Here and Now

Major Learning Points

(1) It is not a matter of *what* justifies the obsessional doubt, but *how* and *when*.

(2) Obsessional doubts always come from you and never from the outside.

(3) Obsessional doubts are 100% irrelevant to the here and now.

Back

OCD Doubt is 100% Irrelevant
to the Here and Now

Exercise

Step 1
At least three times per day, question an obsessional doubt as it occurs. Try to identify the thoughts that come up, which make the doubt seem like a valid concern.

Step 2
Next, determine whether the thoughts that seem to support the doubt go beyond what you can see or sense.

Step 3
Finally, establish what remains of the obsessional doubt, leaving out any information that is not relevant to the here and now.

WORKSHEET 4
HOW OCD BECOMES A 'LIVED-IN' EXPERIENCE

Why do doubts (or obsessions) *feel* so real? To answer this question you will first have to understand why it is that something can feel real to us in the first place. For example, take the activity that you are engaged in right now (reading this page). Why does it feel real to you? It feels real not only because of the information that comes through your senses, but far more importantly, it feels real because there is a story which places this activity in a past, present and future. Ask yourself, how did you come to read this page? Almost immediately a whole story will start to unfold that reads like a novel. You may see yourself in the past struggling with OCD, how you decided to seek help, your trips to the therapist's office, the conversation and questions, the work you did at home, and the hope to overcome your OCD in the future. Imagine for a moment you are engaged in reading this page without the above story. How much would remain of your sense of reality in reading this page?

In a way, listening to your own thoughts is like reading a novel. This is not merely coincidental, but is part of how we organize our opinions and feelings about ourselves and how we experience the world around us. While we are engaged with the world around us, a story is unfolding, and we add elements to this story which make the world around us seem real and convincing, whether on our way to the grocery store, going to work, conversing with friends or family, or obsessing. So, in a way, we go through life being storytellers, and the stories we tell ourselves have an important effect on our experience, what we believe in, and how real these beliefs feel to us. In the same manner, obsessional ideas also come about and appear real to us by the stories we tell ourselves. They have a history and a story attached to them, which make them feel very plausible and real. One of the big and annoying problems in dealing with OCD is that you can be aware it is stupid and give it no credibility, but within the OCD situation you feel compelled to act on the doubt. That is because your OCD story gives the doubt a reality value, no matter whether you believe in it or not outside of the OCD situation.

Of course, you are already quite familiar with the story behind your OCD. After all, in previous sessions, you have identified a lot of thoughts that appear to justify the obsessional doubt. However, all these bits and pieces of information that you have considered so far are organized in the form of a story. This is what makes the doubt feel so real. Like a novel, everything seems to 'fit' almost as if your obsessional doubt has a certain plot to it. This is what makes the OCD feel so real even though all the elements in the story have nothing to do with reality around you in the here and now. The story may contain all kinds of elements like facts or calculations that seem to be *about* reality, but always in the absence of immediate sense information to support it.

You may intellectually agree with all of this, but how do you change the obsessional doubt? Like we said, the doubt feels real because it has a convincing story behind it. It then follows naturally that what needs to be changed is the story. To do this you will be working in the coming weeks on the obsessional story and its elements that make it seem as if the doubt is real, but also, you will be working on alternative stories. By engaging yourself in alternative stories you will automatically weaken the strength of the obsessional story. This will not happen overnight, and requires a lot of practice, but with the proper attitude and techniques you can go a long way, and eventually *live* a different story.

EXERCISE 4
HOW OCD BECOMES A 'LIVED-IN' EXPERIENCE

This exercise sheet contains the instructions on how to work with your obsessional and non-obsessional stories which your therapist has given you in the last session. One of these stories is the justification that you have reported in the last couple of weeks for one of your obsessional doubts. The other story is the beginning of a non-obsessional alternative story opposite to the doubt. Before you continue, take your time to carefully read both stories.

Both stories are likely to change over time and are very much a work in progress. The non-obsessional story will change over time during therapy, because each week you will add new elements to it to make it more real to you. Those elements may contain all sorts of information, but in contrast to the obsessional story you will be able also to add elements that are based in reality or your senses, since this type of information is never part of obsessional stories. The obsessional story may also change over time as you come across ideas and thoughts that you forgot to mention before. At the bottom of each story you will find several places to add new information. Each time that you come up with new elements your therapist will adapt the story for you, and hand it over to you in the next session. However, it is very important that you take the proper attitude towards thinking of new elements that make the non-obsessional alternative more real to you. It would be a big mistake to think of this as solely an intellectual process where you will somehow 'solve' the OCD. Such an attitude will lead the OCD to dismiss everything you come up with. You do not have to *solve* anything. Exploring the non-obsessional alternative is no more than a willingness to creatively imagine and engage yourself in a different story.

Think of your work with the non-obsessional story as a *creative* process. As if your mind is a piece of canvas on which you can paint all kinds of versions of reality through the stories that you tell yourself. A painter doesn't constantly ask himself at each step in the creative process whether this painting is better than the other one, and nor do you have to ask yourself whether the obsessional story is better than the non-obsessional one. The painter simply tries to make this one painting as 'real' or as 'intense' as possible. How well you tell (or paint) that story will be up to you.

To help you locate those elements that are most and least convincing, you can rate each paragraph or sentence in the story and indicate how

---

convincing these elements are to you. The reason for rating each of the elements is to decide at a later stage which elements in the non-obsessional story need to be revised, changed, or perhaps completely dropped.

Don't be discouraged if the obsessional story and its elements in the beginning are far more convincing to you than those in the non-obsessional story. This is entirely normal. Conviction levels in the non-obsessional story may start out low, which is why you have OCD to begin with. Work with the story as described above, and the homework exercises for the coming weeks are geared towards making the story and its elements more real to you. So during the next week, and weeks to come, start by elaborating a bit on the non-obsessional story by introducing new elements, and fill in any missing elements in the obsessional story, if there are any. Use the entries to add this new information, and your therapist will hand you the printed revised story in the next session.

Keep in mind that your therapist won't try to convince you by constantly introducing new elements in order to make you 'see the light'. Your therapist can help you with finding new elements if you have difficulties, and help you to arrange the story in such a way that it makes most sense to you, but he cannot do the real work for you. The only 'magic' solution to overcome your OCD is the magic we perform every day by the stories we tell to ourselves, and how these stories become a lived-in experience. So unless you want someone else to do your living for you, it will be up to you to make the non-obsessional story real and meaningful.

TRAINING CARD 4

Front

> ## How OCD becomes a 'lived-in' experience
>
> ### Major Learning Points
>
> (1) Experiences become real to us by the stories we tell ourselves about them.
> (2) Behind the obsessional doubt there is a convincing story that makes the doubt feel very real.
> (3) To change the doubt you change the story.
> (4) Changing the story is not an intellectual process but a creative one.

Back

> ## How OCD becomes a 'lived-in' experience
>
> ### Exercise
>
> Make yourself very familiar with the non-obsessional story until you know it by heart. Then, at least three times per day, imagine and rehearse the non-obsessional story as vividly as you can. Immerse yourself in it with as much detail as possible. You can do this verbally or use imagery, or both, depending on your preference. Only do this in moments where you are calm, and outside of OCD-type situations. While you imagine it, act as if the non-OCD story is completely true – as if no other possibilities exist. Imagine each of the elements and make them as real as possible to you by going into as much detail as possible. Creatively add new elements to your story. Make it as real and intense as possible!

WORKSHEET 5
CROSSING OVER

It may not seem obvious at first, but you would be surprised how much your OCD is about going beyond the senses. Think of your OCD as a devil's advocate with the goal to make you doubt as much as possible. That's no small feat, especially since there is absolutely nothing in immediate reality around you to back up the doubt. The *only* way for the OCD to make a convincing case is to come up with arguments that make it seem *as if* the doubt has something to do with reality around you. They are those types of arguments that go *beyond* the senses, and make it *seem* as if what your senses tell you is irrelevant. All these elements very quickly become part of the obsessional story and make your doubt seem more real.

For example, let's say you worry about certain dangerous germs on a particular object. Yet, there is no evidence in reality that these germs are present. In fact, all the direct evidence in the here and now seems to suggest there is nothing there at all (it looks clean, there is no smell, the object has been used before without incident, etc.). Following our example, the only way to make it seem as if the doubt has something to do with reality around you is to tell a story about going beyond the senses. Like this:

(1) Germs are too small to be seen . . . *so there might still be germs on it.*
(2) Who knows who else has touched it . . . *so there might still be germs on it.*
(3) People never clean themselves enough . . . *so there might still be germs on it.*

All these arguments may not necessarily be incorrect, yet they do not originate in reality around you. This makes the obsessional doubt 100% irrelevant to the here and now. In other words, obsessional doubt is NEVER kept alive by reality, but ONLY by what your imagination can come up with. An important point is to realize that either we are in the imagination or we are in perception. But in OCD we are confused. Because OCD is such an *all or nothing* process that originates 100% from the imagination, there is an exact point in time where you enter the 'world' of OCD. This point is identifiable and occurs with the first thought that you have that takes you beyond the senses. This can be schematically represented in the following figure:

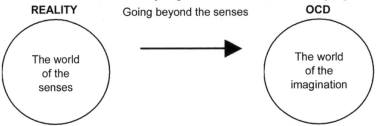

As you can see in the figure above, it is almost like the world of the senses and the world of the imagination are two separate worlds. If, however, you go with the first thought that goes beyond the senses, then you will get sucked into a spiral of drastic imagined consequences, which seem to follow logically from the premise that made you cross into the world of the imagination and so you will feel even more anxious. So there is a cross-over point between those two worlds where you move from reality into a completely imaginary world. This occurs when you have thoughts that go beyond your senses, and makes it seem as if what you *can* sense does not seem to matter any more. You have cut yourself off from the genuine reassuring influence of reality, and once you have crossed, it is very hard to get back. This is because you have left any real criteria behind that could resolve the doubt permanently. Of course, there are rituals that you can perform, but how would you really know that you have checked or washed enough? It is a temporary solution, since if you do finally stop your rituals, it is solely determined by the whims of the OCD.

EXERCISE 5
CROSSING OVER

The following exercise is a full detailed description of the exercise that you will find on your weekly training card. Use this sheet until you are familiar enough with the exercise to only need the training card as a reminder. The goals of the exercise are: (1) to identify the first thought that carries you from reality into the world of the imagination; (2) to slow down the process of crossing over from reality into the imagination; (3) to be able to hold still in between both worlds without reacting to the doubt; and (4) to reflect on how obsessional doubt is resolved. Please keep in mind that the point of this exercise is not to stop you from doing anything! So this is not a frightening exercise, but just a different kind of awareness.

Step 1: You have already had some practice in identifying obsessional doubts, the particular story behind them, and determining whether or not there is any direct evidence in the here and now for the doubts. Ask yourself the following questions whenever a doubt occurs:

(1) What was the first thought that came to mind that took me beyond the senses?
(2) How does this thought make my senses *seem* irrelevant?

Step 2: As soon as you have identified the particular thought that makes you cross from reality into the imagination, do not immediately react with rituals, avoidance, or anything else. Hold off everything for at least one minute. Imagine yourself standing in the middle of a bridge. This bridge is the thought that carries you from the world of the senses into the world of the imagination – the cross-over point. Standing on the bridge makes you feel you need to act upon the doubt. You cannot help but feel that the doubt will be resolved somehow at the other end of the bridge through carrying out a ritual, avoidance, or trying to solve the problem in whatever form. However, look back for a moment into the world of the senses where you came from. Out there, the doubt was irrelevant. There was nothing that supported the doubt to begin with. You can move into the world of OCD, think more about the doubt, and try to solve it somehow, and likely get more upset *or* you can move back to the world of the senses where the doubt is 100% arbitrary and irrelevant. Try to hold your balance like this for at least one minute, and longer if possible without falling off the bridge.

Step 3: Now you can choose what to do. You can move further into the doubt with the hope that you will find some kind of resolution in the world of OCD, or you can decide that the doubt is arbitrary to begin with, and move back to the world of the senses. If you went into the OCD, ask yourself this: Did you eventually stop the rituals as dictated by the whims of the OCD? Do you think the doubt is permanently resolved? Will it come back in similar situations? If you decided to move back to the world of the senses, ask yourself on what basis you decided the doubt was imaginary and not something that needed your attention. Did you use your senses in deciding whether it was imaginary? How permanent is *this* resolution?

Step 4: Write down the most important thoughts that took you beyond the senses and add them to the obsessional story. Hand them to your therapist at the next session so that he can adapt the obsessional story for you.

Don't forget also to continue to rehearse and elaborate on your non-OCD story outside of OCD situations, which is an exercise that will continue throughout therapy!

TRAINING CARD 5

Front

Crossing Over

Major Learning Points

(1) Obsessional doubt can ONLY be maintained by going beyond the senses and NEVER by sensing reality around you.

(2) There is a cross-over point where you move from reality into the imagination.

(3) Crossing over occurs as soon as you go beyond the senses and feel your senses are not really relevant.

(4) Only the senses can provide a permanent resolution to your obsessional doubt and rituals.

Back

Crossing Over

Exercise

Step 1

Identify the thoughts that you have during the day that take you beyond the senses, and make it seem as if your senses do not really matter.

Step 2

Next, hold off every ritual and feeling associated with this thought. You are now at the cross-over point in between the world of the senses and the imagination. Imagine yourself standing on a bridge in between worlds. Look in both directions, and realize there is a choice there.

Step 3

Make your choice, and reflect afterwards on the choice you made.

WORKSHEET 6
THE REASONING 'DEVICES' OF OCD: PART 1

As you saw in the previous worksheet, the key trick of the OCD is to go beyond the senses in order to make it seem as if the obsessional doubt is real and so make you distrust yourself. It is the main device that OCD uses to make you doubt. However, like any salesman of useless goods, OCD has quite a few more tricks up its sleeve. In one way or another, these devices all have something to do with going beyond the senses, and going beyond the senses is always a part of these devices. However, a detailed understanding of each of these devices, and knowing exactly what is going on, can help you distance yourself from your doubt, and make it less real to yourself. These devices are part of the OCD story, and the exercises for this week are geared towards learning to identify them. Below you will find some of these reasoning devices of the OCD:

Category errors
This occurs when you confuse two categories of information or objects as if one has something to do with the other while it does not.

Example: *If this white table is dirty, it means the other white table could need cleaning.*
Feeling angry means I'm a bad person.

Apparently comparable events
Confusing two distinct events separated by time and place.

Example: *My friend often drives off and leaves his garage door open, so mine could be left open.*
I heard of poisoned medicine one time, so my food could be poisoned.

Selective use of out-of-context facts or 'misplaced concreteness'
Abstract facts are inappropriately applied to specific personal contexts.

Example: *Microbes do exist, so therefore there might be microbes infecting my hand.*
I heard on the news that people my age are at risk of heart disease, so I might die now of a heart attack.

Purely imaginary sequences

Making up convincing stories and living them.

Example: *I can imagine the waves entering my head, so they could be infecting my brain.*

I can feel myself getting nauseous and weak when I think I might be ill.

Inverse inference

Inferences about reality precede, rather than follow from, observation of reality.

Example: *A lot of people must have walked on this floor, therefore it could be dirty.*

Chemicals are used everywhere, therefore my hand might be contaminated.

Distrust of normal perception

Disregarding the senses in favor of going deeper into reality.

Example: *Even though my senses tell me there's nothing there, I know by my intelligence something is there.*

I may not see something, but a lot of things are invisible.

EXERCISE 6
THE REASONING 'DEVICES' OF OCD: PART 1

The goal of this week's exercise is to learn how to better identify the devices used by the OCD story that convince you that your particular doubt is real. If you have several doubts, the goal is for now to focus only on the obsessional story that you have been working with in your worksheets. Identifying the particular devices used by the OCD is not easy, since often they will appear to be 'self-evident', or if not self-evident, they may simply feel very real when you're caught up in the emotion of it all. For example, you watch the news and hear about someone having cancer. If your OCD is about illnesses, then you might start to worry about having cancer after watching the news. In that moment, it may be hard to take the time to take a close look at what particular reasoning device you made that caused you to come to doubt your health. Don't worry if you find yourself unable to identify the exact error all the time, since they can overlap at times. Just making the effort of questioning the initial doubt (but not analyzing it) is already a good step in the right direction.

To learn how to identify these devices a little bit better, below you will find several entries to write down examples with each device that applies to your situation. Use your obsessional story to find these reasoning devices, or try to come up with examples by remembering several obsessional situations that occurred today. Then write them down below in each appropriate category:

Category errors: ....
....

Apparently comparable events: ....
....

Selective use of out-of-context facts or 'misplaced concreteness': ....
....

Purely imaginary sequences: ....
....

Inverse inference: ....
....

Distrust of normal perception: ....
....

The training card for this week contains more exercises to further help you locate these devices in as many OCD situations as possible in the course of the week. Focus on those situations that are related to the obsessional story you have been working on in the past weeks, or even situations you have not been working on so far. Each day of the coming week, use your training card to identify the reasoning errors that accompany your obsessional doubts.

TRAINING CARD 6

Front

The Reasoning 'Devices' of OCD: Part 1

Major Learning Points

Reasoning devices to remember:
(a) category errors
(b) apparently comparable events
(c) misplaced concreteness
(d) imaginary sequences
(e) inverse inference
(f) distrust of normal perception

Back

The Reasoning 'Devices' of OCD: Part 1
Exercise

(1) At least four times per day, when an obsessional doubt occurs identify the reasoning devices of the OCD that led to the obsessional doubt.
(2) Ask yourself each time how much would remain of your doubt if you could dismiss it on the basis of the reasoning errors you have identified.
(3) Imagine vividly how the situation in which you have experienced the obsessional doubt would feel without the reasoning devices of the OCD. Identify what is left of the doubt.
(4) Write down the thoughts where you have difficulty deciding on whether the doubt qualifies as a reasoning error, and bring this list with you to the next session with your therapist.

WORKSHEET 7
THE REASONING 'DEVICES' OF OCD: PART 2

An awareness of the reasoning devices in OCD is important, but this is not merely an intellectual exercise. Do you *realize* how the reasoning devices make your obsessional doubt unfounded? All these reasoning devices lead you to distrust evidence from the here and now. The trick is to realize that the initial argument for the doubt is flawed. It is not about there being a small likelihood that the doubt is correct, rather the particular way this doubt comes about is always misconstrued. The obsessional story takes you away from reality and all its reasoning devices go against your objective senses. Your senses will always say the opposite to your doubt. This is why OCD doubt is always mistaken at the time it comes along. Your senses give you *certain* information and only then does the OCD doubt make you less than certain. OCD never comes along, for example, when you genuinely need information. It always puts you in conflict with your senses, which is why you are always in a dilemma unless you decide the doubt is not based on reality at all.

(1) Living a doubt as if it is real does not make it real (purely imaginary sequence).
(2) Someone else having become contaminated or robbed is not relevant to you if your senses say otherwise in the here and now (apparently comparable events).
(3) The fact that germs exist, or that doors are left open, has nothing to do with your situation if you see your hands are clean, or that the door has been closed (selective use of facts).
(4) Starting out with an obsessional doubt, and then trying to find evidence for it, will guarantee that you will always find some evidence that goes beyond the senses, since the doubt came about by going beyond the senses to begin with. It has nothing to do with what is around you, and you could just as well be worrying about meteors landing on your head (inverse inference).
(5) Going beyond the senses will land you in the world of OCD very quickly, and everything you come up with in that SENSEless state is purely determined by your imagination (distrusting the senses).
(6) Just because two objects or two categories have a likeness, they cannot be considered one and the same. For example, I might have run over someone, since the car I'm driving is red, and a red car was in an accident (category error).

As you can see in the above points, there is a definite implication when identifying a particular reasoning device. It makes the obsessional doubt convincing but misguided. At this point, at least at an intellectual level, you should be able to recognize the OCD as incorrect and false. If you still have objections to this idea, which is quite possible, your objections will need to be addressed in therapy with your therapist. On the other hand, you may find yourself already able to sometimes dismiss the obsessional doubt. However, often, dismissing the obsessional doubt is a step that some people with OCD are reluctant to take. They may ask themselves: 'If the doubt is wrong, then what will I have left to rely on? How will I be able to tell if something is clean or dirty if I can't trust my reasoning or the OCD?' The answer, of course, is the non-OCD story that you have been working on in the last weeks. In the non-OCD story you have a completely alternative rationale to that of the OCD story. Moreover, the non-OCD story is in line with the senses in the here and now, whereas the OCD story is not. Therefore, ultimately, there is no misguided reasoning in your non-OCD story.

EXERCISE 7
THE REASONING 'DEVICES' OF OCD: PART 2

To help make what you have learned so far become more apparent to yourself, and not just an intellectual exercise, the exercise for this week is to identify the reasoning devices in situations that are not part of your immediate obsessional concern. Identifying the reasoning devices in the OCD stories of other people can help you, since you will have a little bit more distance and it gives you a feeling of how you can look at your own doubts as a more neutral observer. Take a look at the following two OCD stories and identify the reasoning devices of the OCD in them by writing them between the parentheses. Each time you identify a reasoning device, try to realize why this makes the doubt wrong.

In the following example, a person with OCD recounts a story which convinces her that her hands could be dirty (*primary inference*) and so she must wash her hands:

> *So, I say to myself: Well, my kids were playing outside and like I know it's dirty outside (..........................). I've seen the dirt on the pavement and I think they may have touched something dirty (..........................), like picked up something from the street, dirty paper or dog shit, and then I say, well, if they're dirty then I'm going to be dirty (..........................), and I'm going to make the house dirty, and I imagine the house dirty and me with my dirty hands, so I start to feel dirty (..........................). So I go in and wash and I can't stop, you know, it's like a voice in my head, saying over and over again, you're dirty, even though you're washing and you see nothing (..........................), you could still be dirty (..........................).*

The next example is someone who worries his pool may have become infected, and whether it should be drained and refilled for a second time to avoid animals infecting it:

> *But I look at the pool and it's surrounded by trees and the garden backs onto a field (..........................). Animals could get in during the night. I've heard noises, they could swim in the pool, or do things in it (..........................). It's disgusting, I've seen the mess dogs make, they have fleas and germs on them (..........................). The more I think about it, the more it disgusts me to even look at the pool (..........................). How can I know it's ever clean? (..........................) Once the germs are there, they have the power to infect anything (..........................).*

How quickly were you able to dismiss the above OCD stories? If these stories are different from yours, then you should be able to dismiss them fairly quickly. This is ultimately what we are striving for with your own OCD story. But as you start to dismiss your OCD doubts make sure you do not take on too much of the OCD at once. OCD is like a massive balloon. It contains a lot of air, but even air will push back as hard as you push against it. That is why a well-placed needle prick is a much better way to deal with the OCD rather than face all of the OCD head-on. The exercises for this week on your training card are geared towards dismissing some of your doubts in situations where you feel able to do so at least a couple of times per day. On the training card you will be asked: (1) to uncover the reasoning errors behind the doubt; (2) to realize how the reasoning devices make you doubt; (3) to recount your alternative non-OCD story to replace the obsessional doubt; and (4) to dismiss the doubt. The whole exercise should last no longer than 1–2 minutes each time. If you are unsuccessful at keeping the OCD story at bay, then don't make too much of it, and try again later with an easier situation. The OCD wants you to think it over, one more time, two more times . . . three . . . and it will never be enough. Don't forget to continue to rehearse and elaborate on your non-OCD story also *outside* of OCD situations, and only to do the above exercise in situations where it is relatively easy to keep your distance from the OCD story. The message is: pick only those opportunities where you have a chance of succeeding!

TRAINING CARD 7

Front

The Reasoning 'Devices' of OCD: Part 2

Major Learning Points

(1) Obsessional doubt is always erroneous.
(2) Because obsessional doubt never starts in the senses it takes you further away from what is really there, instead of any closer.
(3) The reasoning devices help the OCD take you away further from reality.
(4) The non-OCD story brings you closer to what is really there since it starts out with your senses.

Back

The Reasoning 'Devices' of OCD: Part 2

Exercise

Do the following exercise for no longer than 2 minutes:
(1) Five times per day when an obsessional doubt occurs, identify the reasoning errors that gave rise to the doubt. Only pick those doubts in situations where you have the feeling you could overcome the doubt.
(2) Realize the implications of the reasoning errors and that the reasoning errors make the doubt wrong. Do NOT analyze this over and over.
(3) Imagine vividly how the situation would feel if the non-OCD story applied. Recount and rehearse the non-OCD story that starts out with the senses.
(4) Let go of the obsessional doubt after you have recounted the non-OCD story. It no longer requires your attention.

WORKSHEET 8
THE SELECTIVE NATURE OF THE OBSESSIONAL DOUBT

One of the greatest oddities of 'obsessional thinking' is the selective nature of the doubt. That is, the doubt is highly specific and applies only to certain situations. It may not feel that way, since, of course, the obsessions and doubts occupy a great deal of time. But look at it this way: of all the situations you regularly encounter in life, how many of them trigger an obsessional doubt? We will argue that they are very few relative to all the other situations you encounter in one day. For example, make a mental list of everything that has occurred in your day. Not just situations that you had obsessions about, but *everything*. You may have picked up a book, looked out of the window, crossed the street, made a telephone call, walked from one room to another, listened to music, closed a drawer, made a note, and breathed air. Did you have obsessions about all of these situations? There may be one, since, curiously, obsessions can truly be about anything. But the great majority of these situations did not cause you any problem. This shows something very important and that is:

IN OTHER ASPECTS OF YOUR LIFE YOU HAVE
NO OBSESSIONAL PROBLEMS AT ALL.

Because you have no problems in such a great variety of situations, your 'reasoning' is actually functioning perfectly fine almost all of the time. You do not confuse the imagined with the real most of the time. So why should the situations where you experience obsessions be any different? One of the reasons is that you may not realize completely that you reason differently in OCD situations than you do in other situations. Habit alone can already be enough to prevent you from dismissing the obsessional doubt as not really relevant. So then it is important to have a close look at how well you reason in non-OCD situations, and whether or not that has any consequences for how you look at your obsessional doubt.

Let's take an example of a situation that very few people with OCD ever have obsessional doubts about, although you may, and then, if so, you and your therapist can look for another situation that is non-OCD for you. Let's say you are about to cross the street. How would you come to the conclusion that it is safe to cross it? What is the information that you use in order to determine if it is safe to cross it? You would have to look left and right to see if there was any traffic, and then you would decide it was safe to cross the street. So, in other words, you would feel no need whatsoever to go beyond the senses: you would not create a story that convinces you that,

Beyond Reasonable Doubt by K. O'Connor, F. Aardema and M.-C. Pélissier.
Copyright © 2005 John Wiley & Sons, Ltd.

despite the fact that you looked, there still might be a car coming. In other words, your senses take precedence over your reasoning, and you would create no doubt in this situation, since after all, here you would know that the idea that it is not safe would be purely *imaginary*.

Now compare this reality-sensing with an obsessional situation that is rather common. You stand in front of the door, and are about to leave the house. How would you come to the conclusion that the door has been properly locked? If you use the same reasoning you use in most of your life, you would say, exactly in the same manner you come to cross the street, that *since I saw myself lock it, it therefore is locked*. It is no different than crossing the street.

You may feel that your OCD situation is different. Perhaps it is, but ask yourself first how your obsessional doubt came about. Did it come from your senses? If you decide it was not based in your senses, then in principle, you should be able to go into an OCD situation with the same confidence as you cross the street. The trick, however, is to realize how similar OCD situations are to all the other situations that you encounter in your life, and that there is no reason to treat the OCD situations any differently.

EXERCISE 8
THE SELECTIVE NATURE OF THE OBSESSIONAL DOUBT

The exercise sheet for this week will be a little bit different from what you have been used to so far. It is really important that you come to a full understanding of what OCD is about, and this week we want you to grab it by the horns. Or, to stay within our metaphorical speak, 'Enter the lion's den'.

Often, when you put a couple of people with OCD together, they look at each other in disbelief when they hear about the other person's obsessions. That is, although it seems natural to doubt in their own situation, they can't believe that anyone would doubt in the other person's OCD situations. However, that disbelief is not entirely justified, since your obsession is really no different from those of the others. The key, of course, is to realize in what way they are similar so that maybe you can start looking at your personal doubts with the same disbelief.

The exercise for this week is to pick a situation together with your therapist that is very *neutral to you*, for example, similar to the one used earlier about crossing the street. It should have no importance to you whatsoever, and an area where you experience no problems whatsoever. Once you have picked the situation, we want you to *make it obsessional*. That is, you think of all the reasons why a particular situation might not be safe, and why a situation might be a problem that to all purposes is neutral to you when looking at it in a non-obsessional way. Write this down in the form of a story of around 5–10 sentences. Make sure that the story contains none of the contents whatsoever that are part of your own unique OCD story. In other words, keep your OCD out of it! For the crossing the street example, it could look like this:

> *It is not safe to cross the street. I heard about an accident happening to someone who was always very careful. So accidents can happen just like that whether or not you pay attention. No one takes any notice of pedestrians any more. So now when I cross the street, I do not look twice or three times to my left or right. Instead, I stand there for half an hour looking to see if there are any cars coming. Even if I don't see any car, one could come out from a corner suddenly. Or it might be a silent car that I cannot hear, since there are even electrical cars now. So I often decide not to cross the street. It just doesn't feel safe, even if I don't see any traffic.*

As you can see, we have just made a situation in which hardly anyone experiences doubt, obsessional. What is going on here? How were we able to make a situation obsessional to the extent that it seems 'reasonable' to never cross the street any more? The answer of course is ... as you have heard many times before ... *by going beyond the senses*. Have a look at the story again and identify exactly those elements that go beyond the senses and create doubt in a situation that to all purposes is safe *if* you use the senses. What is the purpose of this exercise if you do it with your own neutral example and write out an obsessional story for it? It will clarify your personal OCD story. That is, you can start to see that the arguments for your OCD story are no different from the above example. In fact, you could ask yourself the following question: 'Why would I use arguments that go beyond the senses for my OCD doubt in one situation but not in others?' After all, the neutral story is no different from your obsessional story. If you can come to realize that the neutral example which you made obsessional is no different from your OCD story, then maybe you can begin to enter obsessional situations as if they were no different from crossing the street. So once you have written the story where you made a neutral situation obsessional by going beyond the senses, we want you to lay it beside your OCD story, and take a good look at how they are similar.

The training card for this week contains a similar exercise. It will ask you on a daily basis to take note of all the situations around you where you trust your senses and compare it with your OCD reasoning. That is, we want you to come to a full realization how normal your reasoning is in many situations, that in much of your daily life your reasoning is normal, and how you could maybe start to trust your senses in OCD situations too, since they are no different.

TRAINING CARD 8

Front

The Selective Nature of the Obsessional Doubt

Major Learning Points

(1) In other aspects of your life you have no obsessional problems at all.
(2) Obsessional doubt is highly selective and represents only a few aspects of your life.
(3) The reasoning applied in OCD situations is very different from the reasoning you normally apply in situations.
(4) To be aware of your normal reasoning is to be aware how the OCD doubt works against normal reason.

Back

The Selective Nature of the Obsessional Doubt

Exercise

Do the following exercise at least four times per day:
(1) Identify a situation where you experience obsessional doubts or a need to engage in compulsions.
(2) Compare the obsessional situation to another situation where you *do* use your senses and do *not* have obsessional doubts. Ask yourself, would the obsessional situation be any different *if* you used your senses?
(3) Try to imagine how you would act in the obsessional situation if you used and trusted your senses as you do in many other situations.

WORKSHEET 9
THE VULNERABLE SELF-THEME IN OBSESSIONAL STORIES

As we are starting to approach the end of the worksheets, we want to highlight an aspect of obsessional doubts that may help explain the selective nature of the obsessional doubt. Why do you have obsessions in one or some area(s) of your life, but not in others? One way to look at this is to realize that for one reason or another you are very vulnerable to particular types of thoughts which touch a nerve. These thoughts may differ from person to person, since they always follow a different theme that is specifically relevant to you. This theme often runs through the OCD story. For example, if in general you are quite concerned with what other people think of you and feel vulnerable to people's opinions of you, then such a theme may make you vulnerable to developing obsessions in this particular area. You may develop obsessions and doubts about possibly having done embarrassing things even though common sense tells you that you did not. We all have our vulnerabilities, but they express themselves in different ways from person to person and will not always result in OCD. However, if these vulnerabilities become part of the confusion between reality and imagination, then we have a good recipe for OCD. Your vulnerability to OCD is a story about yourself and the person you believe yourself to be – your identity. For example, if you have frequent obsessions about 'having lost something' then in one way or another you consider yourself to be the 'type' of person that could lose something. Or if you have obsessions about something terrible happening to you, then in one way or another, you consider yourself to be the type of person to whom terrible things could happen. Let's look at an example of such a story:

> Despite my good intentions, I could be implicated in something bad, because I'm ignorant about lots of facts, there are dangers out there and I'm not aware all the time. I mean, I'm unaware of unknown dangers, so I have to take precautions because I don't know enough. The unknown, what you can't see, has powers to harm you. The world is a dangerous place, I feel insecure most of the time.

You may or may not identify with this story, but clearly, this person views herself as unaware, or not knowing everything, which she feels makes her more vulnerable to danger. With such a view about herself, it is relatively easy to see how this person will be vulnerable to certain types of obsessions and compulsions.

Beyond Reasonable Doubt by K. O'Connor, F. Aardema and M.-C. Pélissier.
Copyright © 2005 John Wiley & Sons, Ltd.

What is your vulnerability? Below are a couple of examples of how to identify your vulnerable self-theme by starting with your main obsessions and compulsions:

> If you fear contracting illness, then your vulnerability may start with: 'I'm the sort of person who could get sick.'
>
> If you try to memorize things constantly, and worry about forgetting things, then your vulnerability may start with: 'I'm the sort of person who could forget things.'
>
> If you place things symmetrically, and doubt whether they have been aligned correctly, then your vulnerability may start with: 'I'm the kind of person who might not do things neatly enough.'

Once you have identified how your obsession or doubt relates to the particular way you view yourself, the next step is identifying the story that makes you view yourself in that particular way. What are the reasons behind viewing yourself in that particular way?

EXERCISE 9
THE VULNERABLE SELF-THEME IN OBSESSIONAL STORIES

The vulnerable self-theme leads you to give credibility to obsessional doubts. In a way, the OCD tries to do its best to undermine your confidence in yourself exactly in those areas of your life that are meaningful and important to you. Note that the self-theme itself is a doubt ('Maybe I could be the sort of person...?'). Like the OCD doubt it is almost certainly not grounded in real experience. We are not saying this is the cause of OCD. The ultimate cause of OCD is still very much unknown. But for some reason, this self-image of yourself as someone who could 'be contaminated', 'forget to lock the door', or 'have blasphemous thoughts' has taken on a life of its own seemingly beyond your control. Possibly someone repeated it to you or maybe other types of experiences have contributed to this self-image. If you were not concerned with who the OCD says you might be, then you would be unlikely to have obsessions in that area.

So how do you go about changing a self-image of self-doubt? A good place to start is to be aware of exactly what the OCD says that you might be, and also, what the OCD says that you might not be. Start by writing down a story of all those things that the OCD says you might be. Use your main obsession as described on the worksheet, such as 'I'm the sort of person who could get sick if I'm not careful' or 'I'm the sort of person who doesn't know enough'. Next, try to expand as much as possible on all the reasons you could be the type of person as dictated by your OCD. After you have written down this story about who the OCD says you could be, write a second story. But this time, write down the reasons that show this story about you is unfounded. For example, if you wrote down in the previous story 'I'm the sort of person who could hurt others', then you write down in the second story 'I'm the sort of person who is kind and considerate to others'. If you wrote down a reason why you are one sort of person, then write another reason in the second story why you are not that type of person, as dictated by the OCD.

Put both stories next to each other and look at both stories from a common-sense point of view. Which of the two stories really resonates with you when looking at it calmly? In all likelihood, the alternative story is likely to be far more accurate. Take your two stories with you to your therapist for the next session, and share your insights with your therapist as to who you truly are.

Another exercise which is part of your training card is to reposition yourself in the way you use language to describe who you are. Beware of any automatic phrases, metaphors or sayings which you might habitually use to reinforce your position in the world as someone 'more likely to make mistakes' or 'more likely to experience bad things', etc. Every time you find yourself saying things to yourself that reinforce the vulnerable self-theme of your OCD, you can reposition yourself by describing yourself in a different language and placing yourself in a different position regarding the world and its events, for example:

I probably goofed again.

versus

I almost certainly did not goof again.

I'm just not capable of doing a job competently the first time.

versus

I'm capable of doing as good a job as anyone else.

I'm floundering in a mud bath.

versus

I'm like a bird flying though the sky.

TRAINING CARD 9

Front

The Vulnerable Self-Theme in Obsessional Stories

Major Learning Points

(1) You only have certain types of obsessions because you have a specific vulnerability to these obsessions.

(2) You are vulnerable to exactly those obsessions in a particular area that you care about the most.

(3) The vulnerable doubting theme, like the obsessional doubt, is unfounded.

Back

The Vulnerable Self-Theme in Obsessional Stories

Exercise

Make yourself very familiar with the alternative story you wrote about yourself. Then, at least three times per day, take some time to imagine and rehearse this story as vividly as you can. Immerse yourself in it with as much detail as possible. You can do this verbally or use imagery, or both, depending on your preference. Imagine each of the elements and make them as real as possible to yourself by going into as much detail as possible. Creatively add new elements to your story. Reposition yourself by the way you refer to yourself in language, using metaphors.

WORKSHEET 10
REALITY SENSING – TOLERATING THE VOID

We have reached the last worksheet of your therapy. The extent to which you have progressed depends on too many factors to discuss here, but keep in mind that the extent of progress varies greatly from person to person. For example, some people will need considerably more time in therapy, whereas others have already benefited from a therapy of a relatively short duration. Perhaps there are still other obsessions that need further work, and reworking your way through the worksheets from the beginning may be necessary. However, one thing should be clear at this point, and that is that an obsessional doubt is something very different from a normal doubt, and that there are certain implications to this idea that make obsessional doubts not worthy of your attention.

You may think that you agree with all that you have learned in the therapy so far, but yet still have very strong compulsions, and that you can't do anything about them. This is NOT possible. If you agree with all you have learned so far, and we mean *really* agree, then you no longer have obsessional doubts nor compulsions. So you will have to recognize and identify what aspects of the therapy you don't agree with or have difficulty with, since as long as those aspects are not dealt with, you are likely to continue to have a certain amount of OCD. Alternatively, you may have started to notice a change in your compulsions in the course of this therapy. Perhaps your doubts have become less intense and, in a quite natural way without too much effort, you have started to engage in less compulsive behaviors in at least some situations. So how to proceed from there?

It will be important to start to reinforce what you have learned so far for the coming sessions, and perhaps even after therapy on your own. You will have to move in steps where you slowly increase your ability to dismiss obsessional doubts in situations of increasing difficulty. Try to realize one thing. That is, no matter what the OCD may feel like – it is made of brittle glass. It is never reality or your senses that have brought it about, and as much as your OCD will try to escape this fact, your senses will always be on your side.

Reality sensing is about staying with information from the here and now. This means that you will actually look at what is there instead of making assumptions of what is there solely on the basis of an imaginary OCD story. Instead of avoiding a situation or adding doubt to it by going off in the imagination, you will define reality by relying on information from the five senses. And as you have learned in the therapy so far, relying on the senses will leave no room whatsoever for obsessional doubt. For example, do you look at your hands after you feel an urge to wash? Do your senses play any role at all right now? When you check whether you left something unlocked, does it matter whether you heard and felt it lock? Often, for people with OCD, this type of sense information is not given any attention, since the OCD story has found a way around it. But it is the only reality that gives a resolution to your obsessional doubt, and that means learning to trust the senses again – and knowing that this is enough.

Can it be so easy that all it takes is to trust the senses? Yes and no. It's easy, because if you really trust your senses, then there will be no obsessional doubt. It's not so easy, because trusting the senses will give you the feeling you are not doing enough. The OCD has told you for a long time to do more and more, and even then it may still not be enough. So doing less will leave a void and a feeling that you are not doing enough. That may produce anxiety, discomfort, or fear. Yet, you are doing enough, and in fact all that you can do, if you trust the senses. So the anxiety and discomfort are unnecessary to begin with if they are based on an imaginary OCD story. In short, it is time to trust the senses once again.

EXERCISE 10
REALITY SENSING – TOLERATING THE VOID

The exercise on this worksheet is the culmination of all the exercises that you have done so far. It contains a strategy on how to deal with obsessions as they occur. You are not expected to use this strategy in every OCD situation if the OCD is very strong, but only in those situations where you anticipate you will be able to move out of the OCD back into reality where all is safe and secure. The more you do this, the more your confidence will grow, and the better you will be able to tackle situations that used to be difficult. Succeed in doing this often enough, and you will quickly find that the obsessions will not return as frequently and intensely. And if they do not return at all, then you have truly realized the imaginary nature of the obsessional doubt and there is no 'but' or 'what if' which can ever change that.

(1) When an obsession occurs, hold still and don't do anything. Imagine yourself between worlds – a bridge between reality and the imagination.

(2) Focus your attention back to reality, and look at what is there. Only look once and take in the information of what your senses tell you. Don't put any effort into this at all.

(3) Realize for a moment that this is all the information you need and that trying to obtain more information means you have already crossed into OCD-land.

(4) Look down from the bridge you see yourself standing on, and take note that it is the void which makes you feel you are not doing enough. It represents all the anxiety and discomfort you feel by not going into OCD-land and only trusting your senses. Take a moment to realize that this void is merely imaginary, and that there is certainty by remaining in the world of the senses. There is no need to cross the bridge.

(5) Next, act upon the information from your senses by not engaging in compulsive behaviors and dismiss the obsession.

There are a number of things you need to keep in mind while you are doing the exercise, since it may be hard in the beginning to *really* trust your senses and look at what is there, since the OCD will tell you to do more than necessary. Really trusting the senses is allowing the senses to tell you what is there in a natural way – exactly as you trust your senses in non-OCD situations. This excludes:

(1) Staring – if you are staring, you are putting too much effort in to overcome your OCD. In fact, you are in your OCD, the moment you stare.

(2) Fast looking – creating ambiguity by quick looking will reinforce your imagination.
(3) Imposing your imagination on ambiguous percepts – if you can't see something clearly (for example, something in the distance that you may feel justifies the obsessional doubt), be aware that this is not 'real looking'.

The most important element to recognize from this exercise, and in fact all the previous exercises, is that there is certainty where you tend to look the least. It is there already and has always been there. The only thing the OCD does is take you away from the reassuring influence of reality. Reality is there in front of you. You don't have to seek it out especially, or do anything special to get it. It is just there. It's a question of your not giving credibility to the initial OCD questioning, 'Can I be sure?' Eventually the aim is for you to do nothing special in OCD situations, by way of thinking or behavior. Do not, for example, prepare yourself *not* to do the OCD. Be aware of any subtle preparation that in itself involves making special efforts. Just anticipating the OCD can make it special. As you start to act upon this certainty, and your senses, you can increase your confidence in both yourself and the world of the senses. It will start to become more and more apparent that there is nothing more you need to do. And the good part is, the void will slowly disappear, and be filled up with your real personality. So go out there and get to know your real self!

TRAINING CARD 10

Front

Reality Sensing – Tolerating the Void

Major Learning Points

(1) Reality sensing is staying with the information from the here and now.
(2) There already is certainty before the obsessional doubt.
(3) Trusting your senses will add to your confidence each and every time.
(4) The less you do, the more your real personality will emerge to cope naturally with events.

Back

Reality Sensing – Tolerating the Void

Exercise

Do the following exercise three times per day:
(1) When an obsession occurs, hold still and don't do anything. Imagine yourself on a bridge between worlds.
(2) Focus your attention back to reality, and look at what is there. Don't put any effort into this at all.
(3) Realize for a moment that this is all the information you need. Look down from the bridge you see yourself standing on, and take note that it is the void which makes you feel you are not doing enough.
(4) Take a moment to realize that this void is merely imaginary.
(5) Next, act upon the information from your senses by not engaging in compulsive behaviors and dismiss the obsession.

APPENDIX 3

IBA ASSESSMENT AND CASE FORMULATION

General clinical assessment procedures follow guidelines already in place for questionnaire, self-report, semi-structured interview, case history and case formulation (see Taylor, 1998; Clark, 2004). The following assessment procedure is then supplementary and specific to IBA treatment.

Essentially, five clinical scales need to be completed over the evaluation period. First, the hierarchy of compulsion and obsessions needs to be constructed after information on definition of OCD is discussed with the person. The hierarchy is usually ordered according to a self-efficacy type scale (0–100) in answer to the question: At what point do you feel able to resist performing the following compulsion?

Second, associated moods and distress also need to be listed, since they will not always be anxiety, and the exact nature of the discomfort can help identify and nuance the obsessional thought.

Third, primary inference (PI) where the probability of the inference is assessed (0–100), and fourth, strength of secondary inference (SI) where the consequences are assessed as realistic (0–100) given the PI. These two inferences are clearly logically related, since the content of the SI follows logically from the content of the PI. But their values may be independent. Someone could consider it highly likely that their hands could be contaminated but less certain of the consequences. In general, at low and medium levels of the PI there is more chance of independence of PI from SI; at high levels of PI, SI and PI seem linked as part of the same narrative (O'Connor *et al.*, 2003a).

Fifth, we measure conviction (0–100) about the need to perform compulsive actions both in and out of the OCD situation. This scale provides an additional measure of absorption in the narrative and helps clinically for the person to recognize the difference as a way of achieving insight.

Beyond Reasonable Doubt by K. O'Connor, F. Aardema and M.-C. Pélissier.
Copyright © 2005 John Wiley & Sons, Ltd.

ELICITING PRIMARY AND SECONDARY INFERENCES

A convenient format to separate primary and secondary inferences is to use a logical template of the form, 'If..., then...'. For example, 'If the cooker is left on, then the house will burn down'. Here, in logic, the first clause after 'If' is the primary inference (or premise); the clause after 'Then' is the secondary inference (or corollary). If the primary inference is not clear, it is possible to work back from the consequences and ask, '...and that will happen if what state of affairs (is true), or (happens)...?' So, in the following example, the client (C) spontaneously volunteers a consequence to the therapist (T).

C: If I don't check the cooker, the house will burn down.
T: And the house will burn down if what state of affairs is true?
C: Well, if the cooker is left on and catches alight.

The inference can be subsequently refined by asking:

T: So, you are checking the cooker to check for what?
C: Well, to make sure the plates are not left on. Of course I know they aren't really, but I just want to be sure.
T: So, when you go to check, precisely what thought comes into your head?
C: That the plates may still be on.

Primary inference: The plates may still be on. *Secondary inference*: (then) the cooker will catch alight and burn the house.

We also find it clinically useful to complete with the client a personalized crossover sheet marking points where the person's thinking crosses over from reality into the imagination. The completed sheet serves to illustrate how the model applies in the client's case and also to target the point where the client crosses into inferential confusion (see Appendix 4).

Summary of IBA Case Formulation

IBA case formulation requires:

1) Hierarchy of obsessions-compulsions.

2) Strength of primary/secondary inference.

3) Listing of associated moods.

4) Completion of personalized crossing-over diagram to pinpoint operational factors in maintaining inferential confusion.

APPENDIX 4

A personalized crossover sheet marking the points where the client's thinking crosses over from reality into the imagination.

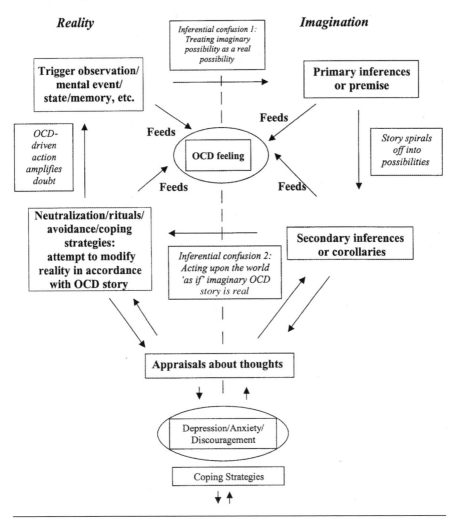

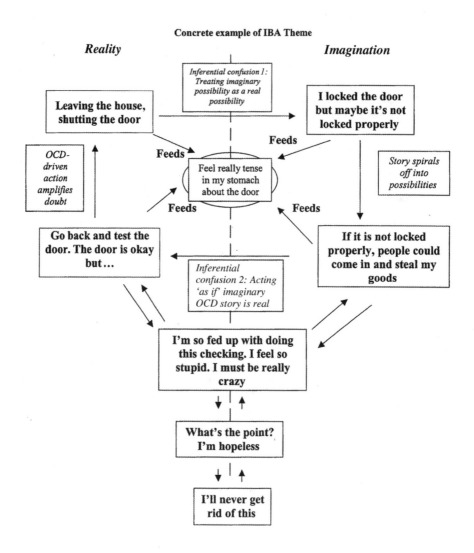

Concrete example of IBA Theme

What the person experiences when entering treatment according to IBA Model:

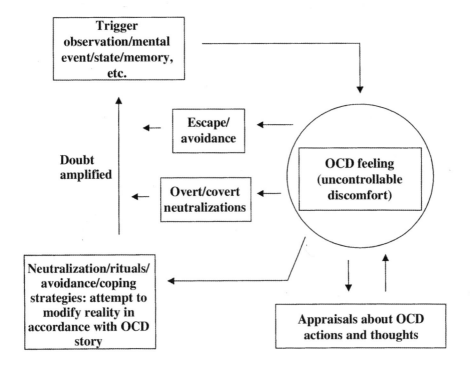

REFERENCES

Aardema, F. (1996). The relationship between cognitive variables and personality. Unpublished Master's thesis. University of Groningen, Groningen.

Aardema, F., & O'Connor, K. (2003). Seeing white bears that are not there: Inference processes in obsessions. *Journal of Cognitive Psychotherapy*, **17**, 23–37.

Aardema, F., Emmelkamp, P., & O'Connor, K. (2004a). Inferential confusion and treatment outcome in obsessive-compulsive disorder. Manuscript submitted for publication.

Aardema, F., O'Connor, K., & Emmelkamp, P.M.G. (2004b). Are obsessive-compulsive beliefs epi-phenomena of inferential confusion? Manuscript submitted for publication.

Aardema, F., O'Connor, K., & Emmelkamp, P. (2004c). Inferential confusion and treatment outcome in obsessive-compulsive disorder. Manuscript in preparation for publication.

Aardema, F., Pélissier, M.-C., & O'Connor, K. (2004d). The quantification of doubt. Ongoing research project.

Aardema, F., Kleijer, T.M.R., Trihey, M., O'Connor, K., & Emmelkamp, P. (2004e). Inference processes, schizotypal thinking and obsessive-compulsive disorder. Manuscript submitted for publication.

Aardema, F., O'Connor K., Emmelkamp, P., Marchand, A., & Todorov, C. (2004f). Inferential confusion in obsessive-compulsive disorder: The inferential confusion questionnaire. *Behaviour Research and Therapy*. Manuscript accepted for publication.

Abramowitz, J.S. (1996). Variants of exposure and response prevention in the treatment of OCD: A meta-analysis. *Behavior Therapy*, **27**, 583–600.

Abramowitz, J.S. (1997). Effectiveness of psychological and pharmacological treatments for obsessive-compulsive disorder: A quantitative review. *Journal of Consulting and Clinical Psychology*, **65**, 44–52.

Abramowitz, J.S. (1998). Does cognitive-behavioral therapy cure obsessive-compulsive disorder? A meta-analytic evaluation of clinical significance. *Behavior Therapy*, **29**, 339–355.

Abrams, D. (1988). Merleau-Ponty and the voice of the earth. *Environmental Ethics*, **10**, 101–120.

American Psychological Association (APA) (1994). *Diagnostic and statistical manual of mental disorders (4th edn)*. Washington DC: Author.

Anderson, H. (ed.) (1997). *Conversation, language, and possibilities. A postmodern approach to therapy*. New York: Basic Books.

Anderson, H., & Goolishian, H. (1996). Systems consultation to agencies dealing with domestic violence. In L. Wynne, S. McDaniel, & T. Weber (eds),

The family therapist as systems consultant (pp. 284–299). New York: The Guilford Press.

Anderson, J.R. (1990). *The adaptive character of thought.* Hillsdale, NJ: Erlbaum.

Angst, J. (1993). Comorbidity of anxiety, phobia, compulsion and depression. *International Clinical Psychopharmacology,* **8,** 21–25.

Arntz, A., Rauner, M., & van den Hout, M. (1995). If I feel anxious, there must be danger: Ex-consequentia reasoning in inferring danger in anxiety disorders. *Behaviour Research and Therapy,* **33**(8), 917–925.

Asch, S.E. (1956). Studies of independence and conformity: 1. A minority of one against a unanimous majority. *Psychological Monographs,* **70**(9), Whole No. 416.

Austin, J.L. (1956–1957/1970). A plea for excuses. *Proceedings of the Aristotelian Society,* **57,** 1–30.

Austin, J.L. (1962). *How to do things with words.* J.O. Urmson (ed.). New York: Oxford University Press.

Baer, L., & Jenike, M.A. (1998). Personality disorders in obsessive-compulsive disorder. In M.A. Jenike, L. Baer, & W.E. Minichiello (eds), *Obsessive-compulsive disorders: Practical management.* St. Louis, MO: Mosby.

Bakhtin, M. (1973). *Problems of Dostoevsky's poetics.* 2nd edn, trans. R.W. Rotzel. Ann Arbor, MI: Ardis (original work published 1929).

Barnard, P. (1985). Interacting cognitive subsystems: A psycholinguistic approach to short-term memory. In A. Ellis (ed.), *Progress in the psychology of language* (vol. 2, pp. 197–258). London: Erlbaum.

Bartlett, F. (1958). *Thinking: An experimental and social study.* London: Unwin University Books.

Basco, M.R. (2000). *Never good enough: How to use perfectionism to your advantage without letting it ruin your life.* New York: Touchstone.

Bechtel, W. (1988). *Philosophy of mind: An overview for cognitive science.* Hillsdale, NJ: Lawrence Erlbaum.

Beck, A.T. (1976). *Cognitive therapy and the emotional disorders.* New York: International Universities Press.

Beck, A.T. (1996). Beyond belief: A theory of modes, personality, and psycho-pathology. In P.M. Salkovskis (ed.), *Frontiers of cognitive therapy* (pp. 1–25). New York: The Guilford Press.

Beck, A.T., & Emery, G. (1985). *Anxiety disorders and phobias: A cognitive perspective.* New York: Basic Books.

Beck, A.T., & Rector, N.A. (2002). Delusions: A cognitive perspective. *Journal of Cognitive Psychotherapy,* **16**(4), 455–468.

Beck, A.T., Rush, A.J., Shaw, B.F., & Emery, G. (1979). *Cognitive therapy of depression.* New York: The Guilford Press.

Bentall, R.P., Kinderman, P., & Kaney, S. (1994). The self, attributional processes and abnormal beliefs: Towards a model of persecutory delusions. *Behavioural Research and Therapy,* **32**(3), 331–341.

Berlin, R.M., Olson, M.E., Cano, C.E., & Engel, S. (1991). Metaphor and psychotherapy. *American Journal of Psychotherapy,* **XLV**(3), 359–367.

Bhar, S.S., & Kyrios, M. (2001). Ambivalent self-esteem as a meta-vulnerability for obsessive-compulsive disorder. In R.G. Craven & H.W. Marsh (eds), *Self-concept theory, research and practice: Advances for the new millennium* (pp. 143–156). Sydney, Australia: SELF.

Bieling, P.J., & Kuyken, W. (2003). Is cognitive case formulation science or science fiction? *Clinical Psychology, Science and Practice*, **10**, 52–69.

Blowers, G., & O'Connor, K.P. (1996). *Personal construct psychology in the clinical context*. Ottawa, ON: University of Ottawa Press.

Bouman, T.K. (2002). Cognitive behavioural group treatment for body dysmorphic disorder. *Abstracts, 32nd EABCT Congress*, Maastricht, The Netherlands.

Brown, H.D., Kosslyn, S.M., Breiter, H.C., Baer, L., & Jenike, M.A. (1994). Can patients with obsessive-compulsive disorder discriminate between percepts and mental images? A signal detection analysis. *Journal of Abnormal Psychology*, **103**(3), 445–454.

Bruner, J. (1986). *Actual minds, possible words*. Cambridge, MA: Harvard University Press.

Bryant, R.A., & Mallard, D. (2003). Seeing is believing: The reality of hypnotic hallucinations. *Consciousness and Cognition*, **12**, 219–230.

Burke, K. (1945). Introduction: The five key terms of dramatism. In K. Burke (ed.), *A grammar of motives* (pp. xv–xxiii). New York: Prentice-Hall.

Burke, K. (1950). *A rhetoric of motives*. New York: Prentice-Hall.

Burkitt, I. (2003). Psychology in the field of being. Merleau-Ponty, ontology and social constructionism. *Theory & Psychology*, **13**(3), 319–338.

Burns, G.L., Keortge, S.G., Formea, G.M., & Sternberger, L.G. (1996). Revision of the Padua Inventory of obsessive compulsive disorder symptoms: Distinctions between worry, obsessions, and compulsions. *Behaviour Research and Therapy*, **34**, 163–173.

Calamari, J.E., Wiegartz, P.S., Riemann, B.C., Cohen, R.J., Greer, A., Jacobi, D.M., John, S.C., & Carmin, C. (2004). Obsessive-compulsive disorder subtypes: An attempted replication and extension of a symptom-based taxonomy. *Behavior Research and Therapy*, **42**, 647–670.

Caro, I. (1991). Theory and practice: An introduction to the cognitive therapy of evaluation [1]. *Counselling Psychology Quarterly*, **4**(2-3), 191–206.

Carr, A.T. (1971). Compulsive neurosis: Two psychological studies. *Bulletin of the British Psychological Society*, **24**, 256–257.

Chia, R. (2002). The production of management knowledge: Philosophical underpinnings of research design. In D. Partington (ed.), *Essential skills for management research*. London: Sage.

Churchland, P.S. (1986). *Neurophilosophy: Toward a unified science of the mind–brain*. Cambridge, MA: MIT Press/Bradford Books.

Clark, D.A. (2002). Commentary on cognitive domains section. In R.O. Frost & G. Steketee (eds), *Cognitive approaches to obsessions and compulsions: Theory, assessment, and treatment*. Oxford: Elsevier.

Clark, D.A. (2004). *Cognitive-behavioral therapy for OCD*. New York: Guilford Press.

Clark, D.A., & O'Connor, K. (2004). Thinking is believing: Ego-dystonic intrusive thoughts in obsessive-compulsive disorder. In D.A. Clark (ed.), *Unwanted intrusive thoughts in clinical disorders*. New York: The Guilford Press.

Clark, D.A., & Steer, R.A. (1996). Empirical status of the cognitive model of anxiety and depression. In P.M. Salkovskis (ed.), *Frontiers of cognitive therapy* (pp. 75–96). New York: The Guilford Press.

Clark, H.H. (1977). Bridging. In P.N. Johnson-Laird & P.C. Wason (eds), *Thinking: Readings in cognitive science* (pp. 411–420). Cambridge: Cambridge University Press.

Cohen, L.J. (1981). Can human irrationality be experimentally demonstrated? *Behavioral and Brain Sciences*, **4**, 317–370.

Coles, M., Bogert, K.V., Krouse, M., Amir, N., Kazak, M., & Foa, E. (1996). Fixity of beliefs in OCD. Paper presented at the *30th Annual Convention of the Association for the Advancement of Behavior Therapy*, New York, November.

De Jong, P.J., Mayer, B., & van den Hout, M. (1997). Conditional reasoning and phobic fear: Evidence for a fear-confirming pattern. *Behaviour Research and Therapy*, **35**(6), 507–516.

De Jong, P.J., Haenen, M.-A., Schmidt, A., & Mayer, B. (1998). Hypochondriasis: The role of fear-confirming reasoning. *Behaviour Research and Therapy*, **36**, 65–74.

Dennett, D.C. (1978). *Brainstorms*. Cambridge, MA: MIT Press/Bradford Books.

De Rivera, J., & Sarbin, T.R. (1998). *Believed-in imaginings: The narrative construction of reality*. Washington, DC: American Psychological Association.

Derrida, J. (1994). The deconstruction of actuality: An interview with Jacques Derrida. *Radical Philosophy*, **68**, 28–41.

Dretske, F.I. (1981). *Knowledge and the flow of information*. Cambridge, MA: MIT Press/Bradford Books.

Dudley, R.E.J., & Over, D.E. (2003). People with delusions jump to conclusions: A theoretical account of research findings on the reasoning of people with delusions. *Clinical Psychology and Psychotherapy*, **10**, 263–274.

Dudley, R.E.J., John, C.H., Young, A.W., & Over, D.E. (1997a). Normal and abnormal reasoning in people with delusions. *British Journal of Clinical Psychology*, **36**, 243–258.

Dudley, R.E.J., John, C.H., Young, A.W., & Over, D.E. (1997b). The effect of self-referent material on the reasoning of people with delusions. *British Journal of Clinical Psychology*, **36**, 575–584.

Dudley, R.E.J., Young, A.W., John, C.H., & Over, D.E. (1998). Conditional reasoning in people with delusions: Performance on the Wason Selection Task. *Cognitive Neuropsychiatry*, **3**(4), 241–258.

Eagleton, T. (1983). *Literary theory: An introduction*. Oxford: Blackwell.

Edwards, A.W.F. (ed.) (1972). *Likelihood: An account of the statistical concept of likelihood and its application to scientific inference*. Cambridge: Cambridge University Press.

Edwards, D., Ashmore, M., & Potter, J. (1995). Death and furniture: The rhetoric, politics and theology of bottom line arguments against relativism. *History of the Human Sciences*, **8**, 25–49.

Ellis, A. (1962). *Reason and emotion in psychotherapy: A comprehensive method of treating human disturbances*. New York: Ellis Citadel Press.

Ellis, A. (1991). Achieving self-actualization: The rational–emotive approach. *Journal of Social Behavior and Personality*, **6**(5), 1–18.

Emmelkamp, P.M.G. (2002). Commentary on treatment. In R.O. Frost & G. Steketee (eds), *Cognitive approaches to obsessions and compulsions: Theory, assessment, and treatment*. Oxford: Elsevier.

Emmelkamp, P.M.G., & Aardema, F. (1999). Metacognition, specific obsessive-compulsive beliefs and obsessive-compulsive behaviour. *Clinical Psychology and Psychotherapy*, **6**, 139–145.

Emmelkamp, P.M.G., & Beens, H. (1991). Cognitive therapy with obsessive-compulsive disorder: A comparative evaluation. *Behaviour Research and Therapy*, **29**, 293–300.

Emmelkamp, P.M.G., Visser, S., & Hoekstra, R.J. (1988). Cognitive therapy vs exposure in vivo in the treatment of obsessive-compulsives. *Cognitive Therapy and Research*, **12**, 103–144.

Emmelkamp, P.M.G., van Oppen, P., & van Balkom, A.J.L.M. (2002). Cognitive changes in patients with obsessive-compulsive rituals treated with exposure in vivo and response prevention. In R.O. Frost & G. Steketee (eds), *Cognitive approaches to obsessions and compulsions: Theory, assessment, and treatment*. Oxford: Elsevier.

Emmelkamp, P.M., van der Helm, M., van Zanten, B.L., & Plochg, I. (1980). Treatment of obsessive-compulsive patients: The contribution of self-instructional training to the effectiveness of exposure. *Behaviour Research and Therapy*, **18**, 61–66.

Emmett, K. (1989). Must intentional states be intenSional? *Behaviorism*, **17**(2), 129–135.

Engelhard, I.M., van den Hout, M.A., Arntz, A., & McNally, R.J. (2002). A longitudinal study of 'intrusion-based reasoning' and posttraumatic stress disorder after exposure to a train disaster. *Behaviour Research and Therapy*, **40**, 1415–1424.

Engelhard, I.M., Macklin, M.L., McNally, R.J., van den Hout, M.A., & Arntz, A. (2001). Emotion- and intrusion-based reasoning in Vietnam veterans with and without chronic posttraumatic stress disorder. *Behaviour Research and Therapy*, **39**, 1339–1348.

Enright, S.J., & Beech, A.R. (1990). Obsessional states: Anxiety disorders or schizotypes? An information processing and personality assessment. *Psychological Medicine*, **20**, 621–627.

Evans, J.St.B.T. (1982). *The psychology of deductive reasoning*. London: Routledge & Kegan Paul.

Evans, J.St.B.T. (1983). The mental model theory of conditional reasoning: Critical appraisal and revision. *Cognition*, **48**, 1–20.

Evans, J.St.B.T. (1989). *Bias in human reasoning: causes and consequences*. Hove: Lawrence Erlbaum.

Evans, J.St.B.T., & Over, D.E. (1996). *Rationality and reasoning*. Hove: Psychology Press.

Evans, J.St.B.T., Newstead, S.E., & Byrne, R.M.J. (1993). *Human reasoning: The psychology of deduction*. Hove: Lawrence Erlbaum.

Fauconnier, G., & Turner, M. (2002). *The way we think: Conceptual blending and the mind's hidden complexities*. New York: Basic Books.

Fear, C.F., & Healy, D. (1997). Probabilistic reasoning in obsessive-compulsive and delusional disorders. *Psychological Medicine*, **27**(1), 199–208.

Feyerabend, P.K. (1963/1970). Materialism and the mind–body problem. *The Review of Metaphysics*, **17**, 49–67.

Foa, E.B., & Franklin, M.E. (2002). Psychotherapies for obsessive-compulsive disorder: A review. In M. Maj, N. Sartorius, A. Okasha, & J. Zohar (eds), *Obsessive-Compulsive Disorder*. Chichester: Wiley.

Foa, E.B., & Kozak, M.J. (1995). DSM-IV field trial: Obsessive-compulsive disorder. *American Journal of Psychiatry*, **152**, 90–96.

Foa, E.B., Steketee, G., Gayson, J.B., & Doppelt, H.G. (1983). Treatment of obsessive-compulsives: When do we fail? In E.B. Foa & P.M.G. Emmelkamp (eds), *Failures in behavior therapy*. New York: John Wiley & Sons.

Fodor, J.A. (1987). *Psychosemantics: The problem of meaning in the philosophy of mind*. Cambridge, MA: MIT Press.

Frank, J.D. (1987). Psychotherapy, rhetoric, and hermeneutics: Implications for practice and research. *Psychotherapy*, **24**, 293–302.

Frauenfeld, A.E. (1937). The power of speech. *Unser Wille und Weg*, August, 16–21.

Freeman, M. (1995). Groping in the light. *Theory & Psychology*, **5**, 353–360.

Freeston, M., & Ladouceur, R. (1997). What do patients do with their obsessive thoughts? *Behavior Research and Therapy*, **35**(4), 335–348.

Freeston, M., & O'Connor, K.P. (1997). *Self-monitoring for OCD studies: Instructional guide for the therapists.* (Available from the Centre de recherche Fernand-Seguin, 7331 Hochelaga St., Montréal, Québec, H1N 3V2.)

Freeston, M.H., Leger, E., & Ladouceur, R. (2001). Cognitive therapy of obsessive thoughts. *Cognitive and Behavioral Practice*, **8**(1), 61–78.

Freeston, M.H., Rhéaume, J., & Ladouceur, R. (1996). Correcting faulty appraisals of obsessive thoughts. *Behaviour Research and Therapy*, **13**, 459–470.

Frenkel-Brunswick, E. (1949). Intolerence of ambiguity as an emotional and perceptual personality variable. In J.S. Bruner & D. Krech (eds), *Perception and Personality*. New York: Greenwood Press.

Frost, R.O., Novara, C., & Rhéaume, J. (2002). Perfectionism and obsessive-compulsive disorder. In R.O. Frost & G. Steketee (eds), *Cognitive approaches to obsessions and compulsions: Theory, assessment, and treatment*. Oxford: Elsevier.

Gadamer, H.-G. (1975). *Truth and method*. Trans. G. Burden & J. Cumming. New York: Seabury Press.

Garety, P.A. (1991). Reasoning and delusions. *British Journal of Psychiatry*, **159** (Suppl. 14), 14–18.

Garety, P.A., & Freeman, D. (1999). Cognitive approaches to delusions: A critical review of theories and evidence. *British Journal of Clinical Psychology*, **38**, 113–154.

Garety, P.A., & Hemsley, D.R. (1994). *Delusions: Investigations into the psychology of delusional reasoning*. Hove: Psychology Press.

Garety, P.A., Hemsley, D.R., & Wessely, S. (1991). Reasoning in deluded schizophrenia and paranoid patients. Biases in performance on a probabilistic task. *The Journal of Nervous and Mental Disease*, **179**(4), 194–201.

Geller, D.A., Biederman, J., Faraone, S., Agranat, A., Cradock, K., Hagermoser, L., Kim, G., Frasier, J., & Coffey, B.J. (2001). Developmental aspects of obsessive compulsive disorder: Findings in children, adolescents, and adults. *Journal of Nervous and Mental Disease*, **189**(7), 471–477.

Georgaca, E. (2003). Exploring signs and voices in the therapeutic space. *Theory & Psychology*, **13**(4), 541–560.

Georgi, A. (ed.) (1985). *Phenomenology and psychological research*. Pittsburgh: Duquesne University Press.

Gergen, K.J. (1994). *Realities and relationships: Soundings in social construction*. Cambridge, MA: Harvard University Press.

Gibson, J.J. (1979). *The ecological approach to visual perception*. Boston: Houghton Mifflin Co.

Ginsberg, M.L., & Smith, D.E. (1988). Reasoning about action I: A possible worlds approach. *Artificial Intelligence*, **35**, 165–195.

Goodman, W.K., Price, L.H., Rasmussen, S.A., Mazure, C., Delgado, P., Heniger, G.R., & Charney, D.S. (1989a). The Yale-Brown Obsessive Compulsive Scale. II. Validity. *Archives of General Psychiatry*, **46**, 1012–1016.

Goodman, W.K., Price, L.H., Rasmussen, S.A., Mazure, C., Fleischman, R.L., Hill, C.L., Heniger, G.R., & Charney, D.S. (1989b). The Yale-Brown Obsessive Compulsive Scale. I. Development, use and reliability. *Archives of General Psychiatry*, **46**, 1006–1011.

Green, M.C., & Brock, T.C. (2000). The role of transportation in the persuasiveness of public narratives. *Journal of Personality and Social Psychology*, **79**(5), 701–721.

Grenier, S., O'Connor, K., & Bélanger, C. (2004). Obsessive-compulsive disorder: Insight and overvalued ideas. Manuscript submitted for publication.

Groves, D.J. (1991). *In the presence of the past*. Eldon: David Groves Seminars.

Guay, S., O'Connor, K.P., Emmelkamp, P., & Todorov, C. (2004, in press). A single belief as a maintaining factor in obsessive-compulsive disorder. *Journal of Cognitive Psychotherapy*.

Guidano, V.F. (1991). *The self in process: Toward a post-rationalist cognitive therapy*. New York: The Guilford Press.

Guidano, V.F., & Liotti, G. (1983). *Cognitive processes and emotional disorders*. New York: The Guilford Press.

Gyoerkoe, K. (2003). *Treatment of homosexual obsessions*. Presented at Anxiety Disorders of America 23rd National Conference, Toronto, Canada.

Hacking, I. (1983). *Representing and intervening*. New York: Cambridge University Press.

Hallam, R.S. & O'Connor, K.P. (2002). A dialogical approach to obsessions. *Psychology and Psychotherapy: Theory, Research and Practice*, **75**, 333–348.

Halliday, M.A.K. (1973). *Explorations in the functions of language*. London: Edward Arnold.

Hamilton, V. (1957). Perceptual and personality dynamics in reactions to ambiguity. *British Journal of Psychology*, **48**, 200–215.

Hansen, E. (2003). Stress, stream of affect, emotions and background variables: Exploratory experiment with poetry reading II. *Stress Research Reports* No. 311. Psychosocial Center, Karolinska Institute, Stockholm, Sweden.

Harré, R. (1991). The discursive production of selves. *Theory and Psychology*, **1**, 51–63.

Hayes, S.C., & Hayes, L.J. (1992). Some clinical implications of contextual behaviorism: The examples: The example of cognition. *Behavior Therapy*, **23**, 225–249.

Heaps, C., & Nash, M. (1999). Individual differences in imagination inflation. *Psychon Bulletin Review*, **6**(2), 313–318.

Heidegger, M. (1962). *Being and time*. New York: Harper.

Heidegger, M. (1987). *An introduction to metaphysics* (trans. R. Mannheim). New Haven, CT: Yale University Press.

Hermans, H.J.M. (1996). Voicing the self: From information processing to dialogical interchange. *Psychological Bulletin*, **119**, 31–50.

Hiss, H., Foa, E.B., & Kozak, M.J. (1994). Relapse prevention program of treatment of obsessive-compulsive disorder. *Journal of Consulting and Clinical Psychology*, **62**, 801–808.

Huq, S.F., Garety, P.A., & Hemsley, D.R. (1988). Probabilistic judgements in deluded and non-deluded subjects. *The Quarterly Journal of Experimental Psychology*, **40A**(4), 801–812.

Husserl, E. (1973). *The phenomenology of internal time consciousness*. Trans. J. Churchill. Bloomington & London: Indiana University Press.

Insel, T.R., & Akiskal, H.S. (1986). Obsessive-compulsive disorder with psychotic features: A phenomenologic analysis. *American Journal of Psychiatry*, **143**(12), 1527–1533.

Jakes, I. (1996). *Theoretical approaches to obsessive-compulsive disorders*. New York: Cambridge University Press.

James, W. (1890). *The principles of psychology*. New York: Holt.

Janet, P. (1903). *Les obsessions et la psychasthénie* (vols 1 and 3, 2nd edn). Paris: Alcan.

Jaspers, K. (1913, 1963). *General psychopathology*. Trans. M.W. Hoenig. Manchester: Manchester University Press.

Johnson-Laird, P.N. (1983). *Mental models: Towards a cognitive science of language, inference and consciousness*. Cambridge, MA: Cambridge University Press.

Johnson-Laird, P.N. (1993). *Human and machine thinking*. Hove: Lawrence Erlbaum.

Johnson-Laird, P.N. (1994a). A model theory of induction. *International Studies in the Philosophy of Science*, **8**(1), 5–29.

Johnson-Laird, P.N. (1994b). Mental models and probabilistic thinking. *Cognition*, **50**, 189–209.

Johnson-Laird, P.N. (1999). Deductive reasoning. *Annual Review of Psychology*, **50**, 109–135.

Johnson-Laird, P.N. (2001). Mental models and deduction. Unpublished document.

Johnson-Laird, P.N., & Byrne, R.M.J. (1991). *Deduction*. Hove: Lawrence Erlbaum.

Johnson-Laird, P.N., & Wason, P.C. (1970). A theoretical analysis of insight into a reasoning task. *Cognitive Psychology*, **1**, 134–148.

Julien, D., O'Connor, K.P., Grenier, S., Aardema, F., & Quevillon, F. (2004). *Do subgroups of obsessive-compulsive disorder (OCD) have specific dysfunctional assumptions?* Poster presented at the Association for the Advancement of Behavior Therapy Annual Meeting, Boston, USA, November.

Kahneman, D., Slovic, P., & Tversky, A. (1982). *Judgement under uncertainty: Heuristics and biases*. Cambridge: Cambridge University Press.

Karno, M., Golding, J.M., Sorenson, S.B., & Burnman, A. (1988). The epidemiology of obsessive-compulsive disorder in five US communities. *Archives of General Psychiatry*, **45**, 1094–1099.

Kelly, G.A. (1955). *The psychology of personal constructs*, 2 vols. New York: Norton.

Knudsen, J.C. (1990). Cognitive models in life histories. *Anthropological Quarterly*, **63**(3), 122–133.

Koopmans, P.C., Sanderman, R., Timmerman, I., & Emmelkamp, P.M.G. (1994). The Irrational Beliefs Inventory: Development and psychometric evaluation. *European Journal of Psychological Assessment*, **10**, 15–17.

Korzybski, A. (1994). *Science and sanity: An introduction to non-Aristotelian systems and general semantics*. 5th edn. European Society for General Semantics.

Kosslyn, S.M., Thompson, W.L., Costantini-Ferrando, M.F., Alpert, N.M., & Spiegel, D. (2000). Hypnotic visual illusion alters color processing in the brain. *American Journal of Psychiatry*, **157**, 1279–1284.

Lacan, J. (1977). The direction of the treatment and the principles of its power. In *Ecrits: A section*. Trans. A. Sheridan. London: Routledge.

Ladouceur, R., Talbot, F., & Dugas, M.J. (1997). Behavioral expressions of intolerance of uncertainty in worry. *Behavior Modification*, **21**(3), 355–371.

Lakoff, G. (1987). *Women, fire, and dangerous things: What categories reveal about the mind.* Chicago, IL: University of Chicago Press.

Lakoff, G., & Johnson, M. (1980). *Metaphors we live by.* Chicago: University of Chicago Press.

Langer, E., & Abelson, R. (1972). The semantics of asking a favor: How to succeed in getting help without really dying. *Journal of Personality and Social Psychology, 24,* 26–32.

Lee, C. (1992). On cognitive theories and causation in human behavior. *Journal of Behaviour and Experimental Psychiatry, 23*(4), 257–268.

Legrenzi, P., Girotto, V., & Johnson-Laird, P.N. (1993). Focussing in reasoning and decision making. Special Issue: Reasoning and decision making. *Cognition, 49*(1–2), 37–66.

Leibniz, G.W. (1682). *Philosophical essays.* Indianapolis & Cambridge: Hackett Publishing Co., 1989.

Levey, A.B., & Martin, I. (1987). Evaluative conditioning. A case for hedonic transfer. In H.J. Eysenck & I. Martin (eds), *Theoretical foundations of behavior therapy.* New York: Plenum Press.

Lowe, R. (1999). Between the 'no longer' and the 'not yet': Postmodernism as a context for critical therapeutic work. In I. Parker (ed.), *Deconstructing psychotherapy.* London: Sage.

Lynn, S.J., Kirsch, I., & Rhue, J.W. (eds) (1996). *Casebook of clinical hypnosis.* Washington, DC: American Psychological Association.

Mahoney, M.J. (2003). *Constructive psychotherapy: A practical guide.* New York: The Guilford Press.

Manktelow, K.I. (1999). *Reasoning and thinking.* Hove: Psychology Press.

Manktelow, K.I., & Over, D.E. (1990). *Inference and understanding: A philosophical and psychological perspective.* New York: Routledge.

Maranhão, T. (2002). *Therapeutic discourse and Socratic dialogue: A cultural critique.* Madison, WI: The University of Wisconsin Press.

Marazziti, D., Dell'Osso, L.D., Masso, E., Pfanner, C., Presta, S., Mungai, F., & Cassano, G.B. (2002). Insight in obsessive-compulsive disorder: A study in an Italian sample. *European Psychiatry, 17,* 407–410.

March, J.S., Frances, A., Carpenter, D., & Kahn, D.A. (1997). Treatment of obsessive compulsive disorders. *The Journal of Clinical Psychiatry, 58* (Suppl. 4), 5–71.

McAdams, D.P. (1997). *The stories we live by: Personal myths and the making of the self.* New York: The Guilford Press.

McClelland, D.C., Koestner, R., & Weinberger, J. (1989). How do self-attributed implicit motives differ? *Psychological Review, 96,* 690–702.

McGill, V.J. (1954). *Emotions and reason.* Springfield, IL: Charles C. Thomas.

McGinn, L.K., & Young, J.E. (1996). Schema-focused therapy. In P.M. Salkovskis (ed.), *Frontiers of cognitive therapy* (pp. 182–207). New York: The Guilford Press.

McGuire, L., Adams, S.G., Jr., Junginger, J., Burright, R., & Donovick, P. (2001). Delusions and delusional reasoning. *Journal of Abnormal Psychology, 110*(2), 259–266.

McKay, D., Abramowitz, J.S., Calamari, J.E., Kyrios, M., Radomsky, A., Sookman, D., Taylor, S., & Wilhelm, S. (2004). A critical evaluation of obsessive-compulsive disorder subtypes: Symptoms versus mechanisms. *Clinical Psychology Review, 24,* 283–313.

Meichenbaum, D. (2001). Cognitive behavioral treatment of post-traumatic stress disorder from a narrative constructivist perspective. In M.F. Hoyt (ed.), *Interviews With Brief Therapy Experts.* Philadelphia: Brunner-Routledge.

Merleau-Ponty, M. (1962). *The phenomenology of perception.* London: Routledge.

Meyer, V. (1966). Modification of expectations in cases with obsessional rituals. *Behavior Research and Therapy,* **9,** 225–238.

Milner, A.D, Beech, H.R., & Walker, V. (1971). Decision processes and obsessional behaviour. *British Journal of Social Clinical Psychology,* **10,** 88–89.

Mullins, S., & Spence, S.A. (2003). Re-examining thought insertion: Semi-structured literature review and conceptual analysis. *British Journal of Psychiatry,* **182,** 293–298.

Myers, T., Brown, K., & McGonigle, B. (1986). *Reasoning and discourse processses.* London: Academic Press.

Newstead, S.E., & Evans, J.St.B.T. (1995). *Perspectives on thinking and reasoning: Essays in honour of Peter Wason.* Hove: Lawrence Erlbaum.

Neziroglu, F., & Stevens, K.P. (2002). Insight: Its conceptualization and assessment. In R.O. Frost & G. Steketee (eds), *Cognitive approaches to obsessions and compulsions: Theory, assessment, and treatment.* Oxford: Elsevier.

Neziroglu, F., McKay, D., Yaryura-Tobias, J.A., Stevens, K.P., & Todaro, J. (1999). The overvalued ideas scale: Development, reliability and validity in obsessive-compulsive disorder. *Behaviour Research and Therapy,* **37,** 881–902.

Nisbett, R.E., & Wilson, T.D. (1977). Telling more than we can know: Verbal reports on mental processes. *Psychological Review,* **84,** 231–259.

Oaksford, M.R., & Chater, N. (1993). Reasoning theories and bounded rationality. In K.I. Manktelow & D.E. Over (eds), *Rationality.* London: Routledge.

Obsessive Compulsive Cognition Working Group (1997). Cognitive assessment of obsessive-compulsive disorder. *Behaviour Research and Therapy,* **35,** 667–681.

Obsessive Compulsive Cognitions Working Group (2001). Development and initial validation of the obsessive beliefs questionnaire and the interpretations of intrusions inventory. *Behaviour Research and Therapy,* **39,** 987–1006.

Obsessive Compulsive Cognitions Working Group (2003). Psychometric validation of the Obsessive Beliefs Questionnaire and the Interpretation of Intrusions Inventory: Part I. *Behaviour Research and Therapy,* **41,** 863–878.

O'Connor, K.P. (1985). The Bayesian inferential approach to defining response processes in psychophysiology. *Psychophysiology,* **22**(4), 464–480.

O'Connor, K.P. (1987). A response model of behaviour. In H.J. Eysenck & I. Martin (eds), *Theoretical foundations of behaviour therapy* (pp. 353–378). New York: Plenum Press.

O'Connor, K.P. (1989). Psychophysiology and skilled behaviour. *Journal of Psychophysiology,* **3,** 219–224.

O'Connor, K.P. (1990). Towards a process paradigm in psychophysiology. *International Journal of Psychophysiology,* **9,** 209–223.

O'Connor, K.P. (1996). Mime and psychology. *The Psychologist,* **9,** 110–113.

O'Connor, K.P. (2001). Clinical and psychological features distinguishing obsessive-compulsive and chronic tic disorders. *Clinical Psychology Review,* **20**(8), 1–30.

O'Connor, K.P. (2002). Intrusions and inferences in obsessive-compulsive disorder. *Clinical Psychology and Psychotherapy,* **9,** 38–46.

O'Connor, K.P. (2004). The relationship between OCD and OCD spectrum disorder. In J.S. Abramowitz (ed.), *Handbook of obsessive-compulsive spectrum disorder.* New York: Kluwer.

O'Connor, K., & Aardema, F. (2003). Fusion or confusion in obsessive-compulsive disorder. *Psychological Reports,* **93,** 227–232.

O'Connor, K.P., & Aardema, F. (in press). The imagination: Cognitive, precognitive and meta-cognitive aspects. *Journal of Consciousness and Cognition.*

O'Connor, K.P., & Grenier, S. (2004). Les troubles obsessionals-compulsifs: appartiennent-ils aux troubles anxieux ou à une autre famille de trouble mentaux? *Santé mentale au Québec,* **1**, 33–51.

O'Connor, K.P., & Hallam, R.S. (2000). Sorcery of the 'self'. (Critical review of the concept of self in cognitive and social psychology.) *Theory and Psychology,* **10**(2), 259–285.

O'Connor, K.P., & Robillard, S. (1995). Inference processes in obsessive-compulsive disorder: Some clinical observations. *Behaviour Research and Therapy,* **33**, 887–896.

O'Connor, K.P., & Robillard, S. (1999). A cognitive approach to modifying primary inferences in obsessive-compulsive disorder. *Journal of Cognitive Psychotherapy,* **13**, 1–17.

O'Connor, K., Aardema, F., Bouthillier, D., Fournier, S., Guay, S., Robillard, S., Landry, P., Todorov, C., Trembley, M., & Pitre, D. (2003a). Evaluation of an inference based approach to treating obsessive-compulsive disorder. Paper presented at the *27th Annual Convention of the Association of Behavior Therapy,* Boston, November.

O'Connor, K.P., Stip, E., Grenier, S., Guay, S., van Haaster, I., Doucet, P., Gaudette, G., & Pélissier, M.-C. (2003b). A randomized controlled trial of cognitive therapy versus attention placebo control in delusional disorder. Symposium, *Annual Conference Association for the Advancement of Behavior Therapy,* Boston, November.

O'Dwyer, A.M., & Marks, I. (2000). Obsessive-compulsive disorder and delusions revisited. *British Journal of Psychiatry,* **176**, 281–284.

Owen, I.R. (1996). Clean language: A linguistic-experiential phenomenology. In A.-T. Tymieniecka (ed.), *Analecta Husserliana,* **XLV**(iii), 271–297.

Oxman, T.E., Rosenberg, S.D., Schnurr, P.P., Tucker, G.J., & Gala, G. (1988). The language of altered states. *The Journal of Nervous and Mental Disease,* **176**(7), 401–408.

Parker, I. (ed.) (1999). *Deconstructing psychotherapy.* London: Sage Publications.

Pélissier, M.-C., & O'Connor, K.P. (2001). Reasoning in obsessive-compulsive disorder. Recent findings. In K.P. O'Connor (Chair), Beyond reasonable doubt: Common inference processes in obsessional, overvalued and delusional ideation. *Symposium conducted at the World Congress of Behavioural and Cognitive Therapies* (WCBCT), Vancouver, BC, Canada, July.

Pélissier, M.-C., & O'Connor, K.P. (2002a). Deductive and inductive reasoning in obsessive-compulsive disorder. *British Journal of Clinical Psychology,* **41**, 15–27.

Pélissier, M.-C., & O'Connor, K.P. (2002b). The role of inductive reasoning in obsessional doubt. In K.P. O'Connor (Chair), Beyond reasonable doubt: Reasoning processes in obsessional, overvalued and delusional ideation. *Symposium conducted at the 32nd European Advancement for Behavioural and Cognitive Therapies* (EABCT), Maastricht, The Netherlands, September.

Pélissier, M.-C., & O'Connor, K. (2002c). The role of inductive reasoning in obsessional doubt. Abstracts, *32nd European Advancement for Behavioural and Cognitive Therapies* (EABCT), Maastricht, The Netherlands.

Persons, J.B., & Foa, E.B. (1984). Processing of fearful and neutral information by obsessive-compulsives. *Behaviour Research and Therapy,* **22**, 259–265.

Phillips, L., & Edwards, W. (1966). Conservatism in a simple probability inference task. *Journal of Experimental Psychology,* **72**(3), 346–354.

Popper, K.R., & Miller, D. (1983). A proof of the impossibility of inductive probability. *Nature*, **302**, 687–688.

Purdon, C., & Clark, D. (1993). New perspectives for a cognitive theory of obsessions. *Australian Psychologist*, **28**, 161–167.

Purdon, C., & Clark, D.A. (2002). Control of thoughts in obsessive-compulsive disorder. In R. Frost & G. Steketee (eds), *Cognitive approaches to obsessive-compulsive disorder* (pp. 28–44). Oxford: Elsevier.

Quine, W.V.O. (ed.) (1969). Ontological relativity. In *Ontological relativity and other essays* (pp. 26–68). New York: Columbia University Press.

Rachman, S. (1983). Obstacles to the successful treatment of obsessions. In E.B. Foa & P.M.G. Emmelkamp (eds), *Failures in behavior therapy*. New York: John Wiley & Sons.

Rachman, S. (1984). Agoraphobia – a safety-signal perspective. *Behaviour Research and Therapy*, **22**, 59–70.

Rachman, S. (1994). Pollution of the mind. *Behaviour Research and Therapy*, **32**, 311–315.

Rachman, S.J. (1997). A cognitive theory of obsessions. *Behaviour Research and Therapy*, **35**, 793–802.

Rachman, S. (1998). A cognitive theory of obsessions: Elaborations. *Behaviour Research and Therapy*, **36**, 385–401.

Rachman, S. (2002). A cognitive theory of compulsive checking. *Behaviour Research and Therapy*, **40**, 625–639.

Rachman, S.J., & DeSilva, P. (1978). Abnormal and normal obsessions. *Behaviour Research and Therapy*, **16**, 233–248.

Rachman, S., & Hodgson, R.J. (eds) (1980). *Obsessions and compulsions*. Englewood Cliffs, NJ: Prentice Hall.

Rachman, S., & Shafran, R. (1999). Cognitive distortions: Thought action fusion. *Clinical Psychology and Psychotherapy*, **6**, 80–85.

Rachman, S., Thordarson, D.S., Shafran, R., & Woody, S.R. (1995). Perceived responsibility: Structure and significance. *Behaviour Research and Therapy*, **33**, 779–784.

Radomsky, A., de Silva, P., Todd, G., Treasure, J., & Murphy, T. (2002). Thought–shape fusion in anorexia nervosa: An experimental investigation. *Behaviour Research and Therapy*, **40**, 1169–1177.

Rasmussen, S.A., & Eisen, J.L. (1992). The epidemiology and differential diagnosis of obsessive-compulsive disorder. *Psychiatric Clinics of North America*, **15**, 743–758.

Rasmussen, S.A., & Tsuang, M.T. (1986). Clinical characteristics and family history in DSM–III obsessive compulsive disorder. *The American Journal of Psychiatry*, **143**, 317–322.

Reed, G. (1977). Obsessional cognition: Performance on two numerical tasks. *British Journal of Psychiatry*, **130**, 184–185.

Reed, G.F. (1985). *Obsessional experience and compulsive behaviour: A cognitive structural approach*. New York: Academic Press.

Reed, G. (1991). The cognitive characteristics of obsessional disorder. In P.A. Magaro (ed.), *Cognitive bases of mental disorders* (pp. 77–99). London: Sage Publications.

Rhéaume, J., Freeston, M.H., Ladouceur, R., Bouchard, C., Gallant, L., Talbot, F., & Vallières, A. (2000). Functional and dysfunctional perfectionists: Are they different on compulsive-like behaviors? *Behaviour Research and Therapy*, **38**, 119–128.

Ribot, T. (1905). *La logique des sentiments*. Paris: Félix Alcan.

Ricoeur, P. (1984). *Time and narrative* (vol. 1). Chicago: University of Chicago Press.

Rieman, B.C., McNally, R.J., & Cox, M. (1992). The comorbidity of obsessive-compulsive disorder and alcoholism. *Journal of Anxiety Disorders*, **6**, 105–110.

Riessman, C.K. (1993). *Narrative analysis*. Newbury Park, CA: Sage Publications, Inc.

Ringler, H. (1937). Heart or reason? What we don't want from our speakers. *Unser Wille und Weg*, **7**, 245–249.

Riskind, J.H. (1997). Looming vulnerability to threat: A cognitive paradigm for anxiety. *Behaviour Research and Therapy*, **35**(5), 386–404.

Riskind, J.H., Abreu, K., Strauss, M., & Holt, R. (1997). Looming vulnerability to spreading contamination in subclinical OCD. *Behavior Research and Therapy*, **35**, 405–414.

Rokeach, M. (1960). *The open and closed mind*. New York: Basic Books.

Russell, R.L. (1991). Narrative in views of humanity, science, and action. Some lessons for cognitive therapy. *Journal of Cognitive Psychotherapy*, **5**(4), 241–256.

Russell, R.L., & van den Broek, P. (1992). Changing narrative schemas in psychotherapy. *Psychotherapy*, **29**(3), 344–354.

Salkovskis, P.M. (1985). Obsessional-compulsive problems: A cognitive-behavioural analysis. *Behaviour Research and Therapy*, **23**, 571–583.

Salkovskis, P.M. (1989). Cognitive-behavioural factors and the persistence of intrusive thoughts in obsessional problems. *Behaviour Research and Therapy*, **27**, 677–682.

Salkovskis, P.M. (1996). Cognitive-behavioural approaches to the understanding of obsessional problems. In R. Rapee (ed.), *Current controversies in the anxiety disorder*. New York: Guilford Press.

Salkovskis, P.M. (1999). Understanding and treating obsessive-compulsive disorder. *Behaviour Research and Therapy*, **37**, S29–S52.

Salkovskis, P.M., & Harrison, J. (1984). Abnormal and normal obsessions: A replication. *Behaviour Research and Therapy*, **22**, 549–552.

Salkovskis, P.M., Forrester, E., Richards, C., & Morrison, N. (1998). The devil is in the detail: Conceptualising and treating obsessional problems. In N. Tarrier, A. Wells, & G. Haddock (eds), *Treating complex cases: The cognitive behavioural therapy approach* (pp. 47–70). Chichester: John Wiley & Sons, Ltd.

Salkovskis, P.M., Wroe, A.L., Gledhill, A., Morrison, N., Forrester, E., Richards, C., Reynolds, M., & Thorpe, S. (2000). Responsibility attitudes and interpretations are characteristic of obsessive compulsive disorder. *Behaviour Research and Therapy*, **38**, 347–372.

Sarbin, T.R. (1996). The poetics of identity. *Theory & Psychology*, **7**(1), 67–82.

Serban, G. (1974). The process of neurotic thinking. *American Journal of Psychotherapy*, **28**(3), 418–427.

Shafir, E., & LeBoeuf, R.A. (2002). Rationality. *Annual Review of Psychology*, **53**, 491–517.

Sharp, H.M., Fear, C.F., Williams, J.M.G., Healy, D., Lowe, C.F., Yeadon, H., & Holden, R. (1996). Delusional phenomenology: dimensions of change. *Behavioural Research and Therapy*, **34**(2), 123–142.

Shiffrin, R.M., & Schneider, W. (1977). Controlled and automatic human information processing: II. Perceptual learning, automatic attending, and a general theory. *Psychological Review*, **84**, 127–190.

Shotter, J. (1994). *Conversational realities: The construction of life through language*. London: Sage Publications.

Skinner, B.F. (1977). Why I am not a cognitive psychologist. *Behaviorism*, **5**, 1–10.

Smeets, G., de Jong, P.J., & Mayer, B. (2000). If you suffer from a headache, then you have a brain tumour: Domain-specific reasoning 'bias' and hypochondriasis. *Behaviour Research and Therapy*, **38**, 763–776.

Smith, C., & Nylund, D. (eds) (1997). *Narrative therapies with children and adolescents*. New York: Guilford Press.

Smith, J.A., Osborn, M., & Jarman, M. (1999). Doing interpretative phenomenological analysis. In M. Murray & K. Chamberlain (eds), *Quantitative health psychology*. London: Sage.

Sookman, D., Pinard, G., & Beck, A.T. (2001). Vulnerability schemas in obsessive-compulsive disorder. *Journal of Cognitive Psychotherapy*, **15**, 109–130.

Spitzer, R.L., Williams, J.B.W., Gibbon, M., & First, M. (1991). *Manual for the structured clinical interview for DSM-III-R with psychotic screen*. Washington, DC: American Psychiatric Press.

Steketee, G.S. (1993). *Treatment of obsessive compulsive disorder*. New York: Guilford Press.

Steketee, G., & Shapiro, L.J. (1993). Obsessive-compulsive disorder. In A.S. Bellack & M. Hersen (eds), *Handbook of behavior therapy in the psychiatric setting* (pp. 199–227). New York: Plenum Press.

Steketee, G., Frost, R., & Wilson, K. (2002). Studying cognition in obsessive-compulsive disorder: Where to from here? In R.O. Frost & G. Steketee (eds), *Cognitive approaches to obsessions and compulsions: Theory, assessment, and treatment*. Oxford: Elsevier.

Taylor, C. (2004). Why San Francisco's brash mayor is taking on Schwarzenegger and Bush over gay marriage. *Time*, March, pp. 24–25.

Taylor, S. (1998). Assessment of obsessive-compulsive disorder. In R.P. Swinson, M.M. Antony, S. Rachman & M.A. Richter (eds), *Obsessive-compulsive disorder: Theory, research and treatment* (pp. 229–257). New York: Guilford Press.

Taylor, S. (2002a). Critical issues and future directions. In R.O. Frost & G. Steketee (eds), *Cognitive approaches to obsessions and compulsions: Theory, assessment, and treatment*. Oxford: Elsevier.

Taylor, S. (2002b). Cognition in obsessive-compulsive behaviour. An overview. In R.O. Frost & G. Steketee (eds), *Cognitive approaches to obsessions and compulsions: Theory, assessment, and treatment*. Oxford: Elsevier.

Taylor, S., Kyrios, M., Thordarson, D.S., Steketee, G., & Frost, R.O. (2002). Development and validation of instruments measuring intrusions and beliefs in obsessive-compulsive disorder. In R.O. Frost & G. Steketee (eds), *Cognitive approaches to obsessions and compulsions: Theory, assessment, and treatment*. Oxford: Elsevier.

Teasdale, J.D. (1996). Clinically relevant theory: Integrating clinical insight with cognitive science. In P.M. Salkovskis (ed.), *Frontiers of cognitive therapy* (pp. 26–47). New York: The Guilford Press.

Teasdale, J.D., Segal, Z.V., & Williams, J.M.G. (1995). How does cognitive therapy prevent depressive relapse and why should attentional control (mindfulness) training help? *Behaviour Research and Therapy*, **33**, 25–39.

Thodarson, D.S., & Shafran, R. (2002). Importance of thoughts. In R.O. Frost & G. Steketee (eds), *Cognitive approaches to obsessions and compulsions: Theory, assessment and treatment* (pp. 15–28). Boston, MA: Pergamon.

Tibbetts, P. (1988). Representation and the realist constructivist controversy. *Human Studies*, **11**, 117–132.

Tolin, D.F., Abramowitz, J.S., Kozak, M.J., & Foa, E.B. (2001). Fixity of belief, perceptual aberration, and magical ideation in obsessive-compulsive disorder. *Anxiety Disorders*, **15**, 501–510.

Trinder, H., & Salkovskis, P.M. (1994). Personally relevant intrusions outside the laboratory: Long-term suppression increases intrusion. *Behaviour Research and Therapy*, **32**, 833–842.

Tversky, A., & Kahneman, D. (1982). Judgement under uncertainty: Heuristics and biases. In D. Kahneman, P. Slovic, & A. Tversky (eds), *Judgement under uncertainty: Heuristics and biases*. Cambridge: Cambridge University Press.

van Balkom, A.J.L.M., van Oppen, P., Vermeulen, A.W.A., van Dyck, R., Nauta, M.C.E., & Vorst, H.C.M. (1994). A meta-analysis on the treatment of obsessive-compulsive disorders: A comparison of antidepressants, behavior, and cognitive therapy. *Clinical Psychology Review*, **14**, 359–381.

van Oppen, P., & Arntz, A. (1994). Cognitive therapy for obsessive-compulsive disorder. *Behaviour Research and Therapy*, **32**, 79–87.

van Oppen, P., de Haan, E., van Balkom, A.J.L., Spinhoven, P., Hoogduin, K., & van Dyck, R. (1995a). Cognitive therapy and exposure in vivo in the treatment of obsessive-compulsive disorder. *Behaviour Research and Therapy*, **33**, 379–390.

van Oppen, P., Hoekstra, R., & Emmelkamp, P.M.G. (1995b). The structure of obsessive-compulsive behaviour. *Behaviour Research and Therapy*, **33**, 15–23.

Veale, D. (2002). Over-valued ideas: a conceptual analysis. *Behaviour Research and Therapy*, **404**, 383–400.

Volans, P.J. (1976). Styles of decision-making and probability appraisal in selected obsessional and phobic patients. *British Journal of Social and Clinical Psychology*, **15**, 305–317.

Wason, P.C. (1960). On the failure to eliminate hypotheses in a conceptual task. *Quarterly Journal of Experimental Psychology*, **12**, 129–140.

Wason, P.C. (1966). Reasoning. In B.M. Foss (ed.), *New Horizons in Psychology* (pp. 135–151). Harmondsworth: Penguin Books.

Wason, P.C. (1968). Reasoning about a rule. *Quarterly Journal of Experimental Psychology*, **20**, 273–281.

Wason, P.C., & Johnson-Laird, P.N. (1972). *Psychology of reasoning: Structure and content*. Cambridge, MA: Harvard University Press.

Weimer, W.B. (1977). Motor theories of mind. In R. Shaw & J. Bransford (eds), *Perceiving, acting and knowing: Toward an ecological psychology* (pp. 270–311). Hillsdale, NJ: Erlbaum.

Weissman, M.M., Bland, R.C., Canino, G.J., Greenwald, S., Hwu, H.-G., Lee, C.K., Newman, S.C., Oakley-Browne, M.A., Rubio-Stipec, M., Wickramarathe, P.J., Wittchen, H.U., & Yeh, E.K. (1994). The cross national epidemiology of obsessive-compulsive disorder. *Journal of Clinical Psychiatry*, **55**, 5–10.

Wells, A. (1997). *Cognitive therapy of anxiety disorders: A practice manual and conceptual guide*. Chichester: John Wiley & Sons, Ltd.

Wells, A. (2000). *Emotional disorders and metacognition. Innovative cognitive therapy*. Chichester: John Wiley & Sons, Ltd.

Wells, A., & Matthews, G. (1994). *Attention and emotion: A clinical perspective*. Hove: Lawrence Erlbaum.

Wells, A., White, J., & Carter, K. (1997). Attention raining: Effects on anxiety and beliefs in panic and social phobia. *Clinical Psychology and Psychotherapy*, 4, 226–232.

Whitehead, A.N., & Russell, B. (1910). *Principia mathematica* (vol. 1). Cambridge: Cambridge University Press.

Williams, J.M.G. (1996). Memory processes in psychotherapy. In P.M. Salkovskis (ed.), *Frontiers of cognitive therapy* (pp. 114–134). New York: The Guilford Press.

Wilson, T.D., & Dunn, E.W. (1986). Effects of introspection on attitude–behavior consistency: Analyzing reasons versus focusing on feelings. *Journal of Experimental and Social Psychology*, 22, 249–263.

Wilson, T.D., & Dunn, E.W. (2003). Self-knowledge: Its limits, value, and potential for improvement. *Annual Review of Psychology*, 55, 17.1–17.26.

Wilson, T.D., & LaFleur, S.J. (1995). Knowing what you'll do: Effects of analyzing reasons on self-prediction. *Journal of Personality and Social Psychology*, 68, 21–35.

Wilson, T.D., & Schooler, J.W. (1991). Thinking too much: Introspection can reduce the quality of preferences and decisions. *Journal of Personality and Social Psychology*, 60, 181–192.

Wilson, T.D., Hodges, S.D., & LaFleur, S.J. (1995). Effects of introspecting about reasons: Inferring attitudes from accessible thoughts. *Journal of Personality and Social Psychology*, 69, 16–28.

Wilson, T.D., Lindsey, S., & Schooler, T.Y. (2000). A model of dual attitudes. *Psychological Review*, 107, 101–126.

Wilson, T.D., Dunn, D.S., Kraft, D., & Lisle, D.J. (1989). Introspection, attitude change, and attitude–behavior consistency: the disruptive effects of explaining why we feel the way we do. In L. Berkowitz (ed.), *Advances in experimental and social psychology* (pp. 287–343). New York: Academic Press.

Wilson, T.D., Dunn, D.S., Bybee, J.A., Hyman, D.B., & Rotondo, J.A. (1984). Effects of analyzing reasons on attitude–behavior consistency. *Journal of Personality and Social Psychology*, 47, 5–16.

Wilson, T.D., Lisle, D.J., Schooler, J.W., Hodges, S.D., Klaaren, K.J., *et al.* (1993). Introspecting about reasons can reduce post-choice satisfaction. *Personal and Social Psychology Bulletin*, 19, 331–339.

Wittgenstein, L. (1953). *Philosophical investigations*. New York: Macmillan.

Wykes, T., & van der Gaag, M. (2001). Is it time to develop a new cognitive therapy for psychosis – cognitive remediation therapy (CRT)? *Clinical Psychology Review*, 21(8), 1227–1256.

Young, H.F., & Bentall, R.P. (1997). Probabilistic reasoning in deluded, depressed and normal subjects: Effects of task difficulty and meaningful versus non-meaningful material. *Psychological Medicine*, 27, 455–465.

Zajonc, R.B. (1980). Feeling and thinking: Preferences need no inferences. *American Psychology*, 35, 151–175.

Zimmerman, J.L., & Dickerson, V.C. (1994). Using a narrative metaphor: Implications for theory and clinical practice. *Family Process*, 33, 233–245.

Zucker, B.G., Craske, M., Barrios, V., & Holguin, M. (2002). Thought action fusion: Can it be corrected? *Behaviour Research and Therapy*, 40, 653–664.

INDEX

absorption 56, 71, 73–5, 77–9, 177
affective and thought disorder 90–1
affirmation of the consequent 18–19
anxiety disorder 3, 71, 86–9, 91–4, 130–1
appraisal
    approach 9, 11, 62
    coping 141, 201
    model 115–16
assumption 55
attention 7, 47
attentional allocation 96
augmented instructions 28
automated and controlled processing 34

Bayes' theorem 83
Bayesian probablistic task 82, 84, 85, 87, 88, 90
Beck
    all-or-nothing thinking 7
    catastrophic thinking 60
    cognitive specificity hypothesis 4, 7, 213
    over-generalization 7, 60
    personalization 7, 60
    psychopathology model 4–5
beliefs 62–3
    bias 28
    challenging 175–6
    disorders 12–13, 15
    fixity of 62
    inflated responsibility 5
    intolerance to ambiguity 5
    intolerance to uncertainty 5, 88
    irrational 6
    narrative and 62–4
    over-estimation of threat 5
    over-importance of thought 5
    perfectionism 5
bias 39
    belief 28
    confirmation 21, 29
    jumping to conclusion (JTC) 85, 90
    matching 21
    omission 201
    reasoning 29
    threat 39
biased coin task 85

bizarre idea formation 86
bridging (given-new contracts) 42, 89

category errors 116
causality 86
certainty 8, 161
cognition 9, 41, 42–5, 209–11
cognitive
    errors 86
    processes 7
    remediation 96
    structure 8, 41
cognitive behavioral therapy (CBT) 4, 16, 41,
    96, 101, 144, 145, 178, 199, 186–7, 204–8
common elements see theory
common-sense philosophy 38
comparable events 116
competence, measures of 81
compulsion 1
    checking 1, 11, 12, 167
    neutralization 150, 180
    subtypes of 2
concept
    attainment 62
    formation 62
conceptual blending 60–1, 67
conditional
    reasoning 20, 28
    rule 21, 205
confirming evidence 16
conjunction fallacy 30
consciousness 46–7, 60–70, 119
constructionism 40, 43–4, 77, 105, 171–2, 211
constructionist
    approach 41
    perspective 40
    version 40
constructivism 42
contamination fears 11–12, 78, 114, 156–7
content 7–8, 90–4
    of reasoning 24, 81
context 15, 21, 45–6, 50, 51
contextual behaviorism 45
conviction
    obsessional 14–15
    strength of 14

crossing over 158–60

data gathering 77
  deficit 86, 87, 95
  excess 87, 95
decision-making 32, 83, 84, 85
deconstructing 65, 104–5
deduction 17–19, 40
deductive
  competence 24
  logic 26, 33, 37
  performance 24, 25
  reasoning 20, 23–5
delusion 84–6
delusional
  belief 79
  disorder 3, 12, 79, 85, 127, 202–3
denial of facts 81
denying the antecedent 19
detachment 74
dialogical approach 107–9, 112
dialogicity 107–9
direct realism 44
discursive approach 104–5
dissociativity 76
distorted perceptions 77
distrust of the senses 116, 118
doubt 8, 114
  obsessional 9, 149–53, 166–9
  primary inference of 150–1
  secondary inference of 150–1

ecological structure 44
emotional engagement 66
emotion-based reasoning 36, 93
evidence 119
ex-consequential reasoning 36, 91, 93
experience 37–42, 42–5
  ego-dystonic 146
  ego-syntonic 146
exposure in vivo 13
exposure and response prevention (ERP) 3–4,
  15, 140
extensionalization 99
external validity 22

facts 56, 116
falsification 21
far-fetched narrative 119
fear 3, 11–12, 174
feelings 120–1
fiction 56
fixed beliefs 62
framing effect 35

gambler's fallacy 30

hallucination 77
heuristic
  affect 35–6
  anchoring (adjustment) 31–2
  availability 26, 31
  representativeness 30–1
hypnosis 75–6
hypnotic
  delusion 76
  illusion 76
hypothetico-deductive reasoning 37

ideation, over-valued 10, 179
illusion 78
imaginary context 46
imaginary beliefs 56, 75–7, 154–5
imaginary sequences 116
imagination 70–1, 169–70
imagined possibilities 154–5
induction
  mechanism 26
  techniques 76
inductive
  behavior 37
  logic 26, 33, 37
  psychology 37
  reasoning 25–7
inference 10–12, 26, 61, 67–71, 118
  primary 118–20, 140, 176–7
Inference Based Approach (IBA) 115–21
  case studies 178–97
  clinical trials 140–6
  future developments 211–13
  idiosyncratic content see obsession
  model 147–8
  step-by-step program 149–66
  treatment 187–94
  Treatment Manual 149–97
  trouble shooting guide 170–8
inferential approach 109
inferential confusion 12–13, 16, 113–15, 117,
  120–1
  distrust of the senses 118
  experimental studies 131–9
  inverse inference 118
  measurement 121–31
  overvalued ideation (OVI) 13, 140
  Questionnaire (ICQ) 123–5, 126, 129, 130–1,
    143, 144, 145, 147, 212
  treatment outcome 144–6
intentionality 40–1, 46, 48, 49, 51, 63, 110
internal modalities 120
interpretation 22
intolerance to ambiguity 5
intolerance to uncertainty 5, 6, 88
introspection 211
intrusion 10–12, 118–20
intrusive thought 10

inverse inference 116, 118, 123
Irrational Beliefs Inventory 6
irrational thinking/belief 86
irrelevant associations 119

judgment of probability 45

knowledge 37–42

language 46–50, 57–8, 110, 174–5
  clean 102
  games 47
laws
  of logic 25
  of thoughts 25
linguistic constructionist model 47
Linda problem 30–1, 58
lived-in experience 76, 78
living "as if" 74–5, 76, 114, 157, 160
logic 22, 28
  experience 32–5
  self-referent ordering 101
logical
  if–then inferences 205
  strategies 102

material realistic 39–40
memory 7, 47, 101
mental
  models 20, 25, 27–8, 32, 44, 138–9
  states 47
  tics see obsession
Mentalese 49
meta-cognition 59, 77, 97
meta-cognitive model 208–9
metaphor 51, 59, 103, 104, 109, 174–5
  as if qualities 74–5, 76, 209
  stance 74, 78
meta-reference 58
metonym 51, 59, 103, 104, 109
mime 45–6
mindfulness 98
mindlessness 98
miscategorization 60, 67
misinterpreted necessity 28
misplaced concreteness 59
models
  cognitive appraisal 140, 199–203
  dual process 34
  multifactorial 85
  realist 39
Modus ponens 18–19, 32
Modus tollens 18–19, 32
mood states 61, 126

narrative 156–8
  –action couplings 62
  approach to thoughts 54–7

believability 56
device 59–61
language of 53, 57–8
misplaced concreteness 59
scripted 51
structure 53, 54–5
theme 189–90
therapies 105–8, 110
unit 51
unspoken 58–9
narrative therapy 105–7, 109
negativity 6, 120
neutralization 2, 12, 150, 180
  covert 140, 150
non-discursive narrative therapy 105–6
"non-logical" issues 28
normalization 8
normative system problem 22

obsession
  content 9
  generalizing 173
  idiosyncratic content see IBA
  occurrence of 9
Obsessive Beliefs Questionnaire (OBG) 5–6, 9
Obsessive-Compulsive Disorder 6
  course 2–3
  devices of 1
  non-phobic characteristic of 12–13
  rituals 1–2
  therapy 3–4
Obsessive-Compulsive Personality Disorder
  (OCPD) 88
otherness 41
overestimation of threat 5, 8
overestimation of the threat scale 212
over-responsibility 209
over-valued
  ideas 13, 62, 145, 202, 203
  Ideas Scale (OVIS) 143
  ideation 12, 144–5

Padua-Revised Inventory 125, 126
Padua Washington State University Revision
  (P1-WSUR) 125, 126, 141, 203
panic attack 100
pathology of doubt 8
perception 7, 44
perceptual disturbances 125–6
perceptual processing 77
perfectionism 5, 6, 89, 175, 206
  dysfunctional 87–8
  functional 87
  pathological 87, 206
personal
  probabilities 37
  utility 37
personal construct psychology 100, 101

personality disorder 170
persuasion 65, 102
phenomenological
    approach 44–5
    descriptive 100
phenomenology 9, 100–2, 146
    interpretative 101
    linguistic-experimental 102–4
physical-out-thereness 38
physicalness 39–40, 41, 68
possibilistic status 68
possibility 67–71
possibility distributions 71–3, 77
post-rationalist cognitive therapy 101, 102
post-traumatic stress disorder 93–4
primary inferences 118–20, 140, 150, 156, 176–7
probabilistic
    mechanism of reasoning 22
    reasoning 82–3, 88
probability 24, 83
psychological reduction 54
psychopathology 4–5, 7, 78–9, 81–112

radical constructionism 43
Rational Emotive Therapy (RET) 4, 97–8
rationality 21–2, 24, 102
    1 and 2 22, 34
reality 41, 78, 119
    sensing 16, 39, 74, 165–6, 193–4
real-life reasoning 22
reasoning 24, 35–6
    biases 28–9
    cognitive structural approach 96–100
    competence 89
    emotion-based 93–4
    errors 15, 97
    faulty 86
    fear-confirming 92–3
    intrusion-based 93–4
    inverted 97
    mechanisms 85, 86–9
    in obsessions 9
    probabilistic 29–30
    studies 81
relevance 21–2, 24
repertory grid technique 100
repetitiveness 81
responsibility 5, 11, 49, 54–5
response bias theory 23
rhetoric 64–7, 111
rhetorical persuasion 66
rhetorician 64
ritual 1–2, 113–14, 150, 171
rule 34

schema 41, 62, 112, 196, 204, 207–8
schizophrenia 84–6
self
    contradiction 81
    deceptions 101, 21
    doubt 63, 164, 197
    fragility 200
    preservation 57
    signaling processes 97
    –society relationship 104
    –world 38, 40, 41, 51, 74, 104
semantic(s) 99, 103
senses 32–51, 170
sequence 116
social constructive approach 43
Socratic dialogue (SD) 206
story 57, 164–5
structural connectedness 56
subjective 56
    probability 29
    utility 29
suggestibility 65, 70
superstition 100
suspicion, hermeneutics of 104
syllogistic reasoning 22–3, 28
syllogism 22–3, 100

task, hypothetico-deductive 81
theory
    of abstraction 20
    atmosphere 23
    common elements 26
    of general semantics 99
    prototype 26
    self-perception 210
thinking 45, 98
thought
    action fusion (TAF) 5, 100, 201, 208–9
    disorder 84–6
    event fusion (TEF) 208–9
    mechanism of 81
    object fusion (TOF) 208–9
tolerance 6
treatment 13–16
    exposure 3–4

vulnerability theme 164–5

Wason Selection Task 20–1, 29–30, 35, 89, 91, 92

Y-BOCS 141, 143, 202